The Mind of Jihad

This book examines contemporary jihad as a cult of violence and power. All jihadi groups, whether Shiite or Sunni, Arab or not, are characterized by a similar bloodlust. Laurent Murawiec characterizes this belief structure as identical to that of Europe's medieval millenarians and apocalyptics, arguing that both jihadis and their European cousins shared in a Gnostic ideology: A God-given mission endowed the Elect with supernatural powers and placed them above the common law of mankind. Although the ideology of jihad is essentially Islamic, Murawiec traces the political technologies used by modern jihad to the Bolsheviks. Their doctrines of terror as a system of rule were appropriated by radical Islam through multiple lines of communication. This book brings history, anthropology, and theology to bear to understand the mind of jihad that has declared war on the West and the world.

Laurent Murawiec taught philosophy, was a foreign correspondent, cofounded and managed a consulting company for geopolitical and geoeconomic affairs, and taught at the Ecole des Hautes Etudes en sciences sociales. He has served as a consultant for the French Ministry of Defense and as a Senior International Policy Analyst with the RAND Corporation and is currently a senior Fellow of the Hudson Institute. He is the author of *La Guerre au XXIè siècle* (2000 [in Chinese, 2004]), *L'Esprit des Nations: Cultures et géopolitique* (2002), *La Guerre d'Après* (2003), *Vulnerabilities in the Chinese Way of War* (2004), and *Princes of Darkness: The Saudi Assault Against the West* (2005) as well as an acclaimed French translation of Clausewitz's *On War* (1999).

L'homme n'est ni ange ni bête, et le malheur veut que qui veut faire l'ange fait la bête.

Blaise Pascal

Though this be madness, yet there is method in't.

William Shakespeare

When people think they possess the secret of a perfect social organization which makes evil impossible, they also think that they can use any means, including violence and deceit, in order to bring that organization into being. Politics then becomes a "secular religion" that operates under the illusion of creating paradise in this world.

John Paul II

There are circumstances in which keeping silence means lying. I have just heard a morbid and senseless cry: Long live death. This barbaric paradox is repugnant to me.

Miguel de Unamuno

If anyone wishes to write against this, I will welcome it. For true and false will in no better way be revealed and uncovered than in resistance to a contradiction, according to the saying: "Iron is sharpened by iron."

Thomas Aquinas

The Mind of Jihad

LAURENT MURAWIEC

CAMBRIDGE UNIVERSITY PRESS
Cambridge, New York, Melbourne, Madrid, Cape Town, Singapore, São Paulo, Delhi

Cambridge University Press
32 Avenue of the Americas, New York, NY 10013–2473, USA

www.cambridge.org
Information on this title: www.cambridge.org/9780521730631

First published 2008

Printed in the United States of America

A catalog record for this publication is available from the British Library.

Library of Congress Cataloging in Publication Data

Murawiec, Laurent.
The mind of Jihad / Laurent Murawiec.
p. cm.
Includes bibliographical references and index.
ISBN 978-0-521-88393-1 (hardback) – ISBN 978-0-521-73063-1 (pbk.)
1. Terrorism – Religious aspects – Islam. 2. Jihad. 3. Islam and world politics. 4. Islamic fundamentalism. I. Title.
HV6431.M865 2008
322.4'2088297–dc22 2008000787

ISBN 978-0-521-88393-1 hardback
ISBN 978-0-521-73063-1 paperback

Contents

Acknowledgments — *page* vii

Introduction — 1
1 "We Love Death" — 5
2 "An Elite of Amoral Supermen" — 59
3 The Gnostic Mahdi — 90
4 Manichean Tribalism — 132
5 The Odd Pedigree of Modern Jihad — 169
6 The Mutated Virus: "Islamic Revolution" — 256
7 Jihad as Terror — 295
Conclusion — 324

Index — 327

Acknowledgments

It is my distinct pleasure to acknowledge the debt I have incurred in researching this subject and putting it on paper. I have received the invaluable help of highly knowledgeable scholars. I have received the benefit of their science, their advice, and their criticism, and this book would have been much poorer without their contribution.

In the first place, Prof. Wolfgang G. Schwanitz introduced me to entire areas and topics of research; his wealth of knowledge always was a prime helper: I could not have connected many dots without his friendly support. Dr. David Wurmser followed step by step the development of the research and the writing and was permanently a stimulating partner in discussion. Prof. Mohamed ibn Guadi's deep well of science and friendship was always open.

For their suggestions, remarks, and criticisms, I would like to thank my friends and colleagues at the Hudson Institute, Dr. S. Enders Wimbush, Mr. Eric Brown, and Dr. Hillel Fradkin; M. Michel Gurfinkiel of the Institut Jean-Jacques Rousseau in Paris; Mr. Praveen Swami of *Frontline* in New Delhi, Prof. Lynn Addington of American University, Washington, D.C.; Ms. Ladan Archin, Dr. Roya Boroumand of the Boroumand Foundation; Prof. Yossi Kostiner and Prof. Azar Gat, both of Tel-Aviv University; Prof. Efraim Inbar of Bar-Ilan University, Prof. Efraim Karsh of King's College, London; my old friend Juliette Minces; Prof. Richard Landes of Boston University; Mr. David Pryce-Jones of London; Prof. Joshua Mitchell of Georgetown University; Mr. Muhammad Akyol; Mr. Paul Goble; Col. Norville "Tex" DeAtkine (U.S. Army, ret.); Prof. Wolfgang Leidhold of the University of Cologne, Germany; Prof. Michael Stürmer of the University of Erlangen-Nürnberg; Dr. Joel Fishman of the Jerusalem Center for Public Affairs; Prof. Emeritus Jean-Paul Charnay of the University of Paris – Sorbonne;

Dr. Shmuel Bar of the Interdisciplinary Center in Herzliya; Mr. Alex Alexiev, Mr. Steven Emerson, and Mr. Ryan Evans of The Investigative Project; Mr. John Taylor of the National Archives of the United States; Prof. Alain Besançon of the Ecole des Hautes Etudes en sciences sociales; Prof. Françoise Thom of the University of Paris; Mr. Ramin Parham; Prof. Hussain Haqqani of Boston University; and Prof. Bernard Lewis of Princeton University. May they all accept the expression of my heartfelt appreciation. I would also like to thank Ms. Maria Farkas, Mrs. Grace Paine Terzian of the Hudson Institute, and my research assistants Ms. Dora Molnár and Dr. Niki Nagy. Particular thanks go to Dr. Ivan Borrello, M.D. I further want to express my gratitude to Prof. Fouad Ajami of Johns Hopkins University (SAIS) and Prof. Robert Lieber of Georgetown University for their support, and to Mr. Lewis Bateman of Cambridge University Press for the interest he took in the project.

Special thanks go to Mr. Andrew Marshall of the Office of Net Assessment at the Department of Defense, who originally commissioned the work this book came from and supported it throughout with unflagging interest. I would not have been able to sustain several years of this research without his support.

This book is, *selbstverständlich*, dedicated to my wife Dr. Claudia Kinkela, first reader, first critic, first in my heart.

Introduction

"It is a riddle, wrapped in a mystery, inside an enigma," Winston Churchill said of Russia in a radio broadcast in October 1939. To forecast its future course he added, "perhaps there is a key. That key is Russian national interest." Today, however, rational self-interest has proven a poor guide to understanding the war waged against the West that so deeply troubles us. The motive force that drives the players, the policies of the players, and the religion that inspires them have all proven altogether immune to the standard calculus of self-interest.

Even several decades into the irregular war waged by the jihadi world against the West, this new Sphinx still transfixes us to the point of making our societies unable to answer the fateful question upon which hinges their fate. Many explanations are proffered, and some do shed light upon the matter, but the nature of modern and contemporary jihad often remains shrouded in darkness: The analyses offered, regrettably, are frequently monocausal and often fit their author's particular agenda more than the facts of the matter. Many cogent approaches have yielded enlightening results but they have made little headway toward informing policy makers and public opinion, both engulfed in confusion.

The expressions "war on terror" or "terrorism" have been justly criticized; they err gravely by focusing upon the tool and do not even properly capture the essence of terror as a continuation of politics, of terror as a system of power: By drawing attention to the terrorist act, they remove it from context, history, and etiology. They not only lose sight of the mind holding the weapon, but they ignore the mind moving the minds: "the mind of jihad."

This research started more than a decade ago, when I began working on a project to chart the "spirit of nations" of important cultures and civilizations. Under that title, a transparent homage to Montesquieu's *L'Esprit des lois*, I published the first results regarding China, Japan, India, and Russia as *L'Esprit des Nations*. A second volume was going to be devoted to the world of Islam. I had been gathering materials for several years when the thunderbolt of September 11, 2001, gave my work greater urgency. The research was equally grounded in the object's history, its theology, its religion, its sociology, and its anthropology. As the analyst of war Bernard Brodie so cogently put it: "Good strategy presumes good anthropology and sociology. Some of the greatest military blunders of all times have resulted from juvenile evaluations in this department." I had hypothesized that the politics of nations was their theology diluted; in no case was this truer than in that of the world of Islam. All my work on the subject is built on that assumption. How could events, trends, and developments that occur in the world of Islam not be based on Islam?

The starting point, though, was an investigation into what could be called "the Arab way of war." Just as Victor Davis Hanson has shown that cultures wage wars in ways that fit their specific outlook and sociology, I sought to establish a causal connection between the tribal and nomadic way of life of the Arabs in history and the way in which terrorist warfare was practiced. This conception soon proved to be too narrow, and I was forced to abandon it, or rather to broaden it considerably: The matter was rooted in Islam, including in the complex relationship between the religion and the people of its birth. It was a matter of the mind.

It was not the last surprise this venture held in store for me: Time and again, I had to jettison my initial hypothesis and feel my way into unexpected pathways. If wonderment is the beginning of science, it never failed to force me to reassess my own conclusions. I discarded the notion of an Arab way of war as I realized in the action of the jihadis the exceptional prevalence of a cult of violence, of a glee to inflict suffering, in short, of a bloodlust that had little if any counterpart. This led to an investigation of an underlying "theology of death," which soon turned out to be the kernel of the jihadi outlook. Chapter 1, "We Love Death," accounts for this discovery.

The next surprise occurred as I sought to find comparable events, conceptions and practices in history. It turned out that the closest peers of the contemporary jihadis were the medieval millenarians of Europe with their Gnostic world-outlook and their own bloodlust. Across the divide of vastly different cultural idioms and religious beliefs, a striking similarity pointed to the etiology of utopia: Sectarian eschatological movements tend to breed behaviors of a similar nature. The conviction that one knows God's will is heady stuff that often leads to shedding torrents of blood in the name of one's mission. Living in a "second reality" deemed superior to the "real" reality shared by the rest of mankind is a recipe for mass murder. This matter is presented in Chapter 2, "An Elite of Amoral Supermen."

The Gnostic inspiration of modern jihad, however similar to its earlier European counterparts, had to make sense within the world of Islam, its law, and its customs. It had to be authentic and organic. One concept emerged to embody revolutionary millenarianism within Islam, that of the Mahdi, the expected and divinely guided one who will appear at the end of times to set the world right. Muslim apocalyptics, I had to discover, were never far from the mind of jihad, to the point that radical Islam was synonymous with Mahdism, the politicized version of the religious concept. This story is developed in Chapter 3, "The Gnostic Mahdi."

Cleaving the world between elects and damned, between the elects' territory and that of the rest, the separation of the human race between an "inside" and an "outside," irresistibly pointed to the spontaneous outlook of tribal societies, the radical split between "us" and "them." A tribal matrix had to be operative: I examined the nature and the implications of the concepts of *dar al-Islam* and *dar al-Harb*, the two abodes into which the world is sundered, and their mutual relationship in Chapter 4, "Manichean Tribalism."

I had long been tantalized by a certain "Leninist" tonality to many texts written by the leading ideologues of radical Islam, such as Abu Ala Maududi or Sayyid Qutb. Lines of communication between Bolsheviks and jihadis were not immediately apparent. What this inquiry dug up was one of the strangest revelations: I uncovered a lavish pattern of relations between radical Islam and Soviet communism, starting in the earliest days of Lenin's putsch, and, essentially, never ending. Strangely, this pattern had started with the First World War's "Jihad Made in Germany" before mutating into a Soviet–Muslim affair: What is reported in Chapter 5, "The Odd Pedigree of Modern Jihad," deserved sustained attention.

It was now possible to address the bizarre concept of "Islamic Revolution," which became so central to radical Islam. The intellectual "greenhouses," the cooperation between Shiites and Sunni, the Muslim Brothers, the ayatollahs, and the South Asian Muslims, which together created the contemporary jihadi ideology is the object of Chapter 6, "The Mutated Virus: 'Islamic Revolution.'"

Finally, reverting to the starting point, it became possible to address the question of "terror." Examining crucial turning points in modern jihadi action, Chapter 7, "Jihad as Terror," tried to establish how the Quranic concept of war – “to strike terror in the heart of the enemy” – has morphed in modern times into a compound of Gnostic cult, tribal outlook, Islamic jihad, and Bolshevik terror. It has been the aim of this book to explore how this happened and what it generated.

Washington, DC, September 2004–September 2007

1

"We Love Death"

You only love talking of death and the dead and I have wearied of all that.
Naguib Mahfuz

Terrorists

The endless Peloponnesian War led to such an erosion of moral values, remarked Greek historian Thucydides, that the "revolutionary passions" it unleashed broke the time-honored boundaries of civility, decency, and respect for human life:

> Revolution thus ran its course from city to city, and the places where it arrived at last, from having heard what had been done before, carried to a still greater extent the refinement of their inventions, as manifested in the cunning of their enterprises and the atrocity of their reprisals. Words had to change their ordinary meaning. [...] In the confusion into which life was now thrown in the cities, human nature, always rebelling against the law and now its master, gladly showed itself ungoverned in passion, above respect for justice... doing away with those general laws to which all alike can look for salvation in adversity.[1]

By exalting the most evil passions, the never-ending war dissolved society into anomie. But what happens if such an inversion of values, instead of a temporary aberration, becomes permanent, if it becomes an influential doctrine, if it reshapes the minds of many? In the modern world, the fateful phrase uttered by Friedrich Nietzsche, "God is dead," turned anomie into nihilism, it turned social cataclysm into doctrine. Drawing radical consequences, Fyodor Dostoyevsky's character Ivan Karamazov's assertion "If

[1] Thucydides, *Peloponnesian War*, 3.82.3–6 and 3.84.2.

God is dead, everything is permitted" encapsulated for the nineteenth century this very inversion of values. Absent moorings of any sort, the disappearance of "God," the fundamental anchor of morality, legitimized the stupendous contention that "everything is permitted." So were overthrown thousands of years of social life.

Some claimed for themselves the privilege – "If God is dead..." – at all times, in the name and for the sake of their good intent. It left their untrammeled personal decision the judge and arbiter of life and death. The Russian terrorists of the late nineteenth century were aptly called "Nihilists."

Starting in the 1860s, in several successive waves (late 1860s, 1878–81, 1887–90, 1902–13), a series of acts of terror stunned Russia. Pistols and bombs felled members of the Russian ruling class. At first, good Russian society treated the terrorists with some respect, as noble rebels with a cause. To effect change, it was said that no way but terror was available. Though they did kill, these young souls loathed killing.[2] Soon enough, however, this "good" terrorism yielded to far more egregious action. Political killing became indiscriminate. Hails of bombs and bullets fell grand dukes, ministers and officials, and senior bureaucrats. Finally, the terrorists murdered Czar Alexander II the Liberator, arguably the most forward-looking and liberalizing monarch in Russian history, who had abolished serfdom.

The political killing spree now seemed to herald a new era of politics, marked by actions wholly disconnected from recognizable moral moorings.[3] Until then, for all its violence, European history had only known two forms of political murder: regicide, which targeted rulers exclusively, and Robespierre's *Terreur* where the state unilaterally cast aside all custom and suspended all laws to decree the death of opponents, in a fashion reminiscent of ancient Roman proscriptions, but in the name of an ideology.[4] Apologists justified both regicide and Terreur by the excellence and purity of the intent: the end justified the means.

In his novel *The Devils* (or *The Possessed*), Dostoyevsky portrayed a group of Nihilists who turned their energies to outright murder. The novelist was drawing from the real-life case of Sergei Nechaev, a young thug and petty delinquent, who coauthored a *Catechism of a Revolutionist* (1869)

[2] Walter Laqueur, *No End to War: Terrorism in the 21st Century*, New York & London, Continuum, 2004, 11. Also see Albert Camus, *Les Justes*, Paris, Gallimard, 1952.

[3] See, inter alia, Ronald Hingley, *Russian Radicals and Revolutionaries in the Reign of Alexander II (1855–1881)*, London, Weidenfeld & Nicolson, 1967; [Général] Alexandre Spiridovich, *Histoire du terrorisme russe* (1886–1917), Paris, Payot, 1930.

[4] Jacob L. Talmon, *Political Messianism: The Romantic Phase,* New York, Frederick A. Prager Publishers, 1960.

with aging anarchist doctrinaire Mikhail Bakunin. It included the famous passage:

The Revolutionist is a doomed man. He has no private interests, no affairs, sentiments, ties, property nor even a name of his own. His entire being is devoured by one purpose, one thought, one passion – the revolution. Heart and soul, not merely by word but by deed, he has severed every link with the social order and with the entire civilized world; with the laws, good manners, conventions, and morality of that world. He is its merciless enemy and continues to inhabit it with only one purpose – to destroy it.

It went on to say:

Our mission is terrible, total, general, pitiless destruction. [...] The goal is but one: the fastest possible destruction of this filthy regime. [...] [Nechaev's new man] is not a revolutionist if he has pity for anything in this world. He must be able to destroy situations, relations or people that belong to this world: all of those must be equally hateful to him [because] he has [waged] a war of cleansing. He does not mix [with them]. He is of another nature. He belongs in the other society. He is not linked to the common morality, for there is no such thing. He does not acknowledge the morality of this filthy society. On the other hand, he is absolutely linked to the morality that stems from the [revolutionary] doctrine and which prevails amongst those who know. [...] He despises and detests the present morality of society in all its motivations and its expressions. To him, moral is what contributes to the triumph of the revolution, immoral and criminal what hinders it.

Nechaev could conclude: "Between [the revolutionary] on the one hand, the State and society on the other, there exists a state of war, visible or invisible, but permanent and implacable, a life and death war." The "filthy society" is divided amongst several categories for purposes of its destruction: The first category includes those sentenced to death without delay, those lower down in the killing order will be killed based "on the degree of usefulness of their death for the cause of the revolution."[5]

In its radical rejection of commonly accepted norms and values, in its methods, Nechaev's terror was a forerunner of the great totalitarian terror of the twentieth century in its various forms, Bolshevism, national socialism, fascism, and Maoism. His were but two-bit assassinations compared to the massive massacres that were to follow, but his short odyssey in murder captured the essence of the phenomenon.[6]

[5] Quoted by Alain Besançon, *Les origines intellectuelles du Léninisme*, Paris, Calmann-Lévy, 1977, 133–8.

[6] See Richard Pipes, *The Unknown Lenin: From the secret Archives*, New Haven, CT, Yale University Press, 1996; V. Zazubrin, *Shchepka* [*Le tchékiste*, Paris, Christian Bourgeois, 1992].

If we replace "revolutionist" by *mujahid* and "filthy society" by *jahiliyya*, the concept of the modern paganism and barbarism developed especially by radical Islamist theoreticians Maududi and Sayyid Qutb, Nihilists and jihadis are a match. In a bizarre twist of history, the Russian Nihilists' departure from the common grounds of accepted norms of human conduct has in turn been turned upside down by Islamic terrorists. The Islamists justify their own denial of the norms that prevail in any society as preconditions for society's own survival – whichever the religion – by invoking God's will: "God wills it, everything is therefore permitted," as one may sum up their apologies *pro suo*, as will be documented, where "everything" means types of crimes loathed by societies everywhere.

Instrumental or accidental crimes, crimes committed in a fit, are "normal" crimes: A burglar kills to protect his anonymity; a gang leader orders a witness to be eliminated to prevent him from testifying; a jealous spouse kills in a fit of rage or passion. Rarely does this involve a positive lust for blood and joy of killing. If so, normal crime has morphed into an abnormal, exceptional form of crime. The lust for blood and killing expresses an infinite lust for power, control, and domination. Is there a greater (if pathological), more intoxicating sense of power than that in which a man tortures, invades, torments, maims the body, severs limbs and more of another one? *Wille zur Macht*, the will to power, the exacerbated desire for overpowering and controlling, expresses itself *in fine* as bloodlust.

Bloodlust

Leon Klinghoffer, a wheelchair-bound 69-year-old, was shot to death and then thrown overboard off the cruise ship *Achille-Lauro* by the Palestinian terrorists of Abu Abbas (the Palestine Liberation Front, a member group of the Palestine Liberation Organization) on October 7, 1985.[7] The throat of a first-class passenger on board American Airlines Flight 11 on September 11, 2001, was needlessly slit. Both cases were gratuitous atrocities, unless some inner urge impelled the killers: What generates this urge is the object of this investigation. Both, however, were witnessed but not recorded. But the decapitation on camera of Nicholas Berg in Iraq, the filmed beheading of Paul Johnson in Saudi Arabia, Daniel Pearl's throat being slit "live" in Pakistan,[8] Margaret Hassan being made to cry and beg for her life in Iraq

[7] Barry Rubin and Judith Kolp Rubin, *Yasir Arafat: A Political Biography*, Oxford, Oxford University Press, 2003, 106.

[8] According to published reports, when Daniel Pearl's throat was first slashed, a technical error caused it not to be captured on film. In the video, Pearl's corpse is shown naked from the

in front of her tormentors' camcorder, and many other such instances of snuff movies shot and spread by Islamists are *prima facie* evidence in the diagnosis: The nature of worldwide Islamist terror is *sui generics*, its nature different from the "usual" forms of terrorism with which it has often been assimilated. This terror is an Islamist innovation, and it has remained mostly an Islamist monopoly.[9]

Not only were many terrorist atrocities filmed, they were publicized, reproduced on videotapes, and aired around the clock by al-Jazeera and other Middle Eastern television channels. This was not just bragging: it was flaunting one's exhilarating sense of total power and offering the viewing public a chance vicariously to partake in it. The killing of Westerners gave viewers, as it gave perpetrators, a sense of identity.

It was a pornography of crime, snuff movies served as political fare, or, even worse, as identity fare: This, O Muslim brothers, is who we are; we slay for our God, our God demands the slaying. I kill, therefore I am. The mass consumption of Islamist snuff movies in most of the Muslim world must be explained. The May 2004 videotaped decapitation of Nicholas Berg, released by the group led by Abu Musab al-Zarqawi, was the most popular search item on the Internet.[10] Demand meets supply: Islamists provide the show; masses of television viewers avidly lap it up. If a wave of revulsion greeted the gruesome show, it would simply not be aired. Viewers recognize something of themselves in the shows, showmasters project and propose a sense of identity: *Allahu akbar* ululated as basso continuo while a human being is being bled like an animal. A conception that treats human beings like animals is one that fails to make a difference between man and beast. It is getting closer to the ancient practice of human sacrifice.[11] "Whoever has

waist up, laying on a blanket; a man's arm is holding his head forward so that his cut neck cannot be seen. With the knife in his other hand, the man proceeds to cut deeper into Pearl's neck, from the back to the front. There is little blood. The remaining 90 seconds of the video consist of a list of demands scrolling by, superimposed over a picture of Pearl's severed head being held by the hair.

9 Explaining Islamist terror with its specific forms by arguing that "occupation" or "grievances" cause it must bear the burden of explaining why other cultures do not cause similar effects or reactions. Short of taking the culture into account, the "explanation" is little more than a peremptory tautology.

10 Ibrahim al-Marashi, "Iraq's Hostage Crisis: Kidnapping, Mass Media and the Iraqi Insurgency," *The Middle East Review of International Affairs* (MERIA), vol. 8 (December 2004), p. 9.

11 The interest in the gory and the macabre often exploited by sensationalist media in the West is of a different nature: It manipulates the prurient for its own sake (or for profit), whereas Islamist snuff systematically shows the "enemies of Allah" being gored, and the "soldiers of Allah" goring them.

lived in the Orient knows how alive the persuasion has remained to this day that the blood spilled is possessed of incontrovertibly purifying virtue."[12]

A 2000 videofilm produced and distributed by the London-based jihadi Azzam Films shows an ambush in Chechnya: The *Mujahideen* parade a lone Russian survivor, a terrified boy who might not be much older than 18. In shock, he staggers and is machine-gunned, while a call to prayer in Arabic is intoned, and a litany of martial songs is played. Bloody corpses are displayed. The scene is in Duba-Yort in Chechnya, "Allahu akbar" is chanted three times in front of the Russian corpses; the snow is red-gored, the Mujahideen show pride, they desecrate the corpses by kicking them.[13]

The Martyrs of Bosnia is a more ambitious and more professional movie. It shows the stories of foreign *Mujahideen* killed in Bosnia.[14] It starts with a quote by Osama bin Laden's mentor Abdullah Azzam: "Indeed the manuscripts of history are not scribed except with the blood of these '*shahada*' [martyrs]." Most of the movie is devoted to close-up mug shots of dead *Mujahideen*, in *rigor mortis*, their mangled bodies, the flies, with purposeful attention upon the caked-up blood on face and body. Every corpse is named; the time of his arrival in Bosnia and that of his death are mentioned. The 72 wives they will have found in paradise are mentioned repeatedly, as is their ability to intercede for their families. Some of the fixed shots show severed heads, eyes gouged out. The movie goes on for dozens of minutes; an erratic, rambling sermon is delivered while more "martyrs" are shown. Sometimes a testimonial from a colleague is read: "He had been hit in the head by a sniper's bullet which led to his death, and I smelled a pleasant smell emanating from him." Evidently, the filmmakers believe that death, not in the abstract, but death in all its anatomical, bodily aspects, fluids and all, is by itself motivational, and the sight of death an appealing inspiration. The movie ends with copious quotes from Abdullah Azzam, Sayyid Qutb, Sheikh Yasin, and other martyrs.

Elsewhere, a videofilm shot in Iraq opens with a martial quote from the Quran; a middle-aged, redheaded man is shown crouching, his hands restrained, the prisoner of two jihadis who are clad in black and clutching submachine guns. The man is blindfolded; his identification is shown to the

[12] Alfred Morabia, *Le Ǧihad dans l'Islam médiéval: le combat sacré des origines au XIIè siècle*, Paris, Albin Michel, 1993, p. 18.

[13] My heartfelt thanks to Steve Emerson and The Investigative Project of Washington, DC, especially Ryan Evans, who helped me into their vast video archives. All the following snapshots were gleaned there.

[14] London, Azzam Publications, BCM Uhud, 2000. See www.azzam.com, accessed November 11, 2005.

camera. He is made to confess his "crimes." After a few long minutes of coerced contrition, both jihadis suddenly pounce on him, press him down on the floor. With a long knife, one of them hacks at his carotid artery – there is a muffled moan, blood spills, the knife hacks away, and the head is severed and brandished, as an inscription and a chant inform the viewer "in the name of Allah the merciful, the compassionate." Another Iraqi movie shows the killing of the Blackwater Co. contractors in Fallujah. "Allahu akhbar" resounds ceaselessly. Time and again, the corpses are kicked, punched, and hit; the blackened bodies are shown repeatedly. Added footage shows the corpses of U.S. servicemen torn to shreds; the severed head of one of them, an African-American, is brandished. They have been kidnapped and tortured. This is not too obscene: It must be shown, just as one dead soldier's gashed rib cage is compulsory viewing. Another severed head is desecrated with the sole of a shoe and toyed with, a supreme insult in the Arab world. "Glory to the *Mujahideen*," intones an off-screen voice.

The "Mujahideen Shura Council," an Al-Qaeda spinoff, produced the following videos: Time and again, a jubilant lynch mob is shown burning the corpse of an Apache pilot, "*Allahu akbar*!" to the sound of martial Islamic music. In another production of the same, a man presented as a "CIA agent" is shown with a sign to that effect around his neck; he has been badly beaten up. He sits behind a table; the "evidence" of his guilt is read out. A Quran is opened. A group of a half a dozen armed and masked men now stands behind him – he is bound to a chair. The slaughterer approaches and hacks perhaps ten times at his neck, until the head is cut off; the small crowd cheers, the head is waved about. "*Allahu akbar*." As the icon of Islamic vengeance, Saladin had said: "The sword of Islam only leaves its scabbard to plunge into the infidels' neck."[15]

Wherever jihadis operate in the world, their delight at killing and displaying the slaughter is pervasive. Stories and reports, films and pictures, all testify to the ubiquity of the practice and the sentiments that go with it. Some of the material that documents the sentiment reveals far more than the explicit content: It brings to light the underlying motivation and the belief structure that enable this behavior. Zarqawi and his fellow jihadis "have chosen a slow, torturous method to terrorize the Western audience."[16]

Aziz Salha, 20, from the village of Dir Jarir on the West Bank, was shot on October 12, 2000, in Ramallah. Two young Israeli reserve soldiers took

[15] Albert Champdor, *Saladin*, Paris, Albin Michel, 1956, 125.

[16] Timothy R. Furnish, "Beheading in the Name of Islam," *Middle East Quarterly*, Spring 2005.

FIGURE 1.1. Ramallah, October 12, 2000: Aziz Salha has dipped his hands in the blood of two lynched Israeli soldiers; Salha and spectators share in the same emotional state.

the wrong turn, drove into the center of town, were cornered by a mob of Palestinians, and lynched when the throng broke into the precarious shelter they had found. The young man shown in Figure 1.1 soaked his hands in their blood and exuberantly displayed it to the jubilant crowd. This was not just plain murder, it was human sacrifice: I (we) kill him (them) so that we can live.

Killing an enemy is part of war. Why revel in it and wallow in the blood, why display ecstatic merriment to the delighted frenzy of the crowd? Why does the crowd applaud and enthuse? There is revenge and elation at avenging a perceived loss of dignity and honor. The slaying is not instrumental: it is an act in itself; it is human sacrifice. The blood of the enemy renews the identity of the lynch mob: To be a Palestinian is to spill the blood of Israelis. Death is not an instrumentality – like the death of the enemy on the battlefield – it has become an end in itself. How else may we fathom the signs on the walls of Hamas kindergarten in Gaza, "The Children Are the Holy Martyrs of Tomorrow"?[17] Death is a source of unalloyed joy: "We love death."

[17] Laqueur, *No End to War*, 94.

Transgression: Thou Shalt Not Murder

Inflicting pain upon another human being is a transgression of the norms that regulate all societies. Elaborate rules are maintained to prohibit the mutual infliction of severe pain, maiming, and killing of members of that society. Morality, the commandment "Thou shalt not murder," reflect and codify an interdict which is a *sine qua non* condition for members of society to maintain orderly lives. Moral rules are the conditioning norms that society rears children to internalize, the social "superego." Their respect guarantees social order. They are an anthropological invariant, in the sense that *homo socialis* is restrained and prevented from murdering. Disregard for this invariant is a severely punished transgression of the social order. Legitimate authority alone is empowered to wield violence upon the members of society (criminal law) or law itself makes provision for the socially approved, regulated usage of private violence (e.g., the rules of vendetta amongst Arabs or the Blood Law amongst Ancient Germans).[18]

The norms are valid in times of peace. Do they remain so in times of war? Wartime killing lifts the moral onus from the individual, by shifting it up onto political power and its military instrument. Legitimate authority instructs and entrusts delegated members of society to do the killing. It is the corporate body that kills legitimately, thus preventing "killing" from being "murder." By killing at the behest of political authority, one accepts the strictures it imposes.

The private killing of members of the group is the object of a sweeping taboo, which wanes when it comes to killing strangers. Killing "them" is always easier than killing "us." Nomadic warriors, such as the Mongols, were known for their utter disrespect of any such prohibition: The world outside the tribe was but a killing field, "outside" people were akin to animals to be culled.[19] The psychocultural precondition for such disdain is the existence in the mind of the killers of an absolute, unbridgeable difference between themselves and those they kill: It is as though they belonged to two different species. We are the humans; they are the animals, the subhumans, the non-Mongols. Killing a Mongol is murder; killing a non-Mongol is disposing of an animal.[20]

18 In Tokugawa Japan, Samurais were entitled to kill commoners they suspected of having disrespected them – death so inflicted was conceived as a punishment for a transgression of the social order rather than as an arbitrary action.

19 See John Keegan, *The History of Warfare*, New York, Vintage Books, 1993.

20 See Laurent Murawiec, "Geopolitics and Strategic Cultures: A Comparison of the Chinese, Nomadic, Islamic and Western Ways of War," London, Routledge & Keegan Paul, 2008 (forthcoming).

Contrary to tribal and nomadic societies, sedentary society has increasingly tried to reject the wanton killing or infliction of violence upon those defined either as "innocent," children, or "weak" or as "incapable of defending themselves," women and old people. Even war against outsiders, however defined, has been subjected to regulation in the form of the Laws of War. By promoting its "Truce of God," the medieval Church sought to make certain categories of population immune to the depredations and wanton savagery of knights.

What traditionally remained was a general, and generally accepted, reluctance to kill those defined as innocent or weak; it is part of what the superego in any society wants the growing human being to internalize: Social rules are made to control the bestial impulse in society's members. In any society, the transgressor must mentally and morally face the whole of society and of society's norms in the guise of his own superego as he contemplates his transgression. The rule holds in the Muslim conception of the Good Life as well as in that of other societies.[21]

An individual who transgresses the taboo crosses a line not only with respect to society but also in his own mind: he knowingly places himself outside society by violating a fundamental norm. Conversely, this violation gives the criminal a new sense of power since he has just overpowered the burdensome superego within himself, and thus placed himself above society. He has freed himself from the heavy shackles of internalized norms. This act of rebellion establishes the guilty individual as the autocrat of his own will; it places his own will above that of society and its norms.

At least in part, this "liberation" cannot but be psychologically lived through as an exhilarating experience: The lifting of the burden "lightens" the individual. Crime will make you free! You have become superior to the rest, the *hoi polloi* who are shackled by conventional rules. Killing – especially the weak and the innocent – is in that sense an intensely satisfactory emotional event, an addictive one: hence serial killings and serial killers. Few events procure the intensity of emotional satisfaction thus encountered, since few liberate the individual from so heavy a burden as that of one of the fundamental commandments of social life: The pleasure is commensurate with the severity of the interdict, and likewise the energy generated and released by the violation. There is an element of hubris in it, which in turn is a great and energetic facilitator of the crime: The killer plays God; he disposes of life and death at his pleasure.

[21] See, infra, Chapter 2.

In their investigations of serial murderers, criminologists have developed a typology that enhances our understanding of Islamic terror. Their six types are summarized next – taking into account the fact that acts of terror are committed by a group rather than an individual (or, in the case of homicide-bombing, an individual acting as the sharp end of a group), as a result of which the sexual element so often encountered in serial murders is largely lessened, and probably sublimated.[22]

The *hedonistic lust killer* is the one least applicable, since it involves a direct sexual element and an active component of sexual necrophilia, neither of which is corroborated by the mass of reports on terror incidents; the *thrill killers* "also derive satisfaction from their murders, but they require a live victim for sexual satisfaction. In contrast to the lust killer, thrill killers receive sexual pleasure from torturing, dominating, terrorizing, and humiliating their victims while they are alive." The *comfort killer* as a type who kills for creature comfort does not concern us here; the *power/control killer* "murders to obtain a sense of domination and total control over the victim. Although sex is sometimes involved, the pleasure is not derived from the sex act in itself (as with lust or thrill killers) but from the complete control that the offender has over the victim"; the *mission killer* "murders because he is on a mission to rid the world of a group of people he perceives as unworthy or inferior in some way"; the *visionary killer* "is characterized by a severe break with reality... frequently driven by voices or images that command them to kill." This type, more of a "psychotic killer" when he is an individual, may change in a terrorist context: Under a charismatic leader, the "break with reality" will be legitimized; the "voices" will emanate from the leader.[23]

This typology places serial murderers in the realm of psychopathology. This does not lessen the murderers' responsibility nor does it imply that the murderers are "insane":

> Most serial killers are not found to suffer from a psychosis and can typically distinguish right from wrong, know exactly what they are doing, and can control their desire to kill – but choose not to. They are more cruel than crazy. Their crimes may be sickening, but their minds are not necessarily sick [...] Indeed, those assailants who are deeply confused or disoriented are generally not capable of the level of planning and organization necessary."[24]

[22] Alex Alvarez and Ronet Bachman, *Murder American Style*, Belmont, CA, Wadsworth/Thomson Learning, 2003, 132–3.

[23] Ibid.

[24] Ibid., 134.

Further study shows that "serial killers tend to kill strangers since killing strangers may also make it easier to dehumanize the victims; the vulnerability of the victim is an essential targeting criterion."[25]

While displaying signs congruent with the psychopathological, the serial killers' mind cannot be reduced to it. Psychopathology itself begs multiple questions – Why? Whence? Criminologists factor in the environmental factors, the "nature" and the "nurture." A phenomenon that flourishes in the political realm like jihadi terror is even more dependent on historical and cultural roots.

This however is only half of the picture: The burden of conscience expressed as remorse and guilt may linger in the mind of the perpetrator. Even the mass-murdering Nazi *Einsatzkommandos* that operated against Eastern European and Russian Jewry in World War II had to be boosted with booze and drugs. Even the SS units assigned to mass extermination needed some furlough to escape the psychological burden of their crimes – for which they had volunteered. Even the powerful grip of national-socialist ideology had to compete with vestiges of the internalized, if rejected, Christian ethic, as SS Reichsführer Heinrich Himmler bitterly complained in his infamous Łodz speech of 1943.[26] This makes the killing frenzy of the Islamists even more significant. Legal sanction is available aplenty to appease scruples. Hear a fatwa by Palestinian radical Abu Qatada "allowing the children of the apostates to be killed in order to live the torment of the children of the mujahideen."[27]

In the killer-in-becoming, knowledge of one's rejection of accepted social norms and customs must be counterbalanced and offset by a power commensurate with the formers' grip on the individual's conscience. In effect, the individual superego must be reconstructed, rewired, so to speak: the *Führer*, the *duce*, the *guru*, the *propheta*, the *Mahdi* will replace the superego. Traditionally, in the psychology of conversion, this is seen as "brainwashing." It entails the subject breaking up with his former self and the former self's attachments – family, friends, studies, profession, environment, cultural habits. The ersatz superego acquired in the course of the conversion is

[25] Ibid., 131–2.

[26] See Christopher R. Browning, *Ordinary Men: Reserve Police Battalion 101 and the Final Solution in Poland*, New York, HarperPerennial, 1993; also Richard Breitman, "Himmler and the 'Terrible Secret' among the Executioners," Journal of Contemporary History, vol. 26, no. 3/4, The Impact of Western Nationalisms: Essays Dedicated to Walter Z. Laqueur on the Occasion of His 70th Birthday (September, 1991), pp. 431–51.

[27] David Cook, *Understanding Jihad*, Berkley, Los Angeles & London, University of California Press, 2005, p. 121.

able to implant its own belief structure (communist, fascist, Nazi, Islamist) in the mind of the convert. New sets of rules replace those commonly accepted by the erstwhile personality.

In the killer's former, precrime life, lived within the prevailing social–moral norms, life was held to be the highest value. In his new self, the killer asserts his freedom from his ancient "servitude" by denying the highest value of the former self, and the society in which the self existed, by actively suppressing life. In the commission of a heinous crime, the element of glee is of prime importance. It is a primitive victory emotion, like a victory dance, an expression of triumph. Deeper down, glee is the expression of unlimited power, the heady elation of pure, sheer power: inflicting pain upon someone and being the master of his life and death. *I kill; therefore I am.* Killing becomes the supreme expression of power. In military ethic, killing is an instrumentality of war.[28] In Islamist *jihad*, killing is not just a means to an end; means and end have merged. The samurai, or the feudal warrior in general, does not derive pleasure from the act of killing itself; the pleasure springs from the feeling of a job well done, according to the requiremments of *bushido*. The Islamist does and broadcasts it.

In wartime, enemy combatants are the target; enemy civilians are incidental victims, "collateral damage," even in the case of the ill thought-out "strategic" bombings of Germany in World War II. We are shocked when Shakespeare's Henry V utters the foulest threats against the civilians of besieged Harfleur.[29] Hence, after the systematic carnage of civilians in the course of the Thirty Year's War, war in Europe was codified.

The Muslim world has elaborated precise rules of jihad.[30] Traditional jihad was not a "license to kill." Let us listen to what even a modern jihadi author, Pakistan's influential brigadier S. K. Malik, has to say:

> The Quran imposed a total ban on the inhuman methods of warfare practiced in Arabia and elsewhere, prior to Islam.... all cruel and torturous ways of killing the enemy are prohibited. The killing of women, minors, servants and slaves, who ought to accompany their masters in war but do not take part in the actual fighting, is also not allowed. The Muslim armies must also spare the blind, the monks, the hermits, the old, the physically deformed and the insane or the mentally deficient. Forbidden also is the decapitation of the prisoners of war; the mutilation of men and beast; treachery and perfidy; devastation and destruction of harvests; and adultery

[28] Shannon E. French, *The Code of the Warrior: Exploring Warrior Values Past and Present*, Lanham, MD, Rowman & Littlefield, 2003.

[29] Act III, Scene 2.

[30] See, inter alia, Jean-Paul Charnay, *L'Islam et la guerre – de la guerre juste à la révolution sainte*, Paris, Fayard, 1986.

and fornication with captive women. The killing of enemy hostages, and resorting to massacres to vanquish an enemy is prohibited. The killing of [relatives] except in absolute self-defense; and the killing of peasants, traders, merchants, contractors and the like who do not take part in actual fighting is also not allowed.[31]

The *ulama* who regulated jihad meant to channel the warriors' recklessness in ways beneficial to the caliphate or whichever Muslim monarch claimed legitimate rulership. Women, children, and other categories were booty, potential slaves, therefore the chattel should be spared; booty was an instrumentality of the tribe. Jihad was not wanton murder but legally regulated (*Sharia*); what killing took place was lawful killing.[32] In the desert, the Bedouins do not condone a member of the tribe who goes off to war on his own but only he who does so at the behest and on behalf of the group.

The prohibition was thus graduated: The closer the individual is to the family, the clan, and the tribe, the greater the prohibition; the more distant the individual is from that center, the weaker the prohibition.

Arguably, Malik prettifies the rules of jihad for apologetic reasons. His jihad is noble, righteous, and innocent. But such is the self-conception of the jihadi, and such is traditional legal norm. In reality, the rationale for sparing the lives of women, children, and other categories is that they are booty for the jihadi raiders. The Quranic concept has no notion of innocent ones or civilians: They are all part of the enemy tribe, even if the "tribe" is now called "heretics" or "unbelievers."[33] The fact remains nonetheless that even if it is for instrumental or utilitarian reasons, and not for principle or humane reasons, the Islamic rules of jihad do not automatically condone the slaughter of the weak. Whether the world of Islam honored it in the breech or only on occasion does not detract from this norm being the promulgated and divinely sanctioned standard. Modern jihad has strayed far from this norm. Al-Qaida's "Training Manual" states:

If God decrees that you are to slaughter, you should dedicate the slaughter to your fathers.... If you slaughter, do not cause the discomfort of those you are killing, because this is one of the practices of the prophet... implement the way of the prophet in taking prisoners. Take prisoners and kill them. As Almighty God said: "No prophet should take prisoners until he has soaked the land with blood."[34]

[31] S. K. Malik, *The Quranic Concept of War*, Lahore, Wajidalis, 1979, 47–8.

[32] Shmuel Bar, *Warrant for Terror: The Fatwas of Radical Islam and the Duty of Jihad*, Lanham, MD, Rowman & Littlefield, 2006, esp. Chapters 3, 4, and 6.

[33] See Ibid., passim.

[34] "Al-Qaida Training Manual," *in* Barry Rubin and Judith Kolp Rubin, eds., *Anti-Americanism and the Middle East: A Documentary Reader*, Oxford, Oxford University Press, 2002, p. 237.

The suicide-killing manual ("Suicide Note") left by Muhammad Atta, leader of the September 11, 2001, killing squads, included this revealing comment: "13. Check your weapon before you leave [for the mission] and long before you leave. (You must make your knife sharp and you must not discomfort your animal during the slaughter.)"[35] The victim is thus degraded to the status of an animal slated for sacrifice. Terror killing is a resumption of the practice of human sacrifice. The power of the victim, which flows out of its body with his blood, enters the sacrificator's system. The victims, animal-like human beings, are a sacrificial offering to God.[36] Bin Laden's hijackers used the box-cutter like the curved dagger, the *khandjar*, used by the Islamic warrior swiftly to cut the throat of the enemy.[37]

We have thus drifted closer and closer to the ancient practice of human sacrifice for bloodthirsty gods. In these, human life is an instrumentality for the gods, and for the societies that abided by the bloodthirsty gods' desires. Human sacrifice propitiates the god. The Incas sacrificed youths to the Sun God, "bestowing considerable prestige on the child's parents and on their local community." The Aztecs thought the blood flowing down the steps of their pyramids was needed to keep the Sun on its daily path. "Human sacrifice is not just a ritual act designed to appease the gods, divine the future, or bring luck and prosperity to those offering the sacrifice. It covers all situations in which a human life is exchanged for a greater cause."[38] By the time the British put it down, the Thug cult of Kali, which supplied its victims' blood to the goddess, had slaughtered up to one million over a period of six centuries.[39]

Baal, sun, lord, god, was a common name for ancient Syrian and Persian deities. The annual rituals of his death and resurrection as a fertility deity included human sacrifice. The practice was frequent. Mesha, for instance, king of Moab, pressed by the Israelites, sacrificed his own son (II Kings 3:27). The Phoenicians sacrificed especially children to Moloch, the great god, and spread the cult around the Mediterranean. In the ancient Phoenician-Punic religion, Diodorus reported how and why the cult of Baal sacrificed human

[35] http://www.mindfully.org/Reform/Photos-Hijackers-DOJ27sep01.htm, translation of the hijacker letter by Hatem Bazian.

[36] "Last Words of a Terrorist," The Observer, London, September 30, 2001, http://www.guardian.co.uk/world/2001/sep/30/terrorism.september113.

[37] My thanks to Dr. Hans-Ulrich Seidt for this suggestive notation.

[38] Dr. Mike Parker-Jones, BBC, March 1, 2003, bbc.co.uk/history/ancient/prehistory/human_sacrifice_03.shtml. Also, Jacques Soustelle, *La vie quotidienne des Aztèques*, Paris, Editions Hachette, 1955.

[39] Barry Cooper, *New Political Religions, or an Analysis of Modern Terrorism*, Columbia & London, University of Missouri Press, 2004, p. 35.

beings: "Vanquished . . . and threatened in their very city . . . the Carthaginians ascribed their defeat to the wrath of the gods and decided to exorcize it to sacrifice to . . . Baal Hammon five hundred children of noble families."[40] Consistent with the arrested sacrifice of Isaac, prophet Elijah discredits King Ahab's belief in the power of Baal and denounced him as a murderer (I Kings 21:17–24).

Islamic terror, in its use of human sacrifice, has strayed farther and farther away from this pivotal event in the history of mankind, the prohibition of human sacrifice enshrined in the biblical story of Abraham and Isaac on Mount Horeb (Genesis 22:19). God's arresting of Abraham's arm symbolizes the sacredness of human life (which Immanuel Kant will rephrase later as: "Act in such a way that you treat humanity, whether in your own person or in the person of any other, always at the same time as an end and never simply as a means"[41]). In Judges 11:39, in fulfillment of a vow, Jephthah offered his daughter in sacrifice: Rabbinical literature treats it as an abomination. In Judaism, a Jew murdered is a *korban*, a martyr; this notion of the martyr was passed on to Christianity: Martyrdom is the willingness to die as a witness to God and never entails the harming of anyone else. Human sacrifice is an abomination because each man is endowed with an immortal soul and has been made "in the image and likeness" of God. Human sacrifice denies precisely that.

In his classic study of the *Assassins* of Hasan-I Sabbah, the Ismaili sect that terrorized the Near East from the late eleventh century until the Mongols exterminated them, Bernard Lewis draws attention to the singularity of the terrorist sect:

> The ancient ideal of tyrannicide, the religious obligation to rid the world of an unrighteous ruler, certainly contributed to the practice of assassination, as adopted and applied by the Ismailis. But there was more to it than that. The killing by the Assassin of his victim was not only an act of piety; it also had a ritual, almost a sacramental quality. It is significant that in all their murders, in both Persia and Syria, the Assassins always used a dagger. [. . .] Human sacrifice and ritual murder have no place in Islamic law, tradition or practice. Yet both are ancient and deep-rooted in human societies, and can reappear in unexpected places.[42]

It is precisely the ritualistic element in Islamic murders performed as snuff movies – the chanting, the ululation, the throat slitting or the neck

[40] André Cacqot, "Les religions des sémites occidentaux," in Henri-Charles Puech, general ed., *Histoire des religions*, vol. 1, Encyclopédie de la Pléiade, Paris, Gallimard, 1970, 335.

[41] Immanuel Kant, *Groundwork for a Metaphysics of Morals.*

[42] Bernard Lewis, *The Assassins: A Radical Sect in Islam*, London, Weidenfeld & Nicolson, 1967; paperback: New York, Basic Books, 2003, 127.

hacking, the black-hooded killers – that unbeknownst to the killers manifests a kinship with human sacrifices.[43]

The brutal reappearance of human sacrifice in the twentieth century reshaped Islamic practice or, in a way, contemporary Islam. We will now follow how that reshaping progressed.

The terrorist draws power from the fear he inspires, from the terror he instills in his victims. It is as though he drew sustenance from the fright of the prey. The complete satisfaction of the *Wille zur Macht* is attained at the orgasmic moment of killing – with a dagger preferably, so that blood spills, so that the integrity of the victim's body is defiled.

The Blood Trail of Islamic Terror

The scent of the blood trail may be traced back one generation ago, on November 28, 1971, at the Sheraton Hotel in Cairo. Jordan's Prime Minister Wasfi al-Tell walked into the lobby of the hotel surrounded by bodyguards: The PLO had threatened to kill him to avenge the Jordanian government's repression of the PLO's "Black September" uprising:

> Five . . . shots, fired at point-blank range, hit [him]. . . . He staggered back against the shattered swing doors, trying to draw his own gun, but his strength had already left him and he fell dying among the shards of glass on the marble floor. As he lay there, one of his killers bent over and lapped the blood that poured from his wounds.[44]

According to another version: "One of the assassins also knelt down and licked the blood that was flowing onto the marble floor."[45]

Something out of the ordinary was occurring, not war in the accepted sense, not political conflict or even guerrilla warfare. Something else was occurring – the object of this investigation.

Inseparable, as will be shown, from contemporary Islamic terrorism are the idolization of blood, the veneration of savagery, the cult of killing, the worship of death. Gruesome murder and gory infliction of pain are lionized and proffered as models, as exemplary actions pleasing to Allah and opening the gates of paradise. The highest religious authorities sanction or condone it, government authorities approve and organize it, intellectuals and the media praise them. From one end of the Muslim world to the other, similar reports abound.

[43] Ronald H. Jones, "Terrorist Beheadings: Cultural and Strategic Implications," SSI Carlisle Barracks, June 2005, passim.

[44] Christopher Dobson, *Black September: Its Short, Violent History*, New York, Macmillan, 1974, p. 1.

[45] Jillian Becker, *The PLO: The Rise and Fall of the Palestine Liberation Organization*, New York, Saint Martin's Press, 1984, p. 77.

Franco-Iranian scholar Farhad Khosrokhavar recounts the following from the Algerian civil war of the 1990s. One of the means used by Islamists to

neutralize the taboo of killing is mentally to train the adherent to murders or massacres described as religious rituals during which "enemies" are assassinated. This is the case of video-cassettes [...] where fighters are seen waging bloody actions against enemies whom they put to death. One of those was recorded by the radical Algerian group Predication and Combat. It is entitled "Algeria." [...] The cassette with the divine injunction "Combat them until the judgment of God is executed on Earth." A comment adds: "Our enemies fight in the name of Satan, you fight in the name of God." The *mujahidin* ambush a unit of the Algerian Army. A military convoy draws near on a road, an explosion is seen which smashes the truck and the soldiers on it. The militants arrive on the site of the explosion. The video-film shows the carnage. The gored bodies of young draftees are shown on screen, one of them beheaded, another reduced to a heap of shredded flesh. Suddenly, a clamor from one of the guerrillas: one of the soldiers is still alive. The fighter unsheathes a dagger and instantly slits the throat of the wounded. The film returns five times to the clip of the blood spurting from the gashed man's carotid artery. The act [slitting the throat] is repeated with the corpses of the other dead soldiers.

Another videocassette entitled "The Mirror of Jihad"

shows the Afghan Talibans in the process of beheading soldiers of the Northern Alliance with daggers.... The cassettes aim, for one, at de-humanizing the enemy, even Muslims...and then, to be a lesson in the apprenticeship of murder. Putting [the victim] to death is displayed as a sacral act or goring a sheep...the enemy is as an animal whose sacrifice is [presented as] sacred. The use of a blade aims, for one, at strengthening this association, and then to connect with the memory of the military exploits of Islam's heroes.[46]

The same author recounts scenes from the Lebanese Civil War and describes "theatralized and solemn executions":

the prisoners are paraded through the streets, sometimes in chains, they are manhandled, tied to cars. The onlookers applaud, they insult and even punch the doomed man.... Often the killers are not content to kill, they relish the death of their prey, they humiliate and torture him prior to the execution. The point is to destroy the other in order to assert oneself. This is why the victim's death is divided in a thousand segments, so it may be savored fully. The ordeal is horror itself, the tormented body has become the individual property of the militiamen. Its destruction implies the destruction of the moral and social values of the opponent and his religion.... The exclusive dominion enjoyed over the person held by the captor gives the latter a

46 Farhad Khosrokhavar, *Les Nouveaux martyrs d'Allah*, Paris, Flammarion, 2002, pp. 112–13.

self-confidence and a euphoric sentiment of unlimited power, of life and death over the victim. His killing begets a renewed thirst for more deaths.[47]

Further:

The militias' slaughter of the victims occurs in a festive atmosphere, even akin to an orgy. The wounded prisoners or their corpses are dragged around, people sing and chant, play music or jump up and down, militiamen sometimes drug themselves before the celebration . . . in order to endow the collective feast with a joyful meaning. The ban is transgressed, cruelty is bliss [in] this blood carnival. The victim's blood brings the members of the clan, the family, the denomination together. Like in scape-goat ceremonies, it strengthens the bonding of the group. . . . In such celebrations, the killers, by transgressing the taboo of killing, place themselves in the position of the Hero.[48]

Not only do terrorists "carry out acts of the most ferocious and indiscriminate murder," noted British journalist Christopher Dobson, but "these acts are greeted with a support which often borders on glee, not only by the terrorists themselves, but also by admiring Arabs and Arab governments."[49]

On July 14, 1958, the Hashemite monarchy of Iraq was overthrown by a coalition led by General Qaseem. The royal family was slaughtered in a show of extreme savagery. A year later, the city of Mosul rose against the new masters:

The events . . . were accompanied by a relatively new phenomenon: mobs on the rampage who were called in to support one side or the other and who indulged in slaughter. The phenomenon first appeared on the day the monarchy was overthrown. Arif occupied the broadcasting station and began inciting the mob to take to the streets and to attack the leading figures of the fallen regime. It was this mob which seized and mutilated the corpse of Crown Prince Abd-al-Ilah, and strung up the remains at the gates of the Ministry of Defense. A few days later, a mob also caught in the street [former prime minister] Nuri al-Said, who was trying to flee disguised as a woman, murdered him, and drove a motor-car over his body, to leave it so horribly mangled as to be unrecognizable.[50]

A more graphic report so relates the death of the deposed King's uncle: He "was dragged through the streets of Baghdad tied with ropes to the back of a truck, then his body was dismembered with axes and his limbs and head tossed about by the hysterical mob. The trunk was hung from a balcony and chunks of his flesh were sliced off and thrown to the crowd below."[51]

[47] Ibid., p. 224.
[48] Ibid., p. 226.
[49] Dobson, *Black September*, pp. 56–7.
[50] Elie Kedourie, *Politics in the Middle East*, Oxford, Oxford University Press, 1992, p. 319.
[51] Becker, *The PLO*, p. 37.

In a frightful episode of the Baathist regime's immersing the Iraqi people in accepted cruelty, it summoned the Baghdadi population to the hanging of nine Iraqi Jews who were strung up on huge gallows in the center of the capital and displayed there for weeks on end in 1968:

> At first, the Iraqi public entered this new world of experiences with great gusto. Later, it grew more reserved as fear took an increasing hold. Estimates on the size of the crowds that came to view the dangling corpses spread seventy meters in Liberation Square – increasing the area of sensual contact between mutilated body and mass – vary from 150,000 to 500,000.[52]

Baghdad radio summoned people to "come and enjoy the feast." Public executions of "convicted" spies became a regular show. Makiya points out that the "hangings, involving only a few victims but permitting mass identification with the ritual, were crucial to the legitimation of Baathism in Iraq."[53] The same party in power

> telev[ized] a lengthy film clip displaying [murdered dictator] Qassem's bullet-ridden corpse. Night after night, they made their gruesome point. The body was propped up on a chair in the studio. A soldier sauntered around, handling its parts. The camera would cut to scenes of devastation at the Ministry of Defense where Qassem had made his last stand. There, on location, it lingered on the mutilated corpses of Qassem's entourage.... Back to the studio, and close ups now of the entry and exit points of each bullet hole. The whole macabre sequence closes with a scene that must forever remain etched in the memory of all those who saw it: the soldier grabbed the lolling head by the hair, came right up close, and spat full face into it.[54]

The Baathists displayed their "unconstrained willingness to use violence."[55]

A "carnival of death," the Lebanese Civil War was called.[56] The same description applies to numerous events in the post-1945 history of the Muslim Middle East.

In Baathist Syria, in retaliation for the targeted slaughter of 83 Alawite artillery cadets in Aleppo in 1979, Rifat al-Assad, brother of president Hafez al-Assad and head of the special *Saraya al-difa* (defense brigades), was given carte blanche.[57] In the small town of Jisr al-Shugur, 200 townspeople were killed in one fell swoop. The 3rd Division of the Army fell upon the great

[52] Samir al-Khalil (Kanaan Makiya), *Republic of Fea: The Inside Story of Saddam's Iraq*, New York, Pantheon Books, 1989, pp. 52–3.

[53] Ibid., p. 58.

[54] Ibid., p. 59.

[55] Ibid., p. 96.

[56] Becker, *The PLO*, p. 124.

[57] Olivier Carré and Gérard Michaud [Michel Seurat], *Les Frères musulmans* (1928–1982) [présenté par], Paris, Julliard, 1983, p. 135.

city of Aleppo: 8,000 were arrested. "The commanding officer, Shafiq Fayad, standing on top of a tank turret, solemnly warned the population that he was ready to exterminate it, 1,000 fatalities a day, as long as he had not freed them from the vermin of the Muslim Brethren."[58] The special brigades were hurled at the Palmyra Prison, where they slaughtered "several thousand opponents, Muslim Brethren or similar." A leader article in the official *Tishrin* signed by Rifat al-Assad explained: "If need be, in order to bring peace and love, we are prepared to engage one hundred battles, to destroy one thousand citadels, and to sacrifice a million martyrs."[59] In reprisal for an attack on an Alawite village nearby in April 1981, a commando unit swooped down on one district of the city of Hama, picked out at random 400 inhabitants whom it shot on the spot. At the trial of Husni Abo, the Syrian leader of the Muslim Brotherhood, the judge said: "We will exterminate you and build the state on your skulls."[60] The climax was to come in 1982 in Hama, which had risen against Baathist rule at the call of the Muslim Brotherhood. This city of 250,000 was shelled and bombarded. Entire districts in the center were razed to the ground. Estimates of fatalities vary from 10,000 to 40,000.

Examples are numerous, composing a long journey through many Islamic countries. The apparatus of state, government itself, is the prominent practitioner of terror: In the modern and contemporary Islamic world, state terror is the rule, not the exception. Privatization has also made it available to nonstate actors.

Violence in the Muslim Middle East, unlike war in Clausewitz's doctrine, is not "the continuation of politics by other means." In the region, violence is politics and politics is violence. Radical Islamists were

> not just murdering the enemy (who often was not an enemy at all) but systematically tortur[ing]. Cases of dismembering the victim, cutting off his genitals, gouging the eyes, and other such practices were reported from Kashmir. The Turkish Hizbullah (also called Ilim) kidnapped their victims in the 1980s and submitted them to systematic torture – which was videotaped. One of the victims was a Turkish feminist, Konca Kuni.... She was tortured for 35 hours before being killed, and it was all recorded on videotape. [61]

Another case cited is that of Algerian intellectual

> Dr. Hammed Boukhobza who was killed by a group of Islamist terrorists in the city of Telemly. [...] He was not just killed in his apartment, but his wife and children

[58] Ibid., p. 145.
[59] July 1, 1980.
[60] Ibid., p. 153.
[61] Laqueur, *No End to War*, pp. 43–4.

who wanted to escape were forced to watch how he was literally cut to pieces, his entrails slowly drawn out while he was just barely alive. The terrorists obviously liked to watch the suffering, and they wanted the family to share their enjoyment.[62]

The civil war there eerily echoed the cruelty of the War of Independence. In an all-too-typical killing of 1961, the Front de libération nationale (FLN) "killed a shop inspector in his car, a man who had never done anything to anyone. They sliced open his skull, took out his brains and carefully placed them on the ground – like a milestone on the roadside."[63]

The question is worth asking: "Why the proclivity toward torture and sadism? It was more than the mere brutalization that occurs in every war. There was the lust of killing, of inflicting pain, of seeing people suffer and slowly die. [...] The underlying motives and urges belong to the realm of psychopathology." Admittedly, instances of sadistic cruelty have occurred elsewhere and everywhere. The more unsettled the environment, the greater the occurrence. "But there were far more incidents in Muslim countries, and the question arises, How could this be squared with the strict Islamic code?" The answer Walter Laqueur proposes will recur in our scrutiny of the problem: "They were convinced that everything was permitted to a mujahid."[64]

Pilgrims to the "waiting room of Paradise" start their guided tour of the Islamic Republic with a visit to the *Behesht Zahra* (Paradise of Flowers) graveyard south of Tehran. They are invited to stand for a minute's silence in front of the Fountain of Blood, a 4.5 meter-high fountain out of which surges a blood-red liquid, symbolizing, in the words of the guide, the essence of Islam's message.[65]

With the image of spurting blood, the revolution that has brought us from atheistic Russian Nihilists to Muslim radicals of the Islamist persuasion is complete. For the former, "Since God is dead, everything is permitted." For the latter, "Gods wills it, everything is permitted." The structural homology is complete even though the specific contents of the belief structure are worlds apart.

62 Ibid.
63 Alastair Horne, *A Savage War of Peace: Algeria 1954–1962*, Hammersworth, Penguin Books, 1979.
64 Ibid. pp. 44–5.
65 Amir Taheri, *Holy Terror: The Inside Story of Islamic Terrorism*, London, Sphere Books, 1987, pp. 113–14.

A Theology of Death

Deeds conform to words; words fit the deeds. The pervasiveness of death in action matches the primacy of death in the mind. After the practice of death, we can study its theoretical underpinnings.

From Saudi mosques rises a veritable din to exalt jihad and killing as the noblest virtues of Islam. Hear for instance Sheikh al-Awaji, formerly the imam at the great mosque at King Saud University, Riyadh:

> The Saudis believe that the glory of the [Islamic] nation appeared when our Prophet taught us the industry of death – when he taught us how to create death. Then life became cheap in our eyes.... When one of the sons of our nation is killed, he says: "I won," and the master of the Ka'aba swears that he had won. This we see as the industry of death. We in Saudi society and in other Islamic societies have finally realized that this is the right path to tread in order to deal with today's deadly strategic weapons. If America has intercontinental missiles and bombs, then our bombs are the *jihad* fighters, whom America has called "suicide attackers" and we call "martyrs." We will develop them because we see them as a strategic weapon.[66]

The sheikh's words are representative of hundreds of sermons and fatwas to the same effect. The "industry of death" is one of the proudest glories of the Wahhabi establishment.[67]

The entire history of the Saudi–Wahhabi nexus was one soaked in the blood of conquest. Ibn Saud had forged a special weapon. He had sent incendiary Wahhabi predicators, the *mutawiya*, to convert and inflame the jihadi zeal of the most backward, deep-desert Bedouins. They were soon turned into ferocious warriors and shaped into a strong raiding force that ibn Saud called the *Ikhwan*, the Brotherhood! As ibn Saud's own grandfather had told a British visitor: "There are two kinds of wars in the desert: war of religion and political war. In political war, you make compromises, but in wars of religion, we exterminate everybody."[68]

Sheikh Wajdi al-Ghazawai, preaching at Al-Manshwai mosque in Mecca:

> The type of terror that Islamic religious law allows consists in terrorizing the cowards, the hypocrites, the non-believers and the rebels by punishing them according to Allah's religious law. The meaning of the word of "terror" that the media use is *jihad* for the sake of Allah. *Jihad* is the zenith of Islam. [...] The *jihad* that defends the Muslims and the land of Islam [...] and the *jihad* which extends the domain

[66] MEMRI, Special Dispatch No. 400, July 18, 2002, Saudi Opposition Sheikhs on America, Bin Laden, and Jihad.

[67] See Shmuel Bar, *The Religious Sources of Islamic Terrorism*, Policy Review, Stanford, June 2004, http://www.policyreview.org/jun04/bar.html#ref2.

[68] Lewis Pelley, *Report on a Journey to Riyadh* (1865), London, 1866, reprint Cambridge, Oleander Falcon, 1978.

of the religion is the pinnacle of terror with respect of the enemies of Allah. The *mujahidin* who go search the martyr's death or victory and come back with their booty are only terrorists for Allah's enemies.[69]

Not just Mecca but Medina and Riyadh echo with the words of death. A zeal for death is an omnipresent feature of the contemporary Muslim world's attitude toward terror. Hear the words of Palestinian writer Nasri ad-Din an-Nashashibi in his 1962 book *Return Ticket*:

I shall see the hatred in the eyes of my son and your sons. I shall see how they take revenge. If they do not know how to take revenge, I shall teach them, and if they agree to a truce or peace, I shall fight against them as I fight against my enemies and theirs. I want them to be callous, to be ruthless, to take revenge. I want them to wash away the disaster of 1948 (*al-Nakba*) with the blood of those who prevent them from entering their land. Their homeland is dear to them, but revenge is dearer. We'll enter their lairs in Tel-Aviv. We'll smash Tel-Aviv with axes, guns, hands, fingernails and teeth. [. . .] We shall sing the hymns of triumphant avenging return.[70]

Whether the enemy is Israeli, American, Western, Indian, or the entire world has no impact on the belief structure and its content: it is ever "me against my brother, me and my brother against our cousins, us and our cousins against the world," as the Arab proverb has it. It is always the deadly, bloody struggle of the victim against a world wholly dedicated to persecuting the victim, who "must" in turn strike "back." Consider this "poem" by the best-known of Palestinian poets, Mahmud Darwish.[71]

If I refuse suicide, you treat
me as a coward; and when I accept
dying in this way, you treat me as
a barbarian. You cannot make up your
minds which manner of death suits
me best so that I can escape my
oppressors. Do you, gentlemen
specialists in genocide, wish to deprive
me even of the liberty of
choosing my death?[72]

[69] MEMRI, Special Dispatch No. 400.

[70] Quoted in Dobson, *Black September*, p. 10.

[71] Traditionally among Arabs, from Bedouin society onwards, the "poet" is a publicist, a polemicist, a man clever at insulting and demeaning his master's enemies and praising his master. He is a herald, a town crier – this poem, rather than anything a Chinese, European, or Indian poet would recognize as his, fulfills those functions. On Darwish, see Kanan Makiya, *Cruelty and Silence: War, Tyranny, Uprising, and the Arab World*, New York & London, W. W. Norton, 1993, 310–11. On the nature of Bedouin poetry, see Rafael Patai, *The Arab Mind*, New York, Scribner and Sons, 1973, esp. pp. 211–15

[72] Quoted in Taheri, *Holy Terror*, p. 90.

The poem is remarkable for its underlying assumptions rather than for any "poetic" quality: nobody, to start with, treats or calls the narrator of the poem a "coward." Or did they? The Arab world displayed its contempt for the Palestinians for "having lost their country" and saw and treated them as losers whose honor had been lost in ignominious defeat. The losers were implicitly or explicitly compared to "women," the height of shame in Arab culture. It was only the internalized Arab shame/honor culture that called the narrator-poet a coward. He was responding to internalized voices.[73]

Nobody had asked him to commit suicide anyway, not at least at that point. But to the creed given vent to in the poem, "suicide" must be posited as the kernel of the political and existential issue posed to Palestinians. Once that is done – arbitrarily, needlessly – the sham symmetry can be completed: To redeem his honor so sullied by them who treat him so, the poet, a metaphor for "all" Palestinians, has to "accept dying in this way," accept suicide. The only possible exit posited to the situation in which the poet-spokesman finds himself is death as escape. Death is the hallowed "liberty" of the "oppressed." Death by homicide or other forms of slaughter is liberation. A few lines reveal the nature of the issue. The poet is an agitprop loudspeaker for an underlying theology of death: the choice made to prefer death over life.

Many Muslims in the contemporary world have intoned such hymns to hatred, blood, and mass murder. The genealogy of this creed must be examined. Jamal al-Din al-Asabadi, a.k.a. al-Afghani (1838–97), the charismatic founder of modern Islamic politics, fathered both pan-Islamism and pan-Arabism as political creeds. Al-Afghani, "the very type of revolutionary conspirator and activist so well-known in Europe in modern times," was a peripatetic "professional revolutionary" seeking and sometimes obtaining influence amongst the civil and religious powers of the world of Islam, among them the shah of Persia, the sultan in Istanbul, the khedive in Egypt. His publications in Arabic and Persian attracted enormous interest in the Muslim world from India to Egypt: "Both the activities and the teaching of al-Afghani contributed to the spread of revolutionary temper and a new attitude toward politics all over the Muslim East. He was everywhere."[74] This Persian claiming to be an Afghan, this Shiite masquerading as a Sunni, was the most seminal intellectual influence in the turn of the Muslim world to

[73] On the shame/honor culture, see David Pryce-Jones, *The Closed Circle: An Interpretation of the Arabs*, New York, Harper Collins, 1989.

[74] Sylvia G. Haim, *Arab Nationalism: An Anthology*, Berkeley & Los Angeles, University of California Press, 1962, p. 8.

violence. We will examine al-Afghani's formative contribution to the modern Muslim ideologies of jihad, salafism, and mahdism later in this study. What is of immediate interest here is his attitude toward violence.

According to the British ideologue of Arabism W. S. Blount, al-Afghani proposed to his disciple Muhammad Abduh (1849–1905), later mufti of Egypt, to arrange the assassination of the Khedive Ismail. Blount reports Abduh as saying: "Sheikh Jamal ed-Din proposed to me that Ismail should be assassinated some day as he passed in his carriage daily over the Kasr-el-Nil bridge, and I strongly approved, but it was only talk between ourselves, and we lacked a person capable of taking the lead in this affair."[75] Failure in Egypt, success in Persia: It was al-Afghani, again, who induced and encouraged the assassin of Nadir al-Din Shah, in 1896, to do his deed. [...] Reportedly, the murderer had exclaimed, as he shot the ruler, "Take this from the hand of Jamal al-Din."[76]

What was it that al-Afghani taught and preached? His Persian friend Mirza Husain Khan reported later that "a fortnight before this assassination, he visited al-Afghani at his house in Istanbul and found him pacing his room, oblivious to his surroundings and shouting with frenzy: 'There is no deliverance except in killing, there is no safety except in killing!'[77] He obsessively repeated "I only want the Shah to die, his belly to be split, and him to be put in his grave."[78] "Al-Afghani believed that violence was the only way to realize his purposes."[79] His influence can be traced through his disciple Abduh and Abduh's own disciple Rashid Rida as the formative influence in modern Islamism: Hasan al-Banna, the Egyptian founder of the Muslim Brotherhood, is his lineal descendent. Abduh copublished *al-Urwa al Wuthqa* (*The Firmest Bond*) with al-Afghani, a journal whose motto was that of returning to the ways of the ancestors, *salaf*, before they parted ways as Abduh decided to eschew grand political action and instead was

[75] W. S. Blount, *Secret History of the British Occupation of Egypt*, London, Fisher Unwin, 1907, p. 489, quoted in Haim, *Arab Nationalism*, p. 8.

[76] Shakib Arslan, *Hadhir al-alam al-Islami*, I, 203, cited by Albert Hourani, *Arabic Thought in the Liberal Age*, Oxford, Oxford University Press, 1962, p. 112. "When the murderer, al-Afghani's former servant, was being interrogated concerning his accomplices and sympathizers, he said: 'When Sayyid Jamal al-Din come to this city, all, whatever their status, hastened to see him and listened to what he had to say.... It was him who sowed the seeds of those high thoughts in their hearts. Then men awoke, understanding burgeoned and now everybody thinks as I do!'"

[77] Mirza Luftallah Khan, *Jamal al-Din al-Asabadi al maruf bil-Afghani*, Cairo, 1957, 134, quoted in Haim, *Arab Nationalism*, pp. 8–9.

[78] Nikki R. Keddie, *Sayyid Jamal al-Din "Al-Afghani": A Political Biography*, Berkeley, Los Angeles & London, University of California Press, 1972, p. 405.

[79] Kedourie, *Politics in the Middle East*, p. 274.

appointed grand mufti of Egypt. Syrian-born Rashid Rida (1865–1935) was until his death the editor of and chief contributor to *al-Manar*, something of the central organ of the new *salafiyya* – the term "reform" in an Islamic context never means the creation of anything new but, to the contrary, a "return to the ways of the ancestors," more often than not a return to the more or less imaginary, and at any rate imagined, ways of the prophet Muhammad and the first four "well-guided" caliphs in the seventh century. Abduh and Rida "may therefore be said to have inaugurated that modern movement of Islamic reform known as the *salafiyya* . . . of which Rashid Rida himself became later the undoubted intellectual leader."[80] Abduh and Rida incubated this phase of modern Islamist ideology. As time went by, salafi ideologists were less and less inclined to accept and adopt anything at all from the West. The more radical they grew, the less able they were to see anything in the West they did not loathe.

Rida was a Hanbalite, the least latitudinarian school of Sunni jurisprudence. He "cast his lot with the Saudis and the Wahhabi revival" to the point that his school "came to be known in certain quarters as 'neo-Wahhabi'."[81] But he also extolled the Arabs against the Ottoman Turks – an essential component of the future chemistry of radical Islam: Contrary to the widespread assumption of some radical opposition and incompatibility between Pan-Arabism and Pan-Islamism, a permanent, if sometimes conflictual, interaction between both movements has shaped the modern Middle East. We will return to this point in the context of the modern sources of political violence. Suffice it here to listen to Rida's own words:

> It is in the countries which were conquered by the Arabs that Islam spread, became firmly established and prospered. Most of the lands which the Turks conquered were a burden on Islam and the Muslims. [. . .] [T]he greatest glory in the Muslim conquests goes to the Arabs, and that religion grew, and became great through them; their foundation is the strongest, their light is the brightest, and they are indeed the best community [*umma*] brought forth to the world.[82]

The concept of Arabs and Arabism and Arabdom (*Uruba*) as the core of Islam carried over even into Arab nationalist secularism. While Rida is fundamentally a salafi thinker, he, like his mentor Abduh and even more so al-Afghani, can be interpreted as, and was, an Arab nationalist:

> To care for the honor of the Arabs and to strive to revive their glory is the same as to work for the Muslim *Umma* which only obtained in past countries thanks to the

[80] Haim, *Arab Nationalism*, pp. 19–20.

[81] H. A. R. Gibbs, *Modern Trends in Islam*, Chicago, University of Chicago Press, 1947, p. 35.

[82] Haim, *Arab Nationalism*, pp. 22–3.

Arabs, and will not return . . . except through them, united and in agreement with all the races. The basis of this union is Islam itself, and Islam is no more than the Book of God Almighty, and the Sunna of His Prophet. . . . Both are in Arabic. No one can understand them properly unless he understands the noble language.[83]

The *Umma al-Muhammadiyya* and the *Umma al-Arabiyya* had large areas of congruence and similarity. It may be, as we will discuss later, that the "secularists" and the Islamists borrowed slightly different items from various European ideologies – fascism, Bolshevism, national socialism – agreeing all the while on what they rejected. In essence, modern Muslim terror has had four endogenous sources that have repeatedly intersected: In the Sunni world, it came from both the Muslim Brotherhood on the Islamist side and the Iraqi nationalist theorists that bloomed from the 1930s onward; on the Shiite side, it came from the 1930s and 1940s *Fidai-e-Islam* led by Navab-Safavi, their clerical mentors, including the young Ruhollah Khomeini, and the Islamo-Marxist Ali Shariati, the Shiite conduit for European left- and right-wing fascism (Georges Sorel, René Guénon, Herbert Marcuse, Franz Fanon, Sartre, Foucault). They will be reviewed in succession.

The Muslim Brotherhood: "The Art of Death"

Both by its immense mass appeal and by the ideological synthesis it achieved, by its intellectual weight and its organizational outreach, the Muslim Brotherhood, in Egypt and in the entire Muslim world, has been one of the principal drivers of modern radical Islam since its establishment in 1928 by the charismatic Hassan al-Banna (1906–49).

The Brothers saw themselves clearly in the line of the modern reform movement identified with the names of Jamal al-Din al-Afghani, Muhammad Abduh and Rashid Rida. . . . Afghani was seen as the "called" or the "announcer" (*muezzin, sarkha*); and Rida as the "archivist" or "historian" . . . Banna, however, was seen as "the builder" (*bani*) of a renaissance, the leader of a generation and the founder of a nation.[84]

The way this lineage was conceived was that "Afghani sees the problem and warns; Abduh teaches and thinks . . . and Rida writes and records." In sum, "[t]oward Afghani the Brothers felt a special kinship. Many felt him to be the spiritual father of the movement."

Hassan al-Banna's father, a student from Al Azhar University, a religious teacher and imam, was a former student of Abduh's and a devotee

[83] Ibid., p. 23, quoted from Rashid Rida, "The Civilization of the Arabs," *al-Manar* III, pp. 290–1.

[84] Richard P. Mitchell, *The Society of the Muslim Brothers*, Oxford & New York, Oxford University Press, 1969, p. 321.

of Rida's.[85] Al Banna Jr. started reading *al-Manar* as a child[86] and "was very much influenced by Rashid Rida's writings," and frequented him assiduously as a young man. "From . . . modest beginnings [. . .] the Society of the Muslim Brothers grew, by the outbreak of the Second World War, into one of the most important political contestants on the Egyptian scene."[87] The Royal Palace of King Faruq, the British Suez Canal Company, and various political leaders and parties all tried to coopt or leverage al-Banna, whose charisma and organizational savvy made the Brotherhood prosper. The movement would grow through a first stage of "propaganda, communication and information"; a second stage of "formation, selection and preparation"; and a third, concluding, phase of "execution," or "the active stage out of which the perfected fruits of the mission of the Muslim Brotherhood will appear."[88] Its creed was summed up as: "(1) Islam as a total system, complete unto itself, and the final arbiter of life in all its categories; (2) an Islam formulated from and based on its two primary sources, the Revelation in the Quran and the wisdom of the Prophet in the Sunna; and (3) an Islam applicable to all times and to all places." The Brotherhood was an militant organization. al-Banna told the Fifth General Conference in 1938:

> At the time there will be ready, O ye Muslim Brothers, 300 battalions, each one equipped spiritually with faith and belief, intellectually with [Islamic] science and learning, and physically with training and athletics, at that time you can demand me to plunge with you through the turbulent oceans and to rend the skies with you and to conquer with you every obstinate tyrant. God willing, I will do it.[89]

Hear the society's motto, an emotionally laden rhyming and rhythmic chant of the type the Arabic language so favors: "God is our goal/the Prophet is our leader/the Quran is our constitution/jihad is our way/Death in the service of God is our loftiest wish/God is God, God is great."[90] The society's emblem was two crossed swords cradling a Quran. The oldest of the institutions that al-Banna had established before creating the Brotherhood and then passed on to his new creature were the "Rovers" or "rover troops," a paramilitary structure. Al-Banna's violence was akin to that of French revolutionary syndicalist Georges Sorel: "How wise was the man who said:

85 Carré and Michaud, *Les Frères musulmans*, p. 15.
86 Ibid.
87 Mitchell, *Muslim Brothers*, p. 5.
88 Ibid., pp. 13–14.
89 Ibid., p. 15.
90 "Allah ghayatuna/Al-rasul zaimuna/Al-Quran dusturuna/Al-Jihad sabiluna/Al-mawt fi sabil Allah asma amanina./Allah akbar." Allah akbar. Ibid., p. 194.

'Force is the surest way of implementing the right, and how beautiful it is that force and right should march side by side.' This striving [...] is another religious duty imposed by God on the Muslims just as he imposed fasting, prayer, pilgrimage and the doing of good and abandonment of evil upon them."[91]

Islam was the message; violence was the method. Al-Banna's "shewd, even cunning caution" was however not going "to come out into the open too soon," rather it followed his staged doctrine. The Muslim Brothers were more effectively violent than other groups on the Egyptian scene. It had raised militancy and martyrdom to central virtues in its ethos. Military terms permeated its literature and speeches. Again and again Banna told members that they were "the army of liberation, carrying on your shoulders the message of liberation, you are the battalions of salvation for this nation afflicted by calamity." They were "the troops of God."[92]

The use of the concept of jihad showed the military quality of the movement. It insisted that jihad, properly, was a variant of *ijtihad* ("interpretation") and connoted intellectual effort. As used in the society's literature, it conveyed the sense of *qital* ("fighting" or "violent use of force in confrontation"), leading, if necessary, to death and martyrdom. "*Jihad* is an obligation for every Muslim" – a duty as firmly established as any of the other pillars of the faith. This view, argued al-Banna, was supported in Quranic texts, the Traditions, and the Four Schools of Law. Those who minimize "the importance of fighting [*qital*] and the preparation for it" are not true to the Faith. God grants "a Noble life" to that nation alone which "knows how to die a noble death."

Jihad – war – was the central element. Its physical component went with the possibility, even the necessity of death and martyrdom. Al-Banna extolled death in his famed formula "the art of death" (*fann al-mawt*) or "death is art" (*al-mawt fann*). "The Quran has commanded people to love death more than life. Unless the philosophy of the Quran on death replaces the love of life which has consumed Muslims, they will reach naught. Victory can only come with the mastery of the art of death."[93]

His organization launched a war of terror in Egypt. Prime Minister Ahmad Maher was assassinated in February 1945 just after reading Egypt's declaration of war on the Axis, against the vociferous opposition of the

[91] Hasan al-Banna, *Five Tracts of al-Banna (1906–1949)*, traslated by Charles Wendell, University of California Press, Berkeley, 1978, p. 80.

[92] Ibid., pp. 206–7.

[93] Ibid.

Brotherhood; government minister Amin Uthman was murdered in January 1946; from 1946 on, British soldiers in the Canal Zone were attacked.[94] Theaters were burned down in Cairo. In March 1948, a respected judge was murdered by two members of the secret apparatus. Two more attempts were made on sometime–Prime Minister Nahhas Pasha. In June, houses were blown up in the Jewish quarter of Cairo, two large Jewish-owned department store were bombed. Cinemas were dynamited, and hotels and restaurants catering to the "infidels and the heretics" were set on fire. Women wearing "inadequate dress" were the victims of knife attacks, and homes said to belong to apostates were raided and ransacked by angry believers gathering for "spontaneous demonstrations."[95] In December, widespread riots brought the university to a stop. The Cairo police chief was killed by a bomb. Dozens of other officials, businessmen, and intellectuals were likewise killed. Prime Minister Nuqrashi Pasha finally ordered the society dissolved – he was gunned down twenty days later. As al-Banna had said, "The dagger, poison, the revolver.... These are the weapons of Islam against its enemies."[96] The Brotherhood had indeed mastered the "art of death."

The last act in the mastery of the insurrectionary art took place after the government-sanctioned killing of al-Banna in 1949. After a bloody incident in the Canal Zone, when British troops stormed the police headquarters in Ismailiyya in late January 1952,

> the heart of modern and Westernized Cairo was left a charred ruin in the wake of the most devastating riot in modern Egyptian history [...] groups, well-organized and well-equipped, began the systematic burning of the center of the city. The fire consumed department stores, cinemas, bars, night-clubs, social clubs, luxury food and clothing establishments, novelty shops, auto-showrooms and garages, airline offices and the like.[97]

The "Arab Street" had been reinvented – none of it through spontaneous acts, all of it painstakingly organized by the Brotherhood. Al-Banna's campaign of terror was to become the model for future fundamentalist movements, notably in Iran and Lebanon but throughout the Muslim world: The "how-to" of an Islamist insurrection had been tested.[98]

A salient feature of the terror campaign was the existence of "a secret committee, headed by [al-Banna] and including two or three other 'judges,'

[94] Ibid., p. 59.
[95] Taheri, *Holy Terror*, p. 43.
[96] Quoted by Taheri, *Holy Terror*, p. 11.
[97] Mitchell, *Muslim Brothers*, pp. 92–3.
[98] Taheri, *Holy Terror*, p. 43.

[that] organized the trial *in absentia* of those in prominent position who were 'causing corruption on earth,'"[99] in the manner of the medieval Vehme in Europe. "A relentless war [was] waged against 'the heathen, the apostate, the deviant' who would, when judged dangerous, be put to death in the name of Allah."[100]

In decades to come, the intellectual and political matrix al-Banna established was to shape not only the organization he had created but the face of Egypt and beyond. Indeed, as the Brotherhood grew, it came not only to loom large on the horizon of Egyptian affairs but to cast a long shadow over the entire Arab and Muslim world. "Scarcely a week passed without witnessing the appearance at the headquarters of one or more dignitaries and many lesser personages from all parts of the Muslim world, as official speakers or merely as listeners at the meetings. [It was also] a kind of haven for the many hundreds of "foreign" students at the Azhar and other Egyptian schools."[101]

In a more specialized vein, "Hundreds of young men from Turkey, India, Afghanistan, Iran and Iraq ... traveled to Egypt to join the Brothers and learn from them the 'art of eliminating the weed.'"[102] Before the society was banned, the Brothers had trained over one hundred foreign terrorists. The society's section for liaison with the Islamic world had nine subcommittees. This section had, amongst other tasks, to act as a "clearing house for the literatures of the various movements throughout the Muslim world," an *Islamintern* of sorts.[103]

Al-Banna had been forthright: "*Jihad* is a collective obligation of the Muslim *umma* in order to spread the Message and an individual obligation when it is necessary to defend from the aggression of the unbelievers," that is, at all times and at all places.

"What I mean with *jihad* is the duty that will last until the Day of Resurrection and which is the object of these words from God's Messenger ... : "He who dies without having fought [*ghaza* = raided] and without having had the intent of going, dies of a

[99] Ibid., p. 44.
[100] Ibid., p. 43.
[101] Ibid., p. 173.
[102] Ibid.
[103] Ibid. (1) North Africa; (2) East and West Africa (Ethiopia, Somaliland, Nigeria, Senegal); (3) the Fertile Crescent (Syria, Palestine, Lebanon, Jordan, Iraq); (4) Saudi Arabia, Yemen, the Gulf; (5) Turkey, Iran, Pakistan, Afghanistan; (6) India, Ceylon, Indonesia, Malaya, the Philippines, China, the Far East and Pacific region; (7) Islamic minorities in America, the USSR, and Europe; (8) an advisory committee and (9) a unit of uncertain functions called "Islamic divisions."

jahiliyya death." [...] Therewith you shall know the meaning of our motto that you must ever retain: *jihad* is our path. [...] [A]t the stage of execution, our movement is one of a merciless war.[104]

After the Guide's death, his intellectual mantle fell upon Sayyid Qutb, whose theories radicalized the master's. The entire world, including all Muslim states and governments, had fallen into a state of *jahiliyya*, the term used to qualify pre-Islamic paganism in Arabia. All the regimes were therefore not only unfaithful to Islam, they were apostates, and worthy of being destroyed, their leaders killed. Jihad was permanent; it was only *qital*, violent, armed struggle. Qutb spread the idea of an "Islamic Revolution" launched by his friend the Indo-Pakistani Abu Ala Maududi. Heavily leaning on thirteenth-century Hanbalite scholar Ibn Taimiyya,[105] Qutb vehemently denied that Islam and its jihad were defensive, and stressed instead the offensive and revolutionary nature of both.[106] Martyrdom was the highest calling. "The death of a believer is in itself an honor."[107] Based on the Quranic verse "Kill the idolaters wherever they are" (9:5), his jihad–qital theory demanded "selective" murder (*qatl*).[108] The next generation of Egptian jihadis, the al-Jihad splinter group led by Abd-al Salaam Farağ, made the *hadith* "Jihad is confronting your enemy and spilling his blood" into a axiom.[109]

Al-Banna's sympathy for the Saudi Wahhabite creed and policy was entirely uncoincidental. After all, Abdul Wahhab himself had reintroduced *takfir* as an active principle in Islamic affairs after centuries of the ulama putting restraints on this divisive and dangerous practice. All relied on the Hanbalite school and ibn Taimiyya's doctrines.

Hassan al-Banna's intellectual father, Rashid Rida, had rallied to the flag of "Amir" Abdulazziz ibn Saud, the future founder of the Saudi kingdom. Rida saw the rise of the Saudi empire as a triumph for a "revival" of true and pure Islam. Al-Banna concurred:[110] Saudi Wahhabis and the Brotherhood were to remain close.[111]

104 Carré and Michaud, *Les Frères musulmans*, p. 44.

105 See Emmanuel Sivan, *Radical Islam: Medieval Theology and Modern Politics*, New Haven, CT, & London, Yale University Press, 1990.

106 Sayyid Qutb, *Milestones*, translated by S. Barul Hasan, Karachi, International Islamic Publications, 1981, pp. 120–1, 137ff.

107 Ibid., p. 262.

108 In Olivier Carré, *Mystique et politique: lecture révolutionnaire du Coron par Ssayyid Qutb, Frère musulman radical*, paris, Ed. du Cerf, 1984, var. pp. 17, 123, 127.

109 Michael Youssef, *Revolt Against Modernity: Muslim Zealots and the West*, Leiden, E. J. Brill, 1985, p. 81. Quran 11:216 was also crucial: "Warfare is ordained to you."

110 Quoted by Carré and Michaud, *Les Frères musulmans*, p. 15.

111 Laurent Murawiec, *La Guerre d'après*, Paris, Albin Michel, 2003.

Iraq: The "Manufacture of Death"

Al-Afghani's doctrines had two sides – pan-Islamic and pan-Arab. Their believers often slaughtered one another with zest, for turf or doctrine, but the beliefs shared a common core that transcended local or temporary enmity.

In the interwar years, Iraq was the epicenter of modern Arab secularism. In the 1930s, Iraq as an "Arab Prussia" was an Arab nationalist trope. A national "culture" was developed: "Iraqi ex-Ottoman officers... acquired from the Young Turk experience what might be called a culture of conspiracy, lawlessness and violence."[112] The oath of the Committee Union and Progress (CUP) committed the member "to kill every person, however near and dear to him, whom [CUP] might condemn to suffer death."[113]

> These tactics were greatly reinforced from the 1930s onwards through the spread of European radical ideologies which came to be greatly and widely admired. This was most true of nazism in the 1930s. The toughness they preached, the quasi-military discipline it sought to instill in its followers, the ideological indoctrination it systematically pursued, its vision of politics as violent conflict in which winners naturally would "liquidate" the losers, the total renovation of society to which it aspired – all of this seemed to young officers, as well as to the teachers through whose hands they passed as schoolboys, to be supremely worthy of emulation. The founders of the Baath Party... all of them secondary school teachers in the 1930s, did not hide their admiration for the ideology of German nationalism as preached, for instance, by Fichte, or for its modern Nazi version.[114]

Dr. Sami Shawkat, Iraqi director-general of education in the 1930s, and a future Nazi agent, told secondary-school boys. "The nation which does not excel in the manufacture of death with iron and fire will be forced to die under the hoofs of the horses and under the boots of a foreign soldiery. If to live is just, then, killing in self-defense is also just." He approved of Mustafa Kemal because he "trained 40,000 officers in the Manufacture of death," of Reza Shah Pahlavi for "thousands of officers well-versed in the sacred Manufacture," and of Mussolini for "tens of thousands of Black Shirts well versed in the Manufacture of death. [...] [I]t is our duty to perfect the Manufacture of Death, the profession of the army, the sacred profession."[115]

Far from this being a lone instance of a senior official's obsessive necromania, the doctrine was spread by schoolteachers; its leading luminary, Sati

[112] Kedourie, *Politics in the Middle East*, 282.
[113] Quoted by Pryce-Jones, *The Closed Circle*, 105.
[114] Ibid., 282–3.
[115] Ibid.

al-Husri (1879–1968), an ex-Ottoman official, was appointed by King Faisal the first director-general of the ministry of education; he had served with him as minister of education in Damascus and came to Baghdad in his train. He "became the first ideologue of Arab nationalism, whose ideas and influence spread all over the Arab world.... His prominence in Baghdad during the 1920s and 1930s... gave his teaching added prestige and resonance."[116] Husri coined the expression "the industry of death" to describe the Arabs' calling.[117]

In World War II, Iraq was the only Arab country where a pro-Nazi coup succeeded in taking power. After the failure of the 1942 putsch, the British purged the pro-Nazi elements around Rashid Ali al-Gailani and expelled Husri who became Syria's top education official and was then appointed to head the cultural department of the new Arab League, whose secretary-general Abd al-Rahman Azzam, was an old friend and confederate of Hassan al-Banna. "Until his death, [Husri] published a large number of books which spread his ideas all over the Arab world. It is said that it was owing to Husri that Nasser became converted to pan-Arabism and made it an ideological pillar of his regime."[118] At the foundation of the Arab League, Hursi became the director of the League's Institute of Arab Studies.

Iraq was the geographic and institutional epicenter, but it was Michel Aflaq, a Syrian Christian, and his fellow founders of the Baath Party, who took upon themselves to devise the Mesopotamian and Levantine doctrines of death. Also under the spell of German nationalist doctrines and impressed with the success of both Nazis and Italian fascism, Aflaq's doctrine demanded a complete refashioning of Arab society that would transfigure the life of the Arab. "This requires cultivation of hatred – hatred and annihilation of everyone whose ideas stand in the way of this transfiguration. This hatred, however, is in reality love – love for Aflaq's fellow Arabs."[119]

Violence was made an article of faith. It was "a priori idolized," Kedourie writes. "In the Arab underground, bearded priest and keyed up youths... celebrate the embrace of the submachine-gun and the Quran," the pro-Nazi former Vichy official Jacques Benost-Méchin, Charles de Gaulle's Middle East guru, whom Aflaq told in 1958 regarding the founding of the Baath that "Nazism was of great interest to us" except for the race theory.

[116] Ibid., p. 295.
[117] Hourani, *Arabic Thought in the Liberal Age*, p. 316.
[118] Ibid.
[119] Ibid., p. 296.

So they added Marxism to their creed, striving for "a general explosion which will sweep everything away like a tornado of fire."[120]

Aflaq's writings have a thinly disguised substratum of raw emotionality. Where those emotions are affixed can be seen as follows: "Any action that does not call forth in us living emotions and does not make us feel the spasm of love, the revulsion of hate, that does not make our blood race in our vein and our pulse beat faster is a sterile action."[121]

Psychoanalysts will diagnose the underlying drives; we may merely state that this was a dangerous starting point. Aflaq's rhetoric was relentlessly violent. "An essential condition for being an Arab," he wrote, "is to have faith in belonging to the Arab nation, and any traitor to Arabism is not an Arab," a statement of anathema close to the Islamic *takfir*, one amongst innumerable examples of the essential religiosity of Arab nationalist thought, where the personal God had been replaced by the deified Arabdom.[122] Aflaq insisted that revolution is "a powerful psychic current . . . a mandatory struggle," for which reason nationalists "are merciless to themselves, merciless to others," for successful nationalist action leads to

> a powerful hate, a hate unto death of those persons who embody an idea contrary to the idea [of the nationalists] . . . An inimical theory is not found on its own, it is embodied in individuals who must be annihilated so that it too may be annihilated. The existence of an enemy of our ideas vivifies it [the idea] and it sends the blood coursing in us.[123]

Aflaq further wrote: "In this struggle we retain our love for all. When we are cruel to others, we know that our cruelty is in order to bring them back to their true selves, of which they are ignorant."[124] The license to kill was exploited *ad libitum* by Aflaq's progeny.

The Blood of "Red Shiism"

Little did Shiites differ in this respect from their Sunni counterparts. The founding hero of the modern Shiite murder cult was Muhammad Navab-Safavi, whose biography exemplified the cooperation of Shia and Sunni radicals: In 1936, an Iranian radical in exile in Cairo, he frequented Muslim Brotherhood mosques and attended their secret meetings; he met Hasan

120 Jacques Benoist-Méchin, *Un Prontemps arabe*, Paris, Albin Michel, 1959, pp. 333–53.

121 Haim, *Arab Nationalism*, pp. 70–1.

122 Ibid., p. 69.

123 Michel Aflaq, *Fi sabil al-Bath*, Beirut, 1959, passim, quoted by Haim, *Arabic Nationalism*, p. 70.

124 Quoted in Samir al-Khalil, *Republic of Fear*, p. 206.

al-Banna in 1937. Though they did not like each other, the meeting did nevertheless convince him that Islam, which he described as "a sword in the shape of a faith" needed a dedicated group of fighters prepared to kill and to die.[125] He set out to establish his terrorist group and called it the "Fedayeen of Islam":

> Islam asks us to command the Good and prevent Evil. Now Good and Evil involve men and women and not objects. All we have to do is to ask followers of Evil to stop and cross over to the side of Good. It is only when our advice is not heeded that we have no choice but to take action, including the elimination of men of Evil.

Most radical authors and predicators use the phrase "we have no choice but [kill]" as if the order of the world dictated murder. In the mind of radical Islam, it does. In the mental disposition of all Muslim terrorists, this Orwellian inversion is critical.[126]

As World War II broke out, Navab-Safavi, back in Najaf, tried but failed to organize a pro-Nazi guerrilla group to murder British. In a momentous encounter, he struck a relationship with a young, ambitious mullah, Ruhollah Khomeini. The young cleric had fulminated against a prominent secularist figure, judge Ahmad Kasravi, whose best-selling books were an assault on Islam's influence on Persia. Khomeini had responded with a book of his own, the tenor of which was to call Kasravi a "son-of-a-bitch," "stupid," "bastard," and "cow dung," and then added: "The rules of Islam do not provide a cure for your diseases, which are the love of debauchery and fornication as well as compulsive lying and cheating. The rule of Islam declares your blood to be worthless and shall cut off your thieving arms."[127]

Khomeini used his religious authority to order Kasravi's assassination. Navab-Safavi now had the necessary licence to kill. Kasravi was to become the first of Islam's many "enemies" murdered by this tiny group of "Soldiers of Allah." Probably formed in 1942, the group was in regular contact with Khomeini. The killer for the first "mission" was directed to use a blade, for "shedding the miscreant's blood" was an important consideration.[128] Through the 1940s and 1950s, the Fedayeen murdered more than a dozen "enemies of Islam" – including a prime minister and a minister of

[125] Quoted in Firuz Akbari, *Tariq Shohada [The Way of the Martyrs]*, Tehran, 1979, in Taheri, *Holy Terror*, pp. 51–2.

[126] Muhammad Navab–Safavi, *Jame'eh va Hokumat Islami* [*Islamic Society and Government*], Qom, 1980, 71. Cited by Taheri, *Holy Terror*, p. 53.

[127] Ruhollah Khomeini, *Kashf al-Asrar [Key to the Secrets]*, Tehran, 1980, 232, quoted by Taheri, *Holy Terror*, p. 232.

[128] Taheri, *Holy Terror*, p. 56.

education – with complete impunity, as various forces – the Shah's government, the SAVAK, the British, and nationalist leader Dr. Mossadeq among others – all found it convenient to lend him a modicum of help or leeway against their own enemies. Navab-Safavi spoke of his "blood-covered path of courage."

On January 10, 1954, the Iranian terrorist arrived in Cairo, where two days later he spoke at a mass meeting of the Muslim Brotherhood at the university. In the evening, he was the main speaker at the evening meeting at the headquarters of the Brotherhood. Al-Banna had been involved in a cooperative effort with radical Shiite clerics to bring Sunni and Shiites together, an Islamic ecumenicism based on radicalism. Navab-Safavi cared to explain himself. This hero of radical Islam, honored after the 1978-9 revolution, wrote:

> We know of no absolute values besides total submission to the will of the Almighty. People say: "don't lie!" but the principle is different when we serve the will of Allah. He taught man to lie so that we can save ourselves at moments of difficulties and confuse our enemies. Should we remain truthful at the cost of defeat and danger to the Faith? People say "don't kill!" But the Almighty Himself taught us how to kill. Without such a skill, Man would have been wiped out long ago by the beasts. Shall we not kill when it is necessary for the triumph of the Faith? We say that killing is tantamount to saying a prayer when those who are harmful [to the Faith] need to be put out of the way. Deceit, trickery, conspiracy, cheating, stealing and killing are nothing but means. On their own, they are neither good nor bad. For no act is either good on its own, isolated from the motivation that motivated it. Look at the kitchen knife. Is it either good or bad? With it a housewife can cut the meat she needs for her daily stew. A miscreant could use it to end the life of a true believer. And a soldier of Islam could use it to pierce the black heart of a harmful one.[129]

Since God exists, everything is permitted! Neither Good nor Bad exist by themselves, Islam states, if they did, their absolute value would bind God's hands, which by definition cannot happen – hence the famous and crucial hadith according to which God "can change good into evil and evil into good, there is no problem." There is therefore no boundary that may not be crossed in pursuit of God's putative Will. Values, again, are negated. What matters is *niyyah*, the believer's intention. To him, Navab-Safavi said, "Throw away your worry beads and buy a gun. For worry beads keep you silent, while guns silence the enemies of Islam."[130] It was incumbent upon the

[129] Muhammad Navab-Safavi, *Collected Speeches, Messages and Edicts*, Tehran, 1983, 51; quoted by Taheri, *Holy Terror*, p. 24.

[130] Quoted in Navab va Yaranash, *Nawab and his Companions*, Tehran, 1981, quoted by Taheri, *Holy Terror*, p. 50.

latter's confederate Khomeini richly to elaborate the theology of brutality: "Muhammad was not only instrumental in bringing the Islamic law: he was also its first executor. [...] He cut off hands, chopped off limbs, stoned adulterers to death."[131] Islam, Khomeini avers, is not a religion of peace:

Islam's *jihad* is a struggle against idolatry, sexual deviation, plunder, repression and cruelty. The war waged by [non-Islamic] conquerors, however, aims at promoting lust and animal pleasures. They care not if whole countries are wiped out and many families left homeless. But those who study *jihad* will understand why Islam wants to conquer the whole world. All the countries conquered by Islam or to be conquered in the future will be marked for everlasting salvation. For they shall live under [God's law].... Those who know nothing of Islam pretend that Islam counsels against war. Those are witless. Islam says: "Kill the unbelievers just as they would kill you all!" Does this mean that Muslims should sit back until they are devoured by [the unbelievers]? Islam says: "Kill them, put them to the sword and scatter their armies!" Does this mean sitting back until [non-Muslims] overcome us? Islam says: "Whatever good there is exists thanks to the sword and in the shadow of the sword!" People cannot be made obedient except with the sword. The sword is the key to Paradise which can be opened only for Holy warriors! There are thousands of other [Quranic] verses and hadiths urging Muslims to value war and to fight. Does all that mean that Islam is a religion that prevents men from waging war? I spit upon those foolish souls who make such a claim.[132]

This cult of force cannot go without a cult of blood:

Islam grew with blood. [...] The great Prophet of Islam in one hand carried the Quran and in the other a sword; the sword for crushing the traitors and the Quran for guidance. For those who could be guided, the Quran was their means of guidance, while as for those who could not be guided and were plotters, the sword descended on their heads. Islam is a religion of blood for the infidels but a religion of guidance for other people. We have sacrificed much blood and many martyrs.... We do not fear giving martyrs. Whatever we give for Islam is not enough and is too little.[133]

Killing is good under all circumstances, *fil sabil Allah* ("in the way of Allah") Khomeini avers:

If one allows the infidels to continue playing their role of corrupters on earth, their eventual moral punishment will be all the stronger. Thus, if we kill infidels in order to put a stop to their [corrupting] activities, we have indeed done them a service. For their eventual punishment will be less. To allow the infidels to stay alive means to let them do more corrupting [activities]. [To kill them] is a surgical operation

[131] Quoted in Hamid Dabashi, *Theology of Discontent: The Ideological Foundation of the Islamic Revolution in Iran*, New York, New York University Press, 1993, p. 440.

[132] Quoted in Rubin and Rubin, *Yasir Arafat*, p. 29.

[133] Speech at Feyziyeh Theological School, Aug. 24, 1979, FBIS, Aug. 27, 1979, quoted in Rubin and Rubin, *Yasir Arafat*, pp. 32–3.

commanded by Allah... those who follow the rules of the Quran are aware that we have to apply the laws of *qissas* [retribution] and that we have to kill.... War is a blessing for the world and for every nation. It is Allah himself who commands men to wage war and kill. The Quran commands: "Wage war until corruption and all disobedience are wiped out!" The wars that our Prophet.... waged against the infidels were divine gifts to humanity. Once we have won the war [with Iraq], we shall turn to other wars. For that would not be enough. We have to wage war until all corruption, all disobedience of Islamic law ceases [throughout the world]. The Quran commands: "War! War until victory!" A religion without war is a crippled religion.... It is war that purifies the earth... Allah be praised, our young warriors are putting this command into effect and fighting. They know that to kill the infidels is one of the noblest missions Allah has reserved for mankind.[134]

This is a Gnostic-Manichean *Weltanschauung*. Likewise, Ali Shariati, with Khomeini the leading ideologue of the revolution, merged the Gnostic version of Shia with the twentieth century's totalitarian ideologies.

Born in 1933, Shariati, "the most ferocious revolutionary among the ideologues of the... revolution" earned his doctorate in Paris, after having worked under Islamologist Louis Massignon, a romantic apologist of Shiite Islam and Sufi mysticism.[135] The starting point of Shariati's "Islamo-Marxism" was a violent rejection of Europe (the West), of European (Western) culture and values. "Come, friends, let us abandon Europe. Let us cease this nauseating apish imitation of Europe. Let us leave behind this Europe that always speaks of humanity but destroys human beings wherever it finds them," Frantz Fanon had written: Shariati repeated.[136] Shariati's was a Manichean pseudohistory of a world divided between the principles of Good and Evil, from Abel and Cain onward, Prophet Muhammad and the quasi-divine figures of Shia Islam, Ali and Husain stood for "the oppressed," the undifferentiated mass of victims, the poor, the exploited.

Shariati's mythography draws on Frantz Fanon's theory of redemptive violence (expounded in particular in *The Wretched of the Earth*), to which Jean-Paul Sartre gave worldwide renown. For "the colonized man," his 1961 preface states, to kill a white man is a double liberation: It frees the colonized man by allowing him to retrieve his identity stolen by the colonizer, and it

[134] Quoted in Taheri, *Holy Terror*, p. 113.

[135] Dabashi, *Theology of Discontent: The Ideological Foundation of the Islamic Revolution in Iran*, New York, New York University Press, 1993, p. 105.

[136] Frantz Fanon, *The Wretched of the Earth*, New York, Grove Press, 1968 (*Les damnés de la terre,* Paris, François Maspéro, 1961), pp. 312–13. Ali Shariati, *On the Sociology of Islam*, Berkeley, CA, Mixan Press, 1979, quoted in Abbas William Samii, "Origins and Implications of Religious Extremism," Parliamentarian Conference on Euro-Atlantic Currents and Future Challenges, Berlin July 6, 1984.

liberates the colonizer by freeing him (in death) of his identity as a colonizer. The Fanon–Sartre doctrine had become an instant hit with the entire intelligentsia of the third world and their Western "anti-imperialist" professors. Shariati's inspirations also included Herbert Marcuse's theory of alienation – he approvingly drew upon the latter's "one-dimension man"[137] – and French occultist–fascist convert to Islam René Guénon. European fascists and Marxists were perfect to prove that Western culture and society were toxic. Shariati could then present his panacea, avidly imbibed by the urban semieducated of prerevolutionary Iran whose idol he became.

Martyrdom was the path to redemption – Marx's proletarians, Fanon's wretched of the earth, Shariati's dispossessed were of a kind, Shariati's in death only. Husain was not just a martyr, he was a revolutionary martyr. "Red Shiism" was thus invented, also called "Ali's Shiism," as opposed to the "official" Shiism that had become the state religion in Iran in the sixteenth century. In Red Shiism, "the color refers to the Shiite tradition of the gored bodies of Husain and his 72 disciples as much as to 'red' Leftism," as "Shia is the religion of rebellion."[138] Red Shiism is "the religion of martyrdom," and, writes Shariati, Husain is "the manifestation of the blood revolution."[139] Drawing upon the legacy of Hasan-I Sabbah's *Assassins* and that of the Gnostic rebellion of the Qarmats, Shariati describes popular uprisings, similar in Persian context to the European *jacqueries*: "The masses have made up their minds. They kill the whole group [of Mongols]. As they know that there is no turning back, as they know that they have already chosen death, they stop wavering. The choice of death gives them such energy that their single-village revolt against that bloodthirsty regime is successful."[140]

Shariati's uprising, ascribing his own mythos to the "masses," is a imaginary morality tale, his "culture of martyrdom" is a cult of death: "Do you not see how sweetly and peacefully a martyr dies?" The Christian martyr dies testifying to God's message, the neo-Shiite martyr dies killing others. "For those not fully accustomed to their everyday routine, death is an awesome tragedy, a horrendous cessation of things; it is becoming lost in nothingness. But the one who intends to migrate from himself begins with death. How great are those men who have heeded the command and acted accordingly: 'Die before you die.'"

[137] Ali Shariati, *Reflections on Humanity: Two Views of Civilization and the Plight of Man*, Houston, Free Islamic Literature, 1974, p. 22.

[138] Khosrokhavar, *Les Neuveaux martyrs*, p. 72.

[139] Ali Shariati, *Red Shiism*, Houston, Free Islamic Literature, 1974, p. 8.

[140] Ibid., p. 16.

In a bizarre parody of Marx's "Theses on Feuerbach," Shariati asserts: "Just as one can only 'understand' a fiery bullet when a fiery bullet hits him, so he can understand a concept precisely when he stand in the current course of the application of that concept. It is in action that truth manifests itself."[141]

In a text devoted to "the philosophy of the rise of the *mujahid*," he extolled the offensive fighter–martyr whose death is not accident but design: "reaching the absolute by one's own death." The death of the martyr:

> brings about the death of the enemy at the hands of the ones who are educated by the blood of a *shahid*. By shedding his own blood, the *shahid* is not in a position to cause the fall of the enemy. He wants to humiliate the enemy and he does so. By his death, he does not choose to flee the hard and uncomfortable environment. He does not choose shame. Instead of a negative flight, he commits a positive attack. By his death, he condemns the oppressor and provides commitment for the oppressed. He exposes aggression and revives what has hitherto been negated. He reminds the people of what has already been forgotten. In the icy hearts of a people, he bestows the blood of life, resurrection, and movement...the blood of a *shahid* is a rescue vessel."[142]

To sum it up, Shariati's "quintessence of martyrdom" was this: "Martyrdom is an invitation at all times and for all the generations: 'If you can, give death. If you cannot, die.'"[143]

The chief clerical theorist of martyrdom, Morteza Mutahhari, was assertive: "Islam is not Christianity.... Islam is the religion of agitation, revolution, blood, liberation and martyrdom."[144] In his opus *The Martyr*, he makes the "self-negation" – the self-destruction – of the individual the highest virtue, jihad the highest calling, and killing the noblest action: "In society at large, the issue is quite clear.... The factor of violence is necessary ... there is no inhibition against the use of violence."[145] Further:

> The Holy Prophet had said: "All good lies under the sword and under the shadow of the sword." He has also said: "Allah has honored my followers because of the hoofs of their horses, and the position of their arrows." This means that the Muslim

[141] Dabashi, *Theology of Discontent*, p. 114.

[142] Ali Shariati, "Blood of the Shahid is the Candlelight that Gives Vision," in Adam Parfrey, ed., *Extreme Islam: Anti-American Propaganda of Muslim Fundamentalism*, Los Angeles, Feral House, 2001, pp. 206–7.

[143] Khosrokhavar, *Les Neuveaux martyrs*, p. 76.

[144] Morteza Mutahhari, *Nehzat Islami dar Sadsal Akhir* [*Islamic Movements in the Last Hundred Tears*], Tehran, 1979, p. 83, quoted by Taheri, *Holy Terror*, p. 77.

[145] Quoted in Dabashi, *Theology of Discontent*, p. 201.

community is the community of power and force. Islam is the religion of power. It produces *mujahids*.[146]

And

What does a martyr do? This function is not confined to resisting the enemy, and in the process, either giving him a blow or receiving a blow from him. Had that been the case, we could say that when his blood is shed it goes to waste. But at no time is a martyr's blood wasted. It does not flow on the ground. Every drop of it is turned into hundreds and thousands of drops, nay, into tons of blood, and is transferred into the body of his society. That is why the Holy Prophet has said: "Allah does not like any drop more than the drop of blood shed in His way." Martyrdom means the transfusion of blood into a society, especially a society suffering from anemia. It is the martyr who infuses fresh blood into the veins of a society.[147]

Based on Ayatollah Khomeini's theology and Ali Shariati's Islamo-Marxist doctrine, Revolutionary Iran has cultivated a systematic worship for blood, death, and killing, to the point of making them a state doctrine, a state religion even. The grip of the doctrine, the object of constant repetition over more than a quarter century, is only matched by its practical implementation, both within and without Iran. The future Supreme Guide Ali Khamenei said in a sermon that "the martyrs are encouraging us, the Quran in one hand and a gun in the other."[148] Khamenei made death the fulcrum and the panacea: "The secret of all this lies in one issue – the secret of the victory of [all prophets] as well as of the victory of the Islamic revolution... is found in one issue, namely, that people among the servants of God are willing to sacrifice their lives."[149] In another sermon, he stated that martyrdom was "by definition" victory because it was better than living in submission. "Remaining alive under the condition of subjugation to the rule of the [evil rulers] is, in reality, death, while [death] through cutting [their] bloody claws is life": life is death and death is life – the Gnostic inversion of reality was perfect. Khamenei had coined the expression of "living

[146] Morteza Motahari [Motah-Hary], *The Martyr*, Houston, Free Islamic Literature, 1980, p. 10.

[147] Ibid., p. 15.

[148] Quoted in Haggay Ram, *Myth and Mobilization in Revolutionary Iran: The Use of the Friday Congregational Sermon*, Washington, DC, The American University Press, 1944, 71. *Khutbah* of March 21, 1980. In a startingly "Orwellian" formulation, he also said that "remaining alive under the condition of subjugation to the rule of [the tyrant] is, in reality, death while [death] through cutting the bloody claws of the [tyrant] is life," khutbah of September 26, 1980.

[149] Ibid., p. 138, from a March 20, 1981, khutbah.

martyrs."[150] Khamenei also sloganeered that the believer should have "the Quran in one hand and a gun in the other."[151] His colleague, future president Ayatollah Hashemi-Rafsanjani, preached that those slain in God's way (that is, in jihad) "do not feel any pain when struck by a bullet, an arrow, a spike, [or] a dagger." He also told a story: "The head of a shahid was cut off...we brought the corpse to Isfahan. His father came, wanting to see his child.... He was told that the corpse had no head. He replied: "It makes no difference." Approaching and seeing the corpse, he placed his lips on the separated head and kissed it. There was not even the slightest sign of emotion on his face. He said: "My God! I thank my child, my son, for becoming a *shahid* in the way of God. He became a *shahid* in the same way [Imam] Husayn...was slain."[152]

Hear Ayatollah Fazlallah Mahalati, once one of the main leaders of Iran's international terror apparatus:

> A believer who sees Islam trampled underfoot and who does nothing to stop it will end up in the seventh layer of Hell. But he who takes up a gun, a kitchen knife or even a pebble with which to arm and kill the enemies of the Faith has his place assured in Heaven, An Islamic state is the sum total of such individual believers. An Islamic state is a state of war until the whole world sees and accepts the light of the True Faith.[153]

Islamic terrorism has played a constant key role in revivalist movements in the past 150 years. The idea of murdering, maiming, and menacing the enemy for the purpose of hastening the final triumph of Islam has always held a very strong appeal among the Muslim masses. Which explains why "[t]o kill the enemies of Allah and to offer the infidels the choice between converting to Islam and being put to death is the duty of every individual believer, as well as the supreme – if not the sole – task of the Islamic state."[154]

The theology of death features a Leninist vanguard, the *mustanbat*, unaware and oppressed masses, the *mustazaf*, and the accursed oppressors, the *mustakbar*. In a companion typology, the Muslim "hypocrites" (*munafeqeen*) refuse to "reform," are warned first, but then "killing a hypocrite who refuses to reform is more worthy than a thousand prayers," or

[150] Ram, *Myth and Mobilization in Revolutionary Iran*, sermon of September 26, 1980, 318–19, p. 72.

[151] Ram, *Myth and Mobilization in Revolutionary Iran*, p. 71.

[152] Ram, *Myth and Mobilization in Revolutionary Iran*, pp. 73–4, Sermon of September 4, 1981.

[153] Taheri, *Holy Terror*, p. 8.

[154] Ibid.

so said Ayatollah Muhammad Muhamadi Guilani, once the Islamic judge at the sinister Evin prison of Tehran, often the scene of great butchery.[155]

He who is designated as an enemy of the Faith becomes *mahdur addamm*, one whose blood must be shed. Non-Muslims, straying Muslims, hypocrites and *dhimmis*, Jews and Christians, will be subjected to anathema:

He who points the finger of *takfir* at a person or a group of persons who refuse to see the light of Islam and embrace it sign the death sentence of that individual or community. For the step that must follow *takfir* is known as *tathir*, which means purification. Could a responsible doctor [of medicine] see microbes in a body through a microscope and do nothing about what he sees? The answer is clearly no. The same can be said of true believers, who cannot see agents of corruption acting within the body of the community without seeking to destroy them.

So wrote radical Abdul-Karim Biazar-Shirazi, in echo of the Nazi obsession with alien contaminations of the *Volk*'s purity.[156] Indeed, for the "enemies of Islam who shall in no circumstance return to the right Path," they should either be disfigured to a point that "they are recognized by the ugliness of their faces that reflects the ugliness of their souls," or "eliminated," writes another master thinker, Muhammad-Taqi Partovi-Sabzevari, a *hadith* authority: "Kill the troublemaker before he can harm you."[157] He explains:

Our own Prophet... was even more of a revolutionary.... Would he hesitate to put the guilty to the sword? Never, three times never! [...] In the Quran's historic vision Allah's support and the revolutionary struggle of the people must come together, so that Satanic rulers are brought down and put to death. A people that is not prepared to kill and to die in order to create a just society cannot expect any support from Allah... that day [of Islam ruling over the entire world] must be hastened through our *jihad*, through our readiness to offer our lives and to shed the unclean blood of those who do not see the light brought from the Heavens by Muhammad.... It is Allah who puts the gun in our hand. But we cannot expect Him to pull the trigger as well simply because we are faint-hearted.[158]

Indeed, as the infamous "killing judge" Ayatollah Sadeq Khalkhali interpreted it (he had been a member of the Navab-Safavi gang in the 1940s): "Those who are against killing have no place in Islam. Our Prophet killed with his own blessed hand. Our Imam Ali killed more than 700 on a single

[155] Ibid., p. 20.

[156] Abdul-Karim Biazar-Shirazi, *Ebadat va Khodsazi [Prayer and Self-Improvement]*, Mashhad, 1986, pp. 118–19, quoted by Taheri, *Holy Terror*, p. 21.

[157] *Ayandeh Nehzat Islami* [*The Future of the Islamic Movement*], Qom, 1986, p. 63. Quoted in Taheri, *Holy Terror*, p. 23.

[158] Ibid., p. 239.

day. If the survival of the Faith requires the shedding of blood, we are here to perform our duty."[159]

Martyropathology

"Martyropathology" is the form taken on by Iranian revolutionary nihilism. "Absent a perspective of self-actualization in the world, [it] offers the possibility of actualizing oneself in death" through a "mortiferous religiosity": The individual acquires an existence in dying:

> This disenchanted segment of the revolutionary youth that joins the *basije* [the revolutionary military mobilization] is not fundamentally concerned with life any longer. It profoundly desires to be annihilated, and destroy an important part of enemy forces in the process of its own destruction. [...] Death thus shifts from being an accepted possibility, or risk, to being "a burning desire," "an unquenchable thirst."[160]

To describe the psychology of the suicidalists:

> In the case of the obsession of death, we are dealing with a state of mind that sees in death a voluptuous embodiment of the ideal, endowed with a value per se, whose accomplishment will fill its adherents with joy... the act of self-immolation and in the process to give death to other humans out of a love for death. [...] In radical Islam... this mortiferous outlook sees life as an inferior level of being compared to the felicity gained by self-annihilation and the annihilation of others – martyrdom.... Martyropathy is a type of behavior that sets up death as the aim, not life.[161]

The suicidalist's blood must be spilled because it burdens him with life; the victims', because their death is good. "The conversion of blood into a mortiferous principle is expressed by using the cultural schemes of Shia [Islam] where [the] blood spilled in Karbala provide the models for the martyrs."[162] This is an inversion of the traditional Shia outlook whereby Ali, Husain, and their companions had "taken the sins of the world upon themselves": They could be admired, symbolically imitated, but they did not push their followers to become martyrs: the function of the bloody *Ashura* celebrations is cathartic and symbolic. Modern radical Islam – Khomeini and Shariati among others – have made the symbol real.

[159] Ibid., p. 36.
[160] Khosrokhavar, *Les Neuveaux martyrs*, pp. 84–5.
[161] Ibid., p. 99.
[162] Ibid., p. 160.

The Iranian regime started training *Enteharis* ("suicide-attackers"). One of the the top trainers, Said Shaykh Ragheeb Harb, a "saint" in the Radical Pantheon, told them:

> You shall begin to live once you have killed yourself. The "you" in you is none other than Satan in disguise. Kill him and you will be saved. Muslims are lucky because they accomplish this self-annihilation in accordance with divine rules. For Islam has an answer for every imaginable question. All an individual needs to do is to obey the rules without posing questions, without seeking variations.[163]

The early sect of Islamic extremists, the Kharijites, had thought no different: "You, who wish to contend with me in a duel, approach that I may hand you the poisoned beverage of death; there is no shame in passing one another the cup which slays those who put their lips to it: pour it out for me, then, and drink it yourself."[164]

The Palestinian Blood Group

The blood-lapping "Black September" assassin was a standard-issue PLO killer. A review of that organization and its components shows that "for Arafat and his Fatah cofounders, violence had assumed from the outset mythic proportions."[165] Like Shariati, the small Palestinian groups that were creating Fatah had been "mesmerized" by Frantz Fanon's notion of "sacred violence." The organization's hymn went:

> Farewell, tears and sorrow.
> Farewell, sighs and grief,
> Our people has come to loathe you,
> Welcome, blood and heroic death.[166]

Likewise, a slogan in high popularity in the Palestinian movement has been: "With our lives and with our blood we will redeem Palestine."[167] A poem recited at the beginning of a summer camp and broadcast on the television of the Palestinian authority proceeds:

> We are your boys, O Palestine
> We will flood you with our blood.[168]

[163] In *Din al-Islam aqwi* [*Islam Is the Strongest Religion*], Beirut, 1983, 22, quoted by Taheri, *Holy Terror*, pp. 131–2.

[164] Quoted in Tilman Nagel, *The History of Islamic Theology*, Princeton, NJ, Markus Wiener Publishers, 2000, p. 43.

[165] Efraim Karsh, *Arafat's War: The Man and His Battle for Israeli Conquest*, New York, Grove Press, 2003, p. 23.

[166] Quoted by Karsh, *Arafat's War*, p. 35.

[167] Ibid., p. 92.

[168] Ibid., p. 101.

The desire to kill is sowed early and often, and with it the love of killing. Sheikh Ibrahim Mahdi from the Sheikh Ijlin Mosque in Gaza said in a sermon broadcast on Palestinian television:

> A young man said to me: "I am fourteen years old, and I have four years left before I blow myself up amongst the Jews." I said to him: "Oh son, I ask Allah to give you and myself martyrdom." He added: "Blessings for whoever has raised his sons on the education of *jihad* and martyrdom; blessings for whoever has saved a bullet in order to stick it in a Jew's head."[169]

Sheikh Ikrimeh Sabri, mufti of Irsim, praised suicide-killing, concluding a sermon: "Whereas the enemies of Islam love life, Muslims love death and strive for martyrdom."[170]

Arafat himself systematically used that rhetoric: "Oh our pure martyrs. Rest in peace, calm and assured. Our blood is cheap for the sake of the goal."[171] He told the family of the June 2001 Tel Aviv disco suicide bomber: "The heroic martyrdom operation [of the man] who turned his body into a bomb [is] the model of manhood and sacrifice for the sake of Allah and the homeland."[172] The bloodlust and the cult of force were congenital to Fatah and the PLO. The Palestinian National Charter (1968) had hammered in its Article 9: "Armed struggle is the only way to liberate Palestine. Thus it is the overall strategy, not merely a tactical phase."[173] A slightly different version read: "Armed struggle is the only way of liberating Palestine and is thus strategic, not tactical."[174]

When Arafat chanted "We have only one motto: victory or death," this might have been downplayed as a rhetorical device or the inflated emotions of an agitated orator.[175] However, his insistence that Palestine can be recovered only "by blood and iron," that "it is the commandos who will decide the future," shows that this represented an "absolute glorification of violence."[176] The initials of the name of the organization Arafat first cofounded, al-Fatah – *Filistin Tahrir Hezb* – Party of the Liberation of Palestine, spelled the acronym *HTF* or *hataf*, which in Arabic means "death," and had to be inverted to *FTH*, *fatah*, or "victory." He established an organic connection

169 Ibid., pp. 104–5.
170 Quoted in Laqueur, *No End to War*, p. 72.
171 Ibid., p. 148.
172 Ibid., p. 213.
173 Y. Harkabi, *The Palestinian Covenant and its Meaning*, London, Vallentine Mitchell, 1979, p. 114.
174 Ibid., p. 120.
175 Quoted by Rubin and Rubin, *Yasir Arafat*, p. 27.
176 Ibid., p. 28.

between violence and identity: "Armed struggle restores a lost personal and national identity, an identity taken by force which can only be restored by force. Palestine has been taken away by fire and steel, and it will be recovered by fire and steel."[177] This was vintage Georges Sorel and Frantz Fanon.

A commando of the Palestine Liberation Front was captured with his cohorts in June 1990 before they could accomplish their mission: They were to land on the TelAviv beachfront and shoot indiscriminately. He reported that his orders were: "Don't leave anyone alive. Kill them all... children, women, elderly people."[178]

It would be tedious to enumerate the litany of attacks on civilians, children, and passers-by that became the hallmark of Palestinian organizations. Bloodlust suffuses them. Hear George Habash, founder and leader of the People's Front for the Liberation of Palestine: "In today's world, no one is innocent, no one is neutral. A man is either with the oppressed or he is with the oppressors."[179] He also said, "The prospect of triggering a Third World War does not bother us,"[180] an echo of sorts to Arafat's own retort to Israeli negotiators: "We can accept a lot of casualties, 30,000 martyrs. Can you accept 500 Israeli soldiers killed?"[181] A macabre calculus echoes much later by al-Qaida's Suleiman Abu Gaith: "We have the right to kill (at least) four million Americans."[182]

The same applies whether those organizations are "secular" or Islamic. The Charter of Hamas – self-defined as "one of the wings of the Muslim Brothers in Palestine" (Part 1, Article 2) – explains:

> Hamas has been looking forward to implementing Allah's promise whatever time it might take. The prophet, prayer and peace be upon him, said: "*The time will not come until Muslims will fight the Jews (and kill them); until the Jews hide behind rocks and trees, which will cry: O Muslim! there is a Jew hiding behind me, come on and kill him! This will not apply to the Gharqad, which is a Jewish tree.*" [cited by Bukhari and Muslim; Part 1, Article 7]

Article 8, "The Slogan of the Hamas," states: "Allah is its [that of Hamas] goal, the Prophet its model, the Qur'an its constitution, *jihad* its path and death for the case of Allah its most sublime belief." Article 15 finally explains:

[177] Al Nahar Arab Report, July 15, 1974, quoted by Rubin and Rubin, *Yasir Arafat*, p. 27.

[178] Jerusalem Post and Haaretz, June 6, 1990, quoted by Rubin and Rubin, *Yasir Arafat*, p. 121.

[179] Quoted by Becker, *The PLO*, p. 106.

[180] Quoted by Dobson, *Black September*, p. 31.

[181] Quoted by Rubin and Rubin, *Yasir Arafat*, p. 157.

[182] MEMRI Special Dispatch, June 12, 2002.

Dwelling one day in the Path of Allah is better than the entire world and everything that exists in it. [...] I swear by that who holds in His Hands the Soul of Muhammad! I indeed wish to go to war for the sake of Allah! I will assault and kill, assault and kill, assault and kill. (Told by Bukhari and Muslim.)[183]

Encapsulating the movement's mind, a Hamas web site was spotted in December 2002 with this statement: "We will use the skulls of Zion's sons [Jews] to build a bridge to heaven."[184] The state-controlled clergy, in another show of cooperation between laity and religion, was itself not shy in expressing the same view. Palestinian Mufti Sheikh Ikrimeh Sabri praises martyrdom in his sermons:

We tell them [the Jews]: in as much as you love life the Muslim loves death and martyrdom. There is a great difference between he who loves the hereafter and he who loves this world. The Muslim loves death and [strives for] martyrdom. He does not fear the oppression of the arrogant or the weapons of the blood-letters. The blessed and sacred soil of Palestine has vomited all the invaders and all the colonialists throughout history and it will soon vomit, with Allah's help, the [present] occupiers.[185]

Sheikh Mudeiris stated in a sermon on May 2, 2003:

No preacher or sermonizer has the right to begin his words without blessing all our martyrs.... The Jews cannot influence the actions of our youth and children. But for you, Allah has chosen martyrdom.... Allah had honored our youth... by choosing you and by choosing from among you the martyrs.... Is the martyr dead like other dead, which requires us to offer condolences and mourn with his family, friend and relatives? Or is the martyr enjoying virtues and the ability to perform miracles, which gives us the right to congratulate the martyr and his family? [...] We have the right to congratulate the martyrs' families, and not extend condolences and sorrow of our martyrs, if they [sacrifice themselves] to Allah.... But the martyr is spared the agony of death. This is one of the miracles of the martyr. Is it not enough that the martyr weds 72 black-eyed [virgins]? [...] When the martyr sees the grace of martyrdom and death for the sake of Allah he will wish to return to this world to be killed in it ten times.... The martyr – is it enough for him that he does not feel the blow of the sword or the pain of death or of the killing, rather as one of you feels a [wasp] sting.[186]

[183] http://www.palestinecenter.org/cpap/documents/charter.html.

[184] http://israel.net/timetospeak/24.htm.

[185] May 25, 2001, Mufti Sheikh Ikrimeh Sabri, Al-Aqsa Mosque in Jerusalem, PA Television, quoted by Steven Stalinsky, MEMRI, Special Report No. 25 Palestinian Authority, December 28, 2003, "Palestinian Authority Sermons 2000–3."

[186] May 2, 2003, Sheikh Ibrahim Mudeiris, Sheikh Ijlin Mosque in Gaza, PA Television, quoted by Stalinsky, ibid.

Equating suicide with martyrdom provided that "enemies of Allah" (i.e., enemies of the Islamists) be killed in the process. Iran set the tone, especially through the ayatollahs' international "Party of God," Hezbollah. The repeated suicide bombings that killed large numbers of American, French, and Israeli soldiers in Lebanon legitimized suicide-killing. Hezbollah also pioneered the use of "snuff movies," videocassettes of bombings and killings.

A Lebanese organization, Shiite by creed but Arab by membership, Hezbollah played a critical role in transferring and transplanting Iranian-Shiite schemes of martyrdom into its surrounding Sunni territory. In another display of ecumenic cooperation, George Habash, himself the Greek Orthodox leader of an Arab terrorist group, agreed in 1972 to give Shiite groups paramilitary training in the PFLP's facilities. When this stopped, it was Sunni-Muslim Arafat who made his facilities available.[187]

Later, the mantle of leadership in Hezbollah fell on the shoulders of Sayyed Hassan Nasrallah, the ideologist of a syncretic blend of Islam, of Marxism, and a fullfledged champion of death. Nasrallah professed: "We have discovered how to hit the Jews where they are the most vulnerable. The Jews love life, so that is what we shall take away from them. We are going to win, because they love life and we love death."[188] In December 2002, addressing Hezbollah military units, he said:

> These suicide operations are the weapon that God gave this nation, and no one can take it away.... Pay no attention to those who say there are civilians and soldiers in Israel. They are all occupiers and invaders, partners in crimes and massacres. [...] Martyrdom operations – suicide bombings – should be exported outside Palestine. I encourage Palestinians to take suicide bombings worldwide. Don't be shy about it.[189]

And in a speech aired by Hezbollah's *al-Manar* television:

> How can death become joyous? How can death become happiness? When Al-Hussein asked his nephew Al-Qassem, when he had not yet reached puberty: "How do you like the taste of death, son?" He answered that it was sweeter than honey. How can the foul taste of death become sweeter than honey? Only through conviction, ideology, and faith, through belief and devotion [...] each of us lives his days and nights hoping more than anything to be killed for the sake of Allah.
>
> The most honorable death is to be killed. [...] The most honorable death is death by killing, and the most honorable killing and the most glorious martyrdom is when

[187] Taheri, *Holy Terror*, pp. 65–7.

[188] Quoted from http://www.templeinstitute.org/archive/02-06-27.htm.

[189] http://qrmapps.com/thugburg/thug.asp?PID=103983013.

a man is killed for the sake of Allah, by the enemies of Allah, the murderers of the prophets [i.e., the Jews].[190]

We Love Death

Love of death is ubiquitous in radical Islam. It is one of its defining traits. "Everyone should know that the killing, massacring, slaughtering, expulsion and taking of captives that we do, these are sacrifices for the sake of Allah. [...] Woe, woe, woe to the enemies of Allah. Blood, blood, destruction, destruction," a communiqué issued by the Algerian GIA stated.[191] In 1972, after the massacre of Israeli athletes at the Munich Olympics, Voice of Palestine had broadcast: "We will the youth of the Arab nation to search for death so that life is given to them, their countries and their people. Each drop of blood spilled from you and from us will be oil to kindle this nation with flames of victory and liberation."[192]

Indeed, at the burial of a Palestinian leader killed in an Israeli raid on Beirut, the eulogist waxed: "Death is the door to a happy future for our people."[193] Arafat himself had assured in 1968: "Our road is the door of death."[194] Osama bin Laden's 1996 "Declaration of War" says:

> Since the sons of the land of the two Holy Places [Saudi Arabia] feel and strongly believe that fighting [jihad] against the unbeliever in every part of the world is absolutely essential.... I say to you: These youths love death as you love life. They inherit dignity, pride, courage, generosity, truthfulness.... Our youth believe in Paradise after death.[195]

The head of al-Qaida adds: "Yes, we kill their innocents, and this is legal religiously and logically. There are two types of terror, good and bad. What we are practicing is good terror. We will not stop killing them."[196]

Osama bin Laden's mentor Abdullah Azzam wanted blood: "The life of the Muslim *umma* is solely dependent on the ink of its scholars and the blood of its martyrs. What is more beautiful than the writing of the *umma*'s history with both... such that [it] becomes colored with two lines, one of

190 MEMRI TV Monitor Project – Hizbullah Leader Hassan Nasrallah: "The American Administration is Our Enemy... Death to America" No. 867, February 22, 2005, http://memri.org/bin/articles.cgi?Page=subjects&Area=jihad&ID=SP86705.

191 Quoted by Cook, *Understanding Jihad*, pp. 171–2.

192 Dobson, *Black September*, p. 87.

193 Ibid., p. 171.

194 *Time Magazine*, Dec. 13, 1968, quoted by Rubin and Rubin, *Yasir Arafat*, p. 45.

195 Quoted in Rubin and Rubin, *Anti-Americanism*, p. 140.

196 *National Post* (Toronto), Nov. 12, 2001, p. A9, quoted by Cooper, *New Political Religions*, p. 155.

them black and the other one red?"[197] The same soundbite was heard at the Finsbury Park Mosque in London from Sheikh Abu Hamza Al-Masri:

The common principle of all these operations, which we find even among the Palestinian youth, the girls, the women, and the children who throw stones at the bulldozers just to stop the destruction of their lands or homes – what unites all of these operations is their love of death for the sake of Allah, their burning desire to meet Allah. They easily sacrifice their lives for Allah. [...] Here is [the example of] Abu Dharr [one of the Prophet Muhammad's companions] who was among those who, when asked what they love best in this world, said: "I love death." He said, "I love illness, I love hunger, and I love death." The Prophet asked him: "Why do you love that which by nature other people hate, Abu Dharr?" And he answered: "I love hunger because when I am hungry my heart becomes gentle; I love illness because when I am ill my sins decrease; and I love death because when I die I shall meet my Lord." [...] The believers may ruin their lives in this world for the sake of the world to come.[198]

Radicals set the tone in the world of Islam. In a widely noticed turnabout, Sheikh Muhammad Tantawi, the highest jurisprudential authority of the Sunni world as rector of al-Azhar University in Cairo, joined the chorus in 2001 since he had earlier queried the Islamic legitimacy of suicide attacks targeting civilians. An al-Azhar web site reported:

The great Imam of Al Azhar Sheikh Muhammad Sayyed Tantawi, demanded that the Palestinian people, of all factions, intensify the martyrdom operations [i.e., suicide attacks] against the Zionist enemy, and described the martyrdom operations as the highest form of *jihad* operations. He says that the young people executing them have sold Allah the most precious thing of all. [...] [He] emphasized that every martyrdom operation against any Israeli, including children, women, and teenagers, is a legitimate act according to [Islamic] religious law, and an Islamic commandment, until the people of Palestine regain their land and cause the cruel Israeli aggression to retreat.[199]

Egypt's new mufti, Sheikh Dr. Ahmad Al-Tayyeb, also expressed his support for suicide attacks. According to his own web site the reported head of the Muslim Brotherhood's international organization, Sheikh Yussuf Qaradawi

[197] Quoted by Cook, *Understanding Jihad*, 128, from www.azzam.com, Nov. 30, 2001.

[198] MEMRI, Special Dispatch No. 762, August 12, 2004, "Sheikh Abu Hamza Al-Masri on Martyrdom and the Love of Death," http://memri.org/bin/arti-cles.cgi?Page=archives&Area=sd&ID=SP76204#_ednref5.

[199] MEMRI, Special Dispatch No. 363, April 7, 2002, "Leading Egyptian Government Cleric Calls For: 'Martyrdom Attacks that Strike Horror into the Hearts of the Enemies of Allah.'"

has confirmed that the operations carried out by the Muslim youth that defend the lands of Islam and the religion and dignity of Islam are the greatest forms of *jihad* for the sake of Allah. They fall under the definition of legitimate terrorization.... "I maintain that it is wrong to consider these acts as 'suicidal,' because these are heroic acts of martyrdom, which are in fact very different from suicide."[200]

There is complete unanimity amongst Muslim radicals: "Slaughtering is an offering on behalf of God.... It is an act of grace conferred by Allah."[201] Bin Laden's mentor Abdullah Azzam had said, "We are terrorists, and terrorism is our friend and companion. Let the West and East know that we are terrorists and that we are terrifying as well. We shall do our best in preparing to terrorize Allah's enemies and our own. Thus terrorism is an obligation in Allah's religion."[202]

Radical, Shiites, Sunnis, Arab and non-Arab radicals, secularists or nationalists and Islamists, each in their idiosyncratic manner recombined aspects of Islam and shards of European totalitarianism to produce a revolutionary creed integrating under the devotion to jihad, the cult of force, the love of death, the enjoyment of killing, and the obsession of blood. Variations exist, but all share a faith in sadistic violence and a necrophiliac vision.

Unbeknownst to its very leaders and theorists, the morbid cult so created merely recreated and repeated – using the cultural idiom of Islam – what vast and bloody insurrections had claimed and done for the better part of a half-millenium in medieval Europe using a Christian idiom. The roots of those insurrections and the belief systems that powered them were Gnostic. Understanding them will vastly enhance our understanding of modern radical Islam.

200 Statement in the Qatari daily Al-Watan, which appeared on Qaradhawi's web site on October 25, 2004, "Martyrdom Operations Are the Greatest Form of Jihad"), in MEMRI, Special Report No. 35, November 11, 2004, http://memri.org/ bin/articles.cgi?Page=archives&Area=sr&ID=SR3504#_ednref15.

201 Laqueur, *No End to War*, p. 95.

202 Quoted in Rubin and Rubin, *Anti-Americanism*, p. 182.

2

"An Elite of Amoral Supermen"

> History is a gallery of pictures with few originals and many copies.
>
> Alexis de Tocqueville

In the Epilogue of his *The Way of Jihad* Hassan al-Banna states:

> My brothers! The *umma* that knows how to die a noble and honorable death is granted an exalted life in this world and eternal felicity in the next. Degradation and dishonor are the results of the love of this world and the fear of death. Therefore prepare for *jihad* and be the lovers of death. Life itself will come searching after you. [...] You should yearn for an honorable death and you will gain perfect happiness. May Allah grant myself and you the honor of Martyrdom in His way.[1]

This clamor is mounting from thousands of madrasas, schools, universities, and mosques; from the mouths of dozens of thousands of predicators and imams; from hundreds of fatwas; from innumerable books, pamphlets, articles, and audio- and videocassettes; and from television shows and small circles and cells. It is a deafening din that crowds out other voices in the Muslim world. Al-Banna's formulaic expression of a trope could have come from any of the radical-Islamic talking heads of the last half century, and many others who drone and psalmodize on the same theme.

The constant repetition of the same stock phrases that prescribe and exalt killing and the veneration of death means that Allah wants blood, needs blood, that blood pleases Allah, whether the blood is that of His martyrs or that of His enemies. Allah demands blood as evidence of worship. In turn, society must be organized according to what Allah demands. A society

[1] In Militant Islam Monitor, http://www.militantislammonitor.org/article/id/39.

that needs blood in so fundamental a way is a society whose mind is set on human sacrifice.

It has set its priorities – death, blood, killing. They are the highest modes of worship – the jihad that powers them is the highest form of worship. They drag along all the other aspects of society. They beg to be extended to other societies. Their demands are absolute because the God from whence they proceed is absolute in its demands. Their *diktat* thus spreads from the core conception outwards.

Inexorably, the this-worldly "life" is depreciated. The otherworldly "death" is exalted. The ceaseless mantra of the worthlessness of life and the infinite felicity of the afterlife establishes a scale of values.

The ratio set between life and afterlife is the determinant of the scale of values. Any religion must strike a durable balance between the call of the afterlife and the reality of life on earth. Overvaluing the this-worldly undermines faith and its normative feedback. Conversely, undervaluing this world, and overvaluing the afterworld, create a massive disequilibrium: It tilts this life toward the afterlife, and that in passing the gate between them should occur the most important act in this life – its termination.

In Judaism and Christianity, Creation is good: "and God saw that it was good" (Genesis 1:10; repeated in Genesis 1:21, and repeated emphatically in Genesis 1:31). "And God saw every thing that he had made, and, behold, it was very good." If Creation is unconditionally "good," then life itself is good. In and of itself, life is an unconditional value. The assertion of life is an anthropological invariant – no society can durably exist without abiding by it, even those religions that aim to abandon what they describe as a cycle of reincarnated body-lives.

The Book of Genesis asserts, "God said, Let us make man in our image, after our likeness" and "God created man in his own image" (1:27). It repeats for good measure "male and female created he them" (1:27). The nature of the "imaging" and the "likeness" has long been adjudicated in Christianity as comprising the twin sparks of reason and love. This is the fundamental reason for the Seventh Commandment, in the Hebrew Bible "*lo tirtzach*" means "Do not murder" (Exodus 20:13 – "Thou shalt not kill" in the King James version): Life is sacred because it is "in the image and likeness of God." Killing *may* happen; murder *must* not. The denial of the goodness of Creation, and the worship of death are two aspects of the same creed.

To the goodness of Creation corresponds the Good Life. In Judaism, to Creation as pure goodness corresponds an unconditional reverence for life as God's gift, as summed up in the toast "*L'chaim*" ("to life"). The Good

Life is defined: "A good life for all, through adherence to God's Teaching (*Torah*) and Commandments (*Mitzvot*), harmony on earth on the individual and social levels culminating in peace and well-being for all humanity."[2]

Jewish thinkers have focused on the ways to lead a good life on earth and improve this world, *tikkun olam*, leaving concerns about death and beyond until the appropriate time. Judaism has stressed the natural fact of death and its role in giving life meaning. Man should develop his human nature, what separates him from beast, since he was created "in God's image and semblance."

Thomas Aquinas, after Aristotle and Augustine, tells us about the Good Life:

> The third good that comes from faith is that right direction which it gives to our present life. Now, in order that one live a good life, it is necessary that he know what is necessary to live rightly; [...] But faith teaches us all that is necessary to live a good life. It teaches us that there is one God who is the rewarder of good and the punisher of evil; that there is a life other than this one and other like truths whereby we are attracted to live rightly and to avoid what evil[3]

And: "We thus see the difference between doing good and doing evil. Good works lead to life, evil drags us to death. For this reason, men ought frequently to recall these things to mind, since they will incite one to do good and withdraw one from evil."[4]

Traditional Islam also develops a concept of the Good Life. It developed a doctrine

> in which the Prophet teaches, in the spirit of the Aristotelian just middle, that "The best among you is not the one who neglects the next world for the sake of this world, nor the one who does the reverse. The best among you is the one who takes from both." In traditional sources examples of excessive asceticism are often related in such a way that the Prophet's disapproval follows immediately upon the tale. "Your body has a claim on you; your wife has a claim on you; your guest has a claim on you."[5]

In several hadiths and stories, the Prophet does not credit fasting, for example, as a work of religious merit – nor torture of the flesh, nor celibacy. Hadith sometimes waxes eloquent on the goods of earthly life: "From every bite that a believer puts into his mouth he receives a reward from God." Or

[2] Midrash Ecclesiastes Rabbah 7:13.
[3] *The Catechism of St. Thomas Aquinas*, The Apostles' Creed, What Is Faith?
[4] Ibid.
[5] Ignaz Goldziher, *Introduction to Islamic Theology and Law*, Princeton, NJ, Princeton University Press, 1981, p. 121.

"God loves the Muslim who keeps up the strength of his body more than he loves the weakling." Or again: "He who eats and is thankful [to God] is as worthy as he who practices renunciation and fasting."[6] This is reflected in countless catechistic or doctrinal outlines, as in the following, unexceptional outline taken from a mainstream Islamic publication:

> Some people think that to live an Islamic life is "restrictive." Islam however, was revealed as a balanced way of living. Allah (The Most High) created all the humans with what is called a *Fitrah* (a natural state/desire). Islam recognizes that within this *Fitrah* there are motivations that influence a man's role on earth, e.g., a desire for good food and drink, to have a home, a desire for love and sex, to protect and be protected and to be successful and strong. Without some form of control and limit, all of these legitimate motives could prove very dangerous. So what constitutes the perfect control for the *Fitrah*? It must be a method that provides an organized yet practical demonstration of how to balance all these natural human desires. It cannot be something that goes against the *Fitrah*, by placing on it extra burdens. Likewise, it cannot be something that allows the human desires to run wild without any form of control. Islam is the perfect control for the *Fitrah*. It provides a divine method that elevates man above animals and the rest of creation.[7]

Compare: "Our lives are not worthy.... Those should fear death who consider the aftermath of death to be obliteration. We, who consider the aftermath of death a life more sublime than this one, what fear have we?" This statement of Ayatollah Ruhollah Khomeini,[8] among innumerable such declarations by radicals, betrays a fundamental devaluation of this life, and conversely, an overvaluation of the afterlife.

The afterlife becomes the sole purpose of life on earth – there is no Good Life, there is no sense of life becoming a preparation for afterlife: Creation is not good, it is bad. Flesh is bad, matter is bad: We are in the thick of a Gnostic-Manichean ideology. Creation itself is corrupt and full of corruption. Life is not a treasure but an evil passage to be terminated, a corrupt blemish, a Satanic plot.

If, then, death is all, and life is nothing; if jihad is the gate to paradise, the implication is that in Allah's determination, there is no Good Life unless it is devoted to jihad. The relationship between the value of life and death is expressed by the dictum heard again and again from the Islamists: "We love death more than you love life; Jihad is the "good" life; nothing else is.

[6] Ibid., p. 122.

[7] *Invitation to Islam*, Issue 2, July 1997, http://thetruereligion.org/modules/wfsection/article.php?articleid=17. Also see Prof. Zeev Magen, Conference Presentation, BESA Center, Bar-Ilan University, Tel-Aviv, May 2006.

[8] Rubin and Rubin, *Anti-Americanism*, 33, "Speech at Feyziyeh Theological School," August 24, 1979, translated by FBIS, August 27, 1979.

Such being the priorities, society should not set its sights on education, public health, technology, or investment. It cannot and must not organize itself in a way that maximizes those choices. It must organize itself in a way that enhances jihad. This may be said of the evolution of, for example, Pakistan since dictator Zia ul-Haq re-Islamized, Saudized, and jihadized the country. As a result, all the foregoing parameters took a nosedive. The brutal re-Islamization of Pakistan created conditions that mortally wounded its future livelihood. A society that makes death, plugged as jihad, as its priority, cannot live long without degenerating into the Hobbesian war of all against all that the unfortunate nation has become.

Of course, countries such as Egypt cannot be said to have been or to be jihadi countries. But their leaders, and their elites, have constantly straddled two worlds and tried to satisfy two contradictory impulses. To remain in power, Sadat and Mubarak made a deal with the Muslim Brotherhood: The despot would keep the political reins; the Brothers would get all of civil society, culture, social policy, and family law. When the latter overdid it to the point of challenging the despot's hold on power, a number were arrested, tortured, and hanged. The jihadi turnout is strong. In Syria or Iraq, totalitarian rule denied the Brothers and their ilk the usufruct of civil society and forced them to re-Islamize clandestinely, or through the path of least resistance, by setting up a countersociety that provides parts of the population with minimum services that corrupt governments deny them, but comes at a price – indoctrination.

Neither the "secular" despot not the "moderate" monarchs could prevent the re-Islamization: They would have had to undermine their own hold on power by setting growth-producing, market-oriented priorities, by giving up a governance based on the exclusive right of the sultan's bureaucracy, and by abolishing the reign of terror of their secret police and their unlimited ability to loot the nation's wealth on behalf of their family, their clan, their tribe, their sect.

The only priority, "secular" or "religious," that remained was jihadi. The absence of a set of priorities designed to enhance the livelihood and freedom of people unleashed a perverse feedback loop upon societies impoverished and sterilized, but that had absorbed enough elementary public health (at the initiative of colonial masters, for example, Lord Cromer in Egypt, or under their influence, as was the case in Pahlevi Iran) to set off population explosions: In spite of the manna generated by Western oil companies and oil consumers for many of these countries, per capita income underwent a historic decline, from levels that were not high to begin with. The frustrations created by the power monopolies that prevented access to lucrative and prestigious careers; the lack, therefore, of upward social mobility; and the sheer misery, the contumely of office, and the like, made avenues of looking at the world other than those offered by the tame religion of official office-holders appear more and more attractive. In the precarious, disorienting world in which increasing numbers of former *fellahs* and peasants now had to live in the city, the chimerical predication of sweeping Islamic Revolution became the one last shining hope. The will to believe exceeds the intelligence of belief.

There are precedents to this loathing for the this-worldly, this militant longing for the otherworldly. It is less in the relationship to God than in the relationship to flesh, matter, and the world and in the attitude toward death and killing, that the would-be jihadi martyr is reminiscent of earlier historical figures and events.

We are constantly told that radical Islam stems from "grievances," which is supposed to magically explain and have created the bloodthirsty creed studied here. Yet the belief-structure we have encountered, the peculiar relationship between life and death, killing and bloodlust, religious war and promised reward, bears an uncanny resemblance to a most unlikely predecessor: medieval Europe's millenarian movements.

Millenarianism

If Muslim terrorism is *sui generis* compared to modern terrorist movements, it bears an odd likeness to ancient events that wreaked havoc upon medieval Europe. Radical Islam is possessed of a striking structural homology with the now largely forgotten, mass-based revolutionary movements that devastated Europe for close to half a millennium.[9]

Those were the apocalyptical, eschatological movements generically termed "millenarian." The standard-bearers of those sects and groups thought that salvation was going to be collective, terrestrial, imminent, total; they believed that it would forever transform life on Earth: The new dispensation would be perfection itself, it would be miraculous and aided by supernatural agencies. Such, in broad brush, were the wreakers of havoc for half a millennium and more.[10]

[9] This conceit bears the hallmarks of Marxist-generated social "science" for which "being determines consciousness" as stimulus determines reaction, in Pavlovian-canine fashion. It is often taken as self-evident without any burden of evidence being required: It testifies more of the sorry state of said sciences than of the purported object of their studies.

[10] Norman Cohn, *The Pursuit of the Millenium: Revolutionary Millenarians and Mystical Anarchists of the Middle Ages*, revised and enlarged edition, Oxford & New York, Oxford University Press, 1961–70, p. 15.

European millenarianism was based on the Christian doctrine of "the last times" or "the last days." This referred to the belief held by some Christians, on the authority of the Book of Revelation (20:4–6), that Christ would establish a messianic kingdom on Earth after His Second Coming and would reign over it for a thousand years before the Last Judgment. According to the Book of Revelation, the citizens of that kingdom would be the Christian martyrs, resurrected for the purpose of a thousand years in advance of the general resurrection of the dead.[11]

In turn, Christian millenarianism rested upon the old Jewish prophecies: They had called for some cosmic catastrophe, the prelude to a new Eden. The central phantasy of revolutionary eschatology portrayed the world as dominated by a demonic, tyrannous power. The tyranny would worsen, the sufferings of its victims would be intolerable – until suddenly the hour would strike when the saints of God are able to rise up and overthrow it. It would occur after a Day of Wrath where misbelievers would be cast down and the righteous resurrected and reassembled in Palestine where Yahweh would dwell amongst them. A rebuilt Jerusalem would be the center of a just world, the poor would be protected, harmony would prevail, iniquity would be abolished: Paradise would be regained. This would be the culmination of history.[12]

In highly charged social and political environments, millenarian exaltation and social unrest tend to intersect at the point of intersection provided by would-be prophets and messiahs.[13] They are adopted as prophetic leaders by groups of the poor who vest them with their "phantasies of a world reborn into innocence through a final, apocalyptical massacre. In medieval Europe, the evil ones – variously identified with the Jews, the clergy or the rich – would be exterminated; after which the Saints – the poor in question – would set up their kingdom, a realm without suffering or sin. Inspired by such fantasies, numbers of poor folk embarked on enterprises which were quite different from the usual revolts of peasants or artisans, with local, limited aims."[14]

Spurred by the widespread belief in the imminent Second Coming of Christ, a profusion of early Christians transferred Jewish millenarianism into the new faith. Prophets and ecstatics abounded, against whom the church fathers fought endlessly. Origen presented the kingdom as an event

[11] Ibid.

[12] Ibid., p. 21

[13] Ibid., p. 16.

[14] Ibid., p. 21

that would take place not in space or time but only in the souls of believers. To collective, millenarian eschatology, he substituted an eschatology of the individual soul: This spiritualization reflected the concerns of a newly organized church. Saint Augustine went further: His *City of God* proposed to see the Book of Revelation as a spiritual allegory only. The Millenium began with Christ and is fully realized in the church, he insisted. This view permeated Western Christianity. The church channeled the emotional energies toward the next life.

The apocalyptic tradition nonetheless lived on even if the official doctrine no longer had an official place for it, "in the obscure underworld of popular religion," as it had such enormous attractions that "no official condemnation could prevent it from recurring again and again in the minds of the underprivileged, the oppressed, the disoriented, the unbalanced."[15]

The "obscure underworld," however, had its ways of reaching the surface: "Particularly at times of general uncertainty or excitement, people were always apt to turn to the Book of Revelation and the innumerable commentaries upon it." The Sybilline Oracles, the fourth century *Tiburtina*, the influential seventh-century *Pseudo-Methodius*, and compounds of Jewish, Christian, and Near Eastern literature ceaselessly fed fervid imaginations. "The particular political situations which had evoked the prophecies passed away and the very memory of them was lost, yet the prophecies themselves kept all their fascination . . . uncanonical as they were, the Sybillines had enormous influence – indeed, save for the Bible and the works of the Fathers they were probably the most influential writings known to Medieval Europe."[16] The lure of holding the keys of the kingdom in one's hands is well-nigh irresistible.

The prophecies also "proved infinitely adaptable: constantly edited and reinterpreted to fit the conditions and appeal to the preoccupations of the moment, they catered at all times for the cravings of anxious mortals for an unquestionable forecast of the future."[17] They were amongst the first books to be printed and, from the fourteenth century on, were translated into every European language and studied everywhere.

The "Johannine" tradition based on the Book of Revelation theorized the figure of God's archenemy in the "prodigious figure of Antichrist." The figure of Antichrist was also merged with those "demonic" beasts – dragon, serpent; later, goat, frog, among others. The coming of Antichrist was anxiously expected, people being forever on the lookout for "signs" – which

[15] Ibid., pp. 29–30.
[16] Ibid., pp. 32–3.
[17] Ibid., p. 33.

included anything and everything: bad rulers, civil discord, war, drought, famine, plagues, comets, sudden deaths of prominent persons, and an increase in general sinfulness, there was never any difficulty in finding them. Invasion or the threat of invasion by Huns, Saracens, Magyars, Mongols, or Turks always stirred memories of those hordes of the Antichrist, the peoples of Gog and Magog. Above all, any ruler who could be regarded as a tyrant was apt to take on the features of Antichrist... *rex iniquus*.[18]

The great church reforms initiated by Pope Gregory VII awakened and released new religious energies. These soon "were beginning to escape from the ecclesiastical control and to turn against the Church.... Unauthorized wandering preachers could expect a following such as they had never known before."[19] Suddenly, circa 1100 A.D., wandering preachers, holy men, and lay preachers, carrying with them apocalyptic prophecy and religious dissent, "became both more numerous and more important."

The early pseudo-Messiahs established a pattern that recurred for over four hundred years. The freelance preacher, hermit, or ascetic claims supernatural gifts of healing and prophecy, people flock to him with their sick, he "heals" some, foretells the future, acquires a "large and devoted" following, and then orders people to worship him. People abandon their priests to gather around the holy man, who exerts a charismatic hold on them.

The charismatic personality organizes some form of a new church and calls himself "Son of God." The more desperate the times are, the greater the faith and the larger the crowd. More often than not, the holy man and his followers turn to violence to impose their rule, which acquires increasing messianic tones. In the end, the holy man claims not only to be a living saint but to be equal or superior to the original apostles.[20] Tanchelm of Antwerpen, circa 1110, a wandering preacher amid areas swept for years by communal insurrections and social risings, acquired a blindly devoted following over which he ruled "like a messianic king." He proclaimed himself "to possess the Holy Spirit in the same sense and to the same degree as Christ and that like Christ he was God." His armed bodyguard acquired "dominion over a large area" until he was finally killed by a priest.[21] While the "messiahs" often acquired support from nobles and prosperous burghers, they "appealed particularly to the lower strata of society." Pope Urban II's call to the Crusade in 1095 unleashed a convulsive spasm throughout Western Christendom. The pope's intent was forthwith usurped by unauthorized

[18] Ibid., p. 35.
[19] Ibid., p. 39.
[20] Ibid., pp. 40–7.
[21] Ibid., pp. 47–50.

wandering preachers who set themselves up as *prophetae*, under the prestigious aura of the pope's summons to Crusade to save the Holy Sepulcher from the Muslims. Armies of crusaders sprang up: Paupers' Crusade, Crusade of the Children, Peter the Hermit, the chief propheta of them all, a charismatic man who exercised an "irresistible fascination upon masses." The hordes were soon joined by "all kinds of nondescript adventurers – by renegade monks, women disguised as men and many robbers and brigands."[22]

Living in a state of chronic frustration and anxiety, such people formed the most impulsive and unstable elements in medieval society. Any disturbing, frightening or exciting event – any kind of a revolt or a revolution, a summons to a crusade, an interregnum, a plague or a famine, anything in fact that disrupted the normal routine of social life – acted on these people with peculiar sharpness and called forth reactions of peculiar violence. And one way in which they attempted to deal with their common plight was to form a salvationist group under a messianic leader.[23]

Defrocked and fugitive priests and monks, semiliterate artisans, and sometimes ambitious noblemen led the crowds by dint of personal charisma, eloquence, "commanding bearing and... personal magnetism."[24] These men who saw themselves as "vessels for the divinity" inspired complete devotion, as if they were the vessel of all the emotions projected by their followers. Joining the eschatological mission of the presumed savior made the followers partake in his superior powers: They turned from humans into saints, infallible in word and deed. "Their final triumph was decreed from all eternity; and meanwhile their every deed, though it were robbery or rape or massacres, not only was guiltless but was a holy act."[25]

God wanted it. God had entrusted them with the stupendous mission, and therefore endowed them with supernatural powers. He had made them pure and placed them above common norms and customs. Authority was deregulated, the eschatological function was privatized. They could neither fail nor fall. They were Nechaev's revolutionaries, they were today's warriors of Allah.

Against them were arrayed the armies of Satan. The dynamic of their movement was compulsive: God had to resort to them in order to face the darkness of the superhuman demon Satan. They underwent a "collective

[22] Ibid., pp. 63–5.
[23] Ibid., pp. 59–60.
[24] Ibid., p. 85.
[25] Ibid., p. 85.

flight into the world of demonological phantasies," Satan's armies being composed of Jews, clerics, the rich and powerful, and sometimes, as in the case of the events that followed the Black Plague of 1348, even the unfortunate lepers. Massacres and extermination ensued. The myths wholly commanded thought and action. Being of the insubstantial nature of ideology, they solved no problem posed by reality, "they often prompted [the believers] to courses of action that proved downright suicidal," but they operated as emotional stabilizers, they turned the believers from angst-ridden ciphers into almighty fighters. "So it came about that multitudes of people acted out with fierce energy a shared fantasy which, though delusional, yet brought them such intense emotional relief that they could live only through it and were perfectly willing to kill and to die for it."[26]

The "Tafurs," an extreme case, but a most telling one that blossomed during the First Crusade illustrates this judgment. From the "Crusade of the paupers," among those who survived the journey on foot through Europe and Asia Minor where so many were slain by the Turks, bands of shaggy vagabonds reached Syria and Palestine, wholly autonomous with respect to the "official" Crusade. Led by prophetae, they were the very example of the hordes described earlier:

> [They] were such a ferocious band that any country they passed through was utterly devastated. [...] When they charge into battle they gnashed their teeth as though they meant to eat their enemies alive as well as dead. The Moslems, though they faced the Crusading barons fearlessly, were terrified of the Tafurs whom they called "no Franks, but living devils."

"Le roi Tafur," their chief, a former Norman knight turned ascetic, led an inner circle, a "college" that was the cadre force of the "army." Money and property had to be renounced. The Tafurs considered themselves elects of destiny. "It was precisely because of their poverty that the Tafurs believed themselves destined to take the Holy City." Poor they were, but cupid too. Loot was a sure sign of God's favor. And "in each captured city the Tafurs looted everything they could lay their hands on, raped the Moslem women and carried out indiscriminate massacres," even to the point of cannibalism. "What do I care if I die, since I am doing what I want to do?" said the "king." The crusader leadership wielded no authority over them at all. The barons seem in fact to have been somewhat frightened of the Tafurs.

In the purely imaginary incidents of stories written about the Tafurs, the beggar-king becomes the symbol of the immense, unreasoning hope that

[26] Ibid., p. 88.

had carried the *plebs pauperum* through unspeakable hardships to the Holy City. The realization of that hope demanded human sacrifice on a vast scale – not only the self-immolation of the crusaders but also the massacre of the infidel. Although pope and princes might intend a campaign with limited objectives, in reality the campaign tended constantly to become what the common people wanted it to be – a war to exterminate "the sons of whores," "the race of Cain," as King Tafur called the Moslems. It was not unknown for crusaders to seize all the peasants of a certain area and offer them the choice of being either converted immediately to Christianity or immediately killed.[27]

Mass Movements

In decades and centuries to come, several major mass movements attract attention as exemplars of the millenarian creed: the "Pastoureaux" of France, or the "Shepherds' Crusade," the Flagellants, the Taborites of Bohemia and Southeast Germany, and the Anabaptists of Westphalia. The intellectual matrix common to all, the prophecies of Joachim de Fiore, will be considered first. The great inventor of the apocalyptic prophecies that powered much of medieval Europe's waves of insurgencies, "the most influential one known to Europe until the appearance of marxism," was Calabrian Abbott Joachim de Fiore (1145–1202), who was strongly encouraged by no fewer than three popes to write down his revelations. His inspiration was that Scripture had "a concealed meaning of unique predictive value."[28]

Regressing to pre-Augustinian times, Joachim was proposing that the Kingdom of God could and would be realized on Earth, that the millenium indeed was coming. Joachim's numerological interpretations indicated that human history would culminate between 1200 and 1260. "Meanwhile however the way must be made straight; and this was to be achieved by a new order of monks who would preach the new gospel throughout the world." One supreme leader, *novus dux*, would "lead all mankind away from the love of earthly things and towards the love of the things of the spirit." Three and half years of reign of Antichrist would chastise and destroy the church, but he in turn would be overthrown.

The extremist wing of the Franciscan order, the so-called "Spirituals," not only appropriated the doctrine, but forged prophecies to adapt the Joachimite eschatology to its own; the Spirituals were now the new order.

[27] Ibid., pp. 65–8.
[28] Ibid., p. 108.

On the fringes of the Spirituals, fanatical extremists flourished and imagined a revolutionary and militant millenarian creed.[29]

This was the doctrine. It was coined in lesser money in the daily life of the insurgents, who often needed, as we have seen, to project their dreams onto a sacral figure that kings and emperors would provide.

The King of France was often the object of messianic expectations. King Louis IX (Saint Louis) was a pious ascetic, solicitous to the poor, and a venerated figure. As his venture in the Seventh Crusade misfired, a renegade monk, Jacob known as "the Master of Hungary" – a sallow, bearded ascetic with a commanding presence – took the lead of a new Crusade in Picardy. The riff-raff flocked to him. They provided the leadership of the "crusade" of the "shepherds" – in French the *Pastoureaux*, whose number reached 60,000.

Soon, Jacob was preaching against the clergy, the mendicants, Rome. The *Pastoureaux* themselves were the embodiment of truth. Jacob prophesied miracles and gave himself the right to grant absolution from every kind of sin, in effect presenting himself as a living Christ. His bodyguard killed contradictors. The army roved around northern France and even to Paris. He was showered with presents by the regent the Queen Mother. The *Pastoureaux* started killing clergy. They left Paris and attacked clergy, looted the religious orders' churches, stormed houses where priests and monks had sought shelter, and killed teachers at the university. "The *Pastoureaux* owed their prestige very largely to their habit of killing and despoiling priests." Their systematic pogroms against Jews continued. Finally when they attacked the rich city of Bourges, they were expelled, Jacob was cut to pieces, the movement was outlawed by the Queen, and the followers hanged in great numbers. The movement soon disintegrated.[30] A similar movement of militant egalitarianism sustained on a vision of the Virgin Mary had agitated southern France in the 1180s under the name *Caputiati*; after they took to slaughtering nobles and clergy, they had to be put down by armed force.[31] In 1309, another people's crusade is recorded with the same pattern, the same crimes, the same inglorious and bloody ending. In 1315, and then in 1320, the pope had to excommunicate crusaders who were threatening Avignon. Again and again from 1320 through 1380, the weavers of the Flemish country rose in revolt, and popular revolts agitated Paris, Picardy, and Normandy with a perennial undercurrent of millenarianism.

[29] Ibid., pp. 110–11.
[30] Ibid., pp. 94–9.
[31] Ibid., p. 102.

"The old eschatology [was] adopted as the vehicle for the new radicalism." Franciscan Jean de Roquetaillade's *Vademecum in Tribulations*, translated into English, Catalan, and Czech, prophesied for 1360–5 the rise of the lowly who would cut down the tyrants and nobles.

"Tempests, floods and plagues will kill off the greatest part of mankind, wiping out hardened sinners and preparing the way for the renewal of the earth. A Western Antichrist will appear in Rome while an Eastern Antichrist will spread his false doctrines from Jerusalem." By 1367, the time of trouble would come to an end, a great reformer would appear and become pope. The king of France would be elected holy emperor. Together they would expel the Saracens and Tatars; convert all Moslems, Jews, and Tatars; reconcile the schismatic Greeks; and "wipe out all heresy from the face of the earth." The king of France would conquer and rule all the world, a thousand years of peace would follow, and so on.[32] In Germany, the messianic monarch was of course German, though the ambit of his world conquests was no less.[33]

The crowning achievement of programmatic millenarianism was the *Book of a Hundred Chapters* written by an anonymous fanatic, the "Revolutionary of the Upper Rhine," one thoroughly familiar with the mass of medieval apocalyptic literature. He elaborated an apocalyptic program of his own, the most comprehensive expression of the popular eschatology of the Middle Ages.[34] God had communicated to him through Archangel Michael. The sins of the world were so great that the world was running into catastrophe. One more chance was given: A pious man would organize an association of like-minded fellows, in order to usher in the one-thousand year reign. However, for the revolutionary, the route to the millenium leads through massacre and terror. God's aim is a world free from sin. If sin continues to flourish, divine punishment will surely be visited upon the world; however, if sin is abolished once and for all, then the world will be ready for the kingdom of the Saints. The most urgent task therefore is to eliminate sin, which in effect means to eliminate sinners. The Brotherhood is a crusading host led by an elite, a "new chivalry" "to smash Babylon in the name of God and bring the whole world under his own rule, so that there shall be only one shepherd, one sheepfold and one faith throughout the whole world."[35]

32 Ibid., pp. 104–7.
33 Ibid., pp. 111–16.
34 Ibid., p. 119.
35 Ibid., pp. 120–1.

To achieve the end envisioned in the slogan *ein Reich, ein Volk, ein Führer*, assassination is wholly legitimate. In the words of the Revolutionary himself: "Whoever strikes a wicked man for his evildoing, for example for blasphemy – if he beats him to death he shall be called a servant of God; for everyone is dutybound to punish wickedness."[36] He calls for the assassination of the ruling emperor. The new one and the Brotherhood will "control the whole world from West to East by force of arms" in "an age of ubiquitous and constant terror," which will implement the prophecy: "Soon we will drink blood for wine." "The fanatical layman never tires of portraying – and in the most lurid possible colors – the chastisement which the future emperor... will inflict upon these children of Satan." The bad priests should be strangled or burned alive; the whole clergy ought to be annihilated: "Go on hitting them from the pope right down to the little students. Kill every one of them!" he insists, and even specifies that 2,300 clerics will be killed every day for four and a half years (one calculates a total of 3,777,750 fatalities) as well as usurers, moneylenders, shopkeepers, unscrupulous lawyers. "The Revolutionary is utterly convinced that God has ordered the great massacre... the holocaust is to be an indispensable purification of the world on the eve of the Millenium."[37]

> Thus society will be entirely recast. Further, sin must be unmasked everywhere, all sin be punished "with cruel severity": For what is mercy toward the sinners but a crime against the community as a whole? [...] If a person will not stop sinning he is better out of the world than in it... therefore he is to be executed forthwith by certain messengers of unquestionable piety.

The Revolutionary's statecraft is straightforward. Talking of the ruler: "By his cruelty he will instill fear into peoples." The conqueror will smash the Turks, conquer Jerusalem, overthrow Islam, and "those who do not accept baptism... are to be killed, then they will be baptized in their blood." An inexorable logic constrains the apocalyptical millenarian to draw such conclusions, whatever his cultural milieu, his religious beliefs, his ethnic background. The homology between the medieval sectarians and their brethren active later and in other settings is entirely uncoincidental.

Shortly after the mid-thirteenth century arose the Flagellant movement, which faithfully followed a virtually preordained trajectory from repentance to mass-based cult convinced that it alone is the path to salvation. They claimed to be "absolved from all sin and assured of heaven, [...]

[36] Ibid., p. 121.
[37] Ibid., p. 122.

empowered to drive out devils, to heal the sick, even to rouse the dead. Some spoke to Christ and the Virgin Mary."[38] The Flagellants made themselves into a substitute for the clergy and turned revolutionary. This army of the Saints believed that their flagellations "had the same redemptive value as the Crucifixion." As the movement slipped out of the control of the church, and as most of the wealthier individuals dropped out, the prophetae assumed leadership, full of enmity for the latter. Soon, sacraments were denied, clerics were assailed, and the Holy Spirit was directly invoked. Jews were slaughtered in great numbers. Rome finally, greatly frightened by this volcanic eruption, issued a Papal Bull, outlawing the movement, which died out in 1357, only to continue in clandestine form and in waves of revival.

The next wave, the Secret Flagellants of Thuringia, saw Christ himself as no more than their precursor; as he had pointed the true way to salvation by enduring flagellation, it was only those who beat themselves who could claim to pursue that way to the end. Now the Christian dispensation was supplanted by a higher dispensation of which they were the only bearers. Just as Christ had changed water to wine, so they had replaced baptism with water by baptism with blood.[39]

The Heresy of the Free Spirit

Not part of the turbulent urban masses, a clandestine movement of heretics wove its web from one end of Europe to the other. No social revolutionaries, its adherents formed the Heresy of the Free Spirit. They were Gnostics intent upon their own individual salvation, but the Gnosis at which they arrived was a quasi-mystical anarchism – an affirmation of freedom so reckless and unqualified that it amounted to a total denial of every kind of restraint and limitation. They were in a sense remote ancestors of Bakunin and Nietzsche[40] The core of the Free Spirit lay in the adept's attitude toward himself: He believed that he had attained a perfection so absolute that he was incapable of sin; as a result, he repudiated moral norms. The "perfect man" would always draw the conclusion that it was permissible and even incumbent upon him to do whatever was commonly regarded as forbidden.[41]

The heresy was also contemporary with and a kin to developments in the Muslim world. Toward the close of the twelfth century, Sufi holy beggars

[38] Ibid., p. 136.
[39] Ibid., p. 143.
[40] Ibid., pp. 148–9.
[41] Ibid., 150.

started spreading to various Spanish cities. Disclaiming book learning and theoretical subtleties, the masters rejoiced in direct contact with God, felt themselves united with the divine essence in a most intimate union. And this in turn liberated them from all restraints. Every impulse was experienced as a divine commandment; they could lie and steal or fornicate without qualms of conscience. For since inwardly the soul was wholly absorbed in God, external acts were of no account.[42]

Here is an essential component of the etiology of self-appointed "elites" and "vanguards" of the sectarian movements. Beyond the verbatim tenets of what each may believe, what matters here is the how of their belief in what they believe. There are invariants to a certain type of quasi-religious ideology, and their effect tend to be very similar.

In the early thirteenth century, the French-based "Amaurians," formed an upper middle-class sect of self-styled holy men with miraculous powers, visions, and trances. Although their doctrine was condemned by Rome and the Sorbonne they held that the incarnation of Christ had now been surpassed, that a last and supreme incarnation was coming to preside over the end of times and the world, and that the Spirit had taken flesh again, in the form of the Spirituals, the Amaurians themselves, who headed mankind toward perfection. One predicted a series of catastrophes for the near future, messianic woes in which the majority of mankind would die; wars and famines, earthquakes and fire would descend from on high. Antichrist would appear but then would be overthrown.

The ability, or not, of the church in its many aspects to retain the trust and loyalty of urban masses determined the extent of the influence found by the holy beggars.

Marguerite Porete, a Frenchwoman and a member of the Free Spirit, wrote a manifesto for the movement, the *Mirouër des Simples Âmes* (*Mirror of the Simple Souls*), which spread throughout Europe and intersected countless millenarian sects and groups. One group called itself the "Blood Friends," another "*Homines Intelligentiae*." As late as 1525, a millenarian leader of Antwerpen sent emissaries to Martin Luther. John Calvin in Paris met the sect of the Quintinists, who enjoyed a huge following amongst artisans and in the refined Humanist court of Marguerite de Navarre. The Free Spirit was to be found from Bavaria to the Rhine, from Northern France to the Flanders, in Umbria in Italy, from England to Bohemia, with extraordinary resilience and continuity.

[42] Ibid., p. 150.

The Free Spirit represents the ideal type of the intellectual construct common to all millenarian, apocalyptical, eschatological schools. Traits characteristic of the Free Spirit will be found in each and every such movement in the future, regardless of the religion or culture of the geographic or ethnic body upon which the ideology has settled.

The adepts of the Free Spirit did not form a single church but rather a string of like-minded groups, each endowed with its particular rites and articles of belief; links between the various groups were often tenuous, but they did keep in touch; and the Free Spirit was at all times clearly recognizable as a quasi-religion with a single basic corpus of doctrine handed down from generation to generation. The doctrine first emerged into full view in the fourteenth century; its features it showed then were to remain almost unmodified throughout the history of the movement.[43]

To have the Holy Spirit incarnated in oneself and to receive the revelation which that brought was to rise from the dead and to possess heaven. A man who had knowledge of the God within himself carried his own heaven about with him. One had only to recognize one's own divinity and one was resurrected as a Spiritual, a denizen of heaven on Earth. To be ignorant of one's divinity was a mortal sin, indeed, it was the only sin.[44] The Free Spirit was set apart from mankind. In practice, adepts knew that the highest spiritual privileges were reserved for their own fraternity. They divided humanity into two groups – the majority, the "crude in spirit," who failed to develop their divine potentialities, and themselves, who were the "subtle in spirit." They attained full absorption in God, not only after death, or at the end of time, but now. The heart of the heresy was not a philosophical idea at all but an aspiration; it was a passionate desire of certain human beings to surpass the condition of humanity and to become God.[45]

The desire to abolish the finite nature of man, the removal of the separateness of the human individual, the "merger" into God, to abolish sin, to possess absolute knowledge – Gnosis – and to do away with doubt and uncertainty, those hallmarks of the human condition were central to the Free Spirit, as it is with those creeds described as "fanatical." In the end, the adept shed the human condition and stood above God. They had acquired prodigious miracle-working powers, the gift of prophecy. They believed that they knew all things in heaven and Earth, that they could perform miracles – cross water dryshod, walk a yard above the ground. But for most of them

[43] Ibid., p. 172.
[44] Ibid.
[45] Ibid., p. 174.

such claims were too petty, for they felt themselves to be quite literally omnipotent.[46]

This belief system was nihilistic and megalomanic. The "supernatural revelation" was apt to feed a paranoid, delusional outlook. But its effects on the real world were very real. A leader of the Free Spirit regarded himself as the "Sword of God," "charged with the task of cleansing the earth of that impurity, the Church of Rome, and saving mankind in the Last Days." The twofold division of mankind was a critical component of the creed: Below the living gods existed a larger class of full initiates, ecstatics without the decisive final step who enjoyed a vicarious superhumanity through contact with the adepts. Between those and the mass of making, the gulf was absolute. Of the latter, the adepts took no account, "no more than of a horse." In their eyes, mankind in general existed only to be exploited by themselves, "the mortified elect." Hence the blithe dishonesty, which was everywhere noted as being characteristic of these sectarians, and a striking similarity with the ethos of the professional revolutionary as developed by the later Russian Gnostics, Chernychevskii or Lenin.[47]

The superhumans concluded that "[t]he truly free man is king and lord of all creatures. All things belong to him, and he has the right to use whatever pleases him. If anyone tries to prevent him, the free man may kill him and take his goods."[48] An adept said: "Cheating, theft, robbery with violence were all justified." If God wills it, everything is permitted. Whatever the Cause may be, it acts as the enabler of the unlimited exercise of the Will of the adept who can do anything he feels since he does it in the name of God, Allah, the Cause – all with the proper intention, *niyyah* in Arabic. Max Weber's distinction between *Verantwortlichkeitsethik* and *Gesinnungsethik* has never been more opposite.[49]

The Bohemian Taborites, radicals influenced by the Free Spirit, created another version of the millenarian movement. They repeated the familiar tale of the messianic woes that are approaching: No longer content to await the destruction of the godless by a miracle, the preachers called upon the faithful to carry out the necessary purification of the Earth themselves. A tract written by one Jan Čapek, a Prague University graduate, was said to have been "fuller of blood than a pond is of water." He proved that it was

46 Ibid., p. 176.

47 Ibid., p. 182. See Alain Besançon, *Les Origines intellectuelles du Léninisme*, Paris, Calmann-Lévy, 1977, *passim.*

48 Cohn, *Pursuit of the Millenium*, pp. 182–3.

49 Max Weber, *Politik als Beruf*, Ditzingen, Reklam, 1992, *passim.*

the inescapable duty of the Elect to kill in the name of the Lord. The work served as a polemical armory for other preachers, who used its arguments to urge their hearers on to massacre. No pity, they declared, must be shown toward sinners, for all sinners are enemies of Christ. "Accursed be the man who withholds his sword from shedding the blood of the enemies of Christ. Every believer must wash his hands in that blood." The preachers themselves joined eagerly in the killing, for "every priest may lawfully pursue, wound and kill sinners."[50]

Sin was to be punished by death, sinners must be exterminated, as one tract said: "The just . . . will now rejoice, seeing vengeance and washing their hands in the blood of sinners." Furthermore, anyone, of whatever status, who did not actively help them in "liberating the truth" and destroying sinners was himself a member of the hosts of Satan and Antichrist and therefore fit only for annihilation. For the hour of vengeance had come, when the imitation of Christ means no longer an imitation of His mercy but only of his rage, cruelty, and vengefulness. As "avenging angels of God and warriors of Christ" the Elect must kill all, without exception, who did not belong to their community.[51]

The Saints were tasked to "go forth to conquer and dominate the rest of the world" as the army sent through all the world to carry the plagues and vengeances and to inflict revenge upon the nations and their cities and towns, and judgment upon every people that shall resist them. "Thereafter, kings shall serve them, and any nation that will not serve them shall be destroyed. [. . .] The Sons of God shall tread on the necks of kings and all realms under heaven shall be given unto them." They considered themselves as avenging angels, whose mission it was to wield the sword throughout the world until all the unclean had been cut down. "Blood, they declared, must flood the world to the height of a horse's head, and despite their small numbers they did their best to achieve this aim . . . their Holy War."[52]

Even after the Czech sect of the Adamites were crushed by force of arms, the Taborite influence was widely felt, notably in this hotbed of sectarian ferment, Southern Germany. In the last quarter of the fifteenth century, a quasi People's Crusade rose from the small town of Niklaushausen, where an illuminated predicator and a defrocked monk partnered together to draw crowds of tens of thousands from as far afield as the Alps and the Rhineland to listen to their violent discourse on repentance, the imminence of the

[50] Cohn, *Pursuit of the Millenium*, p. 212.
[51] Ibid., p. 213.
[52] Ibid., p. 220.

egalitarian millenium. Miracles were duly performed, intense devotion to the propheta was duly produced, while the affair all too predictably ended at the stake. But weaver Taborite Niklas Storch arose from the movement to partner with Thuringian intellectual, monk, erudite, charismatic preacher, and bloodthirsty militant Thomas Müntzer (b. 1488).

One of the most remarkable features of Müntzer's predication was the bloodlust that transpired from it. There was nothing original in the themes of the Last Days being nigh, of the Elects having to rise and annihilate the godless, of his "war of extermination [that] the righteous were to wage against the unrighteous." Contemporaries noted Müntzer's lust for blood which at times expressed itself in "sheer raving"[53]:

> Harvest-time is here, so God himself has hired me for this harvest. I have sharpened my scythe, for my thoughts are most strongly fixed on the truth, and my lips, hands, skin, hair, soul, body, life, curse the unbelievers.... God is sharpening his scythe in me so that later I can cut down the red poppies and the blue cornflowers. Christ is your master. So don't let them live any longer, the evil-doers who turn us away from God. For a godless man has no right to live if he hinders the godly. [...] The sword is necessary to exterminate them, and so that it shall be done honestly and properly, our dear fathers the princes must do it, who confess Christ with us. But if they don't do it, the sword shall be taken from them... if they resist, let them be slaughtered without mercy.... At the harvest-time, one must pluck the weeds out of God's vineyard.... For the ungodly have no right to live, save what the Elect choose to allow them.... I tell you, if you will not suffer for God's sake, then you must be the Devil's martyrs. If there are but three of you who, trusting in God, seek only His name and honor, you will not fear a hundred thousand. [...] Now, go at them.... It is time.... The scoundrels are as dispirited as dogs. Take no notice of the lamentations of the godless! They wil beg you... don't be moved by pity.... At them! At them! While the fire is hot! Don't let your sword get cold! Don't let it go lame! [...] So long as they are alive you will never shake off the fear of men!"[54]

The apocalypse of medieval millenarianism was to take place in 1534–5 in the Westphalian city of Münster where the sect of the Anabaptists took over and proceeded to implement the lessons learned from centuries of millenarianism, in a grotesque *dance macabre*, a rule of terror where the *Narrenschiff's* passengers had taken over the city.

From beginnings where the local artisan and merchant guilds had naively joined forces with the sectarians, the latter gained a strong following, many of whom received "apocalyptic visions in the streets of such intensity that they would throw themselves on the ground, screaming, writhing

[53] Ibid., p. 236.
[54] Ibid., pp. 235–50, *passim*.

and foaming at the mouth. It was in this atmosphere, charged with supernatural expectations, that the Anabaptists made their first armed rising." Soon thereafter, with the help of fellow sectarians freshly immigrated, the Anabaptists established "a theocratic regime in which the divinely inspired community had swallowed up the state [...] [in order to beget] a New Jerusalem purified of all uncleanness."[55] The rich and unbelieving were expelled. New baptism was imposed on the remainder, and it became a capital offense not to be rebaptized. Then began a reign of terror, which *mutatis mutandis* may easily be compared to Lenin's "war communism." Money was abolished and its surrender to authorities made the test of true faith. Offenders were declared fit for extermination; some executions did take place.

An absolute dictatorship ruled the city. "The new government was given authority in all matters, public and private, spiritual and material, and power of life and death over all inhabitants." A very "puritanical" morality was imposed, where lying, slander, avarice and quarreling were made capital offenses. "Death was the punishment for every kind of insubordination."[56] Of course, it was the ruler's destiny to rule the entire world, on God's behalf. He was anointed king of the New Jerusalem and designated the real Messiah:

> Now I am given power over all nations of the earth, and the right to use the sword to the confusion of the wicked and in defense of the righteous. So let no one in this town stain himself with crime or resist the will of God or he shall without delay be put to death with the sword.[57]

Unsurprisingly, the official mottos were: "The Word has become flesh and dwells in us," and "One king over all. One God, one faith, one baptism," and "One king of righteousness over all."

The fixation on oneness is one of the hallmarks of Gnostic political doctrine. Bloodlust, the other marker, was ever present. One of the Anabaptists' pamphleteers explained that supernatural strength was vested with the believers so that "five could kill one hundred of the enemy and ten would kill a thousand. The enemy would flee before them." Big shows – public beheadings – were mounted in town. "All who persisted in sinning against the recognized truth must be ... sentenced to death ... extirpated from the Chosen People." Within days, executions began, and terror intensified. Anyone suspected of wanting to flee the city was beheaded, the king himself

[55] Ibid., p. 261.
[56] Ibid., pp. 268–9.
[57] Ibid., pp. 271–2.

carrying out the sentence, or conducting the quartering of the culprits, the sections of the bodies being hanged in public spaces as a warning. This was the last spasm of insanity in the besieged city, which was taken by storm. The deposed king Jan Bockelson "was led about in a chain and exhibited like a performing bear," and then executed. All surviving Anabaptists were executed.

By adopting Müntzer as a revolutionary icon, Friedrich Engels in his 1850 tome *The Peasant War in Germany* made the Anabaptists as precursors of later revolutionary risings and wars, in more ways than he himself thought. The sought replication of Gnostic ideology, of totalitarian rule, of bloody dictatorship was indeed a harbinger of revolutions to come. In the twentieth century, the fascination for Müntzer continued to imbue various strains of communism, such as utopian Marxist Ernst Bloch.[58] Marxists and anarcho-communists reveled in the doomed figure of the Anabaptist prophet, and often saw themselves as heirs to the "amoral supermen" of the Free Spirit. The desire for the millenarian Apocalypse that would forever release and redeem mankind is central to the Marxist faith.

Etiology

Characteristically, millenarianism sets itself boundless aims. It considers a given social struggle not as a struggle for specific, limited objectives but as an event of unique importance, different in kind from all other struggles known to history, a cataclysm from which the world is to emerge totally transformed and redeemed. This is the essence of the recurrent phenomenon of "revolutionary millenarianism." Authorities lose their credibility. The propheta recruit for such struggles from atomized, marginalized people whose social position has become unsteady and uncertain. Cut off from their traditional social support networks, devoid of institutionalized methods of voicing grievances or conveying disarray, the propheta emerged as a force to reintegrate them in coherent groups. Revolutionary millenarianism took place against a background of disaster. Anguish generated energy. Radicalism injected the apocalyptic element, leading to the final purification of the world.

The propheta was endowed with a personal magnetism that enabled him to claim a special role in bringing history to its apparent consummation. He offered his followers the prospect of carrying out a divinely ordained mission of stupendous, unique importance. What emerged was a new group – a

[58] Ernst Bloch, *Thomas Müntzer als Theologe der Revolution*, Frankfurt, Surkhamp, 1921–67.

restless dynamic and utterly ruthless group that, obsessed by the apocalyptic fantasy and filled with the conviction of its own infallibility, set itself infinitely above the rest of humanity and recognized no claims save that of its own supreme mission and finally subjugated the great mass of the disoriented, the perplexed, and the frightened.[59]

This review of the best-studied type of millenarianism in history, the type that rose and flourished in Western Europe, does not exhaust the history of utopia, of utopian and eschatological movements, or of sectarian insurrection. But before studying the specific form those took in the history of the world of Islam, we must dwell upon what the latter and the former have in common, what – as will be argued here – is their common substratum, the Gnostic ideology.

The origins of gnosis hark back to pagan oriental cults in the Ancient world, and their interaction, by the beginning of the Common Era, with the Hellenistic and Greco-Roman worlds, with Judaism and nascent Christianity. In contents, a gnosis is a doctrine that presents itself as a religious creed. It claims to possess the perfect and complete knowledge about divinity, the universe, man, and man's salvation (different gnoses have elaborated rich speculative mythologies to flesh out their doctrines and rituals to accompany them). Gnosis explains everything, knows all, integrates everything. The believers consider themselves separate from and superior to the rest of ignorant mankind, with considerable practical and ethical consequences.

First and foremost, Gnosticism is a doctrine of salvation: It is salvation through "knowledge" (*gnosis* in Greek) or perhaps a series of doctrines, all of which share a common core. As German philosopher Hans Jonas states in his seminal work on the subject: The Gnostic systems compounded everything – oriental mythologies, astrological doctrines, Iranian theology, elements of Jewish tradition, whether Biblical, rabbinical or occult, Christian salvation-eschatology, Platonic terms and concepts. Syncretism attained in this period [the first centuries of the Common Era] its greatest efficacy.[60]

Being themselves composites from variegated sources accounts for the extraordinary fluidity and plasticity of Gnostic ideologies. The "Gnostic principle" showed remarkable recombinant capabilities that allowed it to mix and mingle with a very broad spectrum of religious ideas and systems. In the end, however, Gnosticism consists of "certain characteristic mental attitudes, which are more or less distinctly exhibited throughout the whole

[59] Cohn, *Pursuit of the Millenium*, pp. 281–5.

[60] Hans Jonas, *The Gnostic Religion: the Message of the Alien God and the Beginnings of Christianity*, 2nd ed., enlarged, Boston, Beacon Press, 1963, p. 25.

group, irrespective of otherwise greatly differing content and intellectual level."[61]

Gnosticism is a radical dualism: An unbridgeable chasm separates God from the world and consequently God from man. The divine is the realm of light; the world is the realm of darkness. "The transcendent God Himself is hidden from all creatures.... Knowledge of Him requires supranatural revelation and illumination."[62] Man is a mix of light and darkness; body and soul are of darkness, spirit (*pneuma*) is of light.

But "the universe... is like a vast prison whose innermost dungeon is the earth, the scene of man's life." The world is ruled by a tyranny of universal Fate, a concept drawn from astrology. The Gnostic "knows" that the world and himself are fallen, that the world is an absurd mix of good and evil. "The world is no longer the well-ordered, the cosmos, in which Hellenic man felt at home, nor is it the Judeo-Christian world that God created and found good."[63] The world is wrong not just because bad things are occurring. It is wrong in its principle, in the way it is organized. It is intrinsically and irretrievably wrong. The world is not a good world that includes flaws and imperfections. It is radically dominated by evil. The way the world is, the way it is constructed, and the very laws of the world are all wrong. It is not that the world is good and human beings are imperfect. Man lives in a "truly dreadful, confusing and oppressive state of the world." As a result, the Gnostic is in revolt against the world.[64] He must disengage from the evil matter in which he is imprisoned.

The means to do so: salvation will come from knowledge (gnosis); the "Gnostics" are "the knowing Ones." But "knowledge" is not a knowledge by reason, a knowledge of rational objects, as was Greek philosophy. It claims to "know" things unknowable, different from faith that has faith in "things invisible" (Saint Paul). Gnosis is a "knowledge" of things unknowable, it claims to be a knowledge of the objects of faith. Gnosis is not scientific knowledge that works by approximation, experimentally, and produces, in Karl Popper's phrase, "falsifiable" truths (that are susceptible of being refuted and proven wrong). Gnosis speculates and claims absolute truth for its speculative assertions. An illumination is required to gain access to this "knowledge," as opposed to simple faith: "It is closely bound up with revelatory experience, so that *reception* of truth either through sacred

[61] Ibid., p. 26.
[62] Ibid.
[63] Eric Voegelin, *Science, Politics and Gnosticism*, Washington, DC, Regnery, 1968–77, p. 7.
[64] Besançon, *Les Origines intellectuelles*, p. 16.

or secret lore or through inner illumination replaces rational arguments and theory. [...] The ultimate "object" of gnosis is God: its event in the soul transforms the knower himself by making him a partaker in the divine existence."[65] Gnosis is the knowledge of the laws of the cosmos and its global structure, macrocosm and microcosm (man). It is the historical knowledge of the evolution of the cosmos, its primeval state, the causes and circumstances of its fall, and the pathways of its redemption that allows it to forecast with certainty its final state. It is a practical knowledge that indicates the means of contributing to salvation and guides the salvational action of the Elect.[66]

Salvation or "the goal of Gnostic striving is the release of the 'inner man' from the bonds of the world and his return to his native realm of light." The Elect will extinguish evil in himself. Gnosis is a morality:

> In this life, the *pneumatics*, as the possessors of gnosis called themselves, are set apart from the great mass of mankind. The immediate illumination not only makes the individual sovereign in the sphere of knowledge (hence the limitless variety of Gnostic doctrines) but also determines the sphere of action. Generally speaking, the pneumatic morality is determined by hostility toward the world and contempt for all mundane ties. From this principle, however, two contrary conclusions could be drawn and both found their extreme representatives: the ascetic and the libertine. The former deduces from the possession of *gnosis* the obligation to avoid further contamination by the world and therefore to reduce contact with it to a minimum; the latter derived from the same possession the privilege of absolute freedom. [...] The law of "Thou shalt" and "Thou shalt not" promulgated by the Creator is just one more form of the "cosmic" tyranny. [...] As the pneumatic is free from the [universal Fate], so he is free from the yoke of the moral law. To him all things are permitted.

So much so that the "intentional violation" of the norms "paradoxically contributes to the work of salvation."[67] The New Man created by the Gnostic is a nihilist. The possession of the absolute key to absolute knowledge cannot go without hubristic pride, arrogance, and conceit – the certainty of thus being superior to all others.

The quest for salvation spills beyond the limits of the individual. As Voegelin writes, oppressive though the dominance of wickedness may be, "salvation from the evil of the world is possible," provided the order of things (Creation) is changed. "From a wretched world a good one must evolve historically. [...] This salvational act is possible through man's own efforts." The Gnostic believes that a state of perfection may be brought

[65] Jonas, *Gnostic Religion*, pp. 34–5.

[66] Besançon, *Les Origines intellectuelles*, pp. 17–18.

[67] Jonas, *Gnostic Religion*, pp. 34–47.

down from the heavens. To him "[i]f it is possible . . . so to work a structural change in the given order of being that we can be satisfied with it as perfect then it becomes the task of the Gnostic to seek out the prescription for such a change. Knowledge – *gnosis* – of the method of altering being is the central concern of the Gnostic."

The "liberal" (in the European sense), "does not think ideologically. He wishes to change reality, within limits, themselves variable. He never thinks of substituting another reality," whereas the Gnostic "is tempted to erect an imaginary world which is the ideal double of a world decreed as absolutely evil." He sets out to implement "a thorough overthrow of the entire structure of the world . . . a radically new life which had never been known to man," a total recasting of the universe.[68] This is not a notion similar to the Jewish notion of *tikkun olam*, nor the Christian notion of preparing the City of God – Christian doctrine believes that perfection can be attained only in the heavenly world, that the world must remain as it is, imperfect, and that one may improve things (persons, society) but not change their nature. Peter Abélard's beautiful phrase "Man is God's gardener" may be used to show the difference between religion and Gnostic creed: To the Judeo-Christian tradition, man cultivates the garden he has received from God; he improves, maintains and repairs it – and enjoys its fruits. Note that Islam traditionally accepts this view that man has received the earth from Allah in "lieutnancy." To the Gnostic, the garden must be upset and overthrown.

Gnosis produces "the construction of a formula for self and world salvation" – hence the appearance of the Gnostic prophet. The Gnostic always shows "a readiness to come forward as a prophet who will proclaim his knowledge about the salvation of mankind."[69] While Gnostic man could simply flee the world altogether, the activist variant of Gnosticism tries to create the perfect social order, "knows" what the final state of perfection is and what the ways and means are that lead to it. The "prophet" is "the intellectual who knows the formula for salvation from the misfortunes of the world and can predict how world history will take its course in the future."[70] To create a new world, the prophet will surround himself with a restricted elite of Elects, initiates who have seen the Perfect Truth and alone possess it, as opposed to the universal ignorance that besieges them. *They* are the *real* mankind. The Gnostic is the carrier of a pathological condition, that of "a thinker who, in his revolt against the world as it has been created

[68] Besançon, *Les Origines intellectuelles*, pp. 88–9.

[69] Voegelin, *Science, Politics, and Gnosticism*, pp. 59–60.

[70] Ibid., p. 67.

by God, arbitrarily omits an element of reality in order to create the fantasy of a new world," which he, or his disciples, will often seek to bring about by turning themselves into the "armed prophets of the new world."[71]

The Gnostic is the great recusant – he who denies any worth and validity to the world as it is, who sets out to destroy it. The Gnostic creeds contrast to its Elect – the New Men, the "Perfect" as the Cathar elite called themselves – as a symmetrical opposite and elective archfoe: the radical evil, the creatures of darkness, the absolute negative. Since this world is the reign of Satan the prince of darkness, the creatures of darkness are the children of Satan and deserve to be treated accordingly. Gnosticism will accordingly develop figures of the archenemies who incarnate this evil. Reality is demonized; the bearers of reality are satanized. They "represent absolute evil. Against it, one may use means similar to those it employs, but whose finality inverts the value." Acts that are crimes if committed by the archenemy become virtuous deeds if committed by the Elect: There are no objective values.[72] This is the creed that twentieth-century philosophy has promoted – Heidegger and Sartre among others – in the first place. In Gnosticism,

> the criterion of good and evil ceases to be a universal one and becomes internal to the doctrine: nothing is right in itself. What is right is relative to the execution of the cosmic plan as *gnosis* has unveiled it, and, therefore, it is relative to *gnosis* itself. It is not the accomplishment of justice that marks the conformity with what is right, but the adequation of behavior to the accomplishment of the cosmogonic scheme. *Gnosis* here splits from religion.[73]

As we will see, however, it does not necessarily split from all religions.

Traditional Christian doctrine properly criticized gnosis for "trespassing beyond any possible limits to human knowledge in its claim to have penetrated the central mystery of the cosmos and man."[74] In so doing, the Gnostics were replacing faith with a pseudoreason that claimed total knowledge: In Gnosticism, "there are no questions, only answers." Saint Augustine had drawn a strict line between Christian doctrine and Gnosticism: At the very beginning of his *City of God*, he emphatically insisted that the kingdom was not, and cold never be, of this world:

> Most glorious will be the City of God, both in this fleeting age of ours, wherein she lives by faith, a stranger among infidels, and the days when she will be established in her eternal home. Now she waits for it with patience, until righteousness returns

[71] Ibid., p. 69.

[72] Besançon, *Les Origines intellectuelles*, p. 105.

[73] Ibid., p. 19.

[74] Ibid., p. 17.

to judgment. Then she shall possess it with preeminence in final victory and perfect peace.[75]

In its dream of earthly perfection, gnosis was the harbinger and the ancestor of modern ideologies. One of the first to draw attention to the resurgenc of the Gnostic millenarian outlook in modern times was German philosopher Karl Löwith, who spotted the doctrine as a crucial component of at least some of the continental Enlightenment: the immensely influential eighteenth-century writer Gotthold Ephraim Lessing revived Joachim de Fiore's doctrine of the three world-ages ending in earthly fulfillment. "Lessing's influence was extraordinarily deep and far-reaching."[76] It influenced early socialism and positivism, Hegel's philosophy of history, and the Marxian form of messianism, all of which postulate that mankind is headed for a final age of fulfillment and earthly perfection. The "father" of modern German nationalism, socialist doctrinaire Johann Gottlieb Fichte, gave vent to a purely Gnostic outlook: "The present age is one of complete sinfulness, preceding a final regeneration in a new age of the spirit, which corresponds to the millennial kingdom of John's Revelation." Friedrich Schlegel followed the same path: "The revolutionary desire to realize the kingdom of God is the flexible starting point... and the principle of modern history."[77] The perfect knowledge attained by the Gnostic then becomes the driver of his action: "At the heart of ideology, there is The Known. Lenin does not know that he believes. He believes that he knows."[78] Does it matter that this postulated knowledge is in fact utterly fantastic? Is it important that the Gnostic, in scientific terms, knows absolutely nothing, neither the end of history, nor God's plan, nor the nature of the order of reality? Ethnological research shows that in the eyes of the believer, this does not matter at all. "That the shaman's mythology does not correspond to an objective reality is of no importance: the sick person [whom the shaman treats] believes in it, and is a member of a society that believes in it. Protective spirits and malfeasant spirits, praeternatural monsters and magic animals, are part of a coherent system which establishes [their] conception of the universe."[79]

German-American philosopher Eric Voegelin charted the underlying commonality between the medieval movements and the twentieth century's

[75] Saint Augustine, *Civitas Dei*, Book I, Preface.
[76] Karl Löwith, *Meaning in History: The Theological Implications of the Philosophy of History*, Chicago, University of Chicago Press, 1949, p. 208.
[77] Ibid., p. 209.
[78] Ibid., p. 15.
[79] Claude Lévi-Stauss, *Anthropologie structurale*, vol. I, Paris, Agora, 1974, p. 226.

totalitarian movement, fascism, communism and national-socialism. These mass movements were rooted in ancient intellectual movements, specifically, he averred, in Gnosticism. At first sight, his claim of filiation seemed outlandish: Were the contemporary movements he referred to not godless? Were they not offsprings of modernity, of the Industrial Revolution, of the French Revolution, of the chaos of World War I? How could they relate in any meaningful way to a two-thousand-year-old religious or quasi-religious creed? Furthermore, can a valid common ground be ascribed between the ancient world's gnosis with its emphasis on individual salvation through knowledge, and the mass-based movements discussed here?

British historian Norman Cohn, plotted the filiation in precise historical detail:

> For the long-term, indirect influence of Joachim [de Fiore]'s speculations can be traced right down to the present day, and most clearly in certain "philosophies of history." [...] It is unmistakably the Joachite phantasy of the Three Ages that reappeared in, for instance, the theories of historical evolution expounded by the German idealist philosophers..., in Auguste Comte's idea as an ascent from the theological through the metaphysical to the scientific phase; and again in the Marxian dialectic of the three phases of primitive communism, class society and a final communism which is to be the realm of freedom...and it is no less true that the phrase "The Third Reich" first coined in 1923 by the publicist Moeller van den Bruck and later adopted as a name for that "new order" which was supposed to last a thousand years, would have had but little emotional significance if the phantasy of a third and most glorious dispensation had not, over the centuries, entered into the common stock of social mythology.[80]

At the very end of his study, Cohn adds a warning that ought to enter the minds of students of Islam, the Middle East, and the Arab world:

> During the half century since 1917 there has been a constant repetition, and on an ever-increasing scale, of the socio-psychological process which once joined the Taborite priests or Thomas Müntzer and the most disoriented and desperate of the poor, in phantasies of a final exterminatory struggle against "the great ones," and of a perfect world in which self-seeking would forever be banished.... The old religious idea has been replaced by a secular one, and this tends to obscure what otherwise would be obvious. For it is the simple truth that stripped of their original supernatural sanction, revolutionary millenarianism and mystical anarchism are with us still.[81]

This brings us back to Voegelin's identification of the common Gnostic roots of those apparently secular Western intellectuals' ideologies and the totalitarian mass movements of the twentieth century. This identification,

[80] Cohn, *Pursuit of the Millenium*, p. 109.
[81] Ibid., 286.

we will argue, is crucial to understanding the nature of the radical Islamic threat today. Beyond the diversity of cultural, religious, and intellectual idioms that these variegated utopias used and spoke, the homology is one of contents, structure, and effects, reaching into real-world action. There is thus a thorough homology between the medieval utopias, that arose in the Christian world, the modern totalitarian utopias, and the current jihadi utopia.

All gnoses structure space and time in a similar way: They all prescribe that there are "two camps, two regions, three times," and so does ideology. The ideologies of radical Islam certainly respond to this characterization as does radical Islam, obsessed as it is with the division of the world into two antithetical camps and regions, *dar al-Islam* and the *dar al-Harb*, and into a ternary division of time: predication, *jahiliyyah*, and apocalypse. Analysts who seek the "root causes of terrorism" ought to dig deeper than the surface. Stripped of its quasi-Christian vestment, which tends to obscure the deeper similarity, the same old outlook is still with us, in the form of radical Islam. Prior to exploring this assertion, it is necessary to describe Gnosticism as it appeared historically and to establish a working definition. We will then show why it is useful, and in fact indispensable, to measure radical Islam according to that yardstick.

3

The Gnostic Mahdi

Modern Islamic Gnosis

Islam is a religion with a universal message, not an esoteric creed reserved to a few Elect. It is an organized religion with institutions, rites, some hierarchy, and mass appeal. Sunni Islam strongly denies that the Quran carries any esoteric or even symbolic meaning. Beyond what God Himself has revealed in His Revelation, man cannot remotely approach the mystery of God. Men, a famous orthodox Sunni saying goes, must believe *bila kayfa*, "without [asking] how," without questioning: "A clearer definition of that how [Muslim theologians believe] passes human understanding, and man ought not to meddle with things that have not been rendered subject to his thought."[1]

Does this place Islam beyond the reach of gnosticism? Hardy Gnostic speculators meet a tall barrier that impedes their fantastic constructs of pseudoknowledge based on the flimsiest of interpretations. Yet Gnosis "attends, like a shadow, late Ancient Judaism, nascent Christianity, later Islam, and the shadow shall never part company from them."[2]

A leader of the revolutionary Iraqi Shiite movement *al-Dawa* explained: "The Muslim people and its leaders are closely linked to the esoteric world, as it is expressed in the form of the Hidden Imam and the divine meaning of the affairs of the world."[3] Islam truly is burdened by a heavy Gnostic content, inherited from the legacies of Persian-Zoroastrian and Manichean religions, from other ancient Middle Eastern mystery religions, from Jewish and

[1] Goldziher, *Introduction*, p. 92.

[2] Besançon, *Les Origines intellectuelles*, p. 17.

[3] Quoted by Emmanuel Sivan, *Mythes politiques arabes*, Paris, Fayard, 1995, p. 240.

Christian apocalyptic religions, and from heresies that preexisted or developed under Byzantine Christianity, itself often gnostically inclined. "The Christian elements of the Koran reached Muhammad mostly through the channel of apocryphal traditions and through heresies scattered in the Eastern Church. In the same way, more than a few elements of each gnosticism are represented in Muhammad's message."[4]

This goes much further than the Gnostic influence so conspicuously claimed in Ismailism and Sufism. The grandiose constructions of ibn Arabi, for instance, owe much to Gnostic, neo-Platonic speculation, as does Gnostic influence upon the generic *zandaqa*, "free-thinking" heresy in Caliphal Islam.[5] A history of Islam cannot be told without examining the repeated blossoming of Gnostic sects within and around it.[6]

Further, there is a strong intimation in Islam that Revelation includes all possible human knowledge. "The old Islamic view of knowledge was not a reaching out to the unknown but a mechanical process of amassing the known."[7] Learned theologians repeat it as often as more mundane speakers. "Popular Egyptian predicator Sheikh Hafiz Salameh, to give but one example, has a ready-made answer: 'Islamic law came down to us from the hands of Almighty Allah; this is why he will bring about the application of sharia as the solution to all our problems.'"[8] Quran and sharia "supply to collective consciousness an exceptionally powerful emotional effect [...]; it is so convenient to assert that 'the Quran provides an answer to all problems.'"[9]

This claim to absolute knowledge, while the speculative extravagances of gnosis is denied, wholly differs from Judaic or Christian concepts of truth and knowledge. For the latter, truth, based on Revelation, is, like revelation itself, the result of a historical process. It is unveiled in the course of a historical process during which God unveils His design to man. Judaic truth and knowledge are the objects of continuous reelaboration and discovery, none of which, admittedly, may contradict canonical knowledge, but which are able to add to it. Beyond the historical nature of Rabbinical Judaism,

4 Goldziher, *Introduction*, p. 14.

5 On the subject of Gnosticism in Islam, see Goldziher, *Introduction*, passim; Jean Doresse, "La Gnose," 364–428, and Henri-Charles Puech, "Le manichéisme," pp. 523–645, in (sous la direction de) Henri-Charles Puech, *Histoire des Religions*, vol. 2, Paris, Bibliothèque de la Pléiade, 1972.

6 See, for example, Henri Laoust, *Les schismes dans l'Islam: Introduction à une étude de la religion musulmane*, Paris, Payot, 1965, especially Chapters II and V.

7 H. A. R. Gibbs, *Modern Trends in Islam*, p. 64.

8 Interview to *al-Shira*, Beirut, July 15, 1985, quoted by Sivan, *Mythes*, p. 227.

9 Mohammed Arkoun, Interview to *Le Monde*, December 22–23, 1985, quoted by Sivan, *Mythes*, p. 236.

the elaboration of the Law continues in the Babylonian Talmud and in the Jerusalem Talmud. The Law is "closed" in its origin, not in its development. Likewise in Christianity, where the entire Patristic and Conciliar efforts were consciously based on a history of salvation, God's word was to be interpreted and developed as human history proceeded.

This is not the case in Islam. The Quran is law and theology: Nothing in Islamic orthodoxy may be added or subtracted from God's verbatim utterances, as reported to Muhammad by archangel Jibril. Islamic theology is a hermeneutics of the letter, not of the spirit. The postulate of the "uncreated" nature of the Quran removes the holy book from any context and history itself. This excision bans any notion of a history of salvation: Salvation in Islam must ever return to the origins, rather than allow the future to actualize itself. The a-temporal nature of the Quran therefore dictates that the knowledge it contains is absolute: It cannot be "bested" or even developed. Since Muhammad is considered the "Seal of the Prophets," that is, the last prophet God will ever send to mankind, he is the last word, he is "the acme of God's revelation to man. [. . .] Everything posterior to Muhammad, therefore, is something of an anti-climax."[10]

Further, it is God's mandate that His kingdom be realized on earth. The crucial notion that "my kingdom is not of this world" is rejected by Islam, which demands not only kingship in heaven in the future, following the end of times, but worldly overlordship, at some real point in a real future. Such is the imperative, that the dar al-Islam will rule over the entire world, and then and there institute the reign of perfect justice. The millenarian impulse is thus fully integrated in the religion where it coexists with the this-world spirit of conquest and rule. "The thought of rejecting this world, coupled with a sense of absolute despondency, had dominated the beginnings of Islam. It was . . . a vision of the end of the world and the Day of Judgment that had awakened Muhammad to prophethood. That vision bred an ascetic mood among those who followed him" even though Islam as it developed included a concept of the Good Life.[11]

The very concept of *dar al-Islam*, the abode of Islam, is perilously close to being in itself a Gnostic concept. It divides the world into two, as all Gnostics do: Gnostics here, Others there. Mankind is divided in two species of unequal worth and value: In Islamic law, the testimony of a Muslim ranks

[10] Sivan, *Mythes*, p. 181.

[11] Ibid., p. 116. See also Ze'ev Maghen, "Islam From Flexibility to Ferocity," in Efraim Inbar, Hillel Frisch, eds., *Radical Islam and International Security: Challenges and Responses*, London, Routledge, 2007, pp. 69–79.

higher than that of an unbeliever. The Muslims are meant to lord over the unbelievers, who are merely *dhimmis*, so-called "protected" people, second-class human beings (not "second-class citizens," as is often said there is no concept of citizenship in Islam).

Granted, the unbeliever can become a believer, change species, and join the Muslim species. Islam does not formally recognize any validity to borders, ethnic groups, and the like within the *umma*. As we mentioned, in spite of its own claims, Islam is a syncretic composite rather than a unified and coherent creed. But the division between an *umma* – the "Islamic nation" – and the rest of the world is of the same nature as the Gnostic division between the Elect (the Perfects) and the mass of mankind. Rather than being a truly universalistic religion, Islam is a tribal religion generalized. The group loyalty (*asabiya*) which once went to the tribe now goes to the *umma*, but the *umma* itself is in turn the tribe generalized. Islamic eschatology is collective more than personal: It is as part of the *umma* that the believer exists at a par with his ritually and socially manifested conformity with the rules and rites of the *umma*. Still, at the Day of Judgment, souls will be weighed and judged individually rather than collectively: Islam indeed is a composite.

Likewise, the emphatic denial in Islam that good and evil are good and evil in themselves – since this would set limits to God's omnipotence – and that they are subject to God's whim and writ is of a Gnostic nature. To take a famous example, Descartes posited in the *Metaphysical Meditations* that God could not possibly alter the fact that 2 + 2 = 4, should the fancy so strike Him; 2 + 2 would never make 5. Good and Evil in the Judeo-Christian tradition are absolute values with absolute contents. God has "limited" His own omnipotence because God is Reason (*logos*), and God is absolute Goodness (love): How could He possibly want the Good not to be so, and 2 + 2 to equal more or less than 4? God is impelled to will 2 + 2 to equal 4 precisely because He is Reason.[12] But in Sunni orthodoxy, a famous hadith tells us: "If God wanted, good would become evil and evil would become good." Creation is thereby not axiomatically oriented to the Good: Its values are arbitrary axioms that are permanently and forever dependent upon God's whim. "Allah behaves like an Oriental despot."[13]

A composite creed is not a stable one: Its different elements will come to the fore according to circumstance. The story of medieval millenarianism has

[12] See Pope Benedict XVI, "Faith, Reason and the University," The Regensburg Lecture, September 12, 2006, Libreria Editrice Vaticana.

[13] Joseph Chelhod, *Introduction à la sociologie de l'Islam*, Paris, Editions Besson Chantemerle/Librarie G. P. Maisonneuve, 1958.

shown that great commotions that upset the normal order of society will tend to push the more unstable fringes of society toward doctrines that address, and relieve, the angst generated in them by precariousness and shocks, and by the loss of authority of normal institutions. In a composite that is partly Gnostic, the Gnostic part will be especially well suited for espousal by the desperate and the angry in times of social ferment and radicalization, at the expense of the non-Gnostic parts of the creed, which are more attuned to life in stable circumstances. The strong Gnostic components present within Islam explain the relative ease with which Gnostic ideas of various forms could historically enter the body of Islam. Gnostic notions saturate radical Islam.

Radical Islam features the essential traits of Gnosticism: the role of the Elect; their stupendous, world-saving mission; their direct entrustment by God of that mission, their shunting of the rest of mankind to the nadir of damnation; the notion that everything is permitted; the ensuing bloodlust; the outbreak of violent hatred and rage; the designation of Satan-like populations to be destroyed; the apocalyptic turn of mind; the coming of the last days; the great, final cosmic battle between Good and Evil.

The starting point in radical Islam may well be the notion of modern *jahiliyyah* developed in the modern age by the Indo-Pakistani Maududi and his Egyptian confederate Sayyid Qutb. According to this view, the entire world, not excepting any Muslim society, has completely reverted to an age of neo-paganism, ignorance, and barbarism similar to the state that prevailed prior to Muhammad's Revelation – and that the prophet called exactly that, *jahiliyyah* in Arabic.[14] As Qutb himself wrote:

> [T]he entire world is steeped in *jahiliyyah*. [...] The basis on which the edifice of this *jahiliyyah* rests is the rebellion against the Sovereignty of God on earth, which is a special attribute of the godhead. This *jahiliyyah* has transferred the reigns of sovereignty to the hands of man and assigned the overlordship of men to some persons... [who assert] the claim that man has the right to create values, legislate rules of collective behavior and prescribe way of life, irrespective of the consideration of what program God has prescribed for human life and in which form he revealed it.[15]

The argument is a closed circle: Only if one believes in Islamic revelation can one believe that the prescriptions of revelation are mandatory. This view of an overwhelmingly jahili world, expresses a marked sense of doom. Laced with apocalyptic overtones, it pervades radical Islam. One Islamist deplores

[14] See Sivan, *Radical Islam, passim.*

[15] Qutb, *Milestones*, translated, by S. Badrul Hasan, Karachi, International Islamic Publishers, 1981, p. 49.

the state of "ordeal and discord" in which the umma and the world find themselves.[16] Sayyid Qutb is despondent about the contemporary state of affairs in the world: "Islam cannot fulfill its role unless it takes the form of a society . . . we can say that the Muslim community has been extinct for many centuries."[17]

From the extravagant assertion that no extant Muslim polity, society, regime, or state is authentically Islamic, Qutb draws his foreordained conclusion: Since the *umma* is not "genuinely" Islamic, there is no *umma* save that formed by the "true" believers, that is, Qutb and his circle, the Egyptian and international Muslim Brotherhood. There is no "real" *umma* in the world of reality. The idea of *umma* that the Brethren carry in their minds is therefore the one and only true *umma*, whereas the (actual) *umma* is unreal: Reality is denied and delegitimized, ideology displaces and supersedes reality. The Gnostic does not believe what he sees; rather, he sees what he believes. Here is his task: "It is necessary to lay the foundation of the campaign of revivalism in one of the Islamic countries. This inevitable struggle of regeneration in a long and a short duration, shall ultimately result in capturing the leadership of mankind."[18]

In a display of Leninist organizing perspective, Qutb writes that this task is incumbent "initially [on] a vanguard," and it will, like Prophet Muhammad's own *hijra* (emigration and retreat) from Mecca to Medina, "keep itself somewhat isolated from this all-encompassing *jahiliyyah*," this "vast ocean of *jahiliyyah* which has encircled the entire world." For Qutb, he and his cohorts are the literal replicas of the prophet's revered companions, "a generation which has no parallel in the entire Islamic history [and] in the entire history of mankind."[19]

Qutb explains, in words reminiscent of medieval apocalyptists fearful that Satan pollute their innocence and sully their purity, that after the prophethood of Muhammad and the first four "well-guided" caliphs of Islam,

> during the subsequent periods it so happened that various offshoots intermingled with the spring [i.e., Islamic Revelation]. The fountain from which later generations imbibed was mingled with Greek philosophy and logic, ancient Persian legends, Jewish scriptures and traditions, Christian theology and remnants of other religions and cultures. . . . All subsequent generations were saturated from this mixed source.[20]

[16] Sivan, *Radical Islam*, esp. chapter 1, quote, pp. 14–15.
[17] Ibid., p. 47.
[18] Ibid., p. 51.
[19] Ibid., p. 53.
[20] Ibid., p. 56.

His phobia of contamination, however, is unevenly applied, though perhaps unwittingly so: For all his virulent loathing of Christianity, Qutb endorses the apocryphal Gospel of Barnaby, a forgery probably composed in the thirteenth or fourteenth century, as well as the equally apocryphal Gospel of Childhood and the Proto-Gospel of James and the so-called Gospel of Thomas, all of which contain elements closer to the Quranic stories.[21] Even more significant, Qutb supports Bishop Arius and his heretical Arianism, which he sees as a prefiguration of Islam with its striving for a form of *tawhid*, of getting away from what Muslims consider the "polytheism" of the Trinity! "At bottom, for Qutb, Islam but restored the trampled and cruelly persecuted Arianism. [...] His kindness for Arius, the Alexandrian of Libyan origins, is obvious. He understands the birth of Islam, quite properly it seems, as a resurgence of the crushed Arianism."[22]

Remarkably, this notion of Islamic purity parallels that of blood purity, the purity of filiation and descent, as it obtains in the tribal world. The inside/outside world of the tribe is replicated in the religion and in the religious ideology. The rot – "the putrid element of human lordship"[23] – has so deeply penetrated that "[a]ll this around us is *jahiliyyah*. People's imaginings, their beliefs, customs and traditions, the sources of the culture, their art and literature, their laws and statutes, much even of what we take to be Islamic culture, Islamic authorities, Islamic philosophy, Islamic thought: all this too is of the making of this *jahiliyyah*.[24]

In typical Gnostic fashion, the sweeping indictment reduces the authentic Muslims to a tiny core of believers. That small core, however, is able to "excommunicate" (*takfir*) all the others. The blanket use of *takfir* dates back to the Kharijites, the early Islamic sect that challenged the Umayyad Caliphate of Damascus from the seventh century A.D. and recurrently thereafter. For the extremists of the sect, any Muslim who had transgressed any part of the Law was a "polytheist" (*mushriq*) and had to be treated with total ruthlessness: He was an apostate, excluded from the *umma* and doomed to eternal damnation. With complete dogmatic and political ruthlessness, the Kharijites branded moderates as major sinners and subjected them to *takfir*. They "advocated and practiced a fanatical terrorism."[25] A Kharijite rebellion rose in the region of al-Kufa in 695 A.D. History has remembered the

[21] Carré, *Mystique et politique*, pp. 109–10.
[22] Ibid., pp. 115, 120.
[23] Ibid., p. 94.
[24] Ibid.
[25] Laoust, *Les schismes*, p. 45.

"bloodthirsty savagery" of their storming of the city and "the savagery with which the faithful who had sought refuge in the [great] mosque of al-Kufa were slaughtered."[26]

The thirteenth-century Hanbalite theologian Ibn Taimiyya integrated this fury in more respectable theological and jurisprudential tradition:

A man who declares himself a Sunni Muslim stops being one if he does not observe (or in the case of a Muslim leader, if he does not apply) *sharia* or if he does not exhaustively abide by the fundamental laws regarding life, the body and property, the statute of *dhimmis*, *jihad*, if he strays from sexual morality, of the ban of alcohol, card games, etc. The list of prescriptions is very large and it is not easy to know from which "degree" of infringement on the believer or the leader reaches the point of no-return. When does he become an apostate who needs to be combated?[27]

If Ibn Taimiyya had any scruple, his disciples did not. The founder of Wahhabism, Hanbalite theologian Muhammad ibn al-Wahhab revived the use of *takfir* against both non-Muslims and those Muslims whom he accused of being hypocrites. "He was also the first to expand the concept of *jahiliyyah* to include Muslim societies of his time that had diverted from the pure truth. Designating Muslims as *jahilis* and *kufr* opened the way for proclaiming jihad against them."[28] Pro-Wahhabi "reformer" Rashid Rida pronounces a form of *takfir* on modern Muslim leaders. In his famous commentary on the Quran, he comments on the Quranic verse "Whoso judges not according to what God has sent down – they are the unbelievers."[29] Rida's words:

In this verse, the matter is with those Muslim [leaders] who have recently instituted new laws and have abandoned *sharia* which was bestowed upon them by Allah.... Thus have they abolished penalties regarded as "detestable," such as the amputation of the thief's hand or the lapidation of adulterous women or prostitutes. Instead, they have edicted laws and penalties invented by Man. Anyone who so acts differs in no way from a heretic.

The number of the True Believers is small indeed. But their small number is offset by the stupendous nature and immense scope of the mission they have received from Allah. The task at hand, according to Qutb, is no less than

[26] Ibid., p. 40.

[27] Sivan, *Mythes*, p. 193.

[28] David Zaiden, "The Islamist Way of Life as a Perennial Battle," in Rubin and Rubin, *Anti-American*, pp. 11–27.

[29] Sura "The Table," 5:50, *The Koran Interpreted*, translated by John Arberry, New York, Touchstone Book, 1955, p. 135.

destroying all the Satanic forces from the face of the earth and making human beings bow down their heads before One God.... [Islam] either completely dynamites the reigning political systems or subjugating them forces to submission and accept *jiziya* [the poll-tax of submission that *dhimmis*, Christians, Jews and other unbelievers have to pay to the Islamic state].[30]

In short, the few Elects will bring to heel the entire world, as Muhammad supposedly did. In radical Islam, the Elect are uniquely possessed of an absolute truth that nobody else is privy to, Muslim or other. This is based on the crucial Quranic verse: "You are the best community ever raised among the people: you advocate righteousness and forbid evil, and you believe in Allah. [...] You are the best community that ever was" (3:110), and on the equally celebrated hadith "my community will never agree on error," that bestows infallibility upon the community. But, since contemporary Islam, to the radical Islamists, is entirely *jahili*, the Islamists themselves are the only real community (*umma*). Ergo, the Islamists are the infallible Elect. In well-known sectarian manner, it is to them an article of faith that their Islam is the only Islam, exclusive of all others.

The Gnostic-Manichean undercurrent emerges in full regalia in Sayyid Qutb's words:

This struggle is not a temporary phase but a perpetual and permanent war. This war is the natural corollary to this eternal verdict that Truth and falsehood cannot coexist on the face of this earth. [...] The struggle between Truth and Falsehood, Light and Darkness, is continuing since the beginning of the universe and the surging tide of the *jihad* for freedom cannot cease until the Satanic forces are put to an end and the religion is purified for God in toto.[31]

Islam is war, and it is at war. It must be interpreted as a struggle, not a spiritual and moral struggle but a military and missionary struggle, military because it is missionary. Qutb's Islam is aggressive and expansionist:

Islam is compelled to fight by its goal, that is, to guide the human race.... There is no system of life but Islam. Thus the Muslim war aims at converting all humans on the entire earth. Men everywhere must be liberated.... Jihad is not, as some "Muslims" claim, a defensive war, it is offensive. It is total revolution.... Who grasps the nature of the religion also grasps how necessary the militant principle of Islam in the form of armed struggle.... It is an expansionist militancy which aims at liberating the whole of mankind.[32]

30 Qutb, *Milestones*, p. 112.

31 Ibid., p. 125.

32 Quoted by Carré, *Mystique et politique*, pp. 123, 127–8.

As a result, "the only possible contact between Islam and its *jahili* environment [the rest of the world] is jihad."[33]

The *jahili* society – the entire world – must be denounced and exposed as heretical, unbelieving, or apostate. Qutb's vision of the world is thoroughly lop-sided. From his sojourn of a few years in the United States, he drew a portrait demonstrating that he had never "seen" America but only observed the figments of his own imagination. He assailed

> this modern and Western ante-Islamic ignorance, with stuttering religious beliefs and disastrous social, economic, moral situations. All the ideas of the "hypostases" of the Trinity, Original Sin, Redemption, which only harm reason and conscience! And this capitalism, made of accumulation, monopolies, usurious interests, all of greed! And this selfish individualism that prevents any spontaneous solidarity beyond what the laws prescribe! This materialistic, measly, dry vision of life! This bestial freedom called "coed"! This slave market called "emancipation of women." [...] This racial discrimination so strong and ferocious! In comparison, what reason, what elevation, what humanity in Islam![34]

This blindness was crucial to the etiology of the jihadi outlook: Qutb's America had to be reconstructed in an unreal and loathsome way in order to be designated as *jahili*, and thus become a detestable object of jihad. The cause of the blindness was a phobia of contamination by the Other. Qutb's Islam must remain like a sterile chamber where not even a speck of dust must be tolerated. "Intrusions into the Islamic legacy" must be banned.[35] The ideology of *tahwid*, unity of God, is exclusive of any form of Otherness. Since the birth of Islam, there has always been, Qutb insists, one and the same religious war. Islam's eternal foes, all in one, are atheists, polytheists, jews, and Christians. Fortunately, in his war against all, the jihadi is merely the instrument of the divine agency: "It is God himself who, in reality, wages war and kills the enemy."[36] The burden of responsibility being thus lifted from the individual, killing becomes easy.

The radicals make systematic use of *takfir*. According to Sharia, the apostate may be, and must be, killed and it is the duty of any Muslim to execute this binding (and automatic) sentence. *Takfir* may be extended to masses of people branded as pagans, not just individuals.[37] "If so, everything was

33 Ibid., p. 130.

34 Sayyid Qutb, *Maalim fi-l-tariq* [*Milestones*], Cairo, 1964, 131, 160, quoted by Carré, *Mystique et politique*, p. 14.

35 Ibid., p. 33.

36 Quoted in Carré, *Mystique et politique*, p. 52.

37 Goldziher, *Introduction*, p. 101.

permitted as far as their treatment was concerned."[38] In practice, "The [Muslim Brotherhood's] secret apparatus had in early days a Mufti of its own to decide on the religious legitimacy of an assassination. On the eve of such an action there would be a ritual trial in the absence of the accused."[39]

The group Takfir wal-Hijra (declaration of apostasy and emigration), also known as Al-Jihad, which plotted the assassination of Egyptian president Anwar al-Sadat, was an offshoot of the Brotherhood – Arab organizations do not abide by the rules of Weberian logic, and membership can be a fluid notion. Its leader and ideologue Abd-al Salaam Farağ "refined the idea of jihad into its purest form: it involves the killing of those deemed infidels."[40] In truth, he was not a lone extremist: on January 7, 1983, the Sheikh Al-Azhar, the leader of the highest spiritual and jurisprudential authority in the Sunni world, had called all non-Muslims *Ahl al-Dhimmi*, people collectively to be enslaved and then "protected."[41] Farağ explicitly, and the sheikh implicitly, wanted to bring back the Pact of Umar, the charter of Muslim enslavement of "infidels," which starts: "We will pay tribute out of hand and be humiliated," and lists all the disabilities inflicted upon them.[42]

Farağ's organization's was a

> typical sect.... [It] rejected the teachings of all the *ulama* past and present because they had been corrupted by the governments of the day and could not be trusted. Like Pol Pot, [the Brotherhood's leader] Shukri Mustafa reached the conclusion that society in general was so corrupt that there was no way to reform it: it had to be destroyed.

At their trial, members of the group "claimed that they firmly believed that they would be the only ones to be saved from Hell."[43]

Qutb was echoing his mentor Hasan al-Banna, who had sliced the world in categories, the believer, the undecided, the opportunist, and the opponent. In the Brotherhood's universe,

> [i]n practice, the line was sharply drawn around "believers" for whom it was necessary to be not merely a Muslim but a Muslim Brother. The consequence of this structuring of the social order was to generate within the Society a current of rigid intolerance which transformed mundane political disputes into elemental social clashes. Independents as well as political opponents became the objects of a violence inspired

38 Laqueur, *No End to War*, p. 43.
39 Ibid., p. 34.
40 Michael Youssef, *Revolt Against Modernity*, p. 6.
41 Ibid., quoting from the official Egyptian daily newspaper *Al-Ahram* of that date.
42 In A. S. Tritton, *The Caliphs and their Non-Muslim Subjects*, London, Fank Cass & Co., 1970.
43 Laqueur, *No End to War*, pp. 34–5.

by a social and religious exclusiveness that could brook no compromise with him who was not a brother.[44]

The party of God led by the Elect was the pivot around which the world revolved; it alone drew the line between "good" and "evil." In turn, this allowed a reinterpretation of the entire history of mankind from the Gnostic viewpoint.

This outlook was by no means limited to the Sunni world; it was rampant in the Shia sect as well, where Ali Shariati's reconstruction of human history has remained a consummate example of the Gnostic outlook. In his *Reflections on Humanity*, the self-styled "Red Shiite" uses Marx's notion of class struggle as the engine of history to paint a vast Gnostic frieze of world history.

His fictitious epos closely resembles the modern para-Christian "theology of liberation." The result of this compound of Christian forms (a Christological obsession for and a cult of victimhood and suffering) and Marxist contents peppered with postmodern philosophy is a fully Gnostic creed.[45] He presents "the oppressed," an ahistorical category that plays the role of Marx's proletariat; they are variously the slaves who built the Pyramids of Egypt, the persecuted Shiites of the seventh or eighth century A.D., or the colonial masses of the mid-twentieth century. The oppressed are the good and embody the principle of the good because they are suffering. Then there are the "oppressors," an equally ahistorical category that embodies Evil. Shiism, as we saw earlier, represents the victims, and Husain the Martyr is their epitome: "Shariati . . . makes of Husain a revolutionary. He describes a character who above all desires to perpetuate the struggle of the partisans of Abel against those of Cain, of Good against Evil."[46]

Likewise, Qutb's view of history was that of eternal essences that forever clash: "[The] one vital element in the question [is that] the crusader spirit . . . runs in the blood of all Westerners"[47] To him, Westerners are literally the same now as in 1099 A.D. History does not occur or unfold; it merely is an eternal repetition, since it has been reduced to the Manichean struggle

44 Mitchell, *Muslim, Brothers*, pp. 318–9.

45 See Claudia Kinkela, "The Case of Rigoberta Menchù," unpublished article, American University, Washington, DC, 2005, and David Stoll, *Rigoberta Menchù and the Story of all Poor Guatemalans*.

46 Khosrokhavar, *Les Neaveaux martyrs*, Boulder, Colorado, Westview Press, 1999, p. 70.

47 Quoted by Mitchell, *op.cit.*, 230, from Sayyid Qutb, *Al-Adalat al-ijtimaiyya fil-Islam*, 3rd ed., n.d., translated by John B. Hardie, *Social Justice in Islam*, Washington, DC, 1955, pp. 236–40.

between the two opposing principles. History is replaced by the Gnostic-Manichean drama, in which men are but puppets of the two principles.

Shariati's is a nonhistory: It is only an eternal repetition of the same, the same cosmic drama replayed again and again, the oppressors oppressing and the oppressed being oppressed – except when arises the Messianic figure to break the logjam and bring an end to tribulations, oppression, and injustice. Save revelation; the martyrdoms of Ali, Husayn, and Hasan; and the eschatological redemption that is to occur on earth when the perfect kingdom will be established and justice will reign, there is no event in history.

Shariati directly refers to Frantz Fanon's "wretched of the earth" as the redeemers. Shariati styles himself as the medieval propheta, or the modern Marxist intellectual, who knows the ends of history. He sets himself up as the spokesman of the immense, anonymous crowd of the oppressed, and makes them speak:

> We lived in despair, but once again, a flash of hope for survival appeared. Great prophets came forth... a gate toward salvation was opened. The "gods" sent us their messengers to save us from the disgrace of slavery. Worship replaced cruelty. Unfortunately, we had bad luck. The prophets, who left their prophetic homes behind and disregarded us, proceeded to the palaces.

Those prophets – Zoroaster, Buddha, and Confucius – were traitors, Shariati asserts. In the holy pseudohistory he is crafting, which may be called a hagiosophy, it is intemporal, an artificial morality tale, a Procustean Bed where events are forced to fit even if they are amputated from all reality. God provides the poor and the oppressed with a new, authentic prophet: "Among all this hopelessness, I learned that a man had descended down from the mountains saying "I have been commissioned by God [...] to have mercy on slaves and those who are weak on earth." His name was Muhammad... he was an orphan who was a shepherd. He was the last in that series [of prophet-shepherds]."[48]

The edifying fairy tale continues. Muhammad has no palace, no riches, nothing. Unfortunately, after his death, his Umayyad successors revert to being oppressors, the Sunnis enslave the world again. Only Ali, the Alids, and their partisans remain faithful to the true faith. The whole world is plunged into a form of jahiliyyah. The message of the Prophet is tamed and subverted; those who govern in his name are but oppressors: "The history of Islam follows a strange path; a path in which hoodlums and ruffians from the Arab, Persian, Turkish, Tatar and Mongol dynasties all enjoy the right of

[48] Shariati, *Reflections on Humanity*, p. 6.

the leadership to the Muslim community and the Caliphate of the Prophet of Islam, to the exclusion of the family of the Prophet and the rightful imams of Islam."[49]

The only besieged, lonely but righteous group is possessed of God's perfect Revelation and mission:

> And Shiism, which begins with a "no," a "no" which opposed the path chosen by history, rebels against history. It rebels against a history which, in the name of the Koran, kings and caesars, follows the path of ignorance [*jahiliyyah*] and in the name of God, sacrifices those brought up in the House of the Koran and the Traditions [hadiths].[50]

The spirit of Negation – Nihilism – speaks. What is Shiism, then? With less elegance, Goethe's Mephistopheles, *Ich bin der Geist, der stets verneint.* "Shiites do not accept the path chosen by history. They negate the leadership which rules over history and deceived the majority of the people through its succession to the Prophet.... Shiites, who represent the oppressed, justice-seeking class in the caliphate system, find, in this house, whatever and whoever they have been seeking."

Gnosis turns to mass movement, to revolution:

> For over eight centuries (until the Safavid era), [Ali's] Shiism was not just a revolutionary sect in history which opposed the autocratic and class-conscious regimes of the Omayyad and Abbasid Caliphates and the kingship of the Ghaznavids, the Seljuks, the Mongols, the Timurids and the Ilkhanids who had made the government version of the Sunni School their official religion and waged a secret struggle of ideas and actions. Like a revolutionary party, Shiism had a well-organized, informed, deep and well-defined idea, with clear-cut and definite slogans and a disciplined and well-formed group organization. It led the deprived and the oppressed masses in their movements for freedom and for the seeking of justice, the rallying point for the demands, pains and rebellions of the intellectuals seeking to gain their rights and the masses in search of justice.[51]

The pseudohistory has morphed into a delirious story where Shiism has magically turned into the Leninist Party. The Sunni confederates of Shariati, for example, al-Banna or Qutb or Maududi, would not use the specifically Shiite references, but the contents are identical.

The end of times is nigh. The great cosmic struggle is now. Salvation is possible in the here and now. "Jihad operates as a substitute to an

[49] Shariati, *Red Shiism*, p. 7.
[50] Ibid., p. 8.
[51] Ibid., p. 10.

Apocalypse that is too long in the coming."[52] The desire for the Apocalypse and belief in its nearness dispense from the longer, less passionate meanderings of politics. And if the hoped for Apocalypse, the Day of Judgment have not arrived yet, the jihadist will create them instead. Shariati's inspiration Frantz Fanon's "ideas derive from millennialism.... In modern garb, adopted by figures like Fanon or [Michel] Aflaq, it issues in the belief that salvation is to be found in the life of politics, and that revolution is the instrument by which it is attained."[53]

A thoroughgoing structural homology binds radical Islam and radical Arab nationalism. "Secular religions" may be secular in the stated aims and concerns and in their expression, but they are steeped in religious and quasi-religious methods, emotions, and aspirations, they parrot religion at every turn. Secular language is used to interact with a secular world, but the emotions conveyed are of a parareligious nature. "Secular" Arab nationalism is a "secular" religion where Uruba, Arabdom, takes the place of the divinity, like Race for Hitler, Class and Communism for Lenin, and the Total State for Mussolini. The same type of religious and quasi-religious emotions and passions are mustered, with like results. Secular Arab nationalism – that of Nasser, Saddam Hussein, Hafez al-Assad, George Habash, the Algerian colonels, and others – are the projection of the essential tenets of Islam upon the screen of modern realities, in a world dominated by non-Arab and non-Muslim powers, modern technology, and administrative methods of rule. The common millenarian quality of radical Islam and radical Arab nationalism is apparent, for instance, in the jaundiced recollections of former Syrian Baath Party leader Sami al-Jundi:

> We thought that the epochs of decadence had come to an end with our predecessors among the politicians, and that we were the glorious beginnings of a new civilization, when in fact we were the last exemplars of backwardness, and a desolating expression of it. We wanted to be a resurrection [*baath* in Arabic] of signal deeds and heroism, but what was resurrected through us when we came to power – was no more than the period of the Mameluks.[54]

The reorganization of the world could only be total. As the Baath Constitution stated:

> The party [is] revolutionary, and its aims could not be achieved except by means of revolution and struggle. To rely on slow evolution and to be satisfied with a

52 Khosrokhavar, *Les Neuveaux martyr*, p. 315.

53 Kedourie, *Politics in the Middle East*, pp. 297–8.

54 Quoted by Elie Kedourie, *Arabic Political Memoirs and other Studies*, London, Routledge, 1974, p. 202.

partial and superficial reform is to threaten those aims and to conduce to their failure and their loss. This is why the party decides in favor of [...] the overthrow of the present, faulty structure, an overthrow which will include all the sectors of intellectual, economic, social and political life.[55]

While Aflaq and his Baathist cohorts were working for the Arab Revolution, Sayyid Qutb was busy launching the idea of "Islamic Revolution," a close kin to Shariati's Red Shiism:

The total revolution against the sovereignty of human creatures in all its guises and in any institution, the total revolt in all parts of our earth, hunting down the usurpers of divine sovereignty who lead men through laws they themselves invented, all this means the destruction of the kingdom of Man on behalf of the kingdom of God on earth. [...] [I]t is Man as such, the human race as a whole that is its purview. [...] Thus is the movement of Muslim struggle a defensive war: it defends Man against all those who alienate his liberty and block his liberation, until the kingdom of the Holy Law will be established upon the human race.[56]

The world as it is has to be destroyed and reconstructed according to the conceit of the autistic sectarian. It never ends: "Belief in Islam means readiness for perpetual Holy War," said Ayatollah Vaez-Tabassi.[57] The view is echoed by Abdullah Azzam, Osama bin Laden's mentor, who was intent on restoring the caliphate, "God's rule on earth": "Azzam believed that jihad should continue until Allah alone is worshipped by all mankind, [his] great contribution was undoubtedly the creation of a mystique of Muslim invincibility."[58]

As Nechaev and Lenin believed, what fosters revolution is good; what hinders it is bad. Nothing matters but the end goal. To Muslim radicals, there is no possible middle ground between Truth, themselves and Error, everything else. The extremities to which the ideology carries its believers may be seen in the difference between Islamic terrorists and what otherwise has proven to be the most proficient terrorist killer group, the Sri Lankan "Tamil Tigers." Even as the Liberation Tigers of Tamil Eelam (LTTE) developed "an elaborate symbolism of death and resurrection and a sacrificial commitment to the nation, a demand for blind faith, a mysticism of blood and an intimate communion of brotherhood, [it] proudly counted the number of suicide attacks in order to commemorate them," which would superficially resemble the Muslim death cult; however, the LTTE never included attacks

55 Article 6 of the Baath Constitution, in Kedourie, *Politics in the Middle East*, p. 298.
56 Qutb, *Milestones*, pp. 50–59.
57 Radio Tehran broadcast, January 11, 1986, cited in Qutb, *Milestones*, p. 85.
58 Laqueur, *No End to War*, p. 50.

against civilians in their count. "The Tigers considered attacks against civilian aims 'terrorist' in character."[59] This was much in contrast to the doctrine of such organizations as Hamas and Islamic Jihad but also al Qaeda, with their belief that jihad gave them a blank check to use all and sundry as a target.

A theorist like Shariati inevitably called upon the example of the sect of the Assassins and their founder Hasan-I Sabbah, the "Old Man on the Mountain"; the romance of terror had a precedent. Discussing the time when "the religious body of the Sunni sect [...] becomes an opiate for the masses," under the Sunni dynasties that ruled Persia, he writes:

> This is what causes Shiism, during that period, to appear as the fountainhead of rebellion and the struggle of the downtrodden and oppressed masses, especially among the rural people. It flourished wondrously in multiple facets and directions, moderate or extreme, in the form of various movements of the masses against the powers of the day, like the terrorism of Hasan Sabah, the communal living of the Qarmats, the extremist cultural and religious beliefs of the Ghaimat and the rebellion for free thinking in some of the Sufi sects of the revolutionary Shiite school of thought.[60]

On the eve of the Iranian Revolution the following popular song, in which "The Imam" stands for any great religious leader, was making the rounds in the streets of Tehran:

> The day the Imam will return
> Nobody will lie any more,
> Nobody will lock the door of his house;
> Men will be Brothers
> They will gaily share their bread
> Justly and sincerely.
> There will be no lines any more
> Lines for bread or meat,
> Lines for gas or cooking gas,
> Lines for the movies or the bus
> Lines to pay taxes,
> Lines for the poison of snakes,
> All will vanish.
> And the dawn of resurrection
> The spring of freedom
> Will smile at us
> The Imam must return...
> So that justice may sit upon its throne,

[59] *Ibid.*, p. 93.
[60] Shariati, *Red Shiism*, p. 12.

So that crime, betrayal and hatred be erased from history.
When the Imam returns,
Iran, this broken and wounded mother
Will be freed forever
From the chains of enslavement and ignorance,
From looting, tyranny and prison.[61]

The jihadists as Gnostics are trapped in the autistic world of their own invention. The evil world they believe they live in – the pseudoworld ideology has crafted – is ruled by Satan. Satan the ruler is everywhere: plots and conspiracies are the drivers of history.[62] Violence is the only way to break the self-made logjam.

Jihad will then be, in Maududi's formulation, the revolutionary struggle to eliminate all evil and establish God's just order on earth. It is the duty of the true believers to "[w]ipe out oppression, wrongdoing, strife, immorality, arrogance and unlawful exploitation from the world by force of arms. It is their objective to shatter the myth of the divinity of the 'demigods' and false deities, and to reinstitute good in place of evil."[63]

The struggle is here and now. All apocalyptic, millenarian dreams of an eschatological bend are summoned. The time has come for the final struggle: the Mahdi will appear; if he does not, his paler version, the "Century Reformer," will hopefully replace him; and, failing the presence of an acknowledged Mahdi or Century Reformer, Mahdism as an ideology will do.

The Mahdi of Islam

Millenarian phantasies move in the realm of the imaginary. Neither physical nor social laws are able to offer much resistance to those flights of apocalyptic and messianic fancy. Their kingdom is not of this world, even if these fanciful castles in the sky project a long shadow on earth. Freed as they are from the constraints of reality, the phantasies are nevertheless a resource to understanding the minds of their faithful. They are, literally, wishful thinking: They tell us what their authors wish. They follow the default paths that criss-cross those minds, they reveal the underlying structures of creeds and ideologies: They inform them on the "geography" and the "geology"

[61] Amir Taheri, *The Spirit of Allah-Khomeini and the Islamic Revolution*, Bethesda, MD, Adler & Adler, 1986, p. 234, quoted by Sivan, *Mythes*, p. 230.

[62] Daniel Pipes, *The Hidden Hand: Middle East Fears of Conspiracy*, New York, St. Martin's Press, 1996, p. 8.

[63] Maulana Maududi, *Jihad fil sabilalla*, pp. 4–6 and 10–11, quoted by D. Zaiden in Rubin and Rubin *Anti-American*, p. 22.

of the believers' minds. As we have seen in the case of medieval Christian apocalyptic, prophetic literature of this kind gives an expression to the hopes, the rages and the hatreds of those it captures and raptures. In their universe, normal causality is abolished and replaced by an erratic, wishful combination of cause and effect: Normal proportions and relations cease to matter. Dream-like, the prophetic utterance represents an invasion of reality by evanescent expectations, utopian yearnings, cravings for revenge, and self-assertion. An identity is sought and asserted in them. To understand the behavior of its sectarians in reality, we need to fathom their creeds, far-fetched as they may be, as they move into the bizarre and often nightmarish landscape of their imaginings: Their life is spent in a Hieronymus Bosch-like mindscape, though the "painting" then spills into our common reality.

In the history of Islam, one myth has powerfully anchored millenarian phantasies of all kinds virtually from the beginnings of the religion: that of the Mahdi. In the history of the world of Islam and today, it has played an essential role. "In Islamic societies a recurrent pattern of phases of belief in an Expected Deliverer may be discerned. It is often designated as 'Mahdism,' since the title given to such a personage is that of *al-Mahdi.*"[64]

The word *al-Mahdi* literally means "the guided one," from the noun *huda*, guidance; as guidance comes from Allah, the guided one evolved to become the divinely guided one. One who is Mahdi or al-Mahdi "is absolutely guided." The term "is used of certain individuals in the past and of an eschatological individual in the future. [...] The name is applied especially to the *Mahdi* of whom the Prophet gave good tidings that he would come at the End of Time."[65]

How is this personage defined? The doctrine has three basic features. He will appear during the period of anarchy and chaos that will precede the coming of the end of the world. During this time, upheavals and dissension will divide the Muslim community and lead to political strife, social disorder, and moral degeneration. Men will turn away from their faith. Instead, they will be greedy, paying no heed to fathers and ancestors. Injustice and oppression will be rampant. The Mahdi will appear with a brief intervening Golden Age in which he will put an end to the trials and the division of the Muslim domain in order to reconfirm the revelation of God and restore the justice of the past through the reestablishment of the original faith and form

[64] Jan-Olaf Blichfeldt, *Early Mahdism: Politics and Religion in the Formative Period of Islam*, Leiden, E. J. Brill, 1985, p. 1.

[65] Duncan Black Macdonald, "Al-Mahdi," in H. A. R. Gibb and J. H. Kramers, eds., *Shorter Encyclopaedia of Islam*, Leiden, E. J. Brill, 1953.

of government. Hence he shall reconcile the weak and the strong, and lavish his gifts upon anyone who asks.[66]

These are the tropes of millenarian literature encountered in late Jewish, early Christian, and medieval apocalyptical and eschatological texts; we likewise recognize the various myths that accreted around imaginings of the Messiah. Ibn Khaldun sums up the power of the myth:

> It has been accepted by all Muslims in every epoch, that at the end of time a man from the family [of the Prophet] will without fail make his appearance, one who will strengthen Islam and make justice triumph. Muslims will follow him, and he will gain domination over the Muslim realm. He will be called the *Mahdi*. Following him, the Antichrist will appear, together with the subsequent signs of the Day of Judgment. After the *Mahdi*, [the Prophet] Isa will descend and kill the Antichrist. Or, Isa will descend together with the *Mahdi* and help him kill the Antichrist. Such statements have been found in the *hadiths* that religious leaders have published.[67]

The output of hadiths concerning the matter is prodigious indeed.

> [The] theme of the Last Days soon became the object of commentaries and enlargements, attracting the attention of both the conventional theologian and the popular preacher. And so immense was this production that a whole literature more or less mythological in character developed, composed not only around the traditional questions of death, resurrections and doomsday, but also around the appearance of the various signs which would occur during the period immediately preceding the actual Day of Judgment... moral degeneracy, and social and political disorder. Yet this literary genre did not confine itself to the foretelling of such signs. Rather these were only considered to be a prelude to other far more ominous signs of physical abnormality, such as the cosmic snake, *addukhan*, the beast, *ad-dabba*, a sunrise in the West, three separate eclipses, and a fire emanating from the city of Aden... all of which drive mankind to the final place of gathering. Summoned there shall also be the one-eyed giant ad-Dajjal and the mythological people Yajuj and Majuj [Gog and Magog] whose previous appearance on earth is connected with an exceptional period of terror and fear.[68]

66 Blichfeldt, *Early Mahdism*, pp. 1–2.

67 Ibn Khaldun, *The Muqqadimah: An Introduction to History*, translated by Franz Rosenthal, edited and abridged by N. J. Dawood, Princeton, NJ, Princeton, University Press, 1967, pp. 257–8. We have replaced "Jesus" by "Isa," his Arabic name, since the "Jesus" of the Quran and Islam, in general, bears no relationship to the Jesus of the New Testament: For Muslims, Jesus is not the Son of God; he did not die on the Cross; he is one Prophet amongst many, the "Prophet of the Gentiles" as Moses was the "Prophet of the Jews." Shorn of his divinity, the Jesus of the Quran and Islamic literature is a Docetist and a Marcionist figure of heresy, with some aspects drawn from the Arian heresy as well. Lest the Western reader projects his or her normal notion of Jesus upon the Muslim Jesus, it seems better to give him his Arabic name.

68 Blichfeldt, *Early Mahdism*, pp. 3–5. Al-Dajjal, the "Antichrist," is the deceiver, who is the negative counterpart to the positive Mahdi.

The framework for Muslim apocalyptic and eschatological conceptions is "general Muslim theory of the deterioration of history,"[69] the notion that "history" reached its absolute climax with the Muhammad's Prophethood and cannot but deteriorate thereafter until the Day of Judgment. "It is characteristic of Islam to take a very pessimistic view of human nature; men always fall away from the faith and have to be brought back."[70] On the entropic notion of history inherent in the Islamic message, a notion of crucial importance to fathom the role of Mahdism in Muslim history and today:

> With the full articulation of the message of Muhammad in a universal community obedient to divine command, what was significant in history came to an end. History could have no more lessons to teach. If there was change, it could only be for the worse, and the worse could only be cured, not by creating something new but by renewing what had once existed. Inherent in this view of the past was a sense of decline. According to a famous *hadith*, the Prophet had said that his generation was the best of all, that the one which would come after him would be the next best, and after that each succeeding generation would be worse.[71]

This rearview-mirror conception of time impels Islam to want to regress toward a Golden Age indelibly located in the past, and to condemn deviation from that past as a harmful and heretical innovation.[72] A world, and especially an umma in perpetual decay and deterioration, is thus the theater in which the Mahdi will appear:

> The apocalyptist and his followers have turned against "formal" Islam, and declared it to have been corrupted. This is a powerful idea in Islam as a whole.... The basic idea is that all faiths are based on a revelation from God, which over a period of time are knowingly or unknowingly corrupted by the followers of that faith.... They introduce changes and corruption to such an extent that the faith is no longer the same as that of the first revelation, and God is obliged to send another prophet/revelation to set things right, whereupon the process is set to occur another time. This revelation/corruption/renewal of revelation view of history is deemed to have ceased with the Revelation of Islam.[73]

Nor did it prevent the popular mind, the mass of the believers, as opposed to the restricted clerical elite, from believing passionately that the notion

69 David Cook, *Studies in Muslim Apocalyptic*, Princeton, NJ, The Darwin Press, 2002, p. 245.

70 Macdonald, "*Al-Mahdi.*"

71 Albert Hourani, *Arabic Thought in the Liberal Age, 1798–1939*, Oxford, Oxford University Press, 1970, p. 8.

72 Bernard Lewis, *Islam in History: Ideas, People and Events in the Middle East*, new ed., revised and expanded, Chicago and La Salle, IL, Open Court, 1993–2001, chapter 22.

73 Cook, *Studies in Muslim Apocalyptic*, p. 235.

of periodic regeneration and renovation did apply to Islam. This raised the wrath of the orthodox *ulama*, an irate echo of which is heard in Ibn Khaldun's sternly negative view of the Mahdi myth uttered in a vindictive, upper-class tone:

> Sufis have other theories concerning the *Mahdi*. The time, the man, and the place [of his appearance], are clearly indicated in them. But the [predicted] time [of appearance] passes, and there is not the slightest trace of [the prediction coming true]. Then, some new suggestion is adopted, which is based upon linguistic equivocations, imaginary ideas and astrological judgments. The life of every one of these people is spent on such suppositions. Most of our contemporary Sufis refer to the [expected] appearance of a man who will renew the Muslim law and the ordinances of the truth. They assume that his appearance will take place at some place near our own period. Some of them say that he will be one of the descendents of [the Prophet's daughter] Fatima. Others speak about him only in general terms.[74]

The stark opposition between popular and official Islam explodes as Ibn Khaldun examines the doctrine:

> The common people, the stupid mass, who make claims with respect to the *Mahdi* and who are not guided by any intelligence or helped by any knowledge, assure that the *Mahdi* may appear in a variety of circumstances and places. They do not understand the real meaning of the matter. [...] Therefore, they firmly imagine that the *Mahdi* will appear [in areas] not under the control of dynasties and [are] out of reach of law and force. Many weak-minded go to those places in order to support a deceptive cause that the human soul in its delusion and stupidity leads them to believe capable of succeeding. Many of them have been killed.[75]

Ibn Khaldun is referring to past events but properly identifies a crucial pattern: In Muslim history, Mahdism always appeared in remote regions that escaped the writ of constituted authority.

The doctrine of the Mahdi largely originated in Jewish, Christian, and Zoroastrian influences. As was mentioned previously, Islam is a syncretic religion, a patchwork of many influences and numerous inputs.

> In all the provinces of [the Middle East] we see Islam at first assuming more or less distinct features, according to the degree of influence which was exerted by the local environment. In the cities of Hijaz it tended to set in the molds of the first generations of practical unspeculative piety; in Syria it began to be influenced by Hellenistic Christian thought; in Iraq it became infected with various Gnostic doctrines; among the unsettled Arab tribesmen of the borderlands it became an instrument of nomadic

[74] Khaldun, *The Muqqadimah*, 258.
[75] Ibid., 259.

cupidity and love of plunder, sublimated into fanaticism; in certain districts of Persia it was adopted as a cloak of a modified dualism.[76]

The religious situation of the late seventh and early eighth centuries had not consolidated into "Sunni" or "Shii" sect, but was highly fluid. To be a "Shii" meant to be a partisan of Ali (*Shiatu Ali*) rather than espouse a given brand of theology or law. Fresh converts among the conquered people carried their religious baggage into their new estate as neo-Muslims. But

at a very early stage . . . the Shiite name was used to cover a number of totally different activities and served as a cloak for the introduction into Islam of all sorts of oriental beliefs, Babylonian, Persian and even Indian. The conversion of large numbers of the earlier inhabitants of the conquered countries necessarily led to a widespread unsettlement of religious belief, which favored the spread of esoteric sects, and led to the religious struggles of the early [Muslim] centuries. The Hellenistic elements as a rule attached themselves to the Sunni or majority party, while the older Asiatic beliefs tended rather to attach themselves to the person of Ali. . . . Such beliefs were held and propagated mainly by the non-Arabs, and more especially by the mixed population of Iraq. . . . Converts from Zoroastrianism adopted in general the Sunni rather than the Shiite faith.[77]

Much of the Hellenistic belief he refers to was largely Gnostic under Byzantine Christian garb. "Iraq" was a largely Persian and Jewish area. "Arab" countries only very gradually became "Arabized" in the course of a centuries-long process of Islamization where many of the converts forgot their earlier identifications and turned into "Arabs" – much in the way that the region forgot its common vernacular, the Aramaic language, and adopted Arabic, the conquerors' tongue and that of their religion.

The accretive process of syncretic religion was operating at full capacity:

In the second century of the *Hijra* [632 A.D., which marks the beginning of the Muslim calendar] it was from the ranks of the ascetics that there arose those popular preachers in whom the zeal of the old Nestorian missionaries was reborn and who were the real missionaries of Islam amongst the people. . . . In the form of sermons or commentaries on Quranic text they stuffed the minds of their hearers with materials derived from the most heterogenous sources – ancient Arab legends, Christian, Zoroastrian, and even Buddhist stories, materials from the Gospel and Jewish Haggada and all the inherited lore of ancient Syria and Babylonia [. . .] among the most significant of these grafts upon the stem of Islam was the transformation of the Second Advent of Christ into a doctrine of the Mahdi, the "rightly guided one," who will effect the final victory of Islam by means of a divine catastrophe.[78]

[76] Gibb, *Mohammedanism*, Oxford, Oxford University Press, 1970, p. 73.
[77] Ibid., pp. 82–3.
[78] Ibid., p. 88.

How this worked:

> This devout hope [of the Imam Mahdi] carried an urgency among pious Muslims; it was like a sigh of longing in the midst of a political and social system against which their religious consciousness constantly rebelled. The circumstances of public life struck them... as a violation of the ideals they upheld, as a continued offense against religion and social justice. They embraced the position, it is true, that in the interest of a united community a good Muslim must not "split the staff" but must, for the common good, resign himself to steadfast endurance of the injustice that by God's decree prevails, and to patient perseverance in the face of evil. All the more intense was their emotional need for a reconcilement of reality with the demands of their devout convictions. Such reconcilement was offered by the firm hope for a *Mahdi*.[79]

The greater was the frustration with the present, the stronger was the emotional transfer into the future. The radical change eschewed for the present was delayed to the hoped-for future, at least as long as the dams containing it all did not break. In Muslim apocalyptics,

> runs the common theme of justice and righteousness lacking in the everyday commonplace world, which can only be restored by a messianic figure by means of the sword. This feeling is summed up by the messianic [hadith] par excellence that "a man will fill the earth with justice and righteousness, just as it has been filled with injustice and oppression." [...] Justice will be the dominant theme of the messianic age, just as the opposite has been true in the age previous to it.... [...] The basic desire [expressed by the messianic literature] is to return to the pristine condition that had existed during the time of [the "well-guided" caliphs] Abu Bakr and Umar, the first two successors of the Prophet.[80]

The figures of the Mahdi and his qualities were taken from "a wide variety of messianic figures, including regional and tribal models, that were available during the first centuries of Islam."[81] The pseudo-"Jesus" of Islam, Isa, was a candidate for Mahdidom for a while, but was gradually restricted to more modest roles, especially in Shia apocalyptic literature. Other earlier prophets also ran. "People of a more realistic bent occasionally supposed the hope for the *Mahdi* to be near fulfillment by certain princes who, so they thought, were about to establish the rule of divine law and righteousness."

As the Abbasid caliphs failed to fulfill those expectations; the "idea of the *Mahdi* then became more and more of a utopian idea, whose realization

[79] Goldziher, *Introduction*, p. 194.
[80] Cook, *Studies in Muslim Apocalyptic*, p. 137.
[81] Ibid., pp. 137–8.

was put off into a dim future, and which proved suited to steady enrichment with crude eschatological fables."[82]

The *Saoshyans* – the mythical "Promised Savior" of the Zoroastrian religion – was combined with motifs from Jewish and Christian apocalyptic writings. "Irresponsible fancy and idle speculation combined their share to the emergence in time of a luxuriant mythology. The *hadith* also took possession of these beliefs.... The Prophet was represented as giving an exact personal description of the one who, he promised, would deliver the world." The etiology of messianism is such that the wish for the end of times becomes the safety valve that allows today's angst to be alleviated; however, in messianic movements, accumulated angst is brutally discharged.

Then as now, people desired to see meaning in the suffering and the uncertainty that they experience constantly. If one knows that suffering is leading somewhere and is part of some divine plan, then it becomes bearable. It becomes even more bearable if one knows that, despite outward appearances, God is on one's side. Muslim apocalypses are designed to encourage the believer, and to show him his place in that plan.[83]

If the present is bad, the assurance of change in the future becomes crucial:

[The apocalypses] are also designed for those who are pessimistic about the ability of Islam to change the world in the short term. If one makes the necessary ideological changes in order to accept the apocalyptic interpretation of events – in other words, to believe that the world is coming to an immediate end – it is a given that the present form of religion is insufficient for the purposes of achieving one's goals. The very adoption of a world-view that leads to a messianic future implies that the present is at least partially a failure. Therefore the Muslim apocalyptist is basically forming a smaller, more dedicated group, in order to accomplish a purification of Islam. He frankly judges Islam, at least the formal side of the faith, to be a failure, and for this reason has harsh words to say about the religious leaders of his time, as well as the political ones.... [To him] Islam has been corrupted by the world.[84]

Like the medieval millenarians of Europe, "One can only be impressed by the sheer megalomania of these apocalyptists, and their arrogance in judging their society in this way." In the realm of action, the utter hubris so manifested defines the difference between Muslim and Christian martyrdom. The one suffers passively, but for the other

martyrdom is achieved through the action of fighting the incredible odds placed against him. Whether he is personally victorious is immaterial, since ultimately the

82 Goldziher, *Introduction*, p. 198.
83 Cook, *Studies in Muslim Apocalyptic*, p. 312.
84 Ibid., p. 313.

Muslim side will win. Therefore his is an active martyrdom.... [The] dominant theme for the genre of Muslim apocalyptic as a whole [is] continual fighting and combat. [...] The Muslim is himself bringing in the messianic age through his actions and his attitudes.... One must constantly desire the End to come. Without this attitude, it will not appear. This leads to a paradox. The Muslim must desire the appearance of his mortal enemies (the *Dajjal* and the *Sufyani*) [the Muslim form of Antichrist and a sort of minor, sub-Antichrist] more than anything else in the world. He must pass them in order to enter the End of Times.[85]

"*Venez! Orages désirés!*" wrote a French poet: Let the End be nigh! Life becomes a paradox since it is the catastrophic End which is expected of it.

The Mahdi mutated from merely religious to political figure, or a mix of both:

The *Mahdi* began as a political leader but rapidly evolved into a messianic pretender. The first characteristic appearance of the doctrine was in the revolt of Mukhtar, who in 685–7 led a rising in Kufa in the name of Muhammad ibn al-Hanafiyya, a son of Ali by a wife other than Fatima. Mukhtar appealed principally to the Mawali [non-Arab converts adopted as "clients"].... After the death of Muhammad ibn al-Hanafiyya, his followers preached that he was not really dead, but had gone into concealment in the mountains near Mecca and would in his own good time return to the world and establish a reign of justice on earth.... The revolt of Mukhtar foundered in blood, but the messianic idea that he had launched took a firm hold, and during the remaining years of the Umayyad Caliphate many Alids and pseudo-Alid pretenders... claimed the allegiance of the Muslims as the sole righteous sovereign of Islam. One after the other these Messianic rebels followed his predecessors in eschatological concealment and each by his career and failure enriched the *Mahdi* legend with some new detail.[86]

The Kharijite movement was another principal source of Mahdism. "*Mahdi*sm grew out of [their] political attitudes and experiences."[87] The rigorist Kharijite interpretation of the believer's duty, their insistence on duty "to be pursued in season and out of season even at the cost of life itself" was extreme and fanatical and "led them to the conclusion that those Muslims who temporized on this point were backsliders and apostates, indeed no Muslims at all, and that they themselves were the only true Muslims. Armed with this principle, they made open war on the [Muslim] community."[88] Indeed, these radical egalitarians

85 Ibid., pp. 314–15.

86 Bernard Lewis, *The Arabs in History*, new ed., Oxford & New York, Oxford University Press, 1993, pp. 74–5.

87 Blichfeldt, *Early Mahdism*, p. 13.

88 Gibb, *Mohammedanism*, p. 81.

carried rebellion against the Umayyads into the farther corners of the vast empire. They did not form a fixed and united community; they did not flock together around a single caliphate. Rather, Kharijite bands that followed different military leaders, scattered throughout the empire, troubled the possessors of power.... The disinherited classes of society readily joined the Kharijites, whose democratic tendencies and whose protest against the rulers' injustice were to their liking. The Kharijite revolt could easily serve as a cover and as a form for every anti-dynastic riot.[89]

Mahdism as a revolutionary doctrine, and would-be Mahdis as insurrectionary leaders, appeared not in times of peace and stability, but in times of trouble and tribulation – just as the Millenarians of Europe or the false pretenders, the many pseudoczars of Russian history. Contrary to its European counterparts, with their clear-cut silhouettes, the figure of the Mahdi curiously appears as somewhat blurred and uncertain, especially in the Sunni narratives. A good reason for this vagueness is that the Prophet "Muhammad ended the series of the prophets forever...he had accomplished for all eternity what his predecessors had prepared.... He was God's messenger delivering God's last message to mankind." No messianic figure may therefore approach his status, that of prophethood. "The 'awaited *Mahdi*,' in this Sunni view, will do no more than re-establish the work of the last prophet, squandered by the corruption of mankind.... He will not himself be a prophet, much less a teacher who transcends Muslim revelation."[90]

The pressing messianic urge nonetheless demanded the elevation of various individuals to some pinnacle of Islamic eminence. The constraint is looser in Shia than in Sunni doctrine, since the Shiite imam returning from his hiding is the Mahdi; the constraint was circumvented by the device of developing a series of infra-prophets who were at the same time endowed with some superhuman qualities. Besides the Shiite imam who sometimes is also the Mahdi, we find the spokesman for the hidden Mahdi, called the *Hujja* ("proof" or "witness"), the silent (or "nonspeaking") imam known as the *natiq*, and the *mujaddid* ("reformer of the century" or "renovator"). Historically, all of these figures represent a tributary flowing into the vast stream of Mahdism as an ideology.

And their appeal came less from their intrinsic content than from their suitability to the troubled times and the stress the troubles imposed upon the believers.

[I]t was in the hearts of the Muslim multitude that the belief in the *Mahdi* was kept alive, so that in times of particular strain, arising from alien domination or from

89 Goldziher, *Introduction*, pp. 171–2.
90 Ibid., p. 221.

inner tension of an unstable society, it could become quite active. That is to say, [his] arrival was expected in the immediate future in order to set things straight. In such circumstances, the ill-defined Sunni conception of the *Mahdi* was made more applicable to the situation at stake by being attached to a claimant at hand, or so formulated that an appropriate candidate could declare himself the Expected One. In this respect, Islamic history shows many instances of claimants to the throne of the Mahdihood, who together with a group of supporters would seek to challenge and overthrow the existing political order by force of arms.[91]

We recognize here the inner workings of contemporary radical Islam. Further, in a striking parallel to (especially) Hasan al-Banna's conception of a three-stage Islamic campaign leading to ultimate takeover,

> [i]f successful, such a *Mahdi* movement has been described to have passed major phases of progression. The movement would be initiated through an intensive propaganda for what we may call Islamic revivalism, having as its prime goal to win support among the restless and the discontented. Secondly, when a sufficient number of adherents had been recruited, a military theocratic organization would be formed. In the course of repeated efforts at propagating its claims, as well as countless military raids and campaigns from inaccessible hiding-places, the movement would change its strategy to openly challenge the sitting regime. As a third and final phase, we may observer the emergence of a territorial state, whose theocratic aspirations will gradually become obsolete until they have faded away.

It is as though Islam inexorably was begetting its Mahdis as the tide of its troubles rose. As in the early centuries of Islam, "[n]umerous pretenders appeared, claiming with varying plausibility to be members or agents of the House of the Prophet.... A recurring feature is the cult of holy men – Imams and *dais* [propagandists] – who were believed to possess miraculous powers and whose doctrine reflects mystical and illuminationist ideas."[92]

The etiology of the rise of Mahdist pretenders and movements parallels that of the millenarians of medieval Europe. In the extremely unsettled times of the decadence of the Abbasid Caliphate in the ninth century A.D. and the takeover of Baghdad by the Shiite dynasty of the Buyids, who made the caliph into their puppet

> there was much that made men seek an alternative. The great social and economic changes of the 8th and 9th century had brought wealth and power to some, hardship and frustration to others. In the countryside, the growth of large and often fiscally privileged estates was accompanied by the impoverishment and subjection of tenants and smallholders; in the towns, the development of commerce and industry created a class of journeyman laborers and attracted an unstable and floating population of

91 Blichfeldt, *Early Mahdism*, p. 10.
92 Lewis, *The Assassins*, p. 24.

rootless and needy migrants. Amid great prosperity, there was also great distress. The dry legalism and remote transcendentalism of the orthodox faith, the cautious conformism of its accredited opponents, offered little comfort to the dispossessed, little scope for the spiritual yearnings of the uprooted and unhappy. There was an intellectual malaise.... There was a loss of confidence in traditional Islamic answers, and a desire, of increasing urgency, for new ones.[93]

French sociologist Emile Durkheim showed that such periods have the effect of creating a situation where all values, social ranks, and individuals' ability to locate themselves within the whole are profoundly upset if not destroyed. Such a situation he called *anomie*, a state of confusion and social deregulation where old norms have ceased to apply. Anomie is a constant in the begetting of revolutionary social movements. The loosening of the social bond and the deregulation of values generate anomic behaviors, which in turn create an angst that begs to be relieved by some grand event, a new dispensation that will reestablish an acceptable sense of rank and value.[94] The Mahdi's "role [is] more easily appropriated by a self-appointed Islamic revolutionary exhibiting what Westerners would call a Messiah complex."[95] The Mahdi foments rebellion against a government declared illegitimate – to mobilize for change in Islam, the religious motif is indispensable; the Mahdists must "deliberately reenact in their own persons the sufferings and triumphs of the early days of Islam and the consciousness of playing in this great drama was an inspiration to them."[96]

The Ismaili sect of Shia had been sending missions to all ends of the Islamic world, as far afield as India, Central Asia, Yemen, North Africa, and the Maghreb. In the late ninth century, "they were strong enough for the hidden *Mahdi* to emerge from hiding and proclaim himself Caliph in North Africa, with the title of al-*Mahdi*, thus founding a state and a dynasty," that of the Fatimids (named after the Prophet's daughter Fatima, wife of Ali).[97] They were not the last, though perhaps the most successful, in the interminable procession of would-be Mahdis and Imam candidates. The Fatimids, who at their high point ruled from Sicily to the Hijaz, were a formidable challenge to both Sunni orthodoxy and the Abbasid caliphate, maintaining themselves until Saladin swept their last representatives from power in Cairo in 1171.

93 Ibid., p. 29.

94 De la division du travail social, Paris, Félix Alcan, 1893–1926. *The Division of Labour in Society*, Paris, 1893.

95 Timothy R. Furnish, *Holiest Wars: Islamic Mahdis, Their Jihads and Osama bin Laden*, Westport, CT, & London, Praeger, 2005, p. 2.

96 Ibid., p. 52.

97 Lewis, *The Assassins*, p. 30.

Next came the triumph of the Almohades. Ibn Tumart (b. ca. 1076), a wandering North African preacher endowed with great charisma, a talent to be expelled from everywhere and a pious busybody compelling each and all to the strict observance of Allah's laws, assumed leadership of large tribal forces opposed to the ruling Almoravid dynasty (itself stemming from an earlier revival). Action followed: "After what may be seen as a ritual withdrawal and due considerations, Ibn Tumart 'reappeared' in public, and declared himself to be the *Mahdi* promised to the Muslim community at the End of Time in order to fill the world with righteousness."[98]

He then retired to his tribe, built a mosque in the high Atlas at Tin Mal where 15,000 locals were slaughtered as a result of his takeover, "and began to work out a doctrine for his Mahdist aspirations and an organization to promote it." In his own words:

> The following is the promise of God, which he made known to the *Mahdi*, the true promise which he does not change. His obeyer is pure, more pure than any before or to come, as it has been seen in no one nor will be again; there is none like him among men, none than can set up against him and contradict him. [...] To none can he remain unknown, none can neglect his command. If any comes against him as an enemy, he is rushing headlong into destruction and has no hope of salvation. He cannot be approached save by what he approves; all things issue from his command. All happens according to his will, but this is also the will of his Lord. To recognize him is an essential religious duty, obedience and devotion to him is an essential religious duty, and to follow him and to be guided by him. [...] The bidding of the *Mahdi* is the bidding of God.[99]

Equipped with that doctrine, the fierce Berber mountain tribesmen swept through the Maghreb and Southern Spain, brought down the decaying Almoravid dynasty, and established the new one. The rough-hewn tribesmen untouched by civilization had converted to the simplistic and inflexible faith that befitted their primitive souls, the better to swoop down for plunder, in the name of the fanatically held belief of the neophyte: the pattern is recurrent in the history of Islam.

Mahdism is messianic and revolutionary. "In the course of Islamic history, this belief could also serve as a justification for religio-political rebels who aspired to overthrow the existing order. It gained them popularity as

[98] Blichfeldt, *Early Mahdism*, p. 11.

[99] "Confession of the *Mahdi*," in "The Collected Works of the *Mahdi* Muhammad ibn Tumart," in I. Goldziher, *Materialen zur Kenntnis der Almohadenbewegung*, NAF, Zeitung der deutschen Morgenländischen Gesellschaft, 1887, pp. 128–9, quoted by Blichfeldt, *Early Mahdism*, p. 12.

embodiments of the idea of the *Mahdi*."[100] Mahdism is radical: "The Muslim apocalyptist ... is extreme in his beliefs, and does not count the cost of his actions. Things must be returned to the simple form that existed during the mythical time of the Prophet and the orthodox Caliphs."[101] A canonical hadith states: "If only one day were left in the world, God would lengthen that day to send a man from my [Muhammad's] descendents who would fill the earth with justice and righteousness, just as it has been filled with injustice and iniquity." This is "a revolutionary statement indicating the end of the rule of Muslim tyrants before the end of the world.... There will be a day of earthly vengeance, when the Muslim community, aided by God and led by His agent, the *Mahdi*, will strike down the evil powers-that-be, so that the world will end on a note of good, just as it began."[102]

The figure of the imam as Mahdi is central to Shiism in general, which has come close to making its great martyrs, Ali and Husain, and the family of the Prophet, into divine figures, and has essentially made its imams "proto-divine." "Belief in the *Mahdi* ... was the vital nerve of the entire Shii system."[103] "In Sunni Islam, the pious awaiting of the *Mahdi* never took the fixed form of dogma, despite its theological treatment and documentation in the *hadith*," whereas "Shia Islam assigns a central theological importance to belief in the future fulfillment of the hope that the *Mahdi* will come. It is the backbone of the Shii system and one with the belief in the return of the Hidden Imam into the visible world."[104] The end of the world will be

> preceded by a long period of chaos and degeneracy to continue with increasing intensity until evil, falsehood and wickedness dominate the earth. The disintegration is to be complete and universal, and will be characterized by political unrest, immorality, falsehood and a total disregard for the principles of religion. Nature will also manifest similar signs of disorder and chaos. Then in the final phase of disintegration, the *Mahdi* will reappear, and he will usher in a new era of restoration. Once here, he will reign for a period of seven years, each year equating ten of our years. Then, at the end of his seventy years of reign, the *Mahdi* will die and forty days later his resurrection will follow.[105]

The many apocalyptic cycles, be they Sunni or Shii, abound in the gory and supernatural details, the epic and credibility-stretching stories. Like their European counterparts they are "a story full of sound and fury." They

[100] Goldziher, *Introduction*, p. 198.
[101] Cook, *Studies in Muslim Apocalyptic*, p. 234.
[102] Ibid.
[103] Goldziher, *Introduction*, p. 199.
[104] Ibid., p. 200.
[105] Blichfeldt, *Early Mahdism*, p. 9.

feature ominous natural and social portents that indicate the unhinging of man's universe and manifest God's intent. They showcase God's herald, the *munadi*, intervening in human affairs. They are brimful of tribulations. The great Christian cities of the Ancient world – Jerusalem, Alexandria, Antioch, Constantinople and Rome – feature prominently, sometimes to be conquered by Muslims, sometimes to be destroyed. Gigantic armies collide, Byzantium sends 800,000 ships sailing against North Africa and 7,000 against Syria, 400,000 captives are taken from Constantinople, 600,000 are killed in Rome, 70,000 virgins from the Byzantine royal palace are ravished – 300 given in booty to each Muslim soldier.

The millennium is brief, 7 or 70 years. The *Dajjal*, contemptible and ugly, arises. He presents an irresistible, quasi-magnetic attraction – his name means "the deceiver." Fantastic details are accumulated: He was born when his mother was already in the grave; when he was born, women aborted. He is curly-haired, hairy, short, walks with his toes turned in, or he is albino, enormously fat, tall, but always one-eyed; his upper chest is broad, his arms hairy. The word *kufr* ("unbelief") is written between his eyes, and only Muslims can read it. He will be followed by 600,000 Jews and 600,000 Bedouins, Turks, weavers, magicians, Uzbeks, and children of prostitutes and half-caste (born of slave women) – the dregs of society. Legions of demonic helpers will be let loose by God on earth. The *Dajjal* will perform miracles in order to deceive his followers and convince the hesitants; he will not only heal lepers, paralytics, and the blind but will also raise the dead. He is really a demon in human form. There is also an inferior Antichrist, the *Sufyani*, named after a family of early opponents of the Prophet, a branch of the Umayyads. He is ugly too. He is joined by an army of 50,000 and gains the allegiance of the Arabs, launching expeditions throughout the empire. Huge numbers are killed: 70,000 or 500,000 in Baghdad and 60,000 in Herazes Kufa. Then the Mahdi appears. The Sufyani attacks Medina and Mecca, sometimes killing most or all of the inhabitants. The Mahdi conquers Hijaz, Constantinople, and Rome; the waters of the Bosphorus open up; Muslims walk on water, with something, presumably Quranic, written on the sole of their shoes. Fortresses and walls fall at the shout of "*Allahu akbar.*" China and India are conquered. Often, the innumerable cruel peoples of Juj and Majuj descend from the Transcaucasia and Transoxania mountain redoubts and slaughter believers; they eat human flesh and corpses but end up being killed under Jericho. One-third of Syria's population has been killed. In Shia Islam, twelve Mahdis rule after the Mahdi-like figure of the *Qaim*; all Shiites gather in Kufa for an era of peace and plenty. They lead long lives, "to the point that a man could father 1,000 children, not one of them will be female."[106] The explicit content always shuffles and reshuffles the same basic material, the kinship of which with Jewish and Christian materials is obvious, in spite of the difference in the cultural, religious, and geographic parameters. What is even more similar is the structure of the myths, and what kind of underlying outlook they impart to those who will believe in them. In other words, who the messianic figure is matters far less than the espousal of messianism. The willingness to believe in fantastical tales is part of the reshaping of the mind of the believer, from "normal" individual to Gnostic.

Whatever the differences between the Sunni and the Shiite Mahdi, what they share in common is Mahdism as the default radical ideology suited to times of trouble and upheaval. Perhaps the epitome of the revolutionary insurgency in Islam was the bloody epic of the sect of the Assassins. What is relevant here is the thoroughly Gnostic substratum of the Assassins organization's Ismaili ideology. "Hasan [-I Sabbah] never claimed to be an Imam – only a representative of the Imam."

> After the disappearance of the Imam, he was the *Hujja*, the Proof, the source of the knowledge of the hidden Imam of his time, the living link between the lines of manifest Imams of the past and the future and the leader of the *dawa* [missionary activity]. [...] This doctrine, with its stress on loyalty and obedience, and by its rejection of the world as it was, became a powerful weapon in the hands of a secret, revolutionary organization.[107]

The formidable challenge launched by the Ismaili Assassins to the Sunni caliphate can be measured in the long list of prominent statesmen, starting with the statesman extraordinary, Grand Vizier Nizam al-Mulk, followed by judges, theologians, governors, senior officials, and military leaders, who all fell victim to the determination of their "emissaries" to kill them at any price, their own life included, which so mesmerized the contemporaries. Fundamentally,

> In one respect the Assassins are without precedent – in the planned, systematic and long-term use of terror as a political weapon. [...] Previous political murders, however dramatic, were the work of individuals or at best of small groups of plotters limited in both purpose and effect. In the skills of murder and conspiracy, the Assassins have countless predecessors; even in the refinement of murder as an art, a rite, and a duty, they have been anticipated and prefigured. But they may well be

[106] All of the above from Cook, *Studies in Muslim Apocalyptic*, *passim*.
[107] Lewis, *The Assassins*, pp. 62–3.

the first terrorists. [. . .] Hasan found a new way, by which a small force, disciplined and devoted, could strike effectively against an overwhelmingly superior enemy.[108]

The Assassins in their time were "regarded as a profound threat"; they were "not an isolated phenomenon, but one of a long series of messianic movements, at once popular and obscure, impelled by deep-rooted anxieties, and from time to time exploding in outbreaks of revolutionary violence"; further "Hasan-I Sabbah and his followers succeeded in reshaping and redirecting the vague desires, wild beliefs and aimless rage of the discontented into an ideology and an organization which, in cohesion, discipline and purposive violence, have no parallel in earlier or in later times." Finally, they shaped "their final and total failure. They did not overthrow the existing order; they did not even succeed in holding a single city of any size."

Yet "the undercurrent of messianic hope and revolutionary violence which has impelled them flowed on, and their ideals and methods found many imitators. For these, the great changes of our time have provided new causes for anger, new dreams of fulfillment, and new tools of attack."[109]

Modern Mahdism

The fall of the shah of Iran in 1978–9 surprised the West. So did the rise of a turban-wearing Rip van Winkle, and the arresting bloody-mindedness of the Iranian Revolution. Once the immediate shock faded away, the temptation often was irresistible to call the event an unpredictable affair and to ascribe it to some mystical and unchangeable "Muslim soul."

Analysts whose lives and minds ignored religion were stunned that the rest of mankind was not like them. What may not be, cannot be. Some sought all kinds of good reasons "why they hate us," and inevitably found explanations galore. Marxism, the method least suitable to understand religious phenomena, in its various academic attires like anthropology, was called to the rescue. Apologists for immoderation and illiberality in the world of Islam blossomed as the demand for explanations and new courses of action increased. The same bent was applied to explaining terrorism, or explaining it away.

The 1979 takeover in Tehran was not the start of an era of "political Islam." It was not "Islam resurgent." It was the volcanic emergence, in the form of an eruption, of tectonic processes that had slowly advanced from

108 Ibid., pp. 129–30.
109 Ibid., p. 140.

various peripheries of Islam toward its centers, over a long period. What was emerging was modern Mahdism.[110] Mahdism was rekindled in the modern era as a result of the encounter with the West and gave birth to the phenomenon of modern jihad, known as radical Islamic terrorism.

Perhaps the relevant starting point in the past is the first instance of Islamic revivalism in the modern world, that is, the world defined by the great expansion of the West.

> Muhammad ibn al-Wahhab, in selecting his native Central Arabia as the scene of his mission, was... adopting the same course as was taken by the leaders of similar reformist movements both before and after his time. This course was to seek out some region that was out of reach of an organized political authority, where there was, therefore, an open field for the propagation of his teaching and where, if successful, he might be able to build up a strong theocratic organization by the aid of war-like tribesmen.[111]

The Ottoman sultan was preoccupied with securing himself from the French and the British, who had successively landed in Egypt, and from the Russians in the northeast. The Ottoman "security perimeter" was reduced, leaving its peripheries vulnerable to fractious adventurers. It enabled a Wahhabi state in Arabia in the late eighteenth century, in the form of the alliance between al-Wahhab and the Al-Saud family. Meanwhile in India, the late-eighteenth century British penetration also led to a reaction: politician-predicator Said Ahmad Barelvi, a Wahhabi convert, declared jihad against the infidel upon his return to India. His forces launched from Patna in 1826, invaded Punjab, and started to massacre Sikhs. In 1830, he took Peshawar and established a short-lived jihadist state, but was killed a year later. His followers, active in Bengal and North India redeclared jihad against the British, ultimately a significant contributing factor to the "Great Rebellion" of 1857–9, which really was the last gasp of Muslim power in the Indian subcontinent. The defeat of the Sepoys in turn set off the establishment by Maulana Abul Qasim Nanotvi of the radical Deobandi movement in 1867. A continuous dialogue connected Islamic radicals from the subcontinent and the Arab Middle East – the dialogue between Maulana Maududi and Sayyid

110 Pryce-Jones, *The Closed Circle*. Daryush Shayegan, *Le regard mutilé: schizophrénie culturelle. Pays tradition-nels face à la modernité*, Paris, Albin Michel, 1989; Published in English as *Cultural Schizophrenia: Islamic Societies Confronting the West*, London, Saqi Books, 1992. Jean-Paul Charnay, inter alia, *Sociologie religieuse de l'Islam*, Paris, Hachette, 1994; *Traumatismes musulmans: Entre charia et géopolitique*, Paris, Afkar, 1993; *Charia et Occident*, Paris, L'Herne, 2001.

111 Gibb, *Modern Trends, in Islam*, p. 26.

Qutb, or the cooperation between Mullah Omar of the Talibans and Osama bin Laden, testify to the continuity.

The Wahhabi reformation and its offshoots were not the only symptoms of renewed activity in Islam during the eighteenth and early nineteenth centuries. There was at the same time a marked revival among the Sufi brotherhoods, accompanied both by the expansion of the older orders and by the formation of new orders.[112] This first wave of Islamic revival also was a first reassertion, after centuries of Ottoman domination, of a properly Arab political claim: "The Wahhabi revival was the first reassertion of the 'Arab Idea.'"[113]

The Wahhabi revival, however, was not consolidated in power. Al-Wahhab proclaimed himself the chief of the worldwide umma in 1787, declared jihad against the Ottomans, and bloodily attacked every state in the entire region, from Yemen and Oman to the Ottoman *vilayets* in what is today Jordan and Iraq, until the ruling Al-Saud exclaimed in a letter in 1800: "Everything West of the Euphrates is mine. Leave what is to the East to the [Ottoman] pasha." The waning of the Napoleonic threat left the Sultan a free hand, which allowed his Egyptian lieutenant, the ambitious Mehmet Ali to take care of the insolent, which was ruthlessly done by 1818.[114] Wahhabism had disappeared for the time being and had been too peripheral to the great centers of the world of Islam – Istanbul, Cairo, Tehran, Delhi – to weigh on events. It was left to lead an underground life, notably in India and Afghanistan, whence it would later reemerge.

The Islamic revival had to wait for its great agitator Jamal al-Din al-Afghani who secularized and politicized the old Mahdist creed and made it into a modern radical ideology:

> There was an element of Mahdism in the pan-Islamic nationalism of al-Afghani, the element in his campaign that appealed to the popular masses and won for him the affection that has clung to his name. Although Muhammad Abduh rejected for himself this revolutionary taint, he did not exorcize it. It has survived in the modern reformist movement as a kind of ground swell, determining the ultimate nature of its thought and reactions, however much surface features may seem to be in contradiction with it and however little the modernists may be conscious of it.[115]

[112] Ibid., pp. 29–30.

[113] Gibb, *Mohammedanism*, p. 115.

[114] Laurent Murawiec, *La Guerre d'après*, Paris, Albin Michel, 2003, pp. 185–8.

[115] Gibb, *Modern Trends in Islam*, p. 119. Gibb adds "And it is this probably which explains the otherwise puzzling fact that so many modernists finding the strain of double-mindedness to be borne or the social cost of modernism to the individual too high, end up as ultra-orthodox bigots," which also applies to the mass "conversions" of Muslim "Marxists" – "Socialists" to Islamic extremists in a more recent period.

With him, "Mahdism has linked up with extreme nationalism to produce the swelling tides of popular discontent and revolutionary ardor which are familiar to all observers of the Muslim world today."[116] Al-Afghani was a critical ingredient in the mix. Better than anyone in his age, he created a synthesis of Mahdism as a political ideology and modern means of waging political warfare.

Just as millennialism became secularized in the modern world, so did the idea of a *Mahdi* become a tool for a secular sort of politics in the hands of one of the most influential Muslim thinkers in modern times. This was Jamal al-Din al-Afghani.... Afghani was [...] very familiar with the Shiite belief in the Hidden Imam, and his awaited appearance. [He], however, changed significantly the original notion of the *Mahdi*, moored as it had been in a long-hallowed religious tradition. This change may have resulted to exposure to Western ideas..., or else stimulated by these Western ideas, he may have worked it out for himself by drawing on certain heterodox currents within Shiism itself.[117]

In December 1883, following the victory of the Sudanese Mahdi over General "China" Gordon, al-Afghani wrote a series of articles in the Paris newspaper *L'Intransigeant*:

Afghani declared that Muslims have a sure belief that a *Mahdi* must come, that every Muslim awaits a *Mahdi* for whom he is ready to sacrifice his life and all his possessions [...] England, Afghani also declares, hopes in vain "to stifle the voice of the *Mahdi*, the most awesome of all voices, since its power is even greater than the voice of the Holy War, which issues from all Muslim mouths. Does England... think herself able to stifle this voice making itself heard in all the East... proudly proclaiming the coming of the Savior whom every son of Islam awaits with such impatience? El *Mahdi*, el *Mahdi*, el *Mahdi*.[118]

Al-Afghani's conclusion was that "[a]ll Muslims await the *Mahdi* and consider his coming as an absolute necessity."

The political savior replaced the superhuman Shiite Mahdi, but they had much in common. The masses could acclaim the would-be political savior who assumed a role akin to Mahdihood. The rather cynical al-Afghani knew it. In words that could have been recited or recreated by every Arab despot and tyrant of the last five or six decades, he wrote:

Man is by nature given to exaggerating all news which come to him from afar so that the figure one traveling from one mouth to the other and augmented by public rumor soon ends up by becoming the figure thousand; the hillock comes to be considered a

[116] Ibid., p. 120.
[117] Kedourie, *Politics in the Middle East*, p. 271.
[118] Ibid., p. 272.

mountain. This is why at the announcement of the coming of a *Mahdi*, the hearts of all those who are waiting for their liberation will be filled by great expectations and will overflow with joy and hope.[119]

Al-Afghani traveled back and forth the wide gray area surrounding the doctrines of the Mahdi in Islam. He was a man who was endowed with an "extraordinary personal magnetism," eloquent, intelligent, and charismatic; he was at ease in Cairo and Moscow, in Paris and Tehran; and his "paradoxical combination of a Sufi mystical streak with extraordinary political activism had considerable precedent in Islamic history."[120] Disciples worshipped him "like a Sufi elder." He succeeded in drawing the best and brightest young students and would-be activists. They referred to him "in worshipful terms... evincing an emotional and almost religious attachment."[121] He never claimed to be the Mahdi, but he behaved as though some Mahdi-like quality was attached to him. The dominant streak of much of his propaganda combined a messianic appeal to Holy War with political Mahdism. His envoys were instructed to "make [the Muslims] await the time and the hour and the arrival of the end period," that is, the advent of the Mahdi.[122] As his biographer put it, Afghani's

strong emphasis on Holy War as the way to achieve pan-Islamist goals is significant. Afghani... saw in Holy War with messianic overtones a sure means for arousing the world's Muslims to action and recreating a strong Islamic state. The use of not only Holy War but even messianic terminology... is surely no accident. It goes along other indications that Afghani and some of his followers saw him as a messianic role.[123]

He was, in sum, the first modern manifestation of political Mahdism – the Mahdi in the era of politics. Many were to follow. "At times [he] saw himself as a messianic savior of the Muslim world," and was often "regarded as a prophet."[124]

No wonder that in the Arab world, candidates rushed headlong after the fall of the Ottoman Empire, and even more after 1945, to volunteer as Mahdi, or quasi-Mahdi, or to assume appropriate Mahdist traits. Among the alternatives present in the Muslim world, a strong one was

[119] Ibid., pp. 272–3.
[120] Keddie, *Sayyid Jamal al-Din "Al-Afghani,"* pp. 52, 61, 50.
[121] Ibid., p. 85.
[122] Ibid., p. 135.
[123] Ibid., pp. 139–40.
[124] Ibid., p. 211.

the revival of Mahdism, the assertion that the Muslim world must be purified and reunited by the sword. In contrast to the modernists and the nationalists, who represent different applications of Western conceptions to the political problems of Islam, this is a popular movement, reflecting the native impulses of the Arab and Muslim mind. It is the true product of primitive Islamic romanticism, with an emotional reason of its own. It is not a rational assertion that one type of political organization is more desirable than another, but a revolt against what is felt to be...an intolerable state of affairs. [...] The alternative attitude toward secular government – a violent assertion of the supremacy of sacred law – is...the kernel of revolutionary Mahdism, which encourages and is itself sustained by the hope of a catastrophic reversal of the existing order and its replacement by the theocratic ideal. In its basic objective it coincides with the political theology of the *ulama*.[125]

We had been warned. Concretely:

The ending of the [second world] war and the resulting relaxation of Western pressures in 1945 were followed by a sudden and tremendous upsurge of religious movements, expressing a messianic radicalism of a kind familiar and recurrent in the Islamic world from the time of the Carmathians and Assassins and those of Shamil of Daghistan and the *Mahdi* of the Sudan.[126]

In content,

[f]or the past 150 years, Europe had provided both the objects of resentment and the ideological means of expressing it. Even now, there were some who began to use the Western doctrines of socialism as the ideological inspiration for the next phase of anti-Western struggle. But far more significant, in the late 1940s and early 1950s, were the religious leagues, whose passionate reassertion of Islamic beliefs, values and standards corresponded far more closely to the feelings of the suppressed lower classes, in their revolt against their own Westernized masters and exploiters as much as against the West itself.[127]

Who could fail to recognize in the behavior and self-conception of a Gamal Abd-al Nasser or a Saddam Hussein, and in the response of Arab masses to them, the identification with Saladin, the victorious one who expelled the crusaders, and, at the deepest level of mass psychology, a passionate desire for them to be some sort of a Mahdi sent for the deliverance, nay, the redemption of the Arabs?[128] That Nasser or Saddam conceived of

[125] Gibb, *Mohammedanism*, pp. 113, 117–18, from Haskell Lecture in comparative religion at the University of Chicago in 1945.

[126] Bernard Lewis, *The Shaping of the Modern Middle East*, New York & Oxford, Oxford University Press, 1994, p. 114.

[127] Ibid., p. 115.

[128] Kanan Makiya's *Republic of Fear*, includes a remarkable treatment of the matter at hand.

themselves as "secular" leaders, that they borrowed the rags of socialist and national-socialist ideologies does not matter much. They were the projection on the plane of modern politics – the state, the army, the United Nations – of the old religious dreams.

As they and their "secular" ideologies faltered, they unsurprisingly reverted to their Islamic default creed. Its shocking defeat in the Six Days' War of 1967 bankrupted Nasserism.[129] Its liquidation was followed by an apparent radicalization in the direction of socialist or Marxist politics, which very quickly yielded to the rising tide. While the Marxists were Mahdists in disguise with a mask of secularism lightly covering their religiosity, the Islamists cluttered themselves with fewer of the ideological flotsam and jetsam – Nazi, fascist, communist or such – that their secularist twin brothers were overburdened with: They were Mahdists without hyphenation and were more able to absorb a bankrupt nationalism than the Arab nationalists were able to absorb Islam, especially in its radical version. Islamists merely borrowed the technologies of power without bothering themselves with dialectical materialism. It was precisely after 1967 that a great revival in the number of books devoted to the Mahdi and Mahdism occurred.[130] In 1976, the Muslim World League, the Wahhabi-run, Saudi-based organization, issued a fatwa to establish that for "the memorizers and scholars of hadith on the Mahdi, the majority of them are narrated through numerous authorities. There is no doubt about their status as unbroken and sound reports and the belief in the appearance of the Mahdi is obligatory . . . none denies it except those who are ignorant of the *Sunna* and innovators in doctrine."[131]

Khomeini's victory, the Saudi-Wahhabi radicalization that resulted from Tehran's challenge to the Saudi monarchy's Islamic credentials, and the attempted 1979 takeover of the Great Mosque in Mecca by Sunni Islamic radicals closed the chapter of the pseudosecular "Arab nationalism." Saddam's turn to Islam in the Iran–Iraq War was a sign of the same. The collapse of the Soviet Union and the discredit of the communist ideology did the rest: Mahdism shed whatever regalia "secular" disguises it had borrowed and appeared in its fully religious – or Gnostic – glory, though it kept all the political and military techniques learned from Soviets and Nazis.

[129] Fouad Ajami, *The Arab Predicament*, Cambridge, Cambridge University Press, 1981; Fouad Ajami, *The Dream Palace of the Arabs*, New York, Vintage Books, 1998.

[130] Furnish, "*Beheading in the Name of Islam*", p. 88.

[131] Ibid., p. 87.

Mahdism

> when first used, provided one of the principal sources of the energy needed to conquer the enormous territory conquered by the Muslims during the first century of Islam, and to establish it as a vital religion. Without this sense of complete self-confidence, this venture would have failed.... The power that drove the first Muslims was the belief that they were living in the last days, and had to accomplish these things before the Day of Judgment.

The apocalyptic fantasies were "an integral part of the ideological foundations of early Islam, and continue to this day to provide Muslims with the energy and inspiration to accomplish incredible deeds."[132] Mahdism is inherently the revolutionary form of the Islamic creed – whether Shiite or Sunni. The very plasticity of the concept has allowed it to be adopted by innumerable pretenders, and, in the contemporary world, to become the political religion that doubles up with Islam.[133] Analyzing the power of the Muslim Brotherhood, a prominent Islamologist diagnosed as early as 1961 that it would be like a yeast whose long-term action would transform Mahdist popular movements, replace "maraboutic" and romantic influences, and generate an organized will to power – Mahdism would merge with Arab nationalism, and create a powerful revolutionary movement.[134] "The heresy of Mahdism is its belief not only that the minds and wills of men can be dominated by force but that truth can be demonstrated by the edge of the sword."[135]

The potency of myth was demonstrated in 1939 by the best-known Turkish poet of the century, Nazim Hikmet, who wrote two remarkable poems called together "The Suras of the Apocalypse." What was most remarkable about the "Sura of the Signs" and the "Sura of the Evaporation" was that their author was a Marxist-Leninist, a prominent communist and Stalinist, a recipient in 1951 of the "International Peace Prize" of the Soviet front organization, the World Peace Council. Hikmet, whose poetry is highly political and ideological, had long nourished the project of writing a "modern Apocalypse" that would draw upon Quran, apocalyptical biblical literature, and the apocryphs such as the so-called Book of Enoch and John's Revelation,

132 Cook, *Studies in Muslim Apocalyptic*, p. 332.

133 See James Darmesteter, *Le Mahdi: depuis les origins de l'Islam jusqu'à nos jours* [First ed. 1885, Paris], reprint Houilles, Ed. Manucius, 2004, p. 68.

134 Louis Gardet, *Laïcité musulmance: vie sociale et politique*, 2nd ed., Paris, Vrin, 1961, p. 362.

135 Gibb, *Modern Trends in Islam*, p. 121.

and merge them with historical prophecy – the coming of the proletarian revolution.[136]

Hikmet combined a central theme of the Quran, the Day of Resurrection, with all the cosmic events that announce it and come with it, with popular beliefs rooted in Islam, to create an imagery of the Apocalypse that he assimilates to the great cataclysm of the wholesale downfall of the established order by class struggle, the great revolution; common to all is the establishment of justice. The "inevitable" face-off between "bourgeoisie" and "proletariat" parallels that of God and Satan. "He has awakened from his slumber/The giant who has but his chains to lose," the poem intones. The Mahdi is present, fighting alongside "the wrestlers without vestment," an image for the proletariat based on the popular Turkish combat sport.

[136] Nedim Gürsel, "L'Apocalypse et Nazim Hikmet," *in* Jean-Pierre Dizard, ed., *Hommage à Maxime Rodinson: Le cuisinier et le philosophe, Etudes d'ethnographie historique du Proche-Orient*, Paris, Maisonneuve & Larose, 1982, pp. 245–82.

4

Manichean Tribalism

Wa la yaslamu as sharafu al-rafiu min al-adha Hatta yuraqu ala jawanibihi al-damu.
High honor is not safe from injury, Until blood is spilled over its flanks.
Al-Mutanabbi, 915–965[1]

Honor and the Honor-Based Society

Honor – no word so insistently recurs in Arab and Arab Muslim political oratory and literature. All commune in unison under the sonorous word of *honor*. The concepts of honor, pride, dignity and their cognates, and their polar opposites of shame and humiliation, occupy a central position in the Muslim political discourse. *Al-sharaf al-arabi* ("Arab honor") and *al-sharaf al-Muslimi* ("Muslim honor") are terms so self-evident as to require no definition for the Arab and Muslim audience: They go directly to the heart and the mind because they express the soul of a society and a culture. They resonate because they are attuned to the inherent "frequency" of their culture.

On October 26, 1954, as Nasser was addressing a crowd in Alexandria, a Muslim Brotherhood sniper shot at him eight times. Nasser was unscathed – his security service had arranged the "plot." Unsurprisingly unfazed, Nasser intoned:[2]

O ye people . . . o ye free men . . . I, Gamal Abdal Nasser, am of your blood and my blood is for you. I will live for your sake and I will die serving you. I will live to

[1] Quoted by Pryce-Jones, *The Closed Circle*.
[2] Dr. Walid Phares, "Saddam's Atrocities of "Honor," FrontPageMagazine, December 19, 2003, http://www.frontpagemagazine.com/Articles/Read Article.asp?ID=11407.

struggle for the sake of your freedom and your dignity. O ye free men, o ye men, even if they kill me now, for I have planted in this nation freedom, self-respect and dignity. For the sake of Egypt and for the sake of Egyptian freedom, I will live and in the service of Egypt I will die.[3]

That was a fine piece of demagoguery, and it had the desired effect: a *rais* whose popularity had been on the wane prior to the incident, emerged triumphant. More than the transient effect, though, what is significant in the incident is the implicit universe of values Nasser was calling forth. All of the notions used by the dictator were self-evident as they operated as undefined axioms of the society from which the audience was drawn.

At the opposite end of the spectrum, Hodjatoleslam Sayyed Hassan Nasrallah, head of the Lebanese Hezbollah, addressed a mass rally of his followers: "You have been present in battlefields for the defense of Lebanon's unity, Lebanon's dignity, Lebanon's Arabism, Lebanon's pride, Lebanon's land, Lebanon's freedom, Lebanon's independence and Lebanon's sovereignty."[4]

Amid the great crisis that rocked Lebanon in the Spring of 2005, following the assassination of former Prime Minister Rafiq Hariri, Nasrallah declared: "We are ready to remain until the end of time a terrorist organization in Bush's view, but we are not ready to give up protection of our country, our people, their blood and their honor."[5]

Regarding Syrian–Lebanese relations, he had stated a few years ago that "Syria and Lebanon are acting wisely with a sense of priority and strong nerves, and are not willing to compromise our honor, destiny, future and those things which we hold sacred."[6] And again,

Our nation despite of its declines in some circumstances regarding many issues is still a better place for living. Go to all over the Arabic and Islamic countries and you will find that the society of the country in the worst situation and circumstances is still holding to its instinctive human values and ethics, and to its proper habits of dignity, honor, generosity, and human sympathy towards other's pains and sufferings.[7]

[3] Quoted by Mitchell, *Muslim Brothers*, p. 151.

[4] Speech made at Riad Solh Square on Tuesday, March 8, 2005, in central Beirut, http://www.cggl.org/scripts/document.asp?id=46225.

[5] Adnan El-Ghoul, "Nasrallah Calls for Arab League Investigation into Hariri Slaying," http://dailystar.com.lb/article.asp?edition_id=1&categ_id=2&article_id=13531, accessed March 18, 2005.

[6] Syrian Television, June 9, 2002, http://www.intelligence.org.il/eng/bu/hizbullah/pb/app7.htm.

[7] Nasrallah, addressing the people on the seventh night of Muharram for the year 1423 (March 20, 2002), http://www.islamicdigest.net/v61/ content/view/388/1/.

In one short chapter of Sayyid Qutb's fundamental essay *Milestones*, "A Muslim's Nationality and His Belief," the word *honor* is used nine times and *dignity* once.[8] The intellectual mooring of the essay is provided by a series of Quranic quotes that are commented upon, after the model of traditional Muslim theological discussion. "Those who risk their lives and go out to fight, and who are prepared to lay down their lives for the cause of God are honorable people, pure of heart, and blessed of soul. But the great surprise is that those among them who are killed in the struggle must not be considered or described as dead. They continue to live, as God Himself clearly states," he wrote, in direct paraphrase of a hadith.[9] And further: "The death of a believer is in itself an honor."[10]

The Charter of the Hamas movement explains: "The nazism of the Jews does not skip women and children, it scares everyone. They make war against people's livelihood, plunder their moneys and threaten their honor."[11] In a *60 Minutes* (CBS) interview, Saddam Hussein, through his translator, explains: "That is why, talking about asylum, we will – whoever decides to forsake his nation from whoever requests is not true to the principles. We will die here. We will die in this country, and we will maintain our honor, the honor that is required of – in front of our people." He adds a few seconds later: "We must maintain the honor of nationalism and pan-Arabism. The importance of that is essential to the nation and to the Arab nation." And again: "We live here in freedom, and our people will continue to defend their freedom, their sanctity, their honor and their country."[12]

Osama bin Laden's August 1996 "Declaration of War," discussing jihad, states: "This humiliation and atheism has ruined and blinded the lands and peoples of Islam. The only way to destroy this atheism is by *jihad*, fighting and bombings that bring martyrdom. Only blood will wipe out the shame and dishonor inflicted on Muslims."[13]

The word *honor* recurs six times in a short "Open Letter from a Saudi Islamist to Those who Shirk Jihad" signed by Abu 'Abd Al-Rahman Al-Athari Sultan Ibn Bijad, self-styled as "of the occupied land of the two

8 Qutb, *Milestones*, Chapter 9.

9 Quoted by Paul Berman, "The Philosopher of Islamic Terror," *New York Times*, March 23, 2003.

10 Qutb, *Milestones*, p. 262.

11 Article 20 of the Hamas Charter Selected Documents Regarding Palestine Hamas Charter (1988), http://www.Palestinecenter.org/Cpap/documents/Charter.html, accessed November 14, 2006.

12 http://www.cbsnews.com/stories/2003/02/26/60II/main542151.shtml.

13 Rubin and Rubin, *Anti-American*, p. 181.

sacred mosques." The style is: "You who shirk *jihad*, how can you enjoy sitting idly while your brethren in Iraq suffer greatly under the oppression of Allah's enemies, while you are with your wives? How can you enjoy life and comfort while your noble sisters are being raped and their honor is defiled in the Abu Ghraib prison." Criticizing the Saudi rulers, he exclaims: "Has anything survived of their manhood and honor, and above all, of their religion?"[14]

In an interview he granted Al-Jazeera television, Yusuf Qaradawi, the international leader of the Muslim Brotherhood, used the term *honor* a dozen times.[15] Talking of the leaders of the Muslim Brotherhood, al-Banna and Qutb, the same Qaradawi states: "They were bold and brave for the religion of Allah, and lovers of public welfare. They had a sense of honor for Islam and were fully active to establish its glory and splendor. They toiled continuously for the rule of Islamic Shari'ah and the leadership of the Muslim Ummah."[16]

The Syrian Foreign Ministry spokeswoman Dr. Buthayna Shaban wrote in her weekly column in the government daily *Teshreen*, "The martyrs represent the conscience of the nation. They are the noblest men in the world and the most respectable of all human beings." She used the word *honor* six times in the article.[17]

Examples are innumerable, and they cover the entire spectrum of Muslim expressed and published opinion (whether secular or religious), all the sects of Islam and all political persuasion: Honor is part of the common cultural stock that each and all possess and draw upon. The fact that all use it shows that it is a central, organizing concept in the cultural and societal warp and woof of the Muslim world.

The "honor" so exalted differs critically from conceptions of honor found in other cultures, be it Europe's or Japan's. In either case, honor is the singular prestige acquired by one as a result of actions of exceptional merit. The warrior's feats, the statesman's courage, and the religious man's steadfastness will be recognized and prized by society. Famously, Napoléon Bonaparte's illustration of it was the creation for his warriors of a *légion*

[14] MEMRI, Special Dispatch No. 820, "An Open Letter from a Aaudi Islamist to those who Shirk Jihad," November 30, 2004.

[15] MEMRI, Special Dispatch No. 858, "Sheikh Yousef Al-Qaradawi on Al-Jazeera," February 4, 2005.

[16] Ama F. Shabazz, "Great Movements of the 20th Century: Al-Ikhwan Al-Muslimeen," http://www.ymouk.com/articles/archive/al_ikhwan_al_mus-limeen.htm.

[17] *Teshreen*, September 6, 2003; MEMRI, Special Dispatch Series 570, "Syrian Foreign Ministry Spokeswoman Glorifies Martyrs & Martyrdom," September 10, 2003.

d'honneur: the recipient of the award was thus individually plucked out of the ranks of the mere mortals and the standard soldiers and inducted into a legion of the noblest. The samurai's view of upholding the Code of the Warrior was of the same nature. In the *bushido*, the warrior's honor is a personal virtue gained through deeds, behavior, and attitude; it is not a collective asset or a group virtue.[18] Nor is it some sort of capital perpetually menaced by thieves, and whose preservation ought to be one's life mission.

In short, the honor the European or the Japanese held dear was, by its very nature, an individual quality. Sometimes this individual quality may also be extended to some corporate body, a regiment, or a city for its exceptional valor. The honor of the people, the nation, was soon metaphorically extolled. But ultimately, honor always reverted to a notion of exceptional deeds. Honor was an attribute gained, not a substance defining a group, including a notion of abiding by one's obligations and living according to an elevated moral code. Western literature abounds in examples of this type of honor, from the French, German, and English versions of the Arthurian cycle to Shakespeare's *Coriolanus* or Corneille's *Le Cid*.

The meaning of the word *honor* used to translate the Arabic *al-sharaf* and the meaning of the Arabic word itself are radically incongruent. *Honor* (like *honneur*, *Ehre*, *onore*, like the Latin equivalent which translates back "honesty," "probity," "integrity," "modesty," "glory," and the Greek *axia*, "glory" and "esteem," or *arête*, "virtue" and "probity" and "dignity") speaks of individual deeds, whereas *al-sharaf* reflects a collective substance claimed by a group, and which is central to its identity. The group, or type of group, for which honor is a central regulator is the family, the clan, the tribe – in short, the kinship-based group.

Kinship versus *Res publica*

The Romans conceived and formulated with great clarity the notion of an entity that stands above society and that encompasses the entire society. This was the *Res publica*, public affairs, as opposed to private affairs. Likewise, to the Greeks, the *polis* stood above its components, as a corporate body that embraced all component parts of society. In Athens, and other Greek city-states, even if the tribes continued to exist and even play a recognized institutional role, the polis and its institutions were not the emanation of the tribes, but impersonal corporate bodies ruled by law.The constitutional

[18] See, for example, *Bushido Shoshinshu (Code of the Samurai)*, part I, 'The Valiant,' translated by Thomas Cleary, Hong Kong & Boston, Tuttle Martial Arts, 1999, pp. 22, 24.

practices of Ancient Greece and Rome were formative of all Western societies, which evolved to be organized according to this distinction. And even though religion was an affair of state for the Romans, the cult rendered to the gods on account of public religion was clearly separated from private religion, a family's worship of its own domestic gods, the Lares. Wealthy and prestigious Roman patricians, supported by their extended families (the *gens*) and their clients, played a powerful role in Roman politics, but Roman politics was nonetheless structured by the impersonal Res publica with its complex power structures generated by constitutional practice and by citizens' suffrage. The noble patricians and the wealthy knights exerted inordinate influence, but they had to exert them through the formalities of the Republic and its elective positions. One may buy an election, but one must be elected praetor, questor, *aedilius,* or consul. The banners of Roman legions did not carry tribal or family names but affirmed *SPQR* (*Senatus Populuque Romanus*), the two basic components of the public entity.

The "Islamic cities are strangely lacking in cohesion," a geographer of Islam explains.

> This is the fundamental difference which separates them as much from the cities of antiquity as from the medieval cities of Europe. [. . .] The Roman city . . . the medieval town . . . [had] a notably pride in the city, and many close forms of cooperation among citizens. There is nothing of the sort in an Islamic city. It has no separate municipal life. No privilege or exemption, no special freedom of action, attaches to citizenship. The price paid for the predominance of religious conceptions in Islamic social organization is the absence of any political interest in the community as such. Nothing intervenes to temper the absolutism of the prince, whose power is the expression of divine might itself, unless it is the moderating but often limited influence of the representative of the faith.[19]

The absence of corporate bodies, sums up the nature of the Islamic polity: Empire at the top – the umma – tribe at the bottom, and nothing in between. The city is traditionally divided among separate, even segregated quarters with their own ethnoreligious character and the trades that go with the ethnoreligious belonging. The trades in turn are organized in guilds that are structurally modeled on tribal organization.[20]

Bureaucratic empire that it was, China similarly was a public concern, as opposed to the expression of some extended family's dynastic power. Chinese society may have rested on clan and village; imperial China boasted

[19] Xavier de Planhol, *The World of Islam* [*Le monde islamique: essai de géographie religieuse*], Ithaca, NY, & London, Cornell University Press, pp. 7–8.

[20] Ibid., pp. 9, 10, 13.

a stability independent of which dynasty sat at the top. Dynasties came and went, the Confucian bureaucracy stayed, and with it the fact that the empire was governed by a hierarchy of civil servants who followed regulated procedure.[21] In contrast:

> As a basis for identity, political allegiance, and behavior, tribe gives primacy to ties of kinship and patrilineal descent, whereas state insists on the loyalty of all the persons to a central authority.... Tribe stresses personal, moral and ascriptive factors in status; state is impersonal and recognizes contract, transaction and achievement. The tribal mode is socially homogenous, egalitarian, and segmentary; the state is heterogenous, stratified and hierarchical. Tribe is within the individual; state is external.[22]

Some agrarian-based polities evolved as bureaucratically ruled impersonal states. Others retained their underlying tribal nature. There is a correlation between honor as a society's dominant value and the persistence of the tribal nature of a society. This correlation governs the access of a given society to modernity. As charted by German sociologist Ferdinand Tönnies, the Industrial Revolution marked the transition from the village to the town, a shift in power and identity from the kinship group to the individual, from personal connections to contract.[23] Granted, networks of kinship, clientelage, and acquaintance did not disappear, but they lost their preeminence. They wove their spells around the institutional framework of society, instead of being its warp and woof. On wings of Western arms and technology, modernity has spread throughout the world, differentially entering and transforming different societies. Some have proven more responsive and adaptive; some have operated as a "closed circle." This is the case of the Arab world.

The following abstracts from a variety of Arab polities mention traits that are common to all, while omitting features that, being of a local or regional nature, differentiate them from one another based on the widely different ethnic, linguistic, religious and civilizational characteristics of the lands that became Arab in the course of the seventh century conquest – Mashrek, Maghreb, Levant, Mesopotamia. The aim is to sketch an ideal type

[21] Etienne Balasz, *La bureaucratie céleste: recherches sur l'économie et la société de la Chine traditionnelle*, Paris, Gallimard, 1968.

[22] Richard Tapper, "Anthropologists, Historians, and Tribespeople on Tribe and State Formation in the Middle East," in Philip S. Khoury and Joseph Kostiner, eds., *Tribes and State Formation in the Middle East*, Berkeley, Los Angeles & Oxford, University of California Press, 1990, 25–47.

[23] Ferdinand Tönnies. *Gemeinschaft und Gesellschaft, Grundbegriffe der reinen Soziologie*, 8th ed., Leipzig 1935, reprint Darmstadt, Wissentschaftliche Buchgesellschaft, 1963.

that represents the core structure of Arabdom, historically and culturally. This is not to deny or otherwise ignore that there are variety and variations in different Arab societies. After all, these societies stretch from Mauritania to the Iranian border and from the Sudan to the Turkish border. The very history of Arab expansion under the banner of Islam generated civilizational hybrids.

The Tribal Matrix

"As ideal types, tribes represent large kin groups organized and regulated according to ties of blood or family lineage."[24] Ibn Khaldun defines the tribe as "a closely knit group of common descent."[25] Only if this is so is the tribe's members' protection assured in the state of nature that desert life is, a war of all tribes against all. As such, the tribe is for its members the fundamental object of identification and loyalty, as opposed to any other unit or entity.

Ibn Khaldun showed that the glue that unites the tribe is its *asabiyya*, its group cohesion or *esprit de corps*, and that it originates in desert life, which is the original habitat of the Arabs, and the source of Islam.[26] In Arabic, *badw* or *badiya* is "desert," its inhabitants the *badwi* or *badawi*, hence "bedouin." The Bedouins are the ur-tribe of Arabdom.

> This strengthens their stamina and makes them feared, since everybody's affection for his family and his group is more important than anything else. Compassion and affection for one's blood relations and relatives exist in human nature as something God put into the hearts of men. It makes for mutual support and increases the fear felt by the enemy. [...] Respect for blood ties is something natural among men.[27]

Further to this definition,

> One feels shame when one's relatives are treated unjustly or attacked, and one wishes to intervene between them and whatever peril or destruction threatens them. [...] If the direct relationship between persons who help each other is very close, so that it leads to close contact and unity, the ties are obvious and clearly require the existence of a feeling of solidarity [*asabiyya*] without any outside prodding.[28]

[24] Khoury and Kostiner, *Tribes and State Formation*, 4. The tribe is characterized by a great deal of endogamy, see Walter Dostal, "The Evolution of Bedouin Life," in Francesco Gabrieli, ed., *L'antica società beduina, studi raccolti da*, Rome, Istituto di studi orientali, 1959, pp. 11–33.

[25] Khaldun, *The Muqqadima*, II, 7; p. 97.

[26] Ernest Gellner, *Muslim Society*, Cambridge, Cambridge University Press, 1981–95, p. 24.

[27] Khaldun, *The Muqqadima*, II, 8; p. 98.

[28] Ibid.

The inside-outside dichotomy is crucial:

Tribal society is a closed order. Those within the tribe are deemed to be relations by blood, a family, by virtue of which they are protected and secure: Those outside are strangers, and therefore suspected to be enemies. Blood relationship provides the closest social bonding, greatly simplifying the common purpose. Aggrandizement and perpetuation of the tribe are ends requiring no justification.[29]

This esprit de corps defines, pervades, and unites it (from the Arabic word that means "spirit of kinship," *asabiyya*, derives from *asaba*, the male relations in the male line of the family or tribe (itself derived from the root verb *asab*, to tie together).[30] But *asabiyya* and the group extend beyond consanguinity. From Arab antiquity, the institution of *wala*, affiliation, allowed nonkin to enter the kinship group. The *mawali*, clients (from *wala*) entered the tribe and became an integral part of it. This principle of affiliation worked for individuals, and also worked at a broader, collective level.[31]

Client and allies belong to the same category. The affection everybody has for his clients and allies results from the feeling of shame that comes to a person when one of his neighbors, relatives or a blood relation in any degree is humiliated. The reason for it is that a client–master relationship leads to close contact exactly, or approximately in the same way, as does common descent. It is in that sense that one must understand [Prophet] Muhammad's remark, "Learn as much of your pedigree as necessary to establish your ties of kindred."[32]

Ibn Khaldun concludes:

The advantage of a common descent consists in the group feeling that derives from it and that leads to affection and mutual help. Wherever the group feeling is truly formidable and its soil kept pure, the advantage of a common descent is most evident, and the group feeling is most effective. It is an additional advantage to have a number of noble ancestors. Thus, prestige and nobility become firmly grounded in those who share in the group feeling of a tribe, because there exists the result of common descent. The nobility of a "house" is in direct proportion to the different degrees of group feeling, because nobility is the secret of group feeling.[33]

The inner, organic connection of the elements of the chain is thus analyzed: *asabiyya*, power, nobility, honor versus shame.

29 Pryce-Jones, *The Closed Circle*, p. 21.

30 Khaldoun, *The Muqqadina*.

31 F. Gabrieli in http://www.muslimphilosophy.com/ei/asbiyah.htm. For Ibn Khaldoun, *asabiyya* is the fundamental bond of human society and the basic motive force of history.

32 Khaldun, *The Muqqadina*, pp. 98–99.

33 Ibid., II, 12; p. 102.

> *Asabiyya* implies boundless and unconditional loyalty to fellow tribesmen.... This ineradicable tribal particularism assumes, of course, that the tribe is a unit by itself, self-sufficient and absolute, and regards every other clan or tribe as its legitimate victim and object of raiding and plunder. These unsocial features, which inevitably accompany *asabiyya* remained imprinted into the Arab character after the rise of Islam.[34]

Power and honor coincide. A large tribe projects power and attracts suitors. The individual tribesman projects his identity into his group and derives identity from it. His only social and juridical status is acquired through membership in the group.[35] This kind of social organization is kin-based and strongly kin-oriented. A cluster of extended families form a subtribe, several of these a tribe, and some of the tribes occasionally constituted a tribal confederation. Cohesion is inversely proportional to size and proximity; "beyond the extended family and the next larger kin group to which it belonged and which made up the wandering unit, there was no power structure, no authority and no protection on which the individual could count. In the desert, it was literally each man and his kin group against the rest of the world."[36]

How was this generated? Kin group cohesion protects the individuals from attacks; conversely, the individual thus protected commits to group solidarity and mutual responsibility as supreme values. This only operates in small groups defined by interpersonal relations and blood relationships. In such a small society, there are considerable pressures to conform, to uphold the group values, and to live by the unwritten but inevitably well-known moral code of the group.What is generated is a "group-being," who has so deeply internalized the supreme value of group cohesion that he exists only as part of the group. "Thus shall we see in this fierce Arab of the desert, an individualist without individuality."[37]

His society bestows little value upon individual nomadic man qua individual. I "am" my group, or a manifestation thereof, and the others are only as concrete, individuated manifestations of their group. The individual exists only as the minimum unit of existence that permits contribution to group defense and its reproduction. The newly born is most often named after an ancestor, grandfather, or great-grandfather. The name he receives is a sort of predestination and plays an integrative function for the group. In turn,

34 Raphael Patai, *The Arab Mind*, New York, Charles Scribner's Sons, 1973–6, pp. 93–4.
35 Chelhod, *Introduction à la sociologie*, p. 23.
36 Patai, *The Arab Mind*, p. 77.
37 Chelhod, *introduction à la sociologic*, p. 27.

even as a child, he is addressed by the name of his future son. "Through this name and surname, the Arab actualizes the past and prepares the future. He is himself the point of intersection between two generations, a simple life in the continuity of the group."[38] In brief, he is not a person by himself but owing to his social-genealogical status.

An investigation of the Kabyles of Algeria found that "the family is the alpha and the omega of the whole system: the primary group and structural model for any possible group, it is the indissoluble atom of society which assigns and assures to each of its members his place, his function, his very reason for existence, to a certain degree, his existence itself."[39] Family, clan, tribe – these are the nested fractal structures that constitute Arab society. The male-consanguinity agnatic clan is based on the *ahl*, the members of a family that live under one roof, under the authority of an elder man. A cluster of *ahl* create a clan, *sira*, subject to the jurisdiction and authority of a *sheikh*, elder, himself subject to those of a higher chief, that of the entire tribe.

The tribe as the aggregation of clans is defined as a domestic unit, all of whose members are *banu amm*, cousins. "In reality, not all are cosanguinous: the clan also includes strangers, a throng of slaves who have been assimilated to the system of kinship by means of formulas of mystic parenthood."[40] The clan as a political unit will be defined as a group all of whose members are held to exert blood revenge. The Arab vendetta comes as no surprise, since

> [l]ike other people in the Mediterranean basin, the Arabs use concepts of shame and honor to sanction their conduct. This shame–honor ranking... stems from the ancient tribalism of the region and predates Islam, though in the course of time merging with it in some respects. Acquisition of honor, pride, dignity, respect and the converse, avoidance of shame, disgrace, and humiliation are key to Arab motivation, clarifying and illuminating behavior in the past as well as in the present.... The institution of the blood feud is common to most Mediterranean cultures and widespread in a wider circle, which includes the Caucasus and Arabia. It is in fact a standard feature of tribal society, one hinged on the pivotal role of shame and honor in allocating rank, status, hierarchy and prestige.[41]

[38] Ibid., p. 40.

[39] Pierre Bourdieu, *The Algerians*, Boston, Beacon Press, 1962; quoted by Pryce-Jones, *The Closed Circle*, p. 27.

[40] Chelhod, *Introduction à la sociologic*, p. 46.

[41] Pryce-Jones, *The Closed Circle*, p. 34.

Hence, we see the role of the feud. Group strength is diminished by the murder of one of their own; its honor is challenged, which beckons revenge; it

> becomes the duty of all the male members of the victim's kin group, all the men within his *khamsa* [kin group to the fifth degree of linkage]. If the avengers cannot find the murderer, any member of the murderer's *khamsa* is a legitimate target for blood revenge. [...] The duties of blood revenge ... are features of the Bedouin ethos which survive in Arab urban society as well.[42]

The operation by which the blood feud is exerted, the raid, *ghazw*, is further developed and becomes jihad: "The *ghawz* (razzia), otherwise considered a form of brigandage, is raised by the economic and social condition of desert life to the rank of national institution. [...] These ideas of *ghazw* and its terminology were carried over by the Arabians into the Islamic conquests."[43] The blood feud is "the most characteristic institution of such institutions" in the "typical Middle East tribal quasistate":

> An offense perpetrated by a member of Group A against a member of Group B is followed by retaliation by *any* member of Group B against *any* member of Group A. If peace is made and compensation paid, members of A all make a contribution, and the members of the receiving Group B all share it. [...] The circular, self-perpetuating, and self-reinforcing mechanism inherent in this situation is obvious.[44]

Honor, group survival, raid, revenge "are strongly connected. Honorable behavior is that which is conducive to group cohesion and group survival, that which strengthens the group and serves its interests; while shameful behavior is that which tends to disrupt, impair, or weaken the social aggregate.[45] Morality is therefore contextual and situational. Further, it is a zero-sum affair. My tribe's loss is your tribe's gain: "failure threatens tribal identity."[46] Violence is called for: "[V]iolence is an essential ingredient in the process of decision-making, it is proof of serious intentions, of the will to proceed in the group interest, no matter what the rights and wrongs. In tribal society, violence is therefore a mechanism of social control. The only way to discover the balance of power is to test it."

42 Patai, *The Arab Mind*, p. 79.

43 Philip K. Hitti, *History of the Arabs: From the Earliest Times to the Present*, 10th ed., London, Macmillan, 1980, p. 25.

44 Ernest Gellner, "Tribalism and the State in the Middle East," in Khoury and Kostiner, *Tribes and State Formation*, pp. 109–26.

45 Patai, *The Arab Mind*, p. 90.

46 Pryce-Jones, *The Closed Circle*, p. 22.

"Feuding is politics rather than war. [...] [T]he reason for indulging in feuding relations is not so much the desire to inflict a loss on a given section, as to use this victory to enhance individual and group prestige within the home community and in the eyes of the world. The prestige acquired is a foremost ingredient of leadership.[47]

This is why "honor" in the Arab–Muslim world, is so ubiquitous in the political discourse.

Honor in the Arab world is a generic concept which embraces many different forms. [...] There is the kind of honor a man derives from his virility as manifested in having numerous sons; another comes to him from engaging in certain types of work and refraining from others: hence it is honorable for the Bedouins to tend their camels, dishonorable to engage in artisanship or agriculture. A third type of honor used to be associated with the sword – the ability to defend oneself against enemies and with bravery in general. To buy protection from a more powerful tribe by paying *khuwwa* (protection money) seriously diminished one's honor. To undertake a raid, within the prescribed rules, is honorable. To refuse participation in a raid is dishonoring. To defend one's livestock against raiders is honorable. Hospitality and generosity are matters of honor. To be inhospitable or ungenerous is shameful. It is honorable to have pure Arab blood, on both one's father and one's mother's side. It is honorable to exhibit a strong sense of kin group adherence. It is honorable to behave with dignity and always be aware of the imperative of *wajh* ["face"]: under all circumstances, a man must beware of allowing his "face" to be "blackened"; he must always endeavor to "whiten his face," as well as the face of the kin group to which he belongs. Cost what it may, one must defend one's public image.

Any injury done to a man's honor must be revenged, or else he becomes permanently dishonored. And, of course, there is the sexual honor of the woman, through which her entire paternal family is constantly and dangerously exposed to the possibility of being dishonored. All these kinds of honor, clearly distinguished in Arab life and operative at various times and on various occasions, interlock to surround the Arab ego like a coat of armor. The smallest chink in the armor can threaten to loosen all the loops and rings, and must therefore be repaired immediately and with determination. There are those who see as paranoid the extreme sensitivity of the Arabs to any infringement of their honor. It [is] an important characteristic

[47] Jacob Black-Michaud, *Cohesive Force: Feud in the Mediterranean and the Middle East*, Oxford, Blackwell, 1975, p. 25. Quoted by Pryce-Jones, *The Closed Cricle*, p. 24.

of the Bedouin mentality which has left its mark on the Arab mind in general.[48]

The implications are pervasive:

> All actions, words, happenings that are not in accordance with the accepted mores of society, result in diminishing a man's honor, or even in bringing about its loss. These, in turn, diminish or destroy the respect he enjoys in the eyes of others and, therefore, ultimately have the same effect on his self-respect. Once honor is impaired, great efforts are needed to restore it. If lost, it is almost impossible to regain. Honor is the collective property of the family: if any single member of the family incurs dishonor, the whole family is disgraced. [...] If a woman loses her honor, this causes her menfolk to lose theirs, which causes them to lose their dignity, which in turns causes them to lose their self-respect.[49]

This in turn often causes the death, by "honor killing," of the next domino, the "culprit," the woman.[50] The extremes to which people will go betray the importance of the matter for their identity:

> Honor is what makes life worthwhile; shame is a living death, not to be endured, requiring that it be avenged. Honor involves recognition, the openly acknowledged esteem of others which renders a person secure and important in his or her own eyes and in front of everyone else. [...] Honor and its recognition set up the strongest possible pattern of conduct, in a hierarchy of deference and respect.[51]

When Osama bin Laden exclaims, as we quoted him doing so, "This humiliation and atheism has ruined and blinded the lands and peoples of Islam. The only way to destroy this atheism is by *jihad*, fighting and bombings that bring martyrdom. Only blood will wipe out the shame and dishonor inflicted on Muslims," he is speaking words that are instantly "readable" for anyone reared in the Arab–Muslim cultural idiom. He argues that the *umma* is being violated by "Crusaders and Jews." Is it an accident that *umma*, the community, is a cognate of *umm*, mother?

In the Middle Eastern culture shaped and pervaded by Islam, the calculus of shame and honor is the primary calculus guiding life decisions.

48 Patai, *Arab Mind*, pp. 90–1.

49 Ibid., p. 95.

50 On Islam, the Arab world, and women, the best literature is: Juliette Minces, *La femme voile: l'Islam au féminin*, Paris, Hachette, 1990 (in English: *Veiled: Women in Islam*, Watertown, MA, Blue Crane Books, 1994) and Juliette Minces, *Le Coran et les femmes*, Paris, Hachette, 1996, which demonstrate how women's virginity is the "geometric center" of Arab society.

51 Pryce-Jones, *The Closed Circle*, pp. 35–6.

The Persistence of the Tribal Matrix

What was true of pre-Islamic Bedouins seems to hold true for today's leaders and peoples. The paradox is multiple: Has Islam not "abolished" tribalism, as we are told in countless textbooks on Islam and the Arab world? Did the Prophet not rail vigorously against *asabiyya*? "The Arabs of the desert are the most hardened in their impiety and hypocrisy," the Quran asserts (9:98).

A first hint: "Occupying the center of social and moral value judgments, shame and honor are a good deal harder to ignore or repudiate than Islam: because they coincide, the two codes enforce identity and conformity of behavior." Furthermore, "[t]ribes did not necessarily cease to exist because new states were formed.... They may remain as they were in spite of state formation" in the region.[52] "Older forms of social identification persisted in new settings."[53]

Persistence of patterns of behavior inscribed in a culture is a normal historical phenomenon. Marx to the contrary, being does not determine consciousness. The chivalric ideal persisted in Europe whose Industrial Revolution made it obsolete – in fact, a first draft of the same idea is one that sets the tone of Miguel de Cervantes's *Don Quixote*[54]: The hero is hopelessly out of sync with a reality that has left behind chivalry, its gratuitous heroics, and its scale of values. Modern history is replete with the repeated story of an old aristocratic elite often incapable of even perceiving change around itself, and being swept aside as a result: the Tokugawa shoguns who fell in the 1860s, the Ottoman Janissaries brushed aside by the Turks, China's Qing dynasty and its disappearance in 1911. The stronger the belief system that goes with the institutional structure is, the more difficult change and adaptation will be. In the case of the Islamic Middle East, the coupling of creed with structure was so strong as to prevent change altogether. Let us hear an especially striking sample of the blood, the soil, and the religion that emanates from them, from an Arab writer whose kinship with the nineteenth century German Romantic nationalism barely needs to be underlined (it is a somber irony to hear an Arab expostulate on Arabness in terms that are simply borrowed from Fichte and the other German reactionary Romantics and were equally used in Russia by the Slavophiles of the nineteenth century and the Bolsheviks of the twentieth century):

52 Khoury and Kostiner, *Tribes and State Formation*, Introduction, p. 2.

53 Ibid., Foreword, p. ix.

54 Albert O. Hirschman, *The Passion and the Interests*, Princeton, NJ, Princeton University Press, 1977.

We are Arabs because we maintain ties with our past, are proud of our traditions, and glory in the heritage of our fathers. Our generation guards this heritage so as to pass it on, pure and complete, to our children and grandchildren. We believe in eternity, the eternity of the spirit and the eternity of the homeland. We are Arabs because we cherish spiritual values; we shall neither renounce them nor exchange them for others, for in the foundations of these values there is something of God; in them are the attributes of God. We are Arabs because we do not cling to a social philosophical outlook which is taken from beyond our horizons, beyond our borders, beyond our great homeland, for such outlooks would shatter our existence and strike a blow at all that is sacred to us. We are Arabs because we adhere to Arab nationalism and are built by it. It belongs to us and we belong to it.[55]

At work here is a factor that prevents the assimilation of the Other, and fanatically insists on the preservation of the Same, reality notwithstanding. What is voiced is a passionate desire for *stasis*, a radical denial of the positive nature, of the very existence, of change in human affairs, a deep-seated conviction of being in possession of Truth unadulterated and perfect. Arab values and homeland are one, they constitute a "closed circle," vouched for by God and tradition. Any interference would sully, pollute, shatter this delicate balance. The theological roots of this attitude are fundamental to Islam. Which fosters the persistence of inadaptive and inadapted creeds and forms of social organization in the modern history of the Arab, and Muslim, world.

"In the inner recesses of the Arab, one almost always finds a complex remnant of nomadism and sedentarism, whatever his lifestyle.... These are the durable legacies of earlier life," it has been asserted; likewise:

In extensive areas ... [of the Middle East], the Ibn Khaldunian formula [about tribe, *asabiyya*, etc.] persisted alive and well. It constituted the normal political condition of a large proportion of Middle Easterners despite the nominal Ottoman overlordship.... In due course, it made its public reappearance, with Abd al-Qadir in Algeria, the *Mahdi*yya in the Sudan, the Wahhabi in the Peninsula, the Sanusiyya in Cyrenaica, the Rashidi in Hail, petty chieftaincies in Eastern Anatolia, the Ibadi Imamate in Oman and the Zaydi in Yemen. In extensive areas it never had been hidden.[56]

Tribal-based Mahdism, in other words, was and remained the underlying ideology of society, under the thin administrative and fiscal net spread by

[55] Nasir al-Din Nashashibi, quoted in Y. Harkabi, *Arab Attitudes to Israel*, Jerusalem, Keter, 1972, p. 356. From Pryce-Jones, *The Closed Circle*, p. 377.

[56] Gellner, "Tribalism and the State," *The Closed Circle*, p. 116.

the Ottomans, whose *millet* system "preserved Arab identity, stabilizing and perpetuating, however unwittingly, the tribal order ands its customs."[57]

Further, under the surface of the Ottoman Empire

> the world of Ibn Khaldun continued to function, it reemerged as the empire declined. It only came to an end when new military and administrative technologies were imported and tilted the balance of power in favor of the state. The subsequent new order has a number of conspicuous features: civil society continues to be weak in the face of the state; political conflict in the state apparatus, even when nominally ideological, is generally a matter of the rivalry of patronage networks, often with a regional or quasi-communal base. This is a kind of tribalism in a new milieu and idiom.[58]

As a result, "Neither in the imperial nor in the territorial state were tribes transformed into a homogenous polity; tribal ties have always been the basic element of group reference, despite the fact that they were suppressed and rhetorically denounced," an analysis that applies no less to Prophet Muhammad's Islam than to twentieth century Arab "nation-states."[59] The body politic that Muhammad directed "did not make pre-Islamic conceptions irrelevant.... The result was to create a federation of tribes in alliance with Muhammad.... Such an alliance meant that the tribe in question became a part of the Islamic state."[60]

The tribe has not remained unaffected by changes in its contemporary environment: a "reemergence of tribal *asabiyya* in the guise of national sovereignty and national legitimacy, which are obviously not related to tribes, but to the modern nation-state." However, few if any Arab countries fail to be ruled by a tribal or tribal-like group. The ever-present domination of tribalism means that Arab polities have ever remained fractious, ever ready to splinter and recombine:

> Division (not unity) has been the salient feature of Islamic history. In Arabia as well as in the Arabized and Islamized provinces of the new imperial state, the tribes remained the basic social unit despite the existing state order. [...] Not... that the tribes did not change. The dilemma of Arab-Islamic history was, and still is, that the structural dissolution of the tribes was not consequential to tribal solidarity. Thus, although the economic basis of the social reproduction of tribes has been undermined by change, the sense of tribal identity continued to thrive.[61]

57 Pryce-Jones, *The Closed Circle*, p. 30.
58 Gellner, "Tribalism and the State," p. 125.
59 Bassam Tibi, "The Simultaneity of the Unsimultaneous: Old Tribes and Imposed Nation-States in the Modern Middle East," in Khoury and Kostiner, *Tribes and State Formation*, pp. 126–42.
60 W. Montgomery Watt, *Islamic Political Thought*, Edinburgh, University Press Edinburgh, 1968, p. 13.
61 Tibi, "*Simultaneity,*" p. 135.

As a result, "Today there exist very few nomadic tribes in the Middle East, yet Middle Eastern structures still display the features of tribal entities, especially tribal loyalty and self-awareness."[62] Consciousness survives being:

> The tribes are not but a small fraction of Arab society... the tribal way of life has been waning in the Arab world as modern transportation, communications and the oil economy have taken root. Today perhaps less than five percent of the Arab world's population is actually nomadic.... A far larger portion, however, retains a degree of tribal identity.[63]

Tribal identity is thus shown to be the default level of Arab–Muslim identity. Kinship trumps all other loyalties, whether based on actual or assumed blood ties, or invented ones, or even, ironically, elective ties – the tribal model becoming the matrix for all kinds of organizations, the "structural model for any possible group." Thus, with respect to the mostly Sufi religious orders and brotherhoods of Islam: "In Islam [...] [t]he hierarchical associations, which most resemble churches, were not shadow states but only disembodied tribes," an insight that begs to be applied to political and paramilitary (terrorist) organizations in the world of Islam. In a "pre-Weberian" society where the impersonal–bureaucratic mode of governance is essentially unknown, or practiced only in its superficial externalities, it is the default layer – tribalism – which will supply the organizational models.[64]

Tribal values and the tribal ethos persisted: "Though the tribe as an actual social structure has declined in significance, the tribe as a referent for social identity and loyalty has persisted."[65]

> Although today the Bedouins constitute probably not more than ten percent of the population of the Arab world, many Arabs, in both the villages and the cities, claim Bedouin origin. What is more important than mere numbers is that a very large sector of the settled population still considers the Bedouin ethos as an ideal to which, in theory at least, it would like to measure up.[66]

Where is identity locating itself? "The emotional intensity of the desert dweller has imposed its ideal on the opulent cities."[67] Likewise, Europe in 1914 was still in the grip of aristocratic values, even though its real life had departed from those values long ago.[68]

[62] Ibid., p. 136.

[63] Michael Hudson, *Arab Politics: In Search of Legitimacy*, New Haven, CT, Yale University Press, 1977, pp. 88–9, quoted by Tibi, "*Simultaneity*," p. 136.

[64] Gellner, *Muslim Society*, p. 56.

[65] Ibid., p. 128.

[66] Patai, *The Arab Mind*, p. 73.

[67] Jacques Berque, *The Arabs: Their History and Future*, New York, Praeger, 1964, p. 174. Quoted by Patai, *The Arab Mind*, p. 73.

[68] See Arno Mayer, *The Persistence of the Ancien Régime*, New York, Pantheon, 1982.

> [T]he Bedouins are looked upon, not only by the Arab cities, but by the entire Arab world . . . as images and figures from the past, as living ancestors, as latter day heirs and witnesses to the ancient glory of the heroic age. Hence the importance of the Bedouin ethos, and of the Bedouins' aristocratic moral code, for the Arab world in general.[69]

This imprint is so indelible that it turns into myth. The desert warrior, with his peculiar characteristics, is the paradigm, the paragon of virtue and potency, the "ideal" Arab. One may live in an urban hovel or a village, "in ideology and scale of values, [the desert and the Bedouins] still loom large; in fact, they still hold the undisputed first place." This was "reinforced by the practice of many generations of Muslim jurists who in their legal decisions relied heavily on Bedouin precedents and by the reliance of Arab philologists on Bedouin usage in deciding the fine points of grammar." This operates for society in general, it works also for more modest social units: "The preservation in many families of a tradition or of a claim to tribal ancestry is another common form of nostalgia for the Bedouin virtues. . . . People of humble circumstances, such as artisans and workers, preserve the tradition of their Bedouin descent carefully and jealously, for it supplies them with the one and only claim they have for a semblance of status and social importance." Those who fail to be absorbed by the urban melting pot "rely on their ethnic–tribal kin-groups; they can survive only through maintaining the network of pre-national tribal loyalties and ties. Social conflicts over scarce resources assume an ethnic, or a tribal [. . .]. Ironically, the national ideology of Arabdom serves as a legitimizing formula" for tribes, sects, clans and families in power – the Alawites of Syria, the Takriti under Saddam.[70]

Islam as the Supertribe

Tribalism and Islam merged, or converged, or became coterminous, at least in part.[71] Tribal mores, customs, and rules were massively integrated into the body of Islamic jurisprudence and practices. This study argues that the tribal element did not have to wait to be absorbed and assimilated: It was present at creation. It is rather a selected body of tribal and quasi-tribal conceptions that presided in part over the birth and rise of Islam.

[69] Patai, *The Arab Mind*, p. 73.

[70] Tibi, *"Simultaneity,"* p. 142.

[71] Patricia Crone, "The Tribe and the State," in J. A. Hall, ed., *States in History*, Oxford, Oxford University Press, 1986.

How could it be otherwise? We have ascertained that the tribe, kinship groups in general, are the substratum for the individual and collective identity of the Arab people, who have for 1,400 years been steeped in the religion of Islam, to the point that in Islam, "[t]he normative function of religion is manifested in the extent to which it regulates everyday behavior through positive and negative commandments, all of which, ideally, must be observed." "Islam permeated life, all of which came under its aegis. Religion was not one aspect of life, but the hub from which all else radiated. All customs and traditions was religion, and religious dos and don'ts extended throughout all activity, thought and feeling.... [Religion was] the central normative force in life."[72]

If tribalism organizes and Islam pervades and prescribes, we must conclude, while taking into account the inevitable tensions and contradictions this implies, that the spectrum of tribalism and the spectrum of Islam intersect and overlap along wide segments of congruence. Must we not conclude that Islam, rather than a universal religion it believes itself to be, is a tribal religion generalized and projected onto a worldwide, specieswide screen?

A number of crucial tenets of Islamic belief in one way or the other represent or reflect the tribal order of things as it was transferred to and subsumed into Islam. This transference was overwhelming: "[E]xcept for a few striking reforms affecting sexual relationships and the position of women, Muhammad the Prophet had himself interfered little with the principles of the social system of his environment. For the tribe he substituted the Muslim community, but in essence his regulations continued to be applicable to the trible way of life."[73]

The ambit of this analysis may not have been appreciated as much as it should: the tribal ways were passed on to the newly created *umma*; the *umma's* ways were essentially tribal.

> They were based in the main on the customs of [Muhammad's] own tribe of the Quraysh and were imposed upon other peoples and communities possessing habits and social laws as firmly established as those of the Prophet's own clan. In many instances, the older system would not be displaced by the newer one, or at any rate a considerable part of the older system survived and played a part in the life of the people equally with Islam.

In essence, then, the jurisprudence of early Islam was an outgrowth of Quraysh tribal law, the law of the victors and the Arab Empire, and of

[72] Patai, *The Arab Mind*, pp. 143, 144.

[73] Reuben Levy, "Usage, Custom and Secular Law Under Islam," in *The Social Structure of Islam*, London & New York, Routledge, 1957, p. 242.

the tribal law of other clans, tribes, and groups that had been subdued by the victorious Muslims. This never went without tensions between the heterogenous components, but an essential continuity obtained. "The law has in numerous places been overridden by traditional usages. It is well established further that in many tribal and other communities in Islam there are native codes of unwritten laws and traditions by which the members have continued to regulate their lives."[74] Historically, tribal law and supertribal law, Sharia, were far from incompatible:

> The unwritten laws of... local custom and practice are known collectively as *Urf* ("what is commonly known and accepted") or *Ada* ("custom"). They have generally been the product of long-standing convention, either deliberately adopted or the result of unconscious adaptation to circumstances, and they have therefore been followed where pratical considerations have been uppermost. There have not been lacking attempts to regard *urf* as one of the "roots" of the *fiqh* [Muslim jurisprudence], but except in the works of the early Sunni *mujtahids* [jurisprudents] the customary laws have generally gone unrecorded by the legists. Yet they have not gone unrecognized.[75]

In fact, "[t]he distinction between the two sources [of values, pre-Islamic and Islamic] is not always clear-cut; certain pre-Islamic Arab ideals have been incorporated into the Quran and Muslim tradition."[76] There is even a hadith that has Muhammad say: "Look to those moral practices you had in the *jahiliyya*, and apply them in Islam." The hadith mentions a few of those – which turn out to be typical of the Bedouin way of life. Muslims must ever return to the origin of their *umma*. As we mentioned repeatedly, just as the Prophets' mores and actions present an unsurpassable model of human action, his ethos and that of the Companions of the Prophet define the highest possible ethos that man may hope to follow. The ethos of the desert warriors is the apex of human ethos.

Islam was created by desert warriors. The very famous hadith of the Prophet reported by the most authoritative of the hadith compilers Bukhari states: "The best of my nation is my generation, then those who follow them and then those who follow them." Islamic history is a downward slope from that Golden Age of the Prophet and the first four "well-guided" caliphs, since each and every generation marks a new step in the entropic distance that constantly increases from the zenith, the point of departure, to the point of arrival, the End of Days. A famous hadith has the Prophet say: "Believe

[74] Ibid., p. 243.
[75] Ibid., p. 248.
[76] Patai, *The Arab Mind*, p. 97.

my Companions, then those who succeed them, and after that those who succeed the Successors. But after them falsehood will prevail when people will swear to the truth without having been asked to swear, and testify without having been asked to testify. Only those who seek the pleasures of Paradise will keep to the Congregation." Sayyid Qutb gives voice to this sense of decay: "[The] message of Islam at one time created a generation which has no parallel in the entire Islamic history, in the entire history of mankind.... After this [the generation of the Prophet and his companions] no generation of this caliber ever came into existence" – a state of affairs that compels the faithful to return to the past in order to find the secret and the path.[77]

"You are the best community raised for the good of mankind you enjoin what is good and forbid what is wrong, and you believe in Allah," said the Quran (3:110). Numerous hadith held for authentic and forever repeated complete the conception implicit in this statement, namely, that the *umma* is in possession of Truth, and that it is, as a community, the embodiment of truth. "Error comes from separation" clearly indicates that truth resides in the body of the community. Another, lengthy saying ascribed to the Prophet concerning the umma asserts: "Allah has granted you protection from three things: your Prophet lays no curse upon you, lest you utterly perish; the party of falsehood among you will never triumph over the party of truth; you will never agree on a false doctrine."[78]

Thus is established the doctrine of the infallibility of the consensus: the community as a community, the *umma* as *umma* is infallible – it is the embodiment of truth: Truth comes from the group, or rather, is carried in and of itself by the group as the group. The consensus of the *umma*, the *ijma*, is immanent to the group. The similarity is striking with the analysis of the sacred (holy) developed by Emile Durkheim.[79] The sacred is the hypostasis of the group, the immaterial embodiment of the group that projects itself into what it considers holy. The holy in turn defines the group and its beliefs. More hadith broaden the sense to be given to *ijma*: "You have to follow the congregation for verily Allah will not make the largest group of Muhammad's community agree on error" and "My Community shall not agree upon misguidance. Therefore, you must stay with the congregation,

[77] Qutb, *Milestones*, 53. On the doom and gloom that affects and colors all contemporary radical Islamists, see Sivan, *Radical Islam*.

[78] Goldziher, *Introduction*, 50.

[79] Emile Durkheim, *Formes Elémen taires de la vie religieuse (Elementary Forms of Religious Life)*, Paris, 1912.

and Allah's hand is over the congregation." And further: "Verily Allah has protected my Community from agreeing upon error." Another hadith avers, "Allah's hand is over the group." And again: "Whoever leaves the community or separates himself from it by the length of a span dies the death of the *jahiliyya*."[80] The proliferation of hadith on the same subject attests the central importance of the doctrine for Islam: The group (*umma*) equals truth, and there is no truth outside the group.

If God's truth is of the group, the dividing line between truth and untruth is the border between the group and the nongroup. By implication, since truth is immanent to the group, there is no objective truth, no unconditionally valid truth independent of the group. Good and Evil are equally of the group, rather than objectively ascertained values. What accords with the group is truth, what does not, does not; what the group holds true is true, what it holds untrue is untrue.

What holds for the True and Untrue holds in equal measure for Good and Evil. One of the most eminent and authoritative formulators of Sunni orthodoxy, Abul Hassan al-Ashari, was a theorist of the absolute power of God, and consequently of the fluidity of Good and Evil, the contents of which could change according to God's will. To postulate an absolute value for Good and Evil would have been to shackle God's omnipotence, or give Good and Evil a quasi-divine status, in turn committing the worst sin imaginable in Islam, *shirk*, giving God "associates," or polytheism.[81]

> If [God] were to send all created beings to Paradise there would be no injustice done, or if He sent them all to Hell there would be no wrong. Wrong consists in usurping rights over that which one does not own or cannot justly claim.... All the duties incumbent upon man are the subject of revelation from God. No essential duty can be dictated by the mind, which cannot in itself determine that an action is good or evil.[82]

Man is radically unable to know good from evil by himself. As the Quran states: "Perchance you hate a thing while it is good for you or love a thing which is bad for you. Allah knows best. You know not" (2:216). But further, as Ahmad Ibn Hazm, a member of the sect of the Zahiris ("literalists")

[80] Shaykh Hisham Muhammad Kabbani, "Questions on *ijma* (consensus), *taqlid* (following qualified opinion), and *ikhtilaf al-fuqaha* (differences of the jurists)." Available at: http://www.sunnah.org/fiqh/usul/ijma.htm#TEXTS%20ON% 20IJMA.

[81] Reuben Levy, "Moral Sentiment in Islam," in *The Social Structure, Accessed of Islam*, London & New York, Routledge, 1957, p. 205.

[82] Ibid., p. 206.

in eleventh century Spain, theorized in a way that encapsulates orthodox Islamic thinking:

Anyone that says that God would do nothing save what is good according to our understanding and would create nothing that our understanding classes as evil, must be told that he has... perversely applied human argument to God. Nothing is good but Allah has made it so, and nothing is evil, but by his doing. Nothing in the world, indeed, is good or bad in its own essence; but what God has called good is good, and the doer is virtuous; and similarly, what God has called evil is evil and the doer is a sinner. All depends on God's decree, for an act that may at one time be good may be bad at another time.[83]

The irrationalist school of Ashari won the day and the millennium thereafter. This concept triumphed over the Free Will school within early Islam, the *mutazila*, also sometimes called the "Rationalists of Islam."

What is pleasing and what is abhorrent [to God]? Orthodoxy answers: good-and-pleasing is what God commands; evil-and-abhorrent is what God forbids. The divine will, which cannot be held accountable, and its dictates are the yardstick for good and evil. Nothing is good and evil because reason makes it so. Murder is reprehensible because God has forbidden it; had the divine law not branded murder as wicked, it would not be wicked.[84]

A much-used hadith states plainly: "If God had wanted evil to be good and good to be evil, there would be no difficulty." Nothing is *zulm* ("wrong") except what God forbids. Good and evil are thus understood through the prism of God's decree. It has been said that Islam, more than an orthodoxy, is an orthopraxy. Indeed, it defines an action, first, not in itself, but according to its intent (*niyya*), which only God and the faithful know, and, second, according to criteria that are not moral but juridical and social: It is approved or not.[85]

Likewise in the tribal environment, it is group-being, group-survival, and group-power that define the rightness or wrongness of a course of action: does it bring honor to the group? Does it bring shame? In the tribal world, morality and ethics are attributes of the group, and subordinate to it. In the *umma*, the supertribe, it is similarly not the correlation with good and evil, but the correlation with the law, *sunna*, that determines the goodness or evil of a course of action. The *umma* is the embodiment of truth, just as the tribe dictates its norms, values, and behaviors.

[83] Ibid., 206–7.

[84] Goldziher, *Introduction*, 91.

[85] See Jean-Paul Charnay, *La Charia et l'Occident*, Paris, l'Herne, 2001, 67–8.

Quran, hadith, sunna: the triad sums up Islam, its creed, doctrine, jurisdiction. The Quran is divine revelation; sunna, the law; and hadith, the documentation of the law. Together they constitute sharia. Originally, "*Sunna* is the custom [*usus*] that prevailed in the first Muslim community concerning any point of law or religion."[86] But upstream:

The Muslims did not have to invent this concept nor its practical scope: it is already in current use amongst the ancient [Arabian] pagans. Those held for *Sunna* what corresponded to the traditions of the Arab world, the mores and customs of the ancestors. It is in this meaning that the word *Sunna* is still used in the Islamic era amongst Arabs little influenced by the Muslim religion.[87]

In brief: "Just as the pagan Arab was bound to his forebears' *Sunna*, the Muslim community held the new *Sunna* in high regard and followed it."[88] The tribe's law, though unwritten, is the body of customs received from the ancestors and that needs to be passed on unaltered to the descendants. It is almighty, hallowed, infrangible. No action may be taken which is outside the boundaries set by the tribal *Sunna*. Its writ is all pervasive. "In primitive society custom stands for law, and even where social organization has made some progress it may still remain the sole rule for conduct."

From time immemorial the Arab's chief criterion for determining propriety and lawfulness in any aspect of life has been conformity in word and deed to ancestral norm and usage. Whatever is true and just must accord with, and be rooted in, inherited opinion and custom. These constitute the *Sunna*. The *Sunna* was their law and sacra. It was the sole source of their legal practice and their religion; to forsake it was to transgress against the inviolable rules of hallowed custom. This applied to actions, and, for the same reasons, to inherited ideas. In the sphere of ideas, too, the group could accept nothing new that was not in harmony with the views of its ancestors. When the Arabs accepted Islam – which had commanded them to break with their authoritative *Sunna* – they brought the concept of *Sunna* with them. From that time forth, it became the main pillar of the Islamic view of law and religion [but] its point of departure shifted; its source now consisted in the doctrines, conceptions and practices of the oldest generations of Muslims, founders of an entirely different *Sunna* from what the original Arab one had been. Henceforth the norm was the demonstrable usage and view first of the Prophet and then of his Companions. People did not so much ask what was, in a given situation, good or proper in itself, as what the Prophet and his Companions had said about the matter, how they had acted, and what had accordingly been passed down as the proper view and the proper action.[89]

[86] Ignaz Goldziher, *Etudes sur la tradition islamique*, Paris, Librairie d'Amérique et d'Orient Adrien Maisonneuve, 1984, p. 13.

[87] Ibid., pp. 14–15.

[88] Ibid., p. 15.

[89] Goldziher, *Introduction*, pp. 230–1.

In other words, just as the tribe ascribed its origin to one common ancestor who gave it its identity, Islam's point of origin provided the *silf* ("ancestral custom"), as practiced by the salaf ("ancients.") As Patricia Crone wrote, "*Sharia* is a tribal code."

It is not coincidental that the elaborate system that Islamic scholars used to authenticate hadith, the *isnad* ("chain of transmission") so much resembles the purity of lineage that is so essential to the tribal life of the Bedouins. The pedigree of divine law operates like the chain of pure tribal blood. "Conduct and judgment were considered correct and their legitimacy was established as a chain of reliable transmissions that ultimately traced them back to a Companion who could testify that they were in harmony with the Prophet's intentions."

Many authorities nonetheless agree that *hadith* were forged in industrial quantities ("the limitless chaos of traditions") and often with the best intent in the world, as they were one of the most potent instruments in the toolkit of Muslims: If the Prophet had said it, it stood above criticism and "acquired a sacred character." As Ibn Khaldun points out, "Muhammad said ... " means, "It is right, it is religiously unassailable."[90] "Learn as much of your pedigree as is necessary to establish your ties of kindred," he quotes the Prophet as saying. In words that might as well concern hadith – most of the gigantic mass of which are forgeries pure and simple, whether vouched for and authenticated or not – he adds that "pedigrees are only useful as they imply the close contact that is a consequence of blood ties and that eventually leads to mutual help and affection. Anything beyond that is superfluous. For a pedigree is something imaginary and devoid of reality.... If the fact of common descent is obvious and clear, it evokes in a man a natural affection."[91]

Isnad is the pedigree of a saying ascribed to the Prophet; what matters with pedigree is that it endows its owner with prestige, the currency that "buys" everything that can be acquired in tribal society. It further establishes who is friend and who is foe; what matters with *isnad* is that it establishes a credible lineage to ideas that are the source of judgments and actions in the world of Islam, what is right and what is wrong, what is true and what is false, since they all depend on their source rather than their content.

The tribal *urf* is sovereign. No man may legislate urf. Islam admits no "sovereignty of man," no "human legislation." What the *urf* ("customary law") dictates is what the sunna of Muhammad dictates: The structural homology is complete. What tradition (*jus consuetudinis*) is to *urf*,

[90] Ibid., pp. 37, 39, 44.

[91] Khaldun, *The Muqqadima*, pp. 98–9.

Revelation is to Islam's sunna. The *umma* is not a tribe, it is a supertribe. Historically, "[t]he concept of *Umma* was fused with concepts of tribal alliance; the image of the religious chief was identified with that of the traditional clan *shaykh*. The early *Umma* was built on an undifferentiated tribal religiopolitical identity and undifferentiated religiopolitical leadership."[92]

"The Islamic *Umma* can be seen as a super-tribe that evolved from a tribal federation."[93] In terms of contents, "[a]t the emotional level, identity and custom join in mutual defense. Loyalty to tribe and religion obliges the Arab and the Muslim to defy and to reject the understanding and acceptance of the outsider and the unbeliever," as well as the ideas, values, and practices they are the carriers of.[94]

The function of pedigree is to vouch for lineage. The function of lineage is to determine who is friend and who is foe. In this sense, the Third Reich's "Crown Jurist" Carl Schmitt was an Islamic thinker; his "friend/foe principle" is sheer tribal thinking. What is at stake here is the nature of the human race – whether it is one, or do the sectional affiliations that have developed trump the oneness. We have already seen how Gnostics divide mankind into slices with different levels of dignity. Gnosticism here lends a hand to tribalism to deny the unity of the species. Islam "is an exclusivism which replaces parentage and race by religion."[95]

Muslim polities and Muslim geopolitics, and, in the end, the Muslim *Weltanschauung*, are determined by this principle:

> The Arab sociopolitical view can best be represented by a series of concentric circles. The smaller the circle the greater the sense of belonging, cohesion and loyalty. In traditional Arab society, the largest such circle was that of the tribe, or, among the settled populations, that of the village. Beyond the tribe and the village loomed the outside world, other tribes or villages which, by and large, constituted a menace rather than kindred aggregates.[96]

As Bernard Lewis wrote:

> In most Muslim countries Islam is still the ultimate criterion of group identity and loyalty. It is Islam that distinguishes between self and other, between insider and outsider, between brother and stranger, [...] just as the insider is defined by his acceptance of Islam, in the same way the outsider is defined by his rejection of Islam.

92 Ira Lapidus, "Tribes and State Formation in Islamic History," in Khoury and Kostiner, *Tribes and States Formation*, p. 30.

93 Ibid., p. 134.

94 Pryce-Jones, *The Closed Circle*, p. 33.

95 Chelhod, *Introduction à la sociologie*, p. 162.

96 Patai, *The Arab Mind*, p. 79.

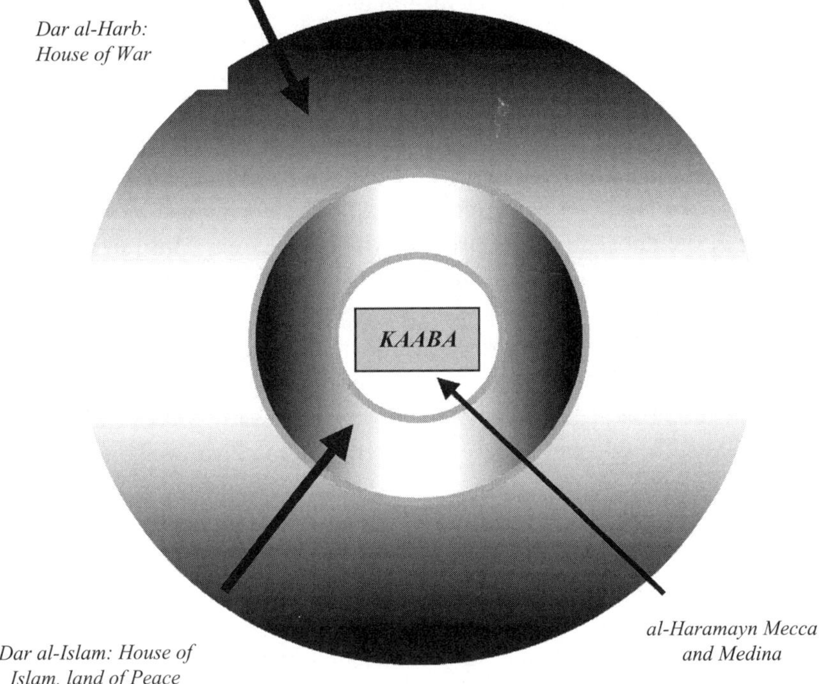

FIGURE 4.1. The concentric circles of Islamo-centered geotheology. There are additional intermediate degrees that depend on the degree of submission and subjection to Islam and the Islamic polity manifested by the locals: *dar al-Dawa* missionary land; *dar al-sulh* [*al-Ahd*]: Treaty lands; *dar al-Kharaj*: Tributary lands. But they are all conceived as not-yet-conquered *dar al-Jahiliyya*, lands of paganism, or *dar al-Kufr*, lands of unbelief.

He is the *kafir*, the "unbeliever." [...] From the time of the Prophet to the present day, the ultimate definition of the Other, the alien outsider and presumptive enemy, has been the *kafir*, the unbeliever.[97]

The ordering of the world will answer those criteria. Relations between the Muslim world and the non-Muslim world are dichotomous: The world is ontologically divided between an inner circle, the *dar al-Islam*, and an outside, the *dar al-Harb*. As shown in Figure 4.1, a series of intermediate circles reflect the realities of the real world, meaning that *dar al-Islam* has not – not yet – expanded and absorbed the rest of the world an Islamo-centered universe is thus created.[98]

[97] Bernard Lewis, "Metaphor and Allusion," *The Political Language of Islam*, Chicago, University of Chicago Press, 1988, pp. 4–5.

[98] Jean-Paul Charnay, *La charîa et l'Occident*, Paris, Ed. de l'Herne, 2001, p. 110.

Jerusalem was the center of the mental universe of medieval Christendom. Medieval cartography placed it at the center not only of its mental universe but of the physical world. It was a mental (or moral) geography rather than a physical or political one. Likewise, the inner, ideological, or theological "map" of Islam is superimposed upon the real world. Just as ancient cosmology placed the Earth (Us) at the center of the universe (Them), the Islamic universe is centered. The absolute center of the universe is located inside the *kaaba*, the cubic structure around which the Great Mosque of Mecca is built: It is the *Hajaru 'l-Aswad* ("The Black Rock"), a 7-inch oval rock supposedly created in heaven 2,000 years ago, erected there by Adam. The kaaba is the axis for the geotheological system of Islam – so much that the prayer rug must be directed to this "magnetic" center of the world: The *qibla* orients those at prayer and their prayers toward Mecca. At the five daily prayers, the Muslim believer "reorients" himself toward the center of his faith.

This Islamo-centrism illustrates the constitutional separation of the world, between the world of Us and the world of Them. Compare it to this other error of Ancient cosmology, whereby different sets of laws ruled the "sublunar" world, that is, the earth and its immediate surroundings, and the extralunar world, the sun, the planets, and the stars. In that conception, and in the geotheology of Islam, the universe is not homogenous, and subject to homogenous rules: The law varies according to the character of the territory. While this kind of collective egocentrism is not uncommon amongst men and nations, it draws a peculiar strength in the Arab world from its pairing with a religion whose underlying logic is based on the self-same logic.

Infidels are banned from entering the *haram* ("the forbidden"), which is at the core of Islam, and its immediate peripheries, variously defined as the Holy Places, *al Haramayn* only, or extended to the entire Arabic Peninsula. From *dar al-Islam* to *dar al-Harb*, the intermediate circles are but shades leading from white to black, from Good to Evil, from our tribe to their tribes – me, my brother, my cousins, the others. The concentric circles represent something of a logarithm of distance: He who belongs in my *asabiyya* group will be treated according to the group's law. He who does not will be treated according to other laws, to the laws of war. The farther an individual is from the core, the farther he will be from its law. It may be that circumstances, tactical turns, balance of forces, and other factors dictate temporary or partial compromises – there are intermediate circles in reality – but the nature of the scheme does not vary. Around the center, *kaaba* and *al-Haramayn*, the Holy Places of Mecca and Medina, lies the *dar al-Islam*, "us." Concentric circles broaden from Islam to unbelief, "them."

Next come *dar al-Kharaj* and *dar al-sulh*: the circle of the tributary territories and the circle of countries that have signed treaties of alliance with Islam. The nations of the *dar al-Kharaj* are vassals and pay tribute, a survival tax as it were, for the unconverted: What the dhimmis are at a personal level – non-Muslims who are not pagans, and are therefore not compelled to choose between conversion and death as pagans are, but have the option of retaining their religion. (In return, they must pay a special tax, the *jaziya*, accept the status of legal inferiors; be subjected to demeaning restrictions in dress, housing, behavior, etc.), the tributary and vassal nations are as states, dhimmi states. The lands of the *dar al-sulh* occupy an intermediate level; they have not yet been vassalized but are coming close: As a result of the *suhl*, an armistice, a settlement, "non-Muslim rulers continue to govern their people through their own agents, with a measure of autonomy under a form of Muslim suzerainty."[99] The next circle, that of *dar al-Dawa* is missionary land – *dawa* is the appeal to convert. *Dar al-Dawa* is the vast march-land of Islam, beyond which starts the lands run by Infidels *dar al-Harb*, which is not an object of *dawa* but of jihad.

The geotheological circles mirror the concentric circles of kinship. This is why the tribal conception of Them and Us prevails. Members of other tribes are of another species. They are prey. In radical Islam, the them are members of a distinct, lower species, the *kufr*, the unbelievers. They do not qualify as full-fledged members of mankind, since only Muslims are part of mankind. "By becoming a Muslim..., a man changes his status: from a slave that he was he becomes a believer.... In fact, Islam does not respect in man the person, but the believer."[100] For the lovers of death of radical Islam, the unbelievers are what *Untermenschen* were to their fellow-Gnostics the Nazis; what the "exploiting classes" were to their fellow-Gnostics the Bolsheviks; what the educated were to their fellow Gnostic Pol Pot. Dhimmis and pagans, heretics and apostates are offerings to God in the giant sacrifice imagined, prepared and sometimes begun by the jihadis. Jihad is the organized expression of that conception. What is called "terrorism" is a tactical expression of the conception.

The love of death of radical Islam is self-directed, it is literally suicidal: Gnosticism is nihilistic and inherently destructive. This necrophilia, or thanatophila[101] is also directed toward the outside, in a fury of destructive

[99] Bernard Lewis, "War and Peace," *The Political Language of Islam*, Chicago, University of Chicago Press, 1988, p. 80.

[100] Chelhod, *Introduction à la sociologie*, p. 162.

[101] A term used by Dr. Shmuel Bar, of the Interdisciplinary Center at Herzliya, Israel, in his own research, which repeatedly intersects mine, and whom I want to thank for his rich input.

rage. This crazed frenzy rests on a megalomania typical of Gnostic-Manichean mass movements and features an intent to exterminate the Other, selected as the Satanic cause for the evils of the world. At the same time, it reflects the all-powerful diktat of a tribal, honor-seeking culture with its pre-modern attitude toward violence, pain, and death. The Gnostic-Manichean division of the world between the Elect of the Good and the doomed cohorts of Satan intersects the tribal division of the world between Us and Them: this is the present-day meaning of *dar al-Islam* and *dar al-Harb*. This singular concatenation creates a deadly combination: that of contemporary jihad, the heir of the nomadic way of war.

Tribal War, Old and New

For, lo, I raise up [a people], that bitter and hasty nation, which shall march through the breadth of the land, to possess the dwelling places that are not theirs. They are terrible and dreadful [...]. Their horses also are swifter than the leopards and are more fierce than the evening wolves: and their horsemen shall spread themselves, and their horsemen shall come from far; they shall fly as the eagle that hasteth to eat. They shall come all for violence: their faces shall sup up as the east wind, and they shall gather the captivity as the sand. Habakkuk 1: 6–9 (King James version)

Much has been written since 2001 about al-Qaeda and international Islamic terrorism. The jihadis' use of the Internet and the apparent decentralization of their operations have led to an analysis of modern jihad and jihadi warfare as "networks." Figure 4.2 was published in 1660 in *La Description d'Ukraine* by Guillaume Le Vasseur de Beauplan. It illustrated the way in which 400 mounted Tatar warriors deployed in the Eurasian steppe.[102] This was "a Tatar strategy for hiding a troop of horsemen in the steppe.... Four hundred men would divide into successively smaller squads and then meet at a prearranged rendezvous. The trails of the smaller groups would soon disappear from the steppe grass leaving no trace for enemy scouts to follow."[103]

Allegorically, the diagram suggests that we may seek some of the organizational and sociological "secrets" of today's jihadis in the historical structures of the societies that generated them, rather than in the silicon instruments they use. It shows a remarkable ability to scatter forces and endow them with great initiative and flexibility, based on what modern

[102] Guillaume Le Vasseur de Beauplan, *La Description d'Ukraine*, Ottawa, Presses de l'Université d'Ottawa, 1990, pp. 116–17.

[103] Eric Hildiger, *Warriors of the Steppe: A Military History of Central Asia 500 BC TO 1700 AD*, New York, Da Capo Press, 1997, p. 118.

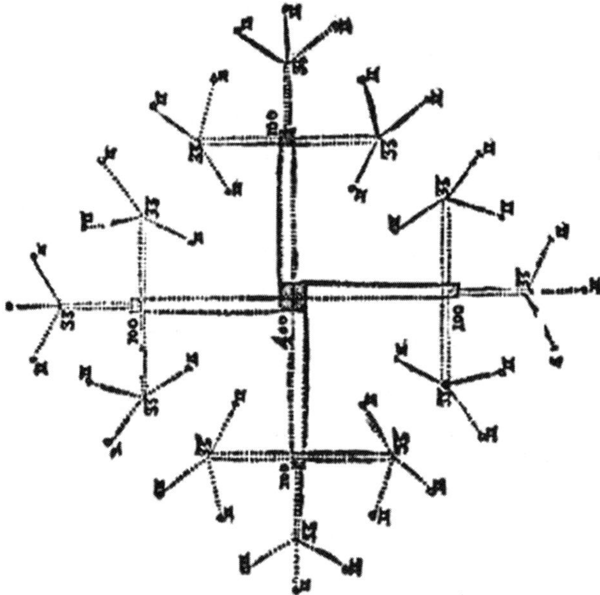

FIGURE 4.2. 400 mounted Tatar warriors deployed in the Eurasian steppe (1660).

military lingo calls "commander's intent," or, in the classical, nineteenth-century German conception, *Auftragstaktik*: the ability of the lower echelons of the officer corps to fathom the strategic sense of the plan they are part of and to take their local decisions within that general framework. Sir Basil Liddell Hart had already pointed out that remarkable characteristic of the Mongol war machine. "To a unique degree, [the Mongol armies] had attained...'intellectual discipline'....The supreme command was in the hands of the Emperor; but once the plan was decided upon, the subordinate generals executed the actual operations without interference and with but the rarest communication with the supreme command." The 10,000-strong *touman* was capable of acting as an independent force. Enormous flexibility was allowed in the execution. Further, "all Mongol campaigns...[were] prepared for by the employment of an extensive spy system, combining propaganda among the enemy peoples with a wonderful service of information....The Mongols were the pioneers of [the] attack on the rear."[104]

All tribally organized societies past the primitive stages of human existence generate essentially similar modes of thought, organization, and action.

[104] B. H. Liddell Hart, "Jengis Khan and Sabutai," *Great Captains Unveiled*, New York, Da Capo, 1996, reprint of 1927, pp. 7ff.

Much of al-Qaida is organized along familial, clan, and tribal lines.[105] The default modes of paramilitary action and organization in the Arab and Muslim world inscribed in the culture's genetic code are the first to be implemented: Everybody in that culture knows how to practice them, and they require little training or education. They are the "spontaneous" way in which things are done.

From the times of Classical Islam, in much of the umma – Syria, the "Jazirah" (Arab Iraq), Persian Iraq, Khurasan – various bodies of townsmen were organized on a more or less permanent militia basis. Sometimes these were sectarian groups. Sometimes they represented the lower-class elements in the towns but could be tied to the established authorities. They formed centers of power to be reckoned with, if they could be effectively mobilized.[106] "Many townsmen came to be organized in socially conscious bodies called most frequently, in Arabic, the *futuwwah*, or men's clubs, ceremonially devoted to the manly virtues. The word *futuwwah*, literally 'young manhood,' expresses manly ideals of comradely loyalty and magnanimity (the term was taken from the Bedouin tradition but was given a special meaning when used to render urban notions)."

A parallel may be drawn with the boisterous, rowdy "circus factions" of the Byzantine Empire – lower-class men's sports clubs that doubled as rent-a-crowd riff-raff for politicotheological factions of the Byzantine power games. Likewise the *futuwwah* had

> militia potentialities; they affected peculiarities of dress and were sometimes even referred to likewise as 'the young men.' Some of the clubs were dedicated to sports, others more to mutual aid. Occasionally the members lived, or at least ate, in a common clubhouse. They were formed among several different social strata; some were youth gangs, bands of adolescents and young men asserting their personal independence, some were general tradesmen's associations. There must have been an unbroken spectrum of such organizations, from one extreme form to another; and certain sorts of ideals and expectations were acknowledged by most of them,

and their common role was their ability to function as the matrix for urban militias.

105 See Laurie Mylroie's documentation of the role of Khaled Sheikh Muhammad's extended family in the 1993 and 2001 World Trade Center attacks: *Study of Revenge: Saddam Hussein's Unfinished War Against America*, Washington, DC, AEI Press, 2000.

106 This discussion of the *futuwwah* is largely drawn from Marshall G. S. Hodgson, *The Venture of Islam*, vol. 2, *The Expansion of Islam in the Middle Periods*, Chicago, University of Chicago Press, 1974, pp. 128ff. All citations in this section refer to this segment of Hodgson's book.

Each town had several independent futuwwah clubs claiming alone to represent true futuwwah. Clubs subdivided into smaller units, within which the ceremonial life chiefly took place. Each futuwwah man had to be unquestioningly obedient to the head of his particular unit. Clubs stressed the ties of mutual loyalty among members at the expense of other social ties; some clubs even insisted on members cutting ties to family, and admitted only bachelors, especially the youth gangs. Unconditional mutual loyalty was a common feature to all futuwwah. Ethical standards, particularly hospitality, were at a premium; in brief, the futuwwah clubs were a highly important network and networking organization.

With sport came military discipline normally directed at least potentially against the established powers. Futuwwah members were ready to bear arms. At times, the clubs carried out military expeditions, they carried out riots, which frightened the wealthier elements. When riots did occur, some made a point of plundering only the houses of the rich. Even their opponents credited them with a strict code of honor in such matters, similar to Mediterranean *bandits d'honneur*. Some clubs undertook "protection rackets." Sometimes even the criminal and beggar elements of a town seem to have assimilated their organizations to the futuwwah; indeed, such elements were likely to be more tightly organized than were more established groups.

Marginal futuwwah could be influential. Rebellious, they were connected to powers. Underground, they could be called upon. There were bridges between them and the rest of society. "Many of the [trade and craftsmen's] guilds seem to have been organized as *futuwwah* clubs – and they maintained an appropriately independent spirit." Further, "[t]he *futuwwah* guilds gained spiritual stability to support such a role through a close association with Sufism. Even in the High Caliphal Period, many Sufis had adopted some of the *futuwwah* language for expressing loyalty and magnanimity.... Some writers interpreted the *futuwwah* as a sort of lesser Sufi way for those unable to achieve the full mystical way." The *futuwwah* had become at least in some places, "essentially the Sufi dimension of guild organization."

The association between futuwwah and Sufism is crucial; Sufism developed as the dimension of popular devotion in Islam that remained unfulfilled by the formalism of the ulama's legalistic version of Islam. Sufism – which took time to be accepted in the mainstream of Sunni orthodoxy – developed as an underground, or at least parallel form of religious organization, and always retained this character. From its early beginnings, circa the middle of the tenth century, Sufis organized themselves in the form of many "schools," or rather, Sufi masters, the *pîrs*, acquired disciples and organized orders (or brotherhoods), the *tariqas* (from a word that means "ways"). The *tariqas* "were loosely organized bodies of *pîrs* and *murids* ["followers," "disciples"] following well-defined and even hierarchically-controlled 'ways' of mystical discipline, each with its rituals, its chiefs, and (of course) its endowments. These were founded on the relationship between master and disciple."[107]

Further,

> "many *tariqa* orders were international and at least at first there was a certain subordination of *pîrs* and *khaniqahs* ["Sufi house"] at a distance to the headquarters of the head of the order – usually at the founder's tomb. In this way, the several *tariqas* formed a flexibly interlocking network of authorities, which paid no attention to the political frontiers of the moment and was readily expandable into new areas.

Sufism and Sufi orders thus were a flexible, international network, sustaining popular devotion and high mysticism, but also representing an alternative social outlook.

Futuwwah, guilds, and Sufi order are facets of similar phenomena – parallel, underground or secret societies. A secret society, with esoteric codes, was endowed with "its own institutions, mores, hierarchies and secret values, its beliefs, its more or less strange non- or infra-Islamic local rituals.... [T]his esoteric proclivity inherent in every self-enclosed grouping... [was] fostered by contacts with the leading political secret societies": Batinites, Qarmats, who more or less leaned toward a terrorism that was all at once anti-Sunni in religious affairs, anti-Caliphal in political affairs, and opposed to big landowners in socioeconomic terms. "[T]he world of craftsmen and trades was...closely related to the criminal underworld," but, being rooted in aboveground commerce and production, it gradually purified the thieves' honor code – "honor and brotherhood, succor to the weak and luckless" – and "exalted it into esoteric and initiatic yearnings."[108]

Field studies would urgently be required today to ascertain whether any such form of organizations has been or is connected to jihadi terror groups. There is extensive evidence of the association of bandits, outlaws, and clandestine guilds of brigands and thugs with modern revolutionary movements. Stalin recruited Russian organized crime to work with the Bolsheviks.[109] Mao Zedong was intimately connected to various Triad gangs.[110] Marxist historian Eric Hobsbawm even devoted a book to the glorification of the coalescence of outcasts, outlaws, and revolutionaries in the form of what

[107] Hodgson, *The Venture of Islam*, pp. 214, 220f.

[108] Jean-Paul Charnay, *Principes de stratégie arabe*, Paris, L'Herne, 1984, p. 8.

[109] Edward Ellis Smith, *The Young Stalin; the Early Years of an Elusive Revolutionary*, New York, Farrar, Straus and Giroux, 1967.

[110] Jean-Louis Margolin, in Stéphane Courtois, Nicolas Werth, and Jean-Louis Panné, *Le livre noir du communisme – Crimes, terreur et repression*, Paris, Robert Laffont, 1998.

he called "social bandits."[111] Many reports have been filed regarding the dealings between al-Qaeda, Hezbollah, and other Islamists on the one hand, and drug, diamond, and smuggling gangs on the other.[112] In periods of great social dislocation and of ensuing anomie, the lower depths rise up to the surface, and tie up with elements in society they would not have known or associated with under normal circumstances – just as the futuwwah used to do. Criminal individuals and organizations that have already broken with the standard norms of social behavior and violated the usual respect for the law and the property and the lives of others can easily slide into the personality and the behavior of the "political" criminal and terrorist. Outlaws and scofflaws, unconnected to legal niceties and independent of existing structures, find it easier to emerge at the top in times of troubles. Both sides, the criminal and the revolutionary, will often find that they share many interests. The borderline between revolutionary terrorist and criminal killer is so gray that it has been crossed back and forth many a time by both sides during the twentieth century's totalitarian and terror wars.

Elsewhere in the Muslim world, Persia's mullahs have traditionally used local toughs, the *luti*, as thugs readily available to rough up designated foes. In his 1851 description of Persia, French traveler Eugène Flandin left a striking description of the *luti* mob of Isfahan recruited by the supreme *mujtahid*: "he had drawn to his banner and paid gangs of hoodlums, thiefs and killers who came from all over Persia to serve under the infamous flag that covered their crimes ... they had become the masters of Isfahan. No power was able to hinder their criminal commands.... This scum of four or five thousand madmen ... terrorized the population."[113] The street ruffians also were used by the mullahs for purposes of religious persecution, such as the assassination of Baha'i; they were "private armies" and associated in this role with "*tullab*, the religious students."[114]

[111] Eric Hobsbawm, *Primitive Rebels: Studies in Archaic Forms of Social Movement in the 19th and 20th Centuries*, Manchester, Manchester University Press, 1959.

[112] Robert Spencer, "Drug Money Sustaining al-Qaeda: US Officials," *Jihad Watch*, December 30, 2003, http://www.jihadwatch.org/archives/000519.php; "Al-Qaeda And Drugs Fuel Afghan Fighting Says NATO Commander," AFP, September 14, 2006, http://www.spacewar.com/reports/Al_Qaeda_And_Drugs_Fuel_Afghan_Fighting_Says_NATO_Commander_999.html. Matthew Levitt, "Hezbollah Drug Ring Broken Up in Ecuador," The Counterterrorism Blog, June 22, 2005, http://counterterror.typepad.com/the_counterterrorism_blog/2005/06/hezbollah_drug_.html.

[113] Eugène N. Flandin, *Voyage en Perse,* vol. 1, Paris, Elibron Classics Repica Edition, 1851, p. 290.

[114] M. Momen, "The Baha'I Community of Ashkhabad: Its Social Basis and Importance in Baha'I History: The Episode of the Murder of Hajji Muhammad Rida Isfahani, 1889," presented at a conference "Cultural Change and Continuity in Central Asia," SOAS, London,

Likewise, a singular nexus of clergy, the bazaar and the semicriminal urban class, played an essential role as an alternative power network in Iran under the Qajar and Pahlevi dynasties; it provided an infrastructure for the Islamic opposition to the shah, for the Islamic Revolution, and for the power centers of the Islamic Republic.[115] With its mosques, religious schools, publics baths, and cafés, the bazaar is traditionally a key center for social gathering and contact. It also includes the traditional athletic clubs, the *zur-khane*, whose members are *luti* of lesser or higher level. Political manifestations and religious ceremonies often started in the bazaar, also the main source of rumor mills and the source of the urban legends. Violence-prone gangs of "heavies" or "hooligans" have loomed large in street movements, whether supportive of or hostile to governments; these *aubach* or *chaku-kechan* have their recruitment pools, among *luti* and low-class layers; they are close to but distinct from the bazaar; they have arrangements with police. They are described as fervent participants in religious manifestations, in particular the flagellations of the *Ashura*.

What kind of connection the toughs have maintained with the principal pillars of the mullahs' regime – *Hezbollahi*, Guardians of the Revolution (*Pasdaran*), *Komitehs*, *Basije* – has not been examined but can be surmised. As default organizations before the revolution, as natural extensions of the regime in power, the complex threads that connect them all, from clergy to bazari, from regime thugs to regime terror apparatus, is coherent with the sociology and the political requirements of the clerical power structure. As such, *luti* and such resemble the Arab futuwwah, the brotherhoods and the lodges in the Muslim world, which in turn serve as underlying default modes of organization, for terror groups inclusively. Muslim jihad is not organized in ways that are not coherent with the sociology of the Muslim world.

April 1987, published in Shirin Akiner, ed., *Cultural Change and Continuity in Central Asia*, London, Kegan Paul International, 1991, pp. 278–305.

115 Soussan Mobasser, "Le bazaar: un acteur principal dans le réseau altrentif de relations et de communication sociales et politiques en Iran," *Cahiers d' études sur la Méditerranée orientale et le monde turco-iranien*, No. 6, juillet-décembre 1988.

5

The Odd Pedigree of Modern Jihad

> A people bewitched
> With a history written with chalks of illusion
>
> Adonis

From Islam to Pan-Islam

There has never been an Islam without jihad: Jihad is an integral part of Islam.[1] In the modern world, jihad has fared no different than the religion it serves. Just as the jihadis use Western technologies to wage their wars, they also use, if more selectively, concepts and practices that originated in the West, all the while extolling the pristine purity of the form of Islam they practice. Its present composition resulted from the splicing of modern messages into the traditional genetic material. This analysis will start from the first impact of sustained Western expansion into the core areas of Islam, toward the end of the eighteenth century.

Islam sees itself as "metahistoric, divinely guided" and "essentially outside and above" history. An article of faith in Muslim orthodoxy determines Islam to be timeless and immutable, in the image of its holy book, the Quran, emphatically defined as "uncreated."[2] Since it sees itself as self-enclosed and self-similar, Islam cannot possibly borrow from the times in which its

[1] L. Murawiec, *The Mind of Jihad*, I. Washington, DC, Hudson Institute, 2005.

[2] On this issue, see, inter alia, Gustav E. von Grunebaum, *Classical Islam:A History, 600 A.D.–1258 A.D.*, Chicago, Aldine Publications Co., 1970, p. 94; Gibb, *Mohammedanism*, p. 76; Christoph Luxenberg, *Die Syro-Aramäische Lesart des Koran, Ein Beitragzur Entschlüssselung der Koransprache*, Berlin, Das Arabische Buch, 2000, *passim*; Tillman Nagel, *Geschichte der islamischen Theologie Von Mohammed bis zur Gegenwart*, Munich, C. H. Beck, 1994; G. E. von Grunebaum, *Modern Islam: The Search for Cultural Identity*, Berkeley, University of California Press, 1972, pp. 180, 186, 209.

adherents live or from alien cultures or peoples. Islam, self-described as perfect from the very inception of its revelation, is as suspended out of time; it rests ever impervious to change in a *stasis* of sameness. "Few culture areas have been subjected to so much and so violent change as that of Islam; none perhaps has so consistently refused to accept the ontological reality of change."[3]

Instead, reverting to an idealized Golden Age that consists of Muhammad's prophethood and his first four flawless successors, the "well-guided" caliphs, allows the actuality of time to be denied. History is not an open-ended development but an entropic process of degeneracy straying ever farther away from the original perfection. For mankind, the only desirable and indeed possible course of action is harking back to that past. In 1925, Al-Azhar in Cairo, the most authoritative institution of theology, law, and learning in Sunni Islam, used a particularly revealing argument to condemn the views expressed by one of its numbers. "According to the unanimous consensus of the Muslims, Islam is the totality of the precepts transmitted by the Prophet in regard to doctrine, and legal relations among the people. These precepts form one whole and cannot be dissociated from one another."[4] Islam is of one piece, and unchanging.

On the Shiite side, Ayatollah Khomeini avers:

> Islam is not constrained by time or space, for it is eternal... what Muhammad permitted is permissible until the Day of Resurrection; what he forbade is forbidden until the Day of Resurrection. It is not permissible that his ordinances (*hudud*) be superseded, or that his teachings fall into disuse, or that the punishments [he set] be abandoned, or that the taxes he levied be discontinued, or that the defense of Muslims and their lands cease.[5]

It is then a great irony that Islam should have been massively drawing upon a modern world that was not of its making, and the workings of which were completely foreign to its very principles. All orthodoxy to the contrary, far from remaining watertight to a constant immersion in its environment, Islam has absorbed elements of a world alien to it. Ever since the relative fortunes of the *dar al-Islam* and the West were reversed more than 250 years ago, osmosis with the modern world has "contaminated" a supposedly hermetically sealed Islam.

3 Quoted by L. Bercher, *Revue des etudes islamiques*, IX, 1935, 75–86, quoted in Grunebaum, *Modern Islam*, p. 228.

4 Ibid.

5 Quoted by Martin Kramer, "Political Islam," *The Washington Papers,* No. 73, vol. VIII, CSIS/Georgetown, Beverly Hills, CA, & London, Sage Publications, 1980, 20.

What goes for Islam in general goes for jihad in particular.

The proclaimed and sought-after ideal of a politically united *dar al-Islam* – one caliphate ruling over all Muslim lands, as had been the case in the times of Muhammad and his successors the *khulafa* – eluded the Muslims as early as a few decades after the establishment of an Islamic polity. Although it lived on as an ideal of undiminished appeal, it was never reconstituted. As long as Muslims lived in a Muslim universe stretching from the Atlantic Ocean to the Bay of Bengal and farther, political fragmentation was an object of sorrow but not of scandal. Alien impingements changed this complacent mood.

Starting with the gradual demise of the Moghul Empire in the eighteenth century, the dynamics unleashed by the West helped dissolve or destroy various Muslim polities; Western expansion spurred on the surviving ones, such as the Ottoman Empire, to change. The retreat of the world of Islam was swift. After centuries of relative stalemate, the British brought to an end close to a millennium of Muslim rule in India; the French effortlessly took Egypt and later Algeria; the Russians advanced along a broad front into the ancestral lands of the Golden Horde and the Turkic lands all around the Black Sea and in Central Asia; the Dutch strengthened their control over the Insulindian archipelago. Gradually, awareness of the changes afoot spread among the faithful: "Muslims in India became aware of the decline of Islam as a world power," notably though the great pilgrimage to Mecca.[6] By the end of the nineteenth century, "the existence of an almost universal Muslim predicament, one of subjugation by the West," was general.[7] The mental map of the world Muslims were able to draw was less and less Muslim, while Muslims in larger and larger numbers stopped inhabiting a world comprised essentially of Muslim empires, as the Muslim tradition had depicted.[8]

In this bygone "natural" Islamic order, under the Ottoman Caliph, Indian Moghul or Qajar Shah, policies and decisions had been arrived at by means of the closed-door interplay of elite groupings. Powerful local notables, imperial lieutenants, and prominent clerics and soldiers were players.

[6] K. H. Ansari, "Pan-Islam and the Making of Early Indian Socialism," *Modern Asian Studies*, vol. 20 (1986), pp. 509–37.

[7] Martin Kramer, *Islam Assembled: The Advent of the Muslim Congresses*, New York, Columbia University Press, 1986, p. 3.

[8] Bernard Lewis, "The Middle East Crisis in Perspective," in *Islam in History: Ideas, People, and Events in the Middle East*, new edition, revised and expanded, Chicago & LaSalle, IL, Open Court, 1993, pp. 405–20; Bernard Lewis, *What Went Wrong: The Clash Between Islam and Modernity in the Middle East*, New York, Perennial, 2003.

Politics in the modern sense did not exist; it did not involve public deliberation nor the engagement of broad social forces. Now, more and more, as a result of the impact of the West, the instruments of rule were political manifestos and programs, books and newspapers, parties and associations, parliamentary assemblies and street demonstrations that competed with increasing vigor with the old instruments of power. What had been dealt with in the secluded privacy of the Topkapı Palace was now increasingly played out in the public realm. Larger masses once kept outside the magic circle were clamoring at gates for some form of participation. Muslims were acceding to politics in the Western sense at the same time as Western politics reached them. As a public life was developing, Islam was less and less able to order it.[9]

The community of Islam was increasingly despoiled of a visible, credible political embodiment. As time went by, no ruler was able any longer credibly to claim and offer leadership to the *umma* and its members. Once the caliph, the last surviving Muslim imperial ruler, was gone, Muslims were released from the Sharia-based political order that had once aggregated them: They now had to recompose their political order. They also were compelled to do so lest all Muslim polity disappear altogether. In spite of themselves, they were thrown into the "free market" of politics. The adaptive change of Muslim societies to the strange new world that now surrounded them first took the form of the rise of Pan-Islam, or Pan-Islamism, in the second part of the nineteenth century. "The idea of Islamic unity remained an alien concept to Muslim rulers until the 19th century, despite the pervasive feelings of religious commonality and brotherhood among the mass of the believers. Prior to the 19th century, in spite of a few, vague and isolated calls for unity, the Islamic states failed to develop a concept of unity."[10]

Birth of Pan-Islam

Pan-Islamism, then, was the notion that the political and religious unity (or union) of Islam was the solution to its distress. The new ideology was based on a few principles: the need for a strong central authority to lead Pan-Islam and impose its ideology; the rallying to the cause of the entire Muslim world; obedience to the caliph; total solidarity with the cause; readiness for

[9] This caused a phenomenon not strictly identical to, but comparable to, the release of newly urbanized masses of peasants and workers from their traditional allegiances and identifications (village, family, church) in nineteenth-century Europe [Mosca, Michels].

[10] Kemal H. Karpat, *The Politicization of Islam: Restructuring Identity, State, Faith and Community in the late Ottoman Empire*, Oxford, Oxford University Press, 2001, p. 48.

common action.[11] A fair outline of the doctrine by Jamal al-Din al-Afghani, considered one of the fathers of the doctrine, went:

> [Under the] rule of Islam over contiguous lands in a single sequence, their government was undefeatable. Their great kings ruled most of the globe . . . : The Kings of China and Europe trembled before a word of their caliphs and princes. Four hundred million Muslims, their hearts stout and ready to die as martyrs in war. Any Muslim under foreign domination is injurious to the *Umma*. After having been the world's teacher, Muslims now lag in knowledge and industry. Muslims have not forgotten that Allah promised they would inherit the earth. But their first problem is their arch-rivalries and internal discord. Unite on the Quran and Islam guarantees success: unity![12]

Pan-Islamism was the form Islam had to assume in order to exist in an international order that it had not made or defined, over which it did not hold sway, and which it needed to fend off. It was the *umma* in politics. It was now the prism through which the world of Islam perceived its new, scandalous situation of worldly inferiority and imagined remedies to rebuild its erstwhile supremacy. As "[t]he expansion of the West into Muslim lands redefined for Muslim peoples the meaning of their universality,"[13] Pan-Islam was the umma's first coherent response to its new situation as a minority in retreat, one that found itself materially and militarily overwhelmed. It was the recombinant form taken by the concept of the *umma* in a world dominated by non-Muslim powers.[14]

The situation of the *umma* thus produced both a global demand for new policies, in response to Western infringements, and a supply in the form of proposed leadership and ideology. Muslim reactions took on two principal and often conflicting forms: Pan-Islam as an official ideology developed by the Ottoman Empire and its rulers and Pan-Islam as a mass movement of religious anti-imperialism.

The caliph was God's shadow on earth, the executant of His decrees, one whose legitimacy was transmitted by an unbroken chain of succession and whom all Muslims should obey and support.[15] This was embodied in his territorial dominion. But in 1774, at the end of a long, lost war the

[11] Jacob M. Landau, *The Politics of Pan-Islam: Ideology and Organization*, Oxford, Clarendon Press, 1990, p. 5.

[12] Jamal al-Din al-Afghani, in an 1884 article in his Paris-based journal *al-Urwa al-Wuthqa*, quoted by Landau, *Pan-Islam*, p. 16.

[13] Kramer, *Islam Assembled, Pan-Islam,* p. 1.

[14] In a limited but useful sense, we may compare the relationship of the imagined community of Islam to the extant Muslim polities, with the relationship between the *Reichsidee* and Germany as a *Kulturnation*, and the actual German-speaking polities of centuries past.

[15] Albert Hourani, *Arabic Thought*, p. 107.

Ottoman Empire signed the Treaty of Kücük Kaynarca with the Russian Empire. One of the treaty's noteworthy features was the assertion by the Ottoman sultan of his spiritual jurisdiction over Muslims living outside the empire. What a change this was! Instead of conquering by force of arms as the Ottomans had done for centuries, and thus asserting his dominion over land and people, the sultan now claimed a lesser form of suzerainty, one modeled on the Christian West: Just as European powers had wrested from the sultans the *capitulations* that made them the "protectors" of the Christian communities inside the Ottoman Empire, the sultan now claimed a religiously grounded relationship to, and "spiritual" dominion over, the Muslims who lived outside his writ, outside the *dar al-Islam*.

The Ottoman court had spread the legend that Sultan Selim I had inherited the caliphate from the last Abbasid Caliph in 1517.[16] Sultan Abdülhamid I had been addressed by the title in 1774 but had not claimed the title himself. The controversial claim was not taken seriously until the reign in the 1860s and 1870s of Sultan Abdülaziz,[17] who was the first to claim the title.

As Muslim uprisings occurred in many places – Syrian rumblings of jihad in 1853; the Great Mutiny in India starting in 1857; Central Asian and Caucasus rebellions and Turkestan wars against Russian rule or incursions; Aceh wars against the Dutch – their leaders looked to the Ottomans for patronage, leadership, and support: There was a convergence of a supply and of a demand for some form of leading political authority in the world of Islam.

The assumption of the caliphal title provided much-needed leverage for the embattled Sultan Abdülhamid II (r. 1876–1909), the "sultan–caliph." As his empire unraveled on its Balkan, Russian, and Mediterranean edges, he was "drawn to claim a spiritual authority no longer dependent upon the possession of the sinews of power. His was a policy intended to conceal weakness, to create an illusion of latent strength."[18] On the other hand, the claim to the caliphate was a powerful means of rallying to the Ottoman cause Muslim nations and leaders fighting against Western powers. The sultan–caliph thus killed many birds with one stone. He himself articulated the creed:

> If we want to rejuvenate, find our previous force and reach our old greatness we ought to remember the fountainhead of our strength. What is beneficial to us is not to imitate the so-called Western civilization but to return to the *sheriat* [Sharia],

[16] *Pan-Islam*, Landau, p. 11.
[17] Hourani, *Arabic Thought*, p. 106.
[18] Kramer, *Islam Assembled*, p. 4.

the source of our strength. [...] Our relations with countries inhabited by Muslims must be expanded and we must strive for togetherness. As long as the unity of Islam continues, England, France, Russia and Holland are in my hands, because with a word the Caliph could unleash the jihad among their Muslim subjects and this would be a tragedy for the Christians.... [O]ne day Muslims will rise and shake off the infidels' yoke. [Millions of them] are beseeching God for delivery from foreign rule. They have pinned their hopes on the Caliph, the deputy of the Prophet Muhammad.[19]

In official conversation Abdülhamid told a Western diplomat:

Unlike the czar, I have abstained till now from stirring up a crusade and profiting from religious fanaticism, but the day may come when I can no longer curb the rights and indignation of my people at seeing their co-religionists butchered [by various Christian rebels] and once their fanaticism is aroused, then the whole Western world, in particular the British Empire, will have reason to fear.[20]

The Sultan broached on the theme again and again: "The entire Islamic world is, so to say, connected by an electric wire. The hand of the great Sultan of Turkey [himself] rests on its button. The least pressure on the button can disturb the whole Islamic world.[21]

In 1882, Colonel Urabi led a revolt against British influence in Egypt; in the Sudan Ahmad Muhammed who called himself the Mahdi started the rising that brought him to power in 1881–2; Tunisia grew restive in opposition to growing French control, and Sultan Abdülhamid was considering sending the Ottoman navy. He was also reportedly considering the establishment of an international Muslim League to assist the Ottoman Empire militarily. The Ottoman press was clamoring that "the Sultan [is] willing to shed his last drop of blood and to spend the last piaster of his treasure to defend the sacred religion of Islam."[22]

Both were saved for another day, but a constant flood of emissaries was streaming out of Istanbul to convey the new creed. Missions were sent to Japan, stopping over in Suez, Aden, Bombay, Ceylon, Singapore, Saigon, and Hong Kong; to China, visiting Muslim countries on the way; and to southern Russia, Iran, Afghanistan, Central Asia, the Philippines, and naturally Morocco, Algeria, Tunisia, Egypt, Sudan, and Arabia as well as the areas adjoining Lake Chad, Tanganyika, Natal, and Zanzibar[23]; emissaries were sent to Muslim communities in an old tradition of propaganda that

[19] Karpat, *The Politicization of Islam*, pp. 162, 176.

[20] From a report by Lord (Henry) Layard, quoted by Joan Haslip, *The Sultan: The Life of Abdülhamid II*, London, Cassell, 1958, p. 124.

[21] Quoted by Kramer, "Political Islam," p. 12.

[22] Landau, *Pan-Islam*, p. 41.

[23] Ibid., pp. 65–66.

went back to the Fatimid caliphs of Cairo: "Messengers in the guise of religious preachers and expounders of the Quran were sent to all quarters of the globe proclaiming the pious feelings of the Khalifa, and exhorting the true believers to persevere in their faith and to unite in a common bond in defense of Islam," a confidante of Abdülhamid wrote. It was "a constant stream of emissaries to and fro Istanbul, bearing the Pan-Islamic message. Many were sheikhs, some of whom were associated with [brotherhoods], other ulama and men of religion. More rarely, they comprised notables, traders and businessmen."[24]

While the caliph turned to Muslims, the converse was equally true: in their hour of need, Muslims turned to him as the sole remaining highly visible and legitimate political authority in the world of Islam. The leader of the Algerian resistance to the French had rallied the caliph as his leader as early as 1840, and called for his help. So did the Sanussi Brotherhood fighting the Italians in Tripolitania, the Aceh Muslims fighting the Dutch, and Yakub Bey, the East Turkestan (Xinjiang) leader in the fight against the Russians. Islam began to acquire a new international dimension that the West described as "Pan-Islam."[25]

Abdülhamid made an especial effort "to harness the entire Sufi structure to his Pan-Islamism under the supervision of the sheikh of the *tarikat*, the *shaykh al-Turuq*." He even personally joined one of them, while reaching out directly to other such important brotherhoods.[26] The Sufi brotherhoods were indeed the most direct and efficient way of reaching the broad masses of the Muslim populations, within and without the empire: Popular Islam was out of the reach of the stale establishment ulama. At the same time, Abdülhamid was ambivalent about popular Pan-Islamism, given the risk that it might escape his control. When Sheikh Shamil, the larger-than-life Chechen hero of Muslim resistance to the infidel Russians, arrived in Istanbul on his way to Mecca (the victorious czar had permitted him to go on the *hajj* after he had surrendered in 1856), "the population gave him an extraordinarily enthusiastic welcome that lasted for days, until the Porte, afraid that the popular demonstrations were escalating into anti-government shows, hastened Shamil's departure."[27]

The caliph was willing to instrumentalize the "Ottoman street," but not to be overwhelmed by it. For rulers, the paradox was powerful and

[24] Arminius Vambéry, quoted by Landau, *Pan-Islam*, p. 64.
[25] Karpat, *The Politicization of Islam*, p. 136.
[26] Landau, *Pan-Islam*, pp. 51–2
[27] Karpat, *The Politcization of Islam*, p. 35.

dangerous: In order to safeguard their realms, they needed to mobilize the masses. In so doing, they ran the risk of letting the genie out of the bottle.[28] He kept Pandora's Box slightly ajar, a difficult enough exercise, enough for the rumbling to frighten partners and opponents, never so wide open that the winds he liberated would sweep him off his throne. In this, he was perhaps a wiser ruler than many later sorcerers' apprentices who recklessly unleashed vast popular movements and were overpowered by the results.

Modernity was at work: It was not enough to rally the ulama. To mobilize the masses, the caliph needed to talk to them – and to do so, to use the literati. The caliph used the printing press, and soon, newspapers were appearing under his benevolent protection to convey a Pan-Islamic message, such as *Basiret*, which "appealed to the world's Muslims, especially in Mecca, India and Central Asia." As for the contents: "*Basiret* claimed that Muslims were endowed with a special inner bond (profound, heartfelt love) which had a permanent religious essence and compelled all Muslims to move toward central union and alliance."[29] Caught between the old and the new, the Muslims' "response [was] largely politicized.... [Their] response had (at least initially), a character of religious anti-imperialism."[30] Religious brotherhood turned into political activism.

The predominant Sunni tradition, best expounded perhaps by al-Ghazali (d. 1111 A.D., known as the "Reviver of the Faith" and whom "Orthodox Islam regards... as the final authority"), was unequivocal on this point:[31] better an injustice than a disorder, better forty years of tyranny than one day of disorder. The fear of disorder was the bugbear of Islamic political thought. As a result, the very thought of organized political action outside the purview of legitimate authority was quite unthinkable. New conditions, however, demanded an ideology capable of moving the masses. What was needed to mobilize the Muslim masses was an ideology that went beyond the narrow bounds of the political quietism in Islam.

Ideology and mobilization: these were key modern ingredients in the new broth now simmering about. These modern creatures, the ideologues and the political agitators, were equally required. The first was the charismatic adventurer Jamala al-Din al-Afghani, whose heady words of jihad we have

[28] The paradox has often occurred: It shook Hohenzollern Prussia faced with extinction at the hands of Napoleon, the Bourbons of Spain, as well as the British ruler who empowered the colonists to fight the French and Indian Wars.

[29] Karpat, *The Politicization of Islam*, pp. 124–5.

[30] Landau, p. 9.

[31] Goldziher, *Introduction*, pp. 161–2.

already heard.[32] His recurrent theme was the mobilization of Muslims (and especially their leaders and intellectuals) simultaneously against European aggression and corrupt tyrannical rule at home.[33] Both appeals were revolutionary, and the combination made them even more so. The problem with the intelligentsia and the demagogues was that they soon were busy developing their own agenda, which did not necessarily include the caliph's. This is likely why Abdülhamid kept Afghani first at arm's length, and finally in a state of gilded captivity in Istanbul (1892–7) until his death. The danger that the populist demagogue would overstep the boundaries was too great.

As early as 1877 or 1878, Afghani had drafted a letter meant for the caliph's eyes, aimed at inciting the ruler to send him on an organizing tour of India to rally Indian Muslims to unity and the caliph. The letter conjures up a messianic vision, comes close to announcing the coming of the Mahdi, includes clever scheming and realpolitik in the cause of Pan-Islam. Afghani outlines a plan to bring together the Ottoman Empire and the Muslims of India and Afghanistan and presents even more ambitious plans for the achievements of Pan-Islam. He offers to send ulama to remote parts of India, others from Afghanistan to Kokand and Bukhara, and yet others to Kashgar and Yark – and all as secret emissaries to mobilize support for the cause, the embryo of a master plan.[34] In his famous 1883 three-part article in *L'Intransigeant*, Afghani first put forth the idea of an outside attack on British India to be carried out by Russia as a means of provoking a mass uprising there, which he argued would be ignited forthwith.[35] The idea remained a tantalizing mirage and a devoutly prepared geostrategic objective for three-quarters of a century, for Turks, pan-Germanist militarymen, and Bolshevik would-be conquerors of the world.

Although there is no indication that the sultan or the Porte entrusted Afghani with its execution the union (or unity) of Islam, in Arabic *Wahdat al-Islam* or *al-Wahda al-Islamiyya* (in Turkish *Ittihad-i Islam*), was becoming a factor in world affairs. To sum up the new doctrine:

1. "All Muslims are part of one country, the head and commander of which is the caliph.
2. Muslim countries all over the world face the danger of subjugation by Europe. The enemies of Islam have gained the upper hand and

[32] See Murawiec, *The Mind of Jihad*, I, ppp. 29f, 163–5.

[33] Landau, p. 14.

[34] Jacob Landau, p. 19; Nikki R. Keddie, *Sayyid Jamal al-Din-al-Afghani: A Political Biography*, Berkeley, San Francisco, & London: University of California Press, 1972, pp. 133–8.

[35] Keddie, *Sayyid Jamal al-Din*, pp. 206–7.

have occupied Muslim lands not because of the inherent inferiority of Islam ... but because the members of the [*umma*] remained disunited, ignorant.

3. The weakness of Muslim society has resulted also from the weakness of *iman* [faith], and the believers' failure to understand properly and obey their faith. Muslims, therefore, should properly interpret Islamic principles in the light of reason and science. Predestination should not be interpreted as fatalism, and Muslims must attach importance to worldly aspects of their existence, such as material progress, rather than solely to the dogma of the faith.
4. The rejuvenation of Islam is possible through a return to its basic principles, and that, in turn, depends first and foremost on achieving the unity of the [*umma*] under the guidance of its leader, the caliph, or *amir al-Muminin*."[36]

The ever-recurring themes of Pan-Islam were summarized: "Damn the Christian hatred of Islam, smash European aggression.... Islamic union is a civilizing force thanks to its humane character.... Islam could shake the entire world with its force, renascent in the near future in a young, united Islamic nation."[37]

The Ottoman Empire itself was soon to take a radically new direction; the sultan was to be sidelined and replaced by an officers' junta, itself based on a secret society. Modernization was relentless, including its ugliest aspects. Events in Turkey foreshadowed the fate of many Muslim nations in the century to come. The Young Turks had first been established in 1889 by cadets. The Committee Union and Progress, a secret society of opponents, was in an symbiotic relationship with the Young Turks. They were not set on a firm ideology. Rather, they alternatively or simultaneously picked from a hodge-podge of different beliefs: a "pan-Turanian" ideology which vaguely aspired to ingather all the Turkic-speaking peoples, or the "Turkic" race, from Western China to Anatolia; "Ottomanism," which meant to continue the Abdülhamid's efforts to rejuvenate the empire; and "Pan-Islamism." Impatience at the sultan's inability to ward off external encroachments would not allow the sultan much time to lead the Ottoman renaisscance he had promised. Anticipating the sorry string of military takeovers that blighted so much of the history of extra-European nations in the twentieth

[36] Karpat, *The Politicization of Islam*, p. 188.

[37] So wrote the eminent Turkish intellectual Celal Nuri (1877–1939) in his 1913 book, *The Past Present and Future of Islam: Views about World Civilization and Its Political and Social Doctrines*, Landau, *Pan-Islam*, p. 83.

century, a secret society plotted to replace him and to do better what he claimed he intended to do.

In 1908, the Young Turks took power, deposed the Sultan and enthroned a puppet monarch. Their policy was unequivocally indicated in the same year, when the island of Crete announced its union with Greece: "The CUP threatened the European powers that, should they support this act, they would have to reckon with the wrath of the Muslims everywhere."[38] The Young Turks used the *hajj* to rouse Muslims energies to that effect. "At the 10th Congress of the CUP, it was decided to continue to employ Pan-Islamist policies; the 1911 Congress, held in Salonica, elaborated on this further." A "more aggressive stance" in activities and propaganda was adopted. By 1913 the CUP had installed a Pan-Islamic league in Istanbul – the Benevolent Islamic Society. The society, which published *The World of Islam,* a fortnightly, which appeared in Turkish, Arabic, Persian, and Urdu, and a nationalist newspaper in Egypt, among other activities, centralized Ottoman Pan-Islamist action: Pan-Islam had become a central tenet of the Young Turks' policy.[39]

When Italy invaded Tripolitania and Cyrenaica in 1913 and found itself at war against the Ottoman Empire, the local tribes rose up under the Senussi Brotherhood, in the name of Pan-Islamism: "It was the first resistance movement inspired by Pan-Islamism against Western occupation." Moreover, "the war was widely considered as a jihad. Enver Pasha [the Ottoman commander in Tripolitania] issued a proclamation to the warriors, urging them to fight the enemies of Islam and assuring them of the support of the world's Muslims. The entire Muslim press in the Ottoman Empire and many Muslim newspapers abroad... supported the Ottoman government and its military forces, on Pan-Islamic grounds, emphasizing the need for unity and union."[40] The Benevolent Islamic Society contributed a big share in the support apparatus. "The war contributed to the institutionalization of Pan-Islamism as a force to be employed."[41]

By 1913, the CUP, the puppeteer for the new caliph and grand vizier, tired of governing at one remove. Through a swift military putsch, it installed a military dictatorship led by a triumvirate of officers – Talaat, Jemal, and Enver – the "Three Pashas." They made the fateful choice of aligning the Ottoman Empire with the central empires and entered World War I against

[38] Landau, *Pan-Islam*, p. 88.
[39] Ibid., pp. 86–93.
[40] Ibid., p. 135.
[41] Ibid., p. 137.

the Allies. All the while, Pan-Islamism had been gaining the upper hand among the spectrum of ideologies available to the Young Turks.[42] The war was going to thoroughly transform Pan-Islamism. The long-threatened Ottoman jihad was indeed declared against the Allies powers, not without the helping hand of the revolutionary Pashas' ally, Wilhelminian Germany.

"Jihad Made in Germany"

Germany's military links with the Ottoman Empire were not new. They harked back to Lieutenant Helmuth von Moltke's ("The Elder") private visit to Istanbul in 1835. A few years later, the Sultan hired Moltke to advise on the training of the new army. More Prussian instructors followed;[43] the military connection only expanded with time. Later, in the course of two missions (1886–95 and 1909–13), General Colmar von der Goltz reorganized the Ottoman army. In 1913, General Liman von Sanders was appointed general instructor of the Ottoman army and, when war broke out in 1914, commander of the Turkish Army Corps of Constantinople. He was later to head the Ottoman general staff. In the Great War no fewer than 30,000 German officers and soldiers came to fight on the Middle Eastern theaters of war on the side of the Ottomans.

Under Bismarck's stewardship, Germany's attitude toward the greater Middle East had been rather detached: The region was of "secondary" interest in the Iron Chancellor's foreign policy, as opposed to his "primary" interest, which lay in Europe, east and west. The Middle East was not worth the bones of a single Pomeranian grenadier.[44] In 1898, having ousted the old statesman, the rash new emperor Wilhelm II was mounting his great challenge to the British Empire. The motto of his *Weltpolitik*, *Ein Platz an der Sonne* (a place in the sun) implied that established imperial powers had to make way for newcomers. The pan-Germanic challenge was multifarious. The German navy was growing at a fast clip, while an aggressive German policy was developing in Latin America, Africa, the Far East, and the Middle East.

[42] On the entrance of the Ottoman Empire in the war, see Efraim Karsh and Inari Karsh, *Empires of the Sand: The Struggle for Mastery in the Middle East, 1789–1923*, Cambridge, MA, Harvard University Press, 2001. On the CUP, see Bernard Lewis, *The Emergence of Modern Turkey*, Oxford, Oxford University Press, 1975.

[43] Lewis, *The Emergence of Modern Turkey*, p. 82.

[44] Wolfgang G. Schwanitz, "The German Middle East Policy, 1871–1945," in Wolfgang G. Schwanitz and Bernard Lewis eds., *Germany and the Middle East, 1871–1945*, Princeton Papers, vol. X–XI, Princeton, NJ, Marcus Wiener Publishers, 2001, pp. 1–23.

In the first place, the Kaiser's policy was anti-British; the Middle East was a primary stage for challenging the British. In 1898, Wilhelm undertook a long tour of the region that led him from a triumphant welcome in Istanbul to highly publicized sojourns in Jerusalem and Damascus. There, on December 8, he proclaimed himself the friend of "300 million Muslims." He let it be known that he had personally paid for a new marble monument at Saladin's tomb in Damascus, visited with much fanfare. German propaganda in the region referred to him as "*Haji* Wilhelm Mohammed" and spread the rumor that he had secretly converted to Islam following an incognito pilgrimage to Mecca. "Passages of the Quran were found that showed the Kaiser had been ordained by God to free Muslims from infidel rule."[45] Sheikh Abdullah, who had welcomed him in Damascus, in return assured him that he had not only earned the gratitude of the "300 million Muslims," but also their love.[46]

The Kaiser was following a script drafted by his chief adviser in the matter, leading Islamologist Baron Max von Oppenheim, whose enthusiastic supporter he was. Wilhelm believed in the latter's thesis regarding the "world-wide importance of the Pan-Islamist movement" and in Germany's ability to harness it for Germany 's own interests. Islam was a revolutionary force and would play an essential role in winning the war against the English, the Russians, and the French.[47] This revolutionary intent fitted in the German Empire's broader war strategy, the *Revolutionierungspolitik*, policy of revolutionizing, which targeted the British and Russian empires in the first place.

"War by revolution" included two main projects. The first was to set off a revolution to knock Russia out of the war. To that effect, Germany would strongly assist the Russian Socialist movement and Nationalist opponents within the empire. The second part was to incite the Ottoman Empire to launch a jihad against Germany's enemies, and to assist Constantinople in order to undermine the colonial possessions of the Allies. Germany's plans also aimed at prompting Mexico to enter the war on the side of the central empires. State Secretary Arthur Zimmermann was in charge of the plan, and made sure that Oppenheim's proposals were read by the top levels of the German military leadership.[48]

45 Thomas L. Hughes, "The German Mission to Afghanistan, 1915–1916," in Schwanitz and Lewis, *Germany and the Middle East*, pp. 25–63.

46 Wolfgang G. Schwanitz, "Djihad 'Made in Germany': Der Streit um den Heilgen Krieg, 1914–1915," *Socialgeschichte, Leiden, 18 (2003)*, p. 24.

47 Fritz Fischer, *Griff nach der Weltmacht: Die Kriegspolitik des kaiserlichen Deutschland 1914–1918*, Düsseldorf, Droste Verlag, 1961–7 (reprint, 2004), p. 11.

48 Hans-Ulrich Seidt, *Berlin Kabul Moskau: Oskar von Niedermayer und Deutschlands Geopolitik*, Munich, Universitas Verlag, 2002, p. 56.

In the margin of a July 30, 1914, telegram, Wilhelm II noted in longhand: We must "publicly tear off the mask of England's Christian peacefulness.... Our consuls in Turkey and India, our agents and so forth, must inflame the entire Muslim world and move them to rise in fierce insurgency against this hated, lying nation of grocers devoid of any conscience; for if we are to bleed, England should at least lose India."[49] There was much emotional energy behind the policy.

On November 11, 1914, the Ottoman Empire declared war on Great Britain and France and their allies.[50] Nine days later, on November 14, signed by the *Şeyhülislam* (*sheikh al-Islam*) Khayri Efendi, the highest religious authority of the empire, a five-part fatwa was promulgated in Istanbul to justify the hostilities.[51]

> When it is verified that the enemies have committed aggression against Islam and the Muslim lands have been seized and plundered and Muslim populations made captive, and the Padishah of Islam thereupon gives orders for the Jihad in the form of a general mobilization, then, in accordance with the beautiful verse "Go forth, light and heavy! Struggle in God's way with your possessions and your selves" ([Quran] 9:41), is the Jihad a duty (*fard*) on all the Muslims and does it become an individual duty (*fard' ayn*) on Muslims in every land, young or old, on foot or mounted...to hasten to the *Jihad* with property and person?
>
> ***Answer*: It does.**
>
> It being verified, by their attacking today...the abode of the Caliphate of Islam and the Imperial Guarded Dominions, that Russia, Britain and France are hostile to the Caliphate of Islam and are striving – God Almighty forfend – to extinguish and destroy the sublime light of Islam, it is a religious duty for all Muslims under the rule of those powers and of states which are aiding and abetting them, to proclaim the *Jihad* against such governments and actively to hasten to the Holy War?
>
> ***Answer*: It is.**
>
> Whereas the achievement of the desired end is dependent on all the Muslims' hastening to the *Jihad*, if – God Almighty forfend – they were to lag behind, would it be a grave act of rebellion fore them to do so

49 Fischer, *Griff nach der Weltmacht*, p. 110.

50 As a belated response to Russia's declaration of war on November 2 and the two Western allies' own declaration of war on November 5.

51 Full text, translation, and presentation by Geoffrey Lewis, "The Ottoman Proclamation of Jihad in 1914," *The Islamic Quarterly*, vol. XIX, nos. 3 and 4 (July–December 1975), pp. 157–63.

and would they incur the wrath of God and the penalty for this gross rebellion?

Answer: **They would.**

Even if the Muslim populations of the aforementioned governments, which are making war on the Islamic government, are compelled and constrained under pain of death for themselves and even of the destruction of all their families, it being totally prohibited in the Law for them to fight the soldiers of Islam, if they do fight them do they merit the fire of hell?

Answer: **They do.**

As Muslims who are under the rule of the governments of England, France, Russia, Serbia and Montenegro and their coadjutors will cause injury to the Caliphate of Islam if, in the present war, they take up arms against Germany and Austria, who are aiding the Imperial Islamic government, this being great sin will they merit painful torment?

Answer: **They will.**[52]

The fatwa accompanied the Proclamation of Jihad against the Allies drafted by the Council of High Learning, also signed by the sheikh and issued under the authority of the sultan–caliph. The Proclamation of jihad itself expanded on the fatwa:

The Moscovite government seeks to reduce mankind to slavery . . . the governments of England and France . . . account it the most agreeable pleasure to keep millions of Muslims under the halter of slavery in the general conflict which is now ablaze. They nourish base aspirations, such as wresting away freedom and ensuring their own interests beneath their unlawful and tyrannical domination.

It skirted the thorny question of allying with one infidel against another in the course of a jihad, especially in the case of the Austrians, the Ottomans' eternal foe in Central Europe and the Balkans. Many earlier Ottoman wars had not been jihad wars. This one was, and it was a world war:

[T]he Muslims in general who are under the oppressive grasp of the aforesaid tyrannical governments in such places as the Crimea, Kazan, Turkestan, Buk hara, Khiva and India, and those dwelling in China, Afghanistan, Iran, Africa and other regions of the earth, are hastening to join in this great Jihad to the best of their ability, with life and property, alongside the Ottomans, in conformity with the relevant holy fatwas. . . . O community [umma] of Muhammad! You have been established as a meritorious community to be taken as an example for emulation among mankind, by following the beautiful way of life of the exalted Prophet . . . of Muslims, who are

[52] Ibid., pp. 157–8.

the obedient servants of God! Of those who go to Jihad for the sake of the happiness and salvation of the believers in God's unity, the lost of those who remain alive is felicity, while the rank of those who depart to the next world is martyrdom. In accordance with God's beautiful promise, those who sacrifice their lives to give life to the truth will have honor in this world and their latter end is paradise....

O Muslims who are athirst and longing for honor and felicity.... The Commander of the Faithful, the Caliph of the Muslims, summons you to the Jihad. O warriors of Islam! By the beautiful divine promise it is corroborated and announced that you will destroy and annihilate the enemies of the Faith and gladden the hearts of the Believers with eternal felicity by the aid and grace of the Almighty and the spiritual assistance of our revered Prophet.[53]

The precedent was thus set in the modern age: It was not some local chieftain or *alim* or mufti who called for religious war against one or the other Western nation. The sultan–caliph was throwing in the full weight of his legitimacy. A worldwide jihad had been enabled. While the fatwa and the Proclamation of Jihad were in the straight continuity of the traditional doctrine and practice of holy Muslim war, new elements were creeping in. Modern jihad was not going to be a carbon copy of traditional jihad.

The "new" jihad was the instrument of the Young Turks' war of choice. The fatwas and the Proclamation were translated and distributed by the *Teshkilat-i Mahsusa* (TM), the intelligence service created by Enver (each of the triumvirs had set up his own intelligence operation) out of Ottoman officers who had served under him in Tripolitania and expanded during the war. A high-powered and efficient operation, it earned a flattering description from Colonel Walter Nicolai, one of the leading figures in German military intelligence: "[a] far-spread, efficient and secret Ottoman political intelligence service, whose field of operations included Central Asia."[54] The TM combined intelligence, counterintelligence, and irregular warfare capabilities, as well as political warfare – and jihad.[55]

[53] Ibid., pp. 160–2.

[54] Walter Nicolai, *Geheime Mächte, Internationale Spionage und ihre Bekämpfung im Weltkrieg und Heute, Berlin, 1923* [*The German Secret Service*, translated, with an additional chapter, by George Renwick, London, S. Paul, 1924], 94. It comes as no surprise that the Turkish Republic asked Walter Nicolai in 1926 to set up a national intelligence service. Nicolai in the meantime had become a fervent advocate of a German alliance with Soviet Russia. Interestingly, in private discussion with the author, a former director of German Military Intelligence (*Militärischer Abschirmdienst*) was still waxing admirative about the Ottoman Intelligence Service [1983].

[55] Tilman Lüdke, *Jihad Made in Germany: Ottoman and German Propaganda and Intelligence Operations in the First World War*, Münster, LIT, 2005, pp. 75–82.

The agency sent agents throughout the Muslim world to spread the jihad; in addition, Muslim societies led by exiled Pan-Islamist figures, such as the Society for the Progress of Islam, were established in Europe to perform the same function.[56]

The call for jihad was also spread by the *Nachrichtenstelle für den Orient* (NfO, News Organization for the Orient), a new political warfare agency for the Muslim world created in Berlin by the Ottomans' ally, the German Imperial government and its military intelligence service. This "translation-cum-agitation office," employing a staff of orientalists, rapidly developed up to forty offshoots from Istanbul on to the rest of the Muslim world.[57]

On the Ottoman side, the chief architect of the jihad policy was Enver Pasha. Born in 1881, the young officer had joined the Young Turks while garrisoned in Salonica. In 1908, Enver's mutiny against the Istanbul authorities made him famous overnight and propelled him into the highest ranks of the CUP. He went to Berlin as military attaché (1909–11), learned German, and became friends with prominent German military leaders, such as General Hans von Seeckt. Enver even grew a handlebar moustache in the style of Kaiser Wilhelm. He was then sent to North Africa to fight the Italian Army – rather ineffectually – though he emerged a propaganda poster boy, a "Hero of Islam." He then returned to the Ottoman capital and applied his military glory to changing the politics of the empire. "On 23 January 1913 . . . the Unionists launched their surprise assault on the Sublime Porte. Led by Enver Bey, a small party of officers forced their way into the cabinet room, shooting the Minister of War Nazim Pasha as they did so. At the point of their guns, the aged [President of the Council of State] Kamil Pasha wrote out his resignation, which Enver triumphantly took to the [Imperial] Palace and presented to the Sultan." Bloody purges ensued. "From then until 1918, Turkey was governed by a virtual military dictatorship, dominated by three men, Enver, Talaat and Cemal Pashas."[58] Enver and his colleagues were the first of the sad cohort of the "Bonapartes" of the twentieth century – more or less victorious military leaders who gore their way to the top of the state and confiscate power in the name of whatever ideology they have chanced upon. After oscillations similar to that of his Young Turk peers he ended up espousing Pan-Islamism. Whether or not his heart was throbbing for it or not, he threw in his lot with it.

[56] Kramer, *Islam Assembled*, p. 55.
[57] Schwanitz, "Djihad 'Made in Germany,'" pp. 2, 7–34.
[58] Lewis, *The Emergence of Modern Turkey*, p. 225.

Enver had been nicknamed *Napoleonlik* by his fellow officers. In 1914, he married a minor princess, daughter of the late Sultan Abdülmejid, which further enhanced his power. In the bizarre, conspiratorial world of the CUP and its triumvirs, Enver played the decisive role in striking the wartime alliance with Imperial Germany: Talaat Pasha was in favor of England until 1913, Cemal was rather pro-French. Enver had become minister of war; he appointed himself chief of the general staff and, on August 2, 1914, signed the momentous accords of alliance between the Ottoman and German Empires, the alliance that promoted jihad as a method to "revolutionize" and debilitate their enemies.[59]

Max von Oppenheim, who engineered the Muslim prong of the strategy, has aptly been called the "German *Abu Jihad*" (father of the jihad).[60] A twenty-year veteran of archeological and ethnological studies in the region, and of the German diplomatic service, Oppenheim could boast as few Westerners could of detailed knowledge of the tribal makeup of much of the Muslim world and personal acquaintance with many of its leading personalities. On August 2, 1914, he was recalled into the Reich's diplomatic service. His ambitious plan for a generalized anti-British, anti-French, and anti-Russian jihad aimed at "fomenting rebellion in the Islamic territories of our enemies."[61] A first version of the project, a cable to the chancellor, submitted in July 1898, had reviewed the potential of the Pan-Islamist movement as a strategic auxiliary for the Reich. It was the inspiration behind the resounding speeches of the Hohenzollern tourist of the Middle East. Oppenheim already then was banking on a pro-German, anti-British jihad.

Both Germany's political and military authorities demanded jihad action on the Middle Eastern front as soon as the war broke out. On August 2, 1914, and again three days later, von Moltke, Jr., nephew of the great field-marshal, now chief of the German general staff, told the German foreign office in no uncertain terms: "[It is] of the highest importance... [to set off] insurrection in India and Egypt, and the Caucasus as well. Thanks to the [war alliance] treaty with Turkey, [we] will be able to implement those ideas and rouse the fanaticism of Islam."[62] The famous Swedish spy-explorer Sven Hedin concurred and reported that the amir of Afghanistan was "raring to

[59] In the chapter of his Constantinople memoirs devoted to the Ottoman genocide against the Armenians, U.S. Ambassador Henry Morgenthau gives very suggestive portraits of especially Enver and Talaat in *The Murder of a Nation*, New York, reprint Armenian General Benevolent Union, 1974, pp. 4, 66–7, 72–86.

[60] By German historian Wolfgang G Schwanitz.

[61] Schwanitz and Lewis, *Germany and the Middle East*, p. 7.

[62] Fischer, *Griff nach der Weltmacht*, p. 113.

conquer India," and only needed German support to do so. A mission to Afghanistan was set into motion; plans to take the Suez Canal were hatched; contacts were renewed with Abbas Hilmi, the ex-Khedive deposed in 1914 by the British; connections were opened to the Senussi leadership in North Africa through Enver Pasha; ideas were developed to gain the alliance of both the *sharif* of Mecca and his rival Abdalaziz ibn Saud.

Von Moltke had urged Minister of War Enver Pasha to proclaim the jihad. As we have seen, the pliant sultan and *sheikh al-Islam*, prodded by a triumvir characterized by "energy, remorselessness, cold-blooded determination, pitiless intention," complied.[63]

Max von Oppenheim's Grand Design

Max von Oppenheim now presented his expanded and updated grand design, a blueprint for joint German–Ottoman action. His 136-page memorandum *Denkschrift betreffend die Revolutionierung des islamischen Gebiete unserer Feinde* (*The Revolutionizing of Our Enemies' Islamic Possessions*) spells out the ways and means of a grand jihad. He neatly outlined the strategic rationale of the grand design, to wit: "England's colonial empire is her most vulnerable spot." Hence, Oppenheim wrote:

> [O]nly when the Turks break into Egypt and when red-hot insurgencies set India ablaze can England be tamed. If it be so, British public opinion will force the government in London . . . either to send a large part of the Fleet, perhaps half of it, to India, to save their many people there and their billions of invested capital, and Britain's world position, or, should [they] not be able to do so, [they would be forced to] sign a peace agreement in our favor. [. . .] The entire way in which our foe is waging war gives us the right and the necessity of our self-preservation the duty to take up such powerful weapons and make use of them in the struggle that has been forced upon us.[64]

The first phase, Oppenheim explained, should be to carry out "systematic and clearly-directed propaganda" which should "use the aura of the Sultan Caliph and be spread in his name," namely as a "call to Holy War." The effort was to be centralized in Istanbul, "but always under German leadership . . . but in such a way that the Turks may believe we are only a friendly

[63] "Enver Pasha and His Times," http://www.geocities.com/enver1908/?20062, accessed June 2, 2006.

[64] Max von Oppenheim, *Denkschrift betreffend die Revolutionierung des islamischen Gebiete unserer Feinde*, Politisches Archiv des Auswärtigen Amtes, Berlin, P Arch AA R 20938, pp. 2–3. My gratitude goes to Dr. Wolfgang Schwanitz who kindly communicated this text to me, as well as many other crucial elements of this story.

adviser." Enver Pasha agreed with it all, he added. Stations would have to be created in Ma'an, Jeddah, Van, Damascus, Basra, Baghdad, Kerbala, Tabriz, Busher, and ten more cities under the elastic rubric of *Nachrichten*; German agents would have to be sent to Mecca, Medina, and Jeddah.[65]

Propaganda and preliminary organizing, recruitment, and so on, should start in Egypt so that, when the Turkish troops approached, a general insurrection would occur. "The whole of Egypt is anti-British," save the Christians.

> We must especially bring to the fore the religious element, the Al-Azhar, the religious brotherhoods. We must launch little putsches, violent actions, etc., whether they succeed or not.... The more cruel the reprisals to be expected, and the more they strike the innocent, the more they will heat up the rage and the fanaticism of the people... [and will] move the urban masses and the fellahin to fight to the death to expel the British. [...] We cannot count on a popular insurrection at present, in spite of the hatred directed at the foreign occupier.

However, the ferment can be helped along; when Enver's troops and a German army enter Egypt, the Khedive will tilt decisively, and then so will the populace. At that point,

> the "Holy War" on the Nile will break out. British civil servants will be killed in town and country. The British garrison in Khartoum will meet the same fate as Gordon.... As soon as the Turks have won the first battle, England's fate in Egypt will have been sealed. The Suez Canal will be locked, and violent risings will take place in India, which in turn will have a major impact on the overall strategic situation.[66]

Similar action was to be taken in the Caucasus where "it would be easy to raise 20 to 30,000 experienced and fanatical warriors against Russia."[67] Persia is not neglected, especially due to "its traditional significance for the Orient" since she "still possesses the greatest spiritual influence upon India, Afghanistan and Russia's Muslim possessions." Persia is "unanimously anti-British and anti-Russian."[68] Oppenheim's otherwise cool, calculating, and well-informed view sometimes veers into wishful thinking, such as when in defiance of all commonsense he assures his reader – the Kaiser – that "Persia would make no difficulty in acknowledging the hegemony of the Turks."[69]

In spite of such arrant fantasy, Oppenheim's grand design was not wholly unrealistic – provided German arms had gained the upper hand in Europe.

65 Ibid., pp. 7–14.
66 Ibid., pp. 20–30.
67 Ibid., p. 54.
68 Ibid., p. 58.
69 Ibid., p. 60.

The plan called for bringing together a Turkish–Persian–Afghan alliance "which would enable an Afghan march on Northwest India ... [that] would cause a mighty revolution in the whole of India, which could mean the end of British rule in the Indian [sub-]continent." Therefore, "the task at hand would be to gain the support of the Porte for this plan. It would not be difficult to set off a rising of the fanatical Persians."

Afghanistan was central to the strategy: "I have long considered that in case of a war opposing Germany to England, the participation of the Amir of Afghanistan and his invasion of India to be of the highest importance. A great general Indian insurrection will only occur as Afghan troops march into the Indus Valley, naturally after India itself has made itself ready for revolution."[70] Hence, the ragged epic of the German mission to Afghanistan, the steppe-and-mountain counterpart to T. E. Lawrence's sand-dunes yarn, will be examined shortly. The differences were that the Germans never had an effective public-relations agent and that they lost the war.[71]

The "fanatically Muslim Afghan people," Oppenheim continued, were enthused by the sultan–caliph's call. "Some Indians will join, members of a committee of fanatical nationalists who have come to Germany to prepare an Indian revolution." Their networks reached far and deep into India, where most educated classes, Oppenheim stated, were anti-British. The *Svadeshi* movement was promoting boycotts and sabotage, while the *Svaraj* movement "aims at bringing about independence by using all possible means, including political assassination.... There is a whole series of revolutionary associations and secret societies." India's Muslims were increasingly dissatisfied, "and they are the most warlike and fervent part of the population."[72] Just as the Great Mutiny of 1857 broke out as a result of England's preoccupation with the Crimean War, the Great War in Europe would open spaces for India, Oppenheim reasoned. And more concretely, he added: "In complete quiet, I have established a committee of Indians who live here and in Switzerland, 18 members strong, highly imbued with our ideas, educated people of high organizing abilities and intelligence, and animated by a burning patriotism." Some of them, he reported, "are ready to participate in our revolutionary propaganda.... Some are chemists, a profession they embraced because of their revolutionary intent. They have sworn themselves

[70] Ibid., p. 71.

[71] See David Fromkin,"The Importance of T. E. Lawrence," *The New Criterion*, vol. 10, no. 1 (September 1991), http://www.newcriterion.com/archive/10/sept91/fromkin.htm, accessed April 3, 2006.

[72] Oppenheim, *Denkschrift betreffend die Revolutionierung*, pp. 81–2.

to die and committed themselves to kill traitors," and were being infiltrated back into India. "I believe it possible to set India afire, to force England to make peace with us.... We must use all possible connections into India, as well as Mecca, the Muslim religious brotherhoods, Hadramut, etc."[73] The German "Abu Jihad" concludes:

In the struggle to the death against England that has been forced upon us, Islam will become one of our mightiest weapons. Egypt and India are the Achilles' heel of the mighty maritime British colossus. This is why England has for long done all she can to prevent us from connecting with the Pan-Islamic and nationalist movements of the Orient. But the ground was being prepared for the rising of Islam in connection with us.... Everywhere [in the Muslim world] prayers are made in mosques for our victory. Such is the disposition, in the Turkish population to start with, but also in the whole world of Islam in today's historical moment where the entire globe is burning with the greatest of all wars, in which for the first time in many centuries the whole of Islam has been called to fight its enemy.... The Sultan-Caliph has now declared Holy War against the enemies of Germany. The world of Islam and the Central Empires fight shoulder to shoulder for their very survival.[74]

Oppenheim vigorously insisted that for a successful implementation of the plan, "[w]e must supply the Turks with personnel, money and equipment, and there, satisfactory results will only be attained if we apply very sizable resources. Half measures would be useless. The success we hope for is however worth a major effort." All assessments concur that the resources never met the requirements. "The actual commitment of resources and personnel in the Islamic world turned out to be... totally insufficient and the result attained nearly zero."[75] The foremost historian of the affair accepts that "[i]n the end, the execution of the jihad was disappointing for Max von Oppenheim [...] it turned out that the majority of Muslims ignored the jihad, although the Germans spent a lot of money for the expeditions... and for Pan-Islamic propaganda printed in Berlin like the weekly *al-Jihad*." One of the leading German participants in the venture, the dragoman Karl Schabinger, concluded that "the seeds of an uprising had been planted. One day there would be an accumulation of colonial people ready to turn against their rulers."[76] The proclamation of jihad was not a total failure: "It certainly did not generate any dramatic results, in terms of numbers" but, as a contemporary French military intelligence report he quotes analyzed: "Turkey, Tripolitania, the Libyan desert, and Darfur have risen for the

[73] Ibid., pp. 90–2.
[74] Ibid., pp. 126–7.
[75] Fischer, *Griff nach der Weltmahcht*, p. 116.
[76] Schwanitz, "The German Middle East Policy," p. 9.

Holy War, without any doubt.... One gets the impression that India has remained loyal, but we know that the Dutch Indies have known some effervescence. Iran has been gravely troubled, Afghanistan excited and Egypt trembling.... There is no doubt that the words 'Holy War' have been pronounced and exploited.... They failed, indeed, but they caused no end of trouble to the Allied powers."

In the long-range perspective of history, "[t]he qualitative gains of the [jihad] proclamation were not so insignificant as the quantitative ones. Quite a few brilliant and dedicated Muslims hurried to Istanbul to share in what they considered the war of Islam"[77] Here may be one of the most significant achievements of the "Jihad Made in Germany:" Even though it helped the German Reich remarkably little, it helped jihad considerably. For the first time in many centuries the whole of Islam has been called to fight its enemy.[78] For the first time, rather than a local or regional holy war, it was a worldwide jihad.

The Pan-Islamist jihadi propaganda had been spread all over the world of Islam in all of its major languages. Much – probably most – of the Pan-Islamist activity during the war years was carried out far from the limelight. The *Teskilat*, the Special Organization originally set up by Abdülhamid for clandestine work, carried out much of this activity. "Its agents continued to serve the [Young Turks], parallel with the agents of the Benevolent Islamic Society.... Indeed, propaganda was the main Pan-Islamic activity of the [Young Turks] (and the Germans) during World War I."[79]

But another, even less quantifiable type of work and of impact may be adjudicated as one of the most significant effects of the "Jihad Made in Germany:" it was the selection, training, and development of a jihadi cadre force, clusters of individuals who, five, ten, or twenty years later, would emerge as the local, regional, national, or international leaders of jihad.

In the geostrategic conception that tended to prevail in the German Reich, Britain was the arch-enemy, the maritime power dead-set against Germany the continental power.[80] India was the keystone of the British Empire, and Afghanistan was the gateway into India. The political and military mission sent by Berlin to Kabul early on in World War I was a tool of the policy to

77 Landau, *Pan-Islam*, pp. 102–3.

78 Ibid.

79 Ibid., pp. 104–5.

80 This was implicitly or explicitly the sense of the geopolitics of Friedrich Rätzel, (*Erdenmacht und Völkerschicksal*, Stuttgart, Kröners Taschenausgabe, 1941), and Karl Haushofer (*Der Kontinentalblock. Mitteleuropa – Eurasien – Japan*, München, Zentralverlag der NSDAP, 1941) the two intellectual leaders of the German school of geopolitics.

pull the Indian prop out from under the British Empire. As an integral part of the German–Ottoman jihad, the Afghan project intended to leverage what its authors called "the fanaticism of Islam" against the British, throwing in Indian nationalism for good measure.

> By Sept. 3, 1914 the [German] Foreign Office had agreed that Germany would assist the Indian nationalists, and for the next few weeks, there were almost daily Indian–German meetings to discuss next steps. On September 9, two months before the jihad was proclaimed, the Kaiser declared that Muslims in Entente [Central Powers] arms would not be treated as belligerents but would be sent to the Caliph in Turkey when taken prisoners.[81]

Oppenheim had assembled a core group of pro-German Indian revolutionaries, and more now flocked into Germany, so that in early 1915, the "Indian Independence Committee" was established at a meeting held in Berlin. The committee was subsidized on a regular basis by the foreign office. "Several prominent Hindu leaders left India in 1914 to campaign abroad for Indian freedom."

But distance was an insuperable obstacle. A forward base was needed closer to the planned theater. Imperial Germany hence threw itself into a new version of the "Great Game," with Afghanistan the centerpiece of the struggle. The Reich's strategists were pressing their Ottoman allies, their Persian friends, their hoped-for Afghan partners to follow in the footsteps of the Muslim conquerors of India, such as Mahmud of Ghazna or Babur, whose tomb General Hans von Seeckt, one of the designers of the anti-British jihadi plans, had reverently visited.

The German ambassador in Constantinople von Wangenheim reported in August 1914 on a meeting with Ottoman members of parliament and Syrian notabilities: "In agreement with Enver Pasha" they had proposed "to support the revolutionary movement in [Egypt] and possibly Afghanistan," news that Oppenheim welcomed as a "godsend."[82] Accordingly, the diplomatic head of the Afghan mission, Werner Otto von Hentig, arrived in the Ottoman capital in April 1915 with an aristocratic and "charismatic" Indian political exile, Kumar Mahendra Pratap, who had been received with some luster by the kaiser in Berlin in February.[83] Together, at Enver Pasha's behest, they were granted an audience by the sultan who bestowed Allah's blessing on the expedition and its purpose.[84] They also spent six hours

81 Hughes, "The German Mission," p. 32.
82 Seidt, p. 49.
83 Hughes, "The German Mission," p. 39.
84 Seidt, *Berlin Kabul Moskau*, p. 77.

weaving plans with the former khedive of Egypt Abbas Hilmi. And off they were to Afghanistan with a group of Germans, Ottomans, and Indians, with the Bavarian geographer and officer Oskar von Niedermayer as military head.

After grueling adventures through deserts and mountain ranges, hounded all the while by the British and their local auxiliaries, the mission arrived in Herat in August 1915 and that October in Kabul, where they were the honored guests of the King (amir) Habibullah, a crafty ruler accustomed to playing balancing games among tribes internally and great powers externally. With an eye on military developments in Europe, the calculating politician responded equivocally to the guests' insistent entreaties to sign a formal alliance. By December, however, his brother Nasrullah Khan was hinting that the king would be ready to sign the treaty, and by January 1916, the draft was indeed autographed by him and by the Germans. The latter were hopeful that the 80,000 men of the regular Afghan army, or at least the 43,000 whom they believed to be combat-ready, would now be dispatched into the Indian Raj's North-West Province and thence into the north Indian valley. A large part of the ruling elite was pressing the king to do so. Shortly after the arrival of the expedition, the king's relative Mahmud Tarzi wrote in his newspaper: "Eat, *Aga*! So that you will not be eaten!"[85]

Military events thousands of miles away interfered: After the Russian Army took Erzurum from the Ottomans, the King' enthusiasm waned, and he went back on his word. The Germans found themselves empty-handed; soon most returned west. As the historian puts it, "The results of the Kabul sojourn... lied with long-term consequences, not in the unfulfilled immediate expectations." For one, the king was murdered twenty-one months after the German delegation's departure and replaced by a decidedly pro-German leader Amanullah, who proceeded in May 1919 to open hostilities against the British, in what became the Third Afghan War. As occurs often in history, the unanticipated consequences of human action override the plans and intents of the actors. Far more important indeed than Germany's absent gains were the developments set into motion by the German mission regarding India.

In Stockholm, whence the India Revolutionary Committee operated; in Berlin, where a number of Indian revolutionaries were active; in San Francisco, where many arrived; in New York, where the Free Hindustan Movement was working with the Irish Fenians (both encouraged by German

[85] Ibid., pp. 84–7.

intelligence, with Major Franz von Papen as paymaster for the arms destined for India), an assault on the British raj was being hatched. The Rajput prince Kumar Mahendra Pratap was an outspoken ally of Germany. As he had said in 1914, "I began to feel decisive sympathy for the Germans who were fighting this dirty British Empire."[86] The prince had been wined and dined by the German military and political elite in Berlin. Regarding the Indian revolutionaries, "it was not a mean achievement on their part to have acquired in Berlin the status of the representatives of a belligerent power, so as to enlist the support of the German government for India's struggle against British imperialism."[87] It was one of them who had recruited Mahendra Pratap.

As a member of the failed German mission to Afghanistan, Pratap had remained in Kabul where he was now joined by Muhamamad Barakatullah, or Barkat-Ullah (1859–1927), an alim who had met Afghani in 1883, a veteran Pan-Islam activist, and publisher of Islamist journals in Japan, who was now the second in command of the Berlin-based Indian National Committee. The German consulate in San Francisco had paid his transatlantic trip toward Berlin. In 1912, Barakatullah had said,

> There is really one man who holds the peace of the world in the hollow of his hand, and that man is Emperor William of Germany. In case of a European war, it is the duty of the Muslims to be united, to stand by the Khalif, and to side with Germany.... All that is required is a leader, and that leader will arise in Central Asia, probably in Afghanistan. The firing of an Afghan gun will give the signal for the rising of all Islam as soon as she [Afghanistan] is ready to open her gates for believers to fight under the green banner of the Prophet.[88]

On December 1, 1915, in Kabul, Mahendra Pratap proclaimed a provisional government of India in exile, with Barakatullah as prime minister; the former Sikh and Muslim convert Maulvi Obeidullah, a Deobandi figure and a future, lifelong Bolshevik fellow-traveler, as minister for home and foreign affairs; the Pan-Islamist figure Muhammad Ali as secretary; and Oskar von Niedermayer as minister of war.[89] This "government" would have been no more than a small historical footnote had it not intersected developments afoot in India, Russia, and Germany. In India, the *Khilafat* movement was transforming the Muslim population; in Germany, ideas of a postwar *revanche* were stirring thoughts of warfare in the Orient against

[86] Hughes, "The German Mission," p. 38.

[87] M. N. Roy, *Memoirs*, New Delhi, Ajanta Publications, 1964 (reprint 1984), p. 286.

[88] Ibid., p. 40.

[89] Seidt, *Berlin Kabul Moskau*, p. 85.

the British – but this time, with the help and cooperation of the new masters of Russia, the Bolsheviks.

The Khilafat Movement

Anti-British ferment had been on the rise in India for a long time; the embers of the Great Mutiny, a war that was largely a jihad, had never been extinguished. A first broad-based movement of support for the Caliph had developed in the years of the Russo-Ottoman War of 1877–8. The Indian Muslim Sayyid Ameer Ali (1849–1928) so described the impact in India:

> Few observers can have forgotten the extraordinary outburst of sympathy among the Mussulmans of India with the wrongs of Turkey and the afflictions to which their co-religionists were subjected in consequence of that war.... [T]he enthusiasm that prevailed amongst all classes to help the Ottoman nation and to relieve the universal suffering and distress among the stricken people of Turkey. Even women in the humbler walks of life sent their earrings, bracelets and anklets to be sold and the proceeds remitted to the Turkish Compassionate Fund... while many Mussulman soldiers offered their services to the Ottoman government.[90]

The momentum of the Pan-Islamist movement was quite irresistible. Far from remaining an elite ideology, "Pan-Islamic ideas filtered into the poorer populations."[91] British-led modernization of Indian society led to greater and faster social differentiation; liberated from Muslim rule and princely despotism. Though nationally oppressed, Indian middle classes, Muslim no less than Hindu, were becoming more assertive. Under the limited political freedoms extended by the British, a modicum of modern political life was developing; Mahatma Gandhi's political acumen was using it to the full.

Originally, the All-India Muslim League – established by the great modernist Sir Sayyid Ahmad Khan (1817–98), founder of the Aligarh College (the Anglo-Indian University) and later led by the Ismaili Aga Khan – had been steered by both in a rather pro-British direction. It now veered sharply in the other direction: By century's end, it had joined the ranks of the proponents of Pan-Islam.

"Between 1908 and [1914], Pan-Islamism in India, which had been simmering steadily beneath the surface, erupted into active opposition to the British.... Under these circumstances, the ideas of Sayyid Jamal al-Din al-Afghani... became popular among sections of Indian Muslims. Of

[90] Landau, *Pan-Islam*, p. 184.
[91] Ibid., p. 198.

particular appeal were his call for Muslim unity, his stress on jihad against Western dominion." His protracted sojourn in India had focused and galvanized energies; some disciples he had recruited now emerged as leaders.

During and after World War I, Gandhi's noncooperation movement, Bal Gangadhar Tilak's violent Hindu nationalism, and a gamut of Muslim movements were grasping for ways to throw off the yoke of British rule. "Resistance to British colonial rule had been growing in the Indian diaspora during the pre-war decade, not only among strident young Indians in Britain and South Africa ... but also among more strident Indians in Japan and in anticolonial circles in the United States."[92] On the Muslim side, the great event of the war had been the sultan-caliph's proclamation of jihad: The Muslim community of India had been the most attuned to and supportive of the Caliph's Pan-Islamism in the nineteenth century. A fever pitch was reached with World War I. Ottoman defeats, the caliphate, and the custodianship of the Holy Places in Mecca and Medina fanned the flames. By September 1919, the Khilafat movement was launched to protect the caliphate and save the caliph's empire; by November, the national Conference for the Caliphate had been held. The movement's main leaders were Muhammad Ali, his brother Shawkat Ali and Maulana Abul Alam Azad. Khilafat conferences were organized in cities in northern India, regional and local committees were set up, a central Khilafat committee was established in Bombay. In 1920, the Ali brothers produced a "Khilafat Manifesto." "The *Khilafat* was a powerful, all-India mass movement of Muslims."

The ulama were coming out of their political isolation and were participating in Pan-Islamist politics.

> [E]very important move of the *Khilafat* was preceded by a fatwa and the ulama, *piris* and other religious dignitaries became political agents for recruiting support ... a growing sentiment pervaded politically aware Muslims in India that ensuring Muslim power and government abroad was a guarantee for their own religious and national survival as a minority group; in other words, Pan-Islam assumed for them a nationalist significance.

For India's Muslims, who had ruled the land and lorded over the Hindus for more than a half a millennium, the sinking feeling of having been reduced to the status of an impotent minority had needed to be allayed: It was their turn to be treated as dhimmi and they disliked it. "The *Khilafat* was rapidly being transformed from an agitational alliance into a religious-political mass

[92] Hughes, "The German Mission," p. 31.

movement."[93] The movement also had an international dimension: "In its heyday [it] had immense prestige among circles inclined toward Pan-Islam not only in India, but also abroad, chiefly in Turkey, in Egypt" and Afghanistan and the Dutch Indies (Indonesia).[94]

Original cooperation with Gandhi's *satyagraha* movement suffered major setbacks with the rise of the *Hijrat* movement. Some ulama ruled that India was not *dar al-Islam*, where Muslims lawfully are permitted to live, but *dar al-Harb*, which Muslims must leave. As a result, between 18,000 and 30,000 Muslim peasants (by some accounts 50,000 to 100,000[95]), mostly from Sind and the North-West Province, sold their possessions and left India, marching westward in the hope of reaching Ottoman territory, a movement inspired by Prophet Muhammad's retreat from Mecca, *hijra*, and his establishment in Medina. Another nail in the coffin of Muslim–Hindu collaboration was the 1921 Moplah Rebellion in South India. Inspired by the Khilafat, a jihad was proclaimed not only against the British, but also against Hindus, who were slaughtered in large numbers by Muslim rioters. One Mohommed Haji was proclaimed the caliph of the Moplah Khilafat, flags of the Islamic caliphate were flown, Khilafat kingdoms were proclaimed.

Anti-British Pan-Islamist Indians themselves were not united.[96] Some Khilafat leaders had a "modernist" reputation, such as the Ali brothers, Muhammad and Shawkat. There were more radical disciples of Afghani such as Abul Kalam Azad, with his inflammatory Urdu-language journal *Al-Hilal*; Azad's circle founded many Pan-Islamist societies, including, in 1913, the *Jamiat-i Hizbollah*, which wanted to unite all Indian Muslims under one Imam, "to form an agreement with the Hindus and declare a jihad against the British." There was a group in Beirut, led by the Pan-Islamist brothers Abdal Jabbar Khairi and Abdal Sattar, that established an "Indian Muslim Committee" in Constantinople in 1915 with German and Ottoman support. Their newspaper *Akhuwat* (*Brotherhood*) appeared in Urdu and English. It urged Indian conscripts in the British Army to "shoot your English officers" and exhorted Muslims in India: "Murder Englishmen, set fire to their houses, destroy railway bridges and help [Germany] in all possible ways." The Kaiser declined to act on a proposal they conveyed to him during a visit to Constantinople in 1917 to the effect that the frontier tribes of Kashmir could be persuaded to

93 Landau, *Pan-Islam*, p. 205.

94 Ibid., p. 214.

95 Roy, *Memoirs*, p. 455.

96 The following is mostly drawn from an article by K. H. Ansari, "Pan-Islam and the Making of Early Indian Socialism," *op.cit.*

declare war on the British if the Germans supplied arms and other assistance. Another group, the ulama of the *darululum* school at Deoband, was intent on returning to the "first principles" of Islam, on fighting for the independence of the Muslim world and the purification and renewal of Islam. They took the lead in branding the *raj* a *dar al-Harb*, which then, of necessity, was a land of jihad. Some ulama decided to leave India themselves and organize jihad from abroad. They joined the departing *Muhajirun*.

The war thus radicalized a diverse array of Islamist and Pan-Islamist groupings. As the Hindu revolutionary M. N. Roy wrote:

> On the outbreak of the First World War in 1914, the Indian revolutionaries in exile looked towards Germany as the land of hope, and pushed there full of expectations. By the end of the year, the news reached us in India that the Indian Revolutionary Committee in Berlin had obtained from the German government the promise of arms and money required to declare the war of independence. The news spread like wildfire to affect the Indian soldiers of the British Army also. Revolution was around the corner . . . independence was within reach.[97]

The defeat of both Germany and Turkey in 1918, the successful Bolshevik putsch in Russia in 1917, and the abolition of the caliphate in 1924 forced the revolutionaries to recast their expectations. "The Muslims in India . . . had expressed Islamic solidarity long before World War I. However, it was the abolition of the Caliphate soon after the end of the war which served as a catalyst for their feelings and activities in the cause of Pan-Islam. It ended the legitimacy of Pan-Islam and compelled Islamists to search for alternative loyalties."[98]

The Khilafat movement correspondingly petered out in the late 1920s. Political defeat, decline or dormancy, yet, has little bearing on the survival of ideological currents. Long periods of latency do not prevent ideas with great emotional pull from persisting. The movement died, but its ideas shaped generations of Muslim activists, journalists, and theorists. A poem by Mohamed Iqbal (1873–1938), the intellectual leader of the Muslims of India from the 1920s until his death, spoke to hearts:" From the banks of the Nile/ To the soil of Kashgar/ The Muslims should be united/ For the protection of their sanctuary."

The forces that had attached themselves to the Khilafat movement were now seeking new political outlets to bring their needs and their demands to bear "with . . . the . . . defeat of Germany . . . their eyes turned to the Soviet

[97] Roy, *Memoirs*, p. 3.
[98] Landau, *Pan-Islam*," p. 176.

Union for help."[99] After its protracted flirtation with pan-Germanism, Pan-Islam now embarked on a tumultuous dalliance with Bolshevism. The Khairi brothers, prominent Indian Pan-Islamist leaders, whom we had left in Constantinople as cohorts of the German–Ottoman jihad, appeared in Moscow in front of the Central Committee of the Soviets on November 25, 1918, "and delivered a long message which echoed the radical changes in Muslim mood toward revolutionary Russia."[100]

Bolsheviks and Pan-Islamists

In the decades that followed, three external factors jointly shaped the destiny of modern jihad. The first was the renascent German ambitions of the early 1920s, formulated and led by General Hans von Seeckt. Although the importance of this element declined as Germany advanced toward national–socialist rule, it received a boost during World War II. The second was the Bolshevik attempt at leveraging Islam against the West, against Britain in particular, leading to intensive interchange between them. The third was the Islamists' own acquisition of Bolshevik know-how, techniques, and methods, by transfer, as it were.

In intellectual and political history, the study of the transfer of ideas is always delicate and difficult. Imported material tools do not change once they cross a border. In the market of ideas, quantification is impossible. Tracing the immaterial can only be done by means of tracing the estimated effects of a cause. If in the "market" of ideologies, a certain technique offered only by one supplier appears in a given market segment and is acquired by a given purchaser, it is a reasonable assumption to infer that the transfer occurred from the known supplier to the known purchaser unless contrary evidence shows that some other pathways and suppliers were involved.[101]

> Ideas – and particularly political ideas – on the other hand, seldom escape being significantly transformed when transmitted from one society to another, from one culture to another. Often, they are molded by the carrier, and by the time they reach their intended destination, much of their original plumage is gone and in its place are new markings which belong to the culture into which the ideas are being transmitted.

We will therefore study the diverse ways in which critical Bolshevik "technologies" were transferred to the modern jihadi movement. No case is made

99 Ansari, "Pan-Islam and the Making of Early Indian Socialism," p. 514.
100 Ibid., p. 518.
101 Alexander A. Benningsen and S. Enders Wimbush, *Muslim National Communism: A Revolutionary Strategy for the Colonial World*, Chicago, University of Illinois Press, 1979.

that the "lines of communication"[102] identified here represent, even by far, the entire span of their transfer to the Muslim world. We merely attempts to identify the principal avenues and channels of the transfer, its leading actors and institutions. We will also attempt to discern ways in which the ideas and practices that were transferred were altered by their recipients.

In the nineteenth century, backward and barbaric Russia had imported what the Russian intelligentsia believed was Marxism, while it was really a simplistic, pared down version of the German ideologue's canon.[103] This ideology, christened "Marxism–Leninism," was a communistic doctrine recombined with the Gnostic heresies inherent to Russia's national religion and ideology.[104] Soviet Russia's role turned out to be the reexporter of this bowdlerized version of Marxism to other areas of the world, especially the extra-European parts. The Russians had absorbed, digested, and broken down the doctrine into bite-size notions of infinite plasticity. One of the dark shadows of modernity, the Marxian revolt against "capitalism," was elastic enough to fit the innumerable variations of the antimodern revolt, especially in traditional societies turned inside out by brutal contact with the West.[105] The Bolshevik ideologues – Lenin, Stalin, and the epigones – were the *terribles simplificateurs*[106] who fed new rhetoric and new intellectual constructs but also new know-how, new techniques of agitation, propaganda, and organization, and the practice of terror as a chief instrument of politics to the "revolutions" of the so-called "third world," in particular the world of Islam. A preponderance of the know-how and technologies acquired by Russia had been German, including the intellectual and political imports. The world of Islam duly acquired the Russian version of German items, including the "Jihad Made in Germany."

In the war, Germany's strategy had included political warfare in her enemies' colonies. The Germans had woven far-flung networks of agents and successfully enabled a revolution; the Russian revolutionaries rapidly

[102] I am grateful to Professor Bernard Lewis for having suggested this very notion.

[103] James H. Billington, *The Icon and the Axe: An Interpretive History of Russian Culture*, New York, Vintage Books, 1970, esp. 456–519; Mikhail Heller and Aleksandr M. Nekrich, *Utopia in Power: The History of the Soviet Union from 1917 to the Present*, New York, Summit Books, 1982; Tomas G. Masaryk, *The Spirit of Russia*, London, Allen & Unwin, 1961.

[104] See Alain Besançon, *Les origines intellectuelles du Léninisme*, Paris, Calmann-Lévy, 1977; René Fülöp-Miller, *Geist und Gesicht des Bolschewismus*, Vienna, Althea, 1929.

[105] See Ian Buruma, Avishai Margalit, *Occidentalism: The West in the Eyes of its Enemies*, New York, Penguin Press, 2004.

[106] A phrase coined by Jacob Burckhardt in a letter of 24 July 1889 to Friedrich von Preen in Jacob Burckhardt, *Briefe*, Max Burckhardt, ed., vol. 9, Basel/Stuttgart, 1980, p. 203.

escaped the control of their Berlin Svengali. In order to bring about Lenin's success, the Germans had developed a rich set of connections in the Russian socialist movement.[107] In this diplomatic demi-monde, ideologues mixed with adventurers, cranks with killers, crooks with activists, spooks with financiers. The pivot of the entire project was Lenin's feared and envied arch-rival, the picaresque Alexander Helphand, a.k.a. Parvus, a Russian socialist who had been Trotsky's master and mentor and was the smartest theorist of the entire Russian Left – its *enfant terrible*. Helphand had lived for years in Germany, moving to Constantinople in 1910. There he developed a trading company dealing in Russian wheat and German machinery and exploited his wide set of acquaintances in Russia, the Balkans, and Central Europe quite mysteriously to rise in record time from rags to riches. He was also apparently involved in selling German weapons to the Ottoman Empire and was rapidly emerging as an influential economic analyst and financial adviser to the Young Turks. By 1912, the newly minted millionaire had been appointed to a semiofficial position as economic editor of the Young Turk daily newspaper *Turk Yurdu*, "[making] him one of the most influential financial advisers of the Young Turks."[108] His direct connections to the regime included the triumvirs (Enver, Talaat, and Cemal) and the finance minister (Djavid Bey).

Parvus was neither the first nor the only Russian socialist approached by the Germans with a view to destabilizing Russia.[109] But he was the gateway to the most radical elements of the ultra-left, including Lenin; his millions allowed him to employ large numbers of ragged Russian émigrés in his political machinery. As the German gold flowed into Helphand's operation, the latter was busy establishing organizations, recruiting Mensheviks and Bolsheviks, and publishing journals and newspapers to further the project. The nerve center of his venture, located in Copenhagen, was the "Research Institute on the Social Consequences of the War." Through it, Helphand funneled large amounts of money into the Bolshevik coffers and employed or influenced a veritable who's who of the Bolshevik leadership, including, most importantly – and most topically – Karl Radek, the future secretary of the Komintern (Communist International) and future herald of the Bolshevik jihad.

[107] Also see Stefan T. Possony, *Lenin: The Compulsive Revolutionary*, London, Allen & Unwin, 1965; Dmitri Volkogonov, *Lenin: Life and Legacy*, London, HarperCollins, 1994; Richard Pipes, *The Russian Revolution*, New York:Vintage Books, 1991, esp. 361–92.

[108] Winfried B. Scharlau and Zbyněk A. Zeman, *Freibeuter der Revolution: Parvus-Helphand, Eine politische Biographie*, Cologne, Verlag Wissenschaft und Politik, 1964, p. 137.

[109] Ibid., p. 248.

Karl Radek was a professional revolutionary and a renowned socialist journalist, equally at ease in Russia, Poland, and Germany. On account of his plasticity, he also had been nicknamed a "revolutionary Harlequin" and "the court jester of Communism." He was a great admirer of Helphand but also a close confederate of Lenin's. In the spring of 1917, as German money flows to the Bolsheviks went from drip to flood, Radek was one of the chief players, having had one last, decisive meeting with Helphand to plan the directing of the flood for Lenin's benefit. Radek was on board the famous train that the German military used to bring Lenin and his entourage from Zurich to St. Petersburg over German and German-controlled territory. On April 17, 1917, the station chief of German military intelligence in Stockholm could send a cable to Berlin: "Lenin successfully arrived in Russia. Is working exactly as we wish."[110] When the Bolsheviks took power, Radek became a member of the party's Central Committee, and was sent to Berlin at the end of 1918 to "advise" (control) the German Communist Party (KPD), also known as the Spartacus League.

Spartacus launched an insurrection on January 5–6 that was put down by the government within a week. The revolutionaries were hunted down, and many of them were killed, including the top leaders Rosa Luxemburg and Karl Liebknecht. On February 12, Radek was nabbed. The German military command did not order Radek summarily executed. Instead, he was interned at the Moabit prison in Berlin and "treated as a respected interlocutor."[111] The Bolshevik leader's opposite number – his negotiating partner – was none other than General Hans von Seeckt.[112] Out of talks then held between Radek and the German military, political, diplomatic, and business elite grew the anti-Western alliance between the Soviet Union and the Reich, the April 1922 Treaty of Rapallo. Out of these talks also grew the Bolshevik jihad.

For the key to the Bolshevik leader's cell was in Seeckt's hand.

Amongst Radek's first visitors in his Moabit jail cell were two old acquaintances: Enver Pasha and Talaat Pasha. The Young Turk leaders had fled [Istanbul] in November 1918 to Odessa and Nikolaev, whence they reached Germany. They had sought

[110] Ibid., p. 266.

[111] Hans-Ulrich Seidt, "When Continents Awake, Island Empires Fall! Germany and the Destabilization of the West 1919–1922," in Andras Hamori and Bernard Lewis, eds., *Germany and the Middle East, 1871–1945*, Princeton Papers, vol. X–XI, Princeton, NJ, Marcus Wiener Publishers, 2001, pp. 65–86.

[112] On Seeckt, his personality, career, views, and power, see John Wheeler-Bennett, *The Nemesis of Power: The German Army in Politics, 1918–1945*, London, Mamillan Press, 1960, esp. pp. 84–120.

asylum in Berlin. Radek knew Talaat Pasha from [the 1918 German–Soviet peace negotiations at] Brest-Litovsk, where the latter had sat on the winners' side.... As a revolutionary he offered Radek the collaboration of the Young Turks refugees: in alliance with the Bolsheviks, the Islamic masses of the East would be liberated from enslavement to the Western powers.[113]

Talaat – until just yesterday one of the leaders of a mighty empire, and one still liable to return to power – was offering Radek, and through him, Lenin, a strategic partnership that inverted the fronts of World War I: Russia would this time fight alongside the Germans and the Turks. Radek liked what he heard, and he invited the Turks to Moscow. "Radek's willingness to bid the Turkish refugees to Moscow was not the tactical gamble of a jailed revolutionary; he acted out of a global strategic concept, which was compatible with Seeckt's aims, interests and instruments." Enver and Talaat were not acting unbeknownst to their German hosts, but at their very urging: "Cooperation with Soviet Russia, based strictly on geopolitical and strategic interests, was to shake the British Empire's foundations and bring about revision of the Treaty of Versailles. The underpinning of these clandestine networks derived from contacts and concepts established during the First World War, particularly the idea of the 'Holy War' – 'Jihad' – against the West."[114]

Late in the war, Seeckt and other Germans had proposed to the Ottoman triumvirs that they shift the center of gravity of their war effort from the futile aim of fighting in Palestine and Mesopotamia to the more substantial and promising theater of the Caucasus and Central Asia. Rather than focusing on the Arabs, who had betrayed the Turks, the "Turanian" perspective should be emphasized. Together with his brother Nuri Pasha, Enver led Turkish troops – renamed the "Army of God" – into the Caucasus. They took Baku in September 1918; the huge oil resources of the Caspian Sea were now theirs. To Seeckt, this meant that those regions could be made into springboards for an attack on "key British positions in the Persian Gulf and India" through Iran.[115] Although the ultimate failure of this "last gasp of Turkish military energy" (Seeckt) sealed the fate of the triumvirs, defeat damped down neither their geopolitical ambitions nor Seeckt's.

The latter's geostrategic design had three pillars: unremitting hostility to the "Anglo-Saxon" powers, Britain and the United States; permanent alliance with Russia – a "continental alliance" against the "maritime

113 Seidt, *Berlin Kabul Moscow*, p. 135.
114 Seidt, "When Continents Awake," p. 65.
115 Seidt, *Berlin Kabul Moscow*, p. 119.

powers;" and the formation of an "indirect empire" dominated by Germany. This latter, new-style Reich was to be based on trade treaties and a customs union rather than on territorial conquests. An "indirect power projection" would make Berlin the hub of a great Eurasian empire able in the long run to challenge Anglo-Saxon power. "This is why the way to Asia must be free.... We need to be the supreme power from the Atlantic Ocean to Persia ... [as] the coalition of interested states that are disposed to be in such a union."[116] This scheme necessitated an entente with Russia. As a senior military commander, Seeckt had disagreed with the policy of destabilizing of the czar and fragmenting his empire. Now Seeckt hastened to collect the threads of a Russian alliance: "Germany's hopes of regaining her position as a world power position can only be fulfilled by means of a firm confederation to Russia," he wrote in 1920. "The staggering colossus will eventually roll over on its side and England will feel its weight in Central and East Asia."[117]

Seeckt had served as chief of general staff of the Ottoman army. A number of German officers who had served under him informally constituted what may be deemed a "Turkish mafia," an old boys' network that worked for him at least as long as he was in charge of the Reichswehr, until 1926. In September 1919, this "mafia" formally incorporated itself as the *Bund der Asienkämpfer* (Union of Asian Fighters). It was the human infrastructure for Seeckt's new chapter of Germany's *Orientpolitik*;[118] its purpose was political and military intelligence regarding the regions where the Germans had been fighting the British, and maintaining action-oriented networks, with British India – the chief target.

In order to get there, Enver had to move to Moscow and work directly with the Soviet and Red Army leadership. Without his Pan-Islamist networks, an assault on the *raj* was inconceivable. In the very testimony of M. N. Roy, who loathed Enver with a passion, "Enver Pasha was the idol of the anti-Imperialist and Pan-Islamist movement in the Middle East and India."[119] In short, the German strategist arranged for Lenin's envoy to send the Ottoman triumvir to Moscow, in order to organize the jihad among oriental Muslims.

A first attempt to smuggle Enver into Soviet Russia ended in failure; inclement weather forced his German military plane to land at Kaunas

[116] Quoted in ibid., p. 131.
[117] Quoted in ibid., p. 133.
[118] Ibid., p. 140.
[119] Roy, *Memoirs*, p. 411.

Airport in Lithuania. One of Seeckt's "Turkish mafia" officers stationed there saved the day by preventing the secret from leaking. Another member of the network, Ernst Kostring, later German military attaché in Moscow, successfully ferried Enver over in a second attempt in the summer of 1920. He delivered Enver to General Tukhachevsky's Red Army then advancing into Poland, and thence to Moscow. By August 25, Enver was able to write a first report to Seeckt. One faction in the Bolshevik leadership, he reported, was focused on a European revolution, but another advocated an attack on British positions in the East. The option to strike a blow against world capitalism in India, its perceived weaker spot, coincided with Seeckt's own geopolitical intents.[120] Enver also asked his friend in Berlin to forward to him an 1883 book by Lord Roberts, *Is An Invasion of India Possible?* With Enver's help, the threads between Berlin, Moscow, and Kabul were tightened.[121] The CUP front organization, the "League of Islamic Revolutionary Societies," which received significant Soviet financial support, moved to Moscow. The league was described as "the foreign policy arm of the Committee." Its last meeting held in Moscow gathered a dozen participants around Enver.[122]

Enver, M. N. Roy reports,

> approached the Russians with the offer to cooperate in the plan of inciting the Muslim peoples of the Middle East to revolt against British imperialism. He would establish contact particularly with the *Khilafat* in India through the cooperation of the Muslim tribes along the Indo-Afghan frontier. He was sure to enlist the support of king Amanullah of Afghanistan and before long take up his headquarters at Kabul. In response to his call, backed up by military operations based on the North–West Frontier tribal territories, India would rise up in a mighty revolt and drive the British rulers out in no time.[123]

In his second Moscow letter to Seeckt, Enver reported having met Efraim Skliansky, War Commissar Leon Trotsky's deputy, who had spoken very favorably about the alliance with Germany. Three hours later, Enver was meeting the president of the Communist International, Grigory Zinoviev, on board a train that was taking them both to Baku, to the "Congress of the People of the East," also known as the "Congress of the Toilers of the East." As a disappointed Roy testified, "The Russians appeared to be taken in by Enver Pasha's diplomacy."[124]

120 Seidt, "When Continents Awake," p. 72.
121 Seidt, *Berlin Kabul Moscow*, p. 146.
122 Kramer, *Islam Assembled*..., pp. 70–1.
123 Roy, *Memoirs*, p. 398.
124 Roy, *Memoirs*, p. 398.

Lenin craftily kept several separate lines of approach to the Muslim world. Besides the Baku crowd, one of the aces in his sleeve was Narendra Nath Bhattacharya, an Indian revolutionary better known under his lifelong alias of M. N. Roy (1887–1954). Roy's role in conveying Bolshevism and Bolshevik known-how to the Muslim world was "crucial."[125] Even though he was born a Hindu of the Brahmin caste and his father's family were hereditary priests of Shakti, Roy exhibited a "radical rejection of India's so-called 'spiritual heritage' and viewed Hinduism as 'an ideology of slavery.'"[126] His *Historical Role of Islam: An Essay on Islamic Culture* is an embarrassing piece of Muslim apologetics. The following offers a taste of Roy's unbridled Islamophilia:

> Mohammad assumed the role of the singular Prophet spreading his Message of Peace.... Every prophet establishes his pretension by the performance of miracles. On that token, Mohammad must be recognized as by far the greatest of all prophets, before or after him. The expansion of Islam is the most miraculous of all miracles.... The phenomenal success of Islam was primarily due to its revolutionary significance and its ability to lead the masses out of the hopeless situation created by the decay of antique civilizations... a tremendously dynamic historical phenomenon. The miraculous performance of the "Army of God" usually dazzles the vision, the nobility of character, purity of purpose and piety of spirit. Their devoutness might have been fortified by superstition, but was not stained by hypocrisy. Their fanaticism was softened by generosity and sound common-sense. Their ambition was remarkably free from selfishness. Godliness, for them, was not a veil for greediness.[127]

From his teens an activist of violent leanings, Roy was a seasoned militant when World War I broke out. The clandestine movements he was working with "planned to arrange armed insurrection all over India.... The revolutionary organizations were extended to [the] Far East, West [Coast] America, and Germany, where [the] Indian revolutionary committee was formed."[128] Contacts with German intelligence were advanced enough that by the end of 1914, Roy headed to Java to rendezvous with German agents, including the consul general there, who gave him large amounts of money though no arms. Roy then met the German ambassador to China, Admiral von Hintze,[129] who strongly recommended that he meet the German

125 Ansari, "Pan-Islam and the Making of Early Indian Socialism," p. 527.

126 Sibnarayan Ray, ed., *Selected Works of M. N. Roy*, vol. 1, Delhi, Oxford University Press, 1987, p. 37.

127 Dr. Farooq's Study Resources Page, http://www.globalwebpost.com/farooqm/study_res/default.html.

128 Banglapedia, http://banglapedia.search.com.bd/HT/R_0243.htm

129 Rear Admiral Paul von Hintze, formerly ambassador to Mexico, had made a secret deal with the former Mexican dictator General Huerta: In return for weapons, the latter had

consulate staff in San Francisco and the Mexican revolutionaries in Mexico, and then go to Berlin. "Since I was to go to Berlin on the advice of the German Ambassador, his subordinates and other influential countrymen were helpful in arranging my trip," Roy recounts.[130] By the summer of 1916, Roy arrived in San Francisco. In Mexico, high-level German emissaries came to see him: He was now secretary general of the Mexican Socialist Party and an influential adviser to president Venustiano Carranza.[131]

In keeping with this spooky world of underground intrigue, Lenin's emissary Mikhail Borodin now arrived in Mexico City and conveyed Lenin's personal invitation to Roy to visit Moscow. After more contacts with German military intelligence, Roy arrived in Berlin late in 1919, where he met the leadership of the Left Socialists and the KPD. The interpenetration between Bolsheviks and German military and intelligence officers ran deep, as the development of the ideology of national Bolshevism shows. Karl Radek was the key exponent of this intersection of extreme, radical nationalism and militarism on the one side and Bolshevism on the other. National Bolshevism was an ideological vehicle for German military officers especially to effect a rapprochement with Soviet Russia – on the basis of a shared hatred for Western liberalism and modernity.[132]

Roy was following in the footsteps of his fellow Indian revolutionists in Berlin. Champakraman Pillai, for instance, was close to Graf zu Reventlow, the "Red Baron," a Prussian aristocrat who championed not only an alliance with Russia, but also some form of national-communist regime in Germany.

Borodin planned Roy's trip to Moscow with the help of national-Bolshevik German officers close to Seeckt.[133] When Roy finally arrived, it was mid-July 1920 and time for the Second World Congress of the Communist International. "Everybody knew that I was 'the wise man from the East' who had come from the New World on Lenin's special invitation." Roy was instantly co-opted into the Commission on the National and Colonial Question chaired by Lenin. The latter needed people like Roy: "the oppressed and exploited masses of Asia have to be mobilized in a gigantic

agreed, to cut off oil supplies to Great Britain in the event of war with Germany; later the admiral became the kaiser's last foreign minister and the negotiator of the "supplementary treaty" of Brest-Litovsk of August 27, 1918, between Soviet Russia and Germany.

130 Roy, *Memoirs*, p. 14.

131 Ibid., pp. 66–81.

132 On national bolshevism, see inter alia, Jean-Pierre Faye, *Langages totalitaires: La raison critique de l'économie narrative,* Paris, Hermann, 1972.

133 Roy, *Memoirs,* p. 295.

revolutionary movement ... [Roy] in practice had anticipated the theory of revolutionary strategy in colonial and semi-colonial countries."

At Lenin's emphatic insistence, his and Roy's own theses on colonial revolutions were jointly presented to the congress (they involved some ideological hair splitting with respect to Marxian theory).[134] The repeated defeats of pro-Bolshevik uprisings in western and central Europe were lending even greater emphasis to extra-European areas for the realization of the Utopia: "The drooping spirit of the Bolsheviks was bucked up by Lenin's declaration that Europe was not all of the world; that London and New York might fall on the Ganges and the Yangtze. The Asiatic provinces of the fallen tsarist empire were still to be brought under the jurisdiction of the Soviet Republic."[135] A kernel of Roy's "Supplementary Theses" was to become the stock in trade of most radical third-worldist movements in the twentieth century, singularly in the Muslim world. This was the doctrine of grievance and victimhood ascribing all of the ills of the extra-European countries to "imperialist" and "colonialist exploitation and plunder." The theses assert that the entire wealth of European capitalism comes from "superprofits" derived from the looting and enslavement of the third world. Later speeches on the issue by a Gamal Abdel Nasser or an Osama bin Laden offer very little that is not already present in Roy's and Lenin's doctrine.[136]

In the eyes of the Bolsheviks, Germany and the rest of Europe were losing their priority status.

> Revolution should have easy victories in the neighboring Muslim countries which, inspired by the message of the liberation of Central Asia, would rise against European imperialism.... [The example of Turkey] was bound to inflame the entire Islamic world. A faint echo of the *khilafat* movement reached Moscow to encourage the view that Pan-Islamism was a revolutionary force and, as such, should be welcomed and supported as an ally of the proletarian world revolution.[137]

Concrete consequences followed. Roy recounts: "I did some hard thinking. The result was a plan for opening the second front of the world revolution," and, from Kabul to India, to "raise an army from the frontier tribes which would be strong enough not only to raid British territory, but to seize certain parts of it and hold them as the base for operations for advancing further."[138] Roy's "hard thinking" consisted in appropriating,

[134] See Ray, *Selected Works of M. N. Roy*, vol. 1, pp. 171–8.
[135] Roy, *Memoirs*, p. 390.
[136] Ray, *Selected Works of M. N. Roy*, vol. 1, pp. 165–9.
[137] Ibid.
[138] Ibid., p. 326.

lock, stock and barrel, the plans developed by Max von Oppenheim, Oskar von Niedermayer, Hans von Seeckt, and Enver Pasha! Given Roy's persistent association with German military intelligence, and the Germans' osmosis with the Bolsheviks, this was not surprising.

Deputy Soviet foreign minister Lev Karakhan approved of the plan, Deputy War Minister Skliansky liked it, and Lenin supported it. As a result, "the strategy of revolution in Asia was given a prominent place in the agenda of the 'Small Bureau' [of the Communist International]," and two decisions were taken: A Central Asiatic Bureau of the Communist International run by Roy would be set up in Tashkent, and a "Congress of the Oppressed People of the East" would be held in Baku.

The affair was Zinoviev's own idea, although Karl Radek, by now secretary of the Communist International, "was very enthusiastic." Of course Radek would have been enthused, as he most likely originated the idea, together with his bosom friend Enver Pasha. The congress was meant to celebrate in grand style the official alliance between the Bolsheviks and the Pan-Islamists. To achieve this kind of marital bliss, however, Enver, who was despised by any number of Central Asia leftists, nationalists, and Islamists, had to be given a certificate of revolutionary virginity signed by the Bolshevik experts. In the end, Enver's past was amnestied, the Bolsheviks gained a powerful ally, and Enver joined Zinoviev and Radek on the train to Baku.

Lenin's Jihad

In words dripping with demagogy, the Second Congress of the Communist International issued a summons inviting the "enslaved popular masses of Persia, Armenia and Turkey" and of Mesopotamia, Syria, Arabia, and more, to gather in Baku. "Spare no effort to ensure that as many as possible may be present on Sept 1 [1920] in Baku. Formerly you traveled across deserts to reach the holy places – now make your way over mountains and rivers, through forests and deserts." This was a new *hajj*, it was hinted. The "peasants and workers of Persia," appealed to in the name of Sharia, were told that they were being "robbed and exploited" by local reactionaries "who have sold [out] to Britain the rich oilfields of South Persia, thereby cooperating in the plundering of your country." The "peasants of Mesopotamia" were told: "80,000 British soldiers stand upon your soil, robbing and killing you and violating your women." The "peasants of Anatolia" were told that Allied powers "dictated their alien laws" and had "made the Sultan prisoner and forced him to agree to the partition of purely Turkish territory." Every sectional, national, or ethnic group was addressed in the same way,[139] setting the tone. The Bolsheviks were ready to go very far indeed to meet the world of Islam, whatever they themselves were doing domestically to "their" Muslims.

During the first session of the congress, Zinoviev gave a speech that called five times for a "Holy War." He argued for it as an attack on "the policy which conferred the colonies syphilis, opium and a debauched caste of officers, the policy which turned these countries into the bourgeoisie's rubbish dump and which plundered them relentlessly." The Bolsheviks "respect the religious feelings of the masses," Zinoviev proclaimed, though they "must educate the masses of the East to hate and to want to fight against the rich in general – Russian, Jewish, German, French." What was Zinoviev suggesting?

> We are now faced with the task of kindling a real holy war against the British and French capitalists.... Comrades, you... for the first time assembled in a congress of peoples of the East, must here proclaim a real holy war against the robbers and oppressors.... The time has come when you can act about organizing a true people's holy war, in the first place against British imperialism!

At this point the stenographic report notes: "Tumultuous applause, prolonged shouts of 'Hurrah!' Members of the congress stand up, brandishing their weapons. The speaker is unable to continue for some time. All the delegates stand up and applaud! Shouts of 'We swear it!'"[140] The congress was attended by 1,891 participants, two-thirds Bolshevik party members. The largest contingents were from Turkey (235), Persia (192), Armenia (157), Russia (104), Georgia (100), and Chechnya (82).[141] In time-tested Bolshevik manner, the "delegates" were self-appointed and delegated by nobody in particular. Still, from what is known of the biography of a number of them, some had access to groups, networks, and associations in various countries.

At the next session of this highly choreographed congress, the main speech came from Communist International secretary Karl Radek, whose presence was not due to any particular knowledge of or acquaintance with the East – he was a quintessential *Mitteleuropa* intellectual – but rather his close connection to Enver Pasha. Radek's speech sounded like an ideologized, and

[139] *Congress of the People of the East, Baku, September 1920*. Stenographic Report, translated and annotated by Brian Pearce, London, New Park Publications, 1977, 4, 1, 2.

[140] Ibid., pp. 25–37.

[141] Ibid., p. 192. Other attendees included 61 Tadzhiks, 47 Kirghiz, 41 Jews, 35 Turkmens, 33 Kumyks, 25 Lesgians, 14 Indians, a few Arabs, some Kurds, and some Hazaras (from Afghanistan).

less lyrical, version of the infamous 1918 poem "Scythians," by Russian writer Aleksandr Blok, a Russian declaration of hatred against the West:

You are millions. We are hordes and hordes and hordes. Try and take us on! Yes, we are Scythians! Yes, we are Asians – With slanted and greedy eyes! [...]

The time is come. Trouble beats its wings – And every day our grudges grow, And the day will come when every trace Of your Paestums may vanish! [...]

Russia is a Sphinx. Rejoicing, grieving, And drenched in black blood, It gazes, gazes, gazes at you, With hatred and with love! [...]

We love the flesh – its flavor and its color, And the stifling, mortal scent of flesh.... Is it our fault if your skeleton cracks In our heavy, tender paws? [...]

[W]e have nothing to lose, And we are not above treachery! For ages and ages you will be cursed By your sickly, belated offspring! [...]

We will not lift a finger when the cruel Huns Rummage the pockets of corpses, Burn cities, drive cattle into churches, And roast the meat of our white brothers!...

Come to your senses for the last time, old world! Our barbaric lyre is calling you One final time, to a joyous brotherly feast To a brotherly feast of labor and of peace!

Radek the Bolshevik offered the same kind of brotherly love as Blok the poet, who had welcomed the Bolshevik Revolution as the Apocalypse. The Muslim East was being taught by its new teachers a new rhetoric as well as new concepts, such as "imperialism," "colonialism," "plundering" of their countries, and so on.[142] The occasion was "historic," Radek told the congress, because

[T]he representatives of the [laboring] masses [of the East] here present, all moved by the same emotion, rose and swore an oath to wage holy war... against the oppressors of the world of labor.... We appeal, comrades, to the warlike feelings which once inspired the people of the East when these peoples, led by their great conquerors advanced upon Europe. We know, comrades, that our enemies will say that we are appealing to the memory of Genghis Khan and to the mercy of the great conquering Caliphs of Islam. But we are convinced that yesterday you drew your daggers and your revolvers not for aims of conquest... long live the Red East, which together with the workers of Europe will create a new civilization under the banner of Communism.[143]

142 Provision must also be made for the influence of the Fabian socialist doctrines, which were immensely influential amongst less radical and more upper-class elements of the colonial world. There was however a coherence between the radical (bolshevik) and the moderate (Fabian) socialism: The theory of "imperialism" originated with the British liberal Hobson and was then adopted by Fabians and bolsheviks alike, before being retreaded for the colonials. See Laurent Murawiec,""Impérialisme?," *Le Débat*, Paris, Winter 2004.

143 Ibid, pp. 38–52.

The principal problem the Bolsheviks had to tackle to gain control over the Muslims was the latter's mistrust of Russian imperial designs. The suspicions transpired quickly. At the third session, one Narbutabekov flatly stated, "The Muslims will not abandon the Soviet power, but this on condition that the peculiarities of the Eastern peoples be recognized.... We need a special yardstick in [the] case of [the 400 million Muslims]." He suggested that "only the paying of close attention to the life of the Eastern peoples" would allow the Bolsheviks to acquire and keep influence, and he reminded them of the terms of the November 1917 Council of People's Commissars' "Appeal to All the Toiling Muslims of Russia and the East": "Henceforward your beliefs and customs, your national and cultural institutions are declared free and inviolable. Build your national life freely and without hindrance."[144] The contradiction between Islam and Bolshevism as ideologies was real and would continue to haunt both Islamists and Bolsheviks. There was enough kinship between the two groups for cooperation and limited osmosis, but too much difference for a full merger. The amity would forever be conflict-laden.

After Radek finished speaking, Comrade Korkmasov was happy to inform the crowd that "[a]ssembled in their own congress a month ago, the [Caucasus] Highland poor, and even the ulama, issued a call for a *ghazawat*, a holy war, against all the oppressors of the East."

The crux of the congress came the next day at the fourth session. Zinoviev announced:

> Next, comrades, two prominent Turkish leaders, not delegates to our congress, who are here in Baku [quite a bold lie by omission since he and Enver had traveled thither together!] have sent the Presidium a statement in writing, and as these statements are of great political importance, the presidium has decided to make them public, both from this tribune and in the press. One of these statements is by Enver Pasha.[145]

Enver's declaration read to the congress was a virtuoso piece of mendacity; he complained that "German imperialism used us for its bandit aims" – a tall story from a man who only days before had been writing intelligence reports to Hans von Seeckt!

> But our desire was only to safeguard our independence. Comrades, the sentiment which caused us to leave a calm, refuge-seeking life for the burning deserts of Tripoli and the poor tents of the Bedouin and forced us to spend there the most difficult time of our life, was no sentiment of imperialism.... Comrades, during the world

[144] Ibid., pp. 61–3.
[145] Ibid., pp. 75–6.

war I occupied a very important post. I assure you that I regret that we were obliged to fight on the side of German imperialism. I hate and curse German imperialists as much as I hate and curse British imperialism and the British imperialists.

Completing this piece of oriental farce, Enver announced: "Comrades, I declare to you that the Union of revolutionary organizations of Morocco, Algeria,Tunisia, Tripoli, Egypt, Arabia and India, which has sent me here as its representative, is in full solidarity with you in this respect." By this, Enver meant his once-powerful personal intelligence network, the *Teshkilat-i Mahsusa*.[146]

After this show, the Hungarian communist leader Bela Kun "propose[d] to [Enver and his friends] that they prove in deeds that they are now ready to serve the toiling people and make amends for their false steps of the past." Uproar followed, since many participants were still upset by Enver's association with Kaiser Wilhelm. In a fine display of Bolshevik manipulation, the presidium then drowned these voices by proposing an immediate vote, with Zinoviev screaming, "holy war!"

The Bolshevik jihad continued to be elaborated on. Comrade Utushev, in his praise of Islam, this "colossal ideological stock of spiritual culture," quoted a poem by Bolshevik writer Sergei Gorodetsky: "This is why, when the black coffee bubbles with a golden glint in the porcelain cup, there rises to the brain a wave of desire for violent actions, and the heart suddenly yearns for catastrophe. Blow up Europe! Sweep away with fierce will the evil shamelessness of buying and selling!"[147] The apocalyptic messianists of Russia held out their arms to their Muslim counterparts. Both recognized one another because they partook in similar Gnostic belief structures, with similar political consequences. Both exuded a seething hatred for the "materialist West"; the diverse ideological conceits used to drape the hatred mattered less than the driving emotion itself. Thus, Zinoviev concluded, "that moment . . . when the assembled representatives of the peoples of the East swore to begin a Holy War, that moment will be preserved in our hearts as a sacred experience. . . . Yes, a Holy War against the plunderers and capitalists."[148]

Accordingly, the "Manifesto of the Congress of the Peoples of the East" stated:

Peoples of the East! You have often heard the call to holy war from your governments, you have marched under the green banner of the Prophet, but all these holy wars were fraudulent, serving only the interests of your self-serving rulers, and you, the

[146] Ibid., pp. 76–9.
[147] Ibid., pp. 113–14.
[148] Ibid., p. 161.

peasants and workers, remained in slavery and want after these wars.... Now we summon you to the first real holy war under the red banner of the Communist International. We summon you to a holy war for your own wellbeing, for your own freedom, for your own life!

No less that fifteen times the manifesto contained the call for a Holy War:

[W]e – representatives of the toiling masses of all the peoples of the East... united in unbreakable union among ourselves and we revolutionary workers of the West – summon our peoples to a holy war.... Go forward as one man into a holy war against the British conquerors! High waves the banner of the holy war!... This is a holy war for the liberation of the peoples of the East... into the holy war...! Into the holy war for the liberation of all mankind from the yoke of capitalist and imperialist slavery, for the ending of all forms of oppression of one people by another and all forms of exploitation of man by man! Into the holy war against the last citadel of imperialism in Europe, against the nest of pirates and bandits by sea and land, against the age-old oppression of all the peoples of the East, against imperialist Britain! Into the holy war for freedom.... Peoples of the East! In this holy war all the revolutionary workers and all the oppressed peasants of the East will be with you.... May the holy war of the peoples of the East and the toilers of the whole world against imperial Britain burn with unquenchable fire![149]

One other part of the manifesto deserves special mention in view of later events – the early injection of communist anti-Semitism into the Muslim East, and the supplying by the former to the latter of rhetorical and propaganda themes that were to have a singular fortune in decades to come: "Peoples of the East!... What has Britain done to Palestine? There, at first, acting for the benefit of Anglo-Jewish capitalists, it drove Arabs from the land in order to give the latter to Jewish settlers. Then, trying to appease the discontent of the Arabs, it incited them against these same Jewish settlers." This sanctimonious analysis was music to the ears of such leaders of the Palestinian movement as Amin Husayni, whom the British governor-general had just appointed to be grand mufti of Jerusalem. As later events proved, this was not to remain the only case of anti-Jewish collaboration between communists and Islamic radicals.

The congress – or its Bolshevik masterminds – decided to set up a "permanent executive committee of the Congress of the People of the East" under the name of "Council for Propaganda of the People of the East." The council included a close associate of Roy's, a prominent Tatar Islamic revolutionary, two of Joseph Stalin's close cohorts, a Persian Muslim, and a few others lesser lights. A decision was also made to publish a journal, *Narody Vostoka*

[149] Ibid., pp. 167–73.

(*Nations of the East*), and to establish a "university of the social sciences for activists in the East," which took the form of the Communist University of the Toilers of the East (*Kommunisticheskii universitiet trudiashchikhsya vostoka*).

The congress had struck a powerful blow for the Bolsheviks. Their crude but effective anti-imperialist rhetoric and the blending of the Islamic concept of jihad with their own design could now be spread far and wide. The homeward-bound participants were armed with new rhetorical, conceptual, agitational, and organizational instruments unknown in their lands of origin.

In Germany, the journal of the Union of Asian Fighters was unsurprisingly all praise for Baku and the Bolsheviks: "Lenin and [Soviet foreign minister Georgy] Chicherin have identified Britain's weak spot – India. [...] The Congress of Baku must be considered as the prelude of the fight to the death [with Britain]."[150] Enver Pasha returned to Berlin in mid-October 1920. There, in a safe-house kept by a member of Seeckt's group, Enver received a large number of "officers, professors and diplomats," including the Soviet "trade" representative in Berlin, Viktor Kopp, an operative very close to Trotsky's war commissariat.

In great secrecy, Seeckt was creating the high-powered *Sondergruppe R* (where "R" stood for Russia) that brought together all the threads of the secret collaboration between the *Reichswehr* and the Red Army. As Oskar von Niedermayer had written, action against the British in their Muslim sphere of influence "can only be carried out under the leadership of Moscow."[151] And, as he was to write later, "Afghanistan is the intersection of Russian expansion and Indian revolution."[152] In mid-January 1921, having conferred with Seeckt, Enver left Berlin to return to Moscow. In February, Seeckt secretly asked his loyal aide Niedermayer to present a paper at a private – secret – "assessment of military geographic conditions of an attack on India." Seeckt attended his subordinate's presentation. "We will wait for the opportunity, and the opportunity must arise, when Britain must fight to save her position of power in the world takes on the most violent forms," and "she will pay for [a situation] where a people of 50 million fools itself that it can lord it over and plunder 400 million of the people of the world.... When continents awake, Island-empires collapse," Niedermayer grandly concluded.[153]

150 Seidt, *Berlin Kabul Moscow*, p. 140.
151 Ibid., p. 142.
152 Ibid., p. 144.
153 Ibid., p. 143.

Enver helped further tighten the connections between Berlin, Moscow, and Kabul. He soon announced to Seeckt the forthcoming visit of General Mehmed Veli Khan, a senior Afghan military figure, who was tasked with developing military cooperation. The Afghan mission arrived in Berlin in April and was received by no lesser figures than German president Friedrich Ebert and Foreign Minister Walter Simon. Enver continued to send visitors, all relating to the planned operation in India. A member of Seeckt's group, Günther Voigt, was also sent, with the help of the Soviet trade delegation in Berlin, to Kabul via Moscow to dispose the Afghan government favorably toward Moscow. In Moscow, Voigt met with Foreign Minister Chicherin, Trotsky became directly involved with *Sondergruppe R*, and Niedermayer was assigned as a permanent delegate to Moscow. Among those attending the first meetings he held there were Radek, Trotsky, and Lenin!

"The best laid schemes o' Mice an' Men, / Gang aft agley," Robert Burns wrote in his "Ode to a Mouse." So went this multifangled scheme. By the summer, Enver Pasha had determined that there was a greater empire for him to carve out by working with the Afghans against the Soviets than by working with Moscow. He was drifting away from the deal of mutual instrumentalization he had made with the Bolsheviks. Initially, in the first months of 1922, with the support of the Afghan army, Enver scored successes against the Red Army – to the great annoyance of his old German friends. By May 1922, Enver had conquered Ashkhabad, but on August 4, he was killed on the battlefield. As Seeckt put it, "*Que voulez-vous, c'est la fin d'un révolutionnaire.*"[154] The Indian operation was stillborn, but in the intervening time, the Germans and the Soviets had signed the Rapallo Treaty. With respect to the Muslim world, Enver had been Lenin's joker card. Yet Lenin still held some aces, as Baku had shown, and as M. N. Roy was about to show.

Red Jihad, Green Jihad

Out of loathing for, and personal rivalry with, Enver Pasha, whom he called "the dangerous Turk," M. N. Roy had disagreed with the idea of the Baku Congress, which he derisively called "Zinoviev's Circus." Although Roy himself ostentatiously refused to attend, he sent at least one of his trusted lieutenants, Acharya, who was included among the new organization's leadership. His self-serving protests to the contrary, Roy was at one with the

[154] Ibid., pp. 146–55.

Bolshevik strategy of using Pan-Islamist jihad as the mainstay of their strategy in the Muslim world.

The Communist International duly established a Central Asia Bureau (CAB) in Tashkent, immediately tasked to foster revolution in the vast region of "Turkestan," including the Emirates of Bokhara and Shiva, earlier protectorates of the czar. The CAB was led by prominent Bolshevik Fyodor Raskolnikov, the commander of the Red Army in Central Asia and chairman of the Turkestan Committee of the Soviet government; Georgi Safarov, "a passionate believer in the revolutionary significance of the colonial nationalist movement, particularly of the Islamic countries"; M. N. Roy himself; the Latvian leader of the Cheka, the Bolshevik terror police, Jakob Peters; the administrator Lazar Kaganovich; and the president of the Turkestan Soviet, a Tajik named Abduqadir Rahimbaev.

On the strength of Enver Pasha's plan to attack the British in India, Raskolnikov was appointed ambassador to Kabul. Roy reports that Raskolnikov was of the belief that the Khilafat movement was going to overthrow the *raj*. "The breakdown of British rule in India would open the floodgates of revolution.... That was my old idea, which still fascinated me," Roy adds, naively claiming authorship of the Oppenheim–Seeckt strategy. Further, "I submitted the plan for Lenin's consideration and approval.... He was interested."[155] The plan to raise an "Army of Liberation" then suddenly received a fillip – the Muslims who had left India in the framework of the *Hijrat* movement.

> A new factor had appeared on the scene.... Reports had reached Moscow that, responding to the call of the *Khilafat* Committee, thousands of Muslims, including many educated young men, were leaving India for Turkey.... It was a religious Pan-Islamist movement, but it gave me an opportunity to contact a large number of possible recruits for an army to fight for the liberation of India instead of a lost cause.[156]

Roy describes his intent as consisting less in enlisting the "religious fanaticism" of the "ignorant masses" than the

> politically motivated educated youth... the educated amongst the Indian *Mujaheers* might realize the pointlessness of a pilgrimage to Turkey to fight for the cause of secular nationalism. My plan was to raise, equip and train such an army of liberation. Using the [Indo-Afghan] frontier territories as the base of the operation and with the mercenary support of the tribesmen, the liberation army would march into India

155 Roy, *Memoirs*, p. 417.
156 Ibid., p. 420.

and occupy some territory where a civil government should be established as soon as possible.... It would call upon the people to rise in the rear of the enemy, so that the liberation army could advance further and further into the country. The requirements for implementing the plan were obvious: a sufficiently large quantity of arms, field equipment, training personnel and plenty of money. The last item was sanctioned by the Council of People's Commissars on the recommendation of the Communist Party.[157]

The German jihad plan had been recast as a Bolshevik enterprise, but the underlying jihad remained. "Who will guard the guardians?" the wise Romans asked. "Manipulator, beware being manipulated" would be the challenge for the modern sorcerer's apprentices of jihad.

Ill-treated by the Afghan amir, a large number of *muhajirun* walked the whole distance across Afghanistan, joined along the way by Indian deserters from the British Army. "The position of the Indian *muhajirun* was transformed by the Russian Revolution."[158] Some had made their way to the Baku congress. Turkmen tribesmen had taken a large number of them prisoner. Bolshevik authorities in turn arranged for the release of this promising prey that they could work over. Roy was also counting on the support of a number of prominent Pan-Islamists turned pro-Bolsheviks. Maulana Barakatullah, for one, already a character in the cast of the pro-German Indians in Berlin, and the "prime minister" of the provisional Indian government proclaimed in 1915 in Kabul, "though a staunch Muslim throughout his life... was permanently involved in developing the new relationship with the Bolsheviks.... Though he never claimed to be a Bolshevik... his views on most temporal matters became almost identical with those of the Bolsheviks." Barakatullah's book *Bolshevism and the Islamic Body Politick*, appearing in several languages, appealed to the Muslims of the world "to understand the noble principles of Russian Socialism and to embrace it seriously and enthusiastically.... O Muhameddans, listen to this divine cry. Respond to the call of liberty, equality and brotherhood which comrade Lenin and the Soviet Government of Russia are offering to you."[159]

By March 1919, Barakatullah was the ambassador extraordinary of Afghan king Amanullah to Soviet Russia, "and for the rest of his life, he worked closely with the Soviet Union in the struggle for Indian freedom."

[157] Ibid., pp. 419–21.
[158] Ansari, "Pan-Islam and the Making of Early Indian Socialism," p. 518.
[159] Ibid., p. 519.

With him at first was Abd al-Rab Peshawari, who then moved with Roy from Moscow to Tashkent, where he joined the Oriental Propaganda Bureau along with other Indian revolutionaries. Peshawari, M. P. B. T. Acharya – of the Baku Congress secretariat – and others created the *Inqilabiun-i Hind*, the Indian revolutionary association. Acharya also moved to Tashkent, where, with lavish funding from the Bolsheviks, he published a newspaper, *Zamindar*, and recruited support from wealthy Indian merchants plying their trade in Central Asia.

One of the most significant figures connecting the Bolsheviks and the Khilafat was Maulana Ubaidullah, or Obeidullah. The Maulana was a prominent Deobandi – quite a jump from the school to Bolshevism, as M. N. Roy put it, "a respected Muslim divine," with whom he collaborated closely.[160] Ubaidullah Sindhi (1872–1944) was a Sikh convert who had been trained at the highly politicized school in Deoband Dar-ul Uloom. There he had reinterpreted the traditional Deobandi creed in a radical way and given it a revolutionary content.[161] In 1913, he had set up a madrasa, the *Nizarat al-Marif*, in New Delhi that aspired "to mobilize India's Pan-Islamists to take up jihad against the British." The *sheikh al-Hind* Mahmud al-Hassan, the principal of the Deobandi Dar-ul Uloom, however, instructed Ubaidullah to enter clandestine political activity as a more effective way to struggle for Pan-Islamist goals. Hence Ubaidullah's plan of action, which was the plan of action of the Deobandi leadership: to seek revolution abroad. Al-Hassan would go to Hijaz, the stronghold of the Wahhabi, while Ubaidullah would go to Kabul with the purpose of persuading the king of Afghanistan to declare war on Britain, while a Muslim insurrection would be started in the tribal belt to spill over into India proper. In September 1915, Ubaidullah set out to Kabul with a retinue of followers as an advisory group. In the Afghan capital, he met of course with Barakatullah and the other pro-German revolutionists.[162] From there, he called for the unification of the Muslim world in the form of a hierarchical league: "This is a special Islamic society based on military principles. Its first object is to create an alliance among Islamic kingdoms." This was to be called *Jund al-Rabbaniyya*, the Army of God.[163]

160 Roy, *Memoirs*, p. 468.

161 Ansari, "Pan-Islam and the Making of Early Indian Socialism," p. 515.

162 Pursuing his own track, Hasan succeeded in convincing the Ottoman governor of Hijaz Ghalib Pasha to issue a letter to all Muslims all over the world proclaiming jihad on behalf of the caliph against the enemies of Islam. "[A]ttack the tyrannical Christian government" wherever they suffer under its "bondage." Ibid., pp. 515–17.

163 Kramer, *Islam Assembled*, p. 59.

The welcoming committee for the *muhajirun* was in place. "The general strategy of the Bolsheviks toward the *muhajirun* recognized the very considerable power of Pan-Islamism."[164] At Tashkent, Roy established a military school (*Induskii kurs*) to start training one hundred of the muhajirun. As the Bolshevik schooling proceeded, an emotional transfer of identity occurred. At first,"[t]hey understood the world only in Pan-Islamist terms" but were impressed with the efficiency of the Bolsheviks' anti-British power. The product of the confluence of Islam and Bolshevism was a novelty. According to Roy, "Islamic ideas were so strongly entrenched in the minds of the *mujahirun* that even when some of them adopted Socialist ideas, it did not mean that they totally rejected their identification with Islam. 'Islam preaches equality, so does Communism, that is why I am a Communist,'" one of them said.[165] By the end of 1920, a number of them had become convinced Communists. "I was very much surprised to find that a few of the educated youth were more fanatical than the emigrant mass.... My preliminary efforts with the educated minority produced greater results than I expected and wanted. Most of them transferred their fanatical allegiance from Islam to Communism."[166] For two species to be able to cross and hybridize, they must have enough in common – and they did.

Roy had successfully transformed his raw material, or a part of it. He established "the first international brigade of the Red Army," which was used to harass British troops on the Ashkhabad–Meshed road connecting to Persia. The Red Army soon elevated a number of Indians to officer rank, which had an "incalculable" effect on morale, notably that of prompting Indian soldiers and noncommissioned officers to desert from the British Army. "The international brigade soon became an effective auxiliary of the Red Army. In less than a year, the Indo-British Army evacuated Meshed and the entire Persian province of Khorasan was cleared of British influence."[167] No wonder that the Bolsheviks "believed that Pan-Islamism could be a powerful anti-British movement, provided its reactionary leaders were isolated by clever diplomacy and devious political maneuvers."[168]

The Bolshevik leader explains: "I made a careful study of the Quran and other classics of Islamic theology. In public meetings I could justify the Revolution on scriptural authority."[169] The convergence was deep. As Roy

[164] Ansari, "Pan-Islam and the Making of Early Indian Socialism," p. 525.
[165] Ibid., p. 530.
[166] Roy, *Memoirs*, p. 464.
[167] Ibid., pp. 436–7.
[168] Ibid., p. 439.
[169] Ibid., p. 447.

himself stated, "The Soviet Republic was not a national state." It was like the *umma*, an ideology embodied in a polity.[170]

Roy returned to Moscow to take charge of the Eastern Section of the Communist International. "I conceived the idea of establishing in Moscow a center for the political training of revolutionaries from various Asiatic countries," he writes with some exaggeration – since a number of other Bolsheviks had come up with the same idea, including at the Baku Congress. "Lenin enthusiastically approved the idea and advised me to consult Stalin about its execution."[171] Roy then had his first meeting with Stalin, the crafty Georgian who knew about Muslims in a way none of his European Bolshevik colleagues did. Stalin's opener was brutal: "So you do not see the revolutionary significance of Pan-Islamism?"[172] The people's commissar for nationalities outlined a fully formed strategy: "Not only the national bourgeoisie in less backward colonial countries like India and China, but even the feudal landlords, *ulama* and mullahs in the Islamic countries must also be helped."[173]

Social–political movements in the Muslim and "colonial" world "must be strengthened by a well-trained revolutionary cadre," Stalin continued, a perspective with which Lenin agreed. The Communist University of the Toilers of the East (KUTVa) was to be founded to serve that purpose. Indeed, KUTVa was launched in April 1921 and effectively opened for business in September. It was "[t]he most important center for transmission of these ideas" and "remained an extremely active and influential forum" for years[174] as the cadre school for high-level Bolshevik operatives in the orient. At various points, the student body included, among others, Ho Chi-Minh; Deng Xiaoping; Liu Shaoqi; Tan Malaka, founder of the Communist Party of Indonesia; Japan's Sen Katayama; the Turkish communist leader and poet Nazim Hikmet; Khalid Bagdash, decades-long head of the Syrian Communist Party; and "Fahd," head of the Iraqi Communist Party. Courses included the theory of historical materialism, the history of class struggle and the Western labor movement, the program of the Communist Party and its tactics, a history of India and Russia, problems of nationalism, the history of the French Revolution, and the evolution of modern capitalism. Until its dissolution in the 1930s during the great Soviet purges, KUTVa

[170] Ibid., p. 326.
[171] Ibid., p. 526.
[172] Ibid., p. 537.
[173] Ibid., p. 538.
[174] Alexander A. Benningsen and S. Enders Wimbush, *Muslim National Communism*, p. 110.

trained hundreds of Muslim cadre for the holy war – red jihad, green jihad, but mostly jihad.

Sultan Galiev, the Hybrid

Muslims could very well become Bolsheviks, and in Russia many did. But Muslim Bolsheviks could with equal ease shuttle back to their roots. In such adventures, however, the mind of the traveler is not static: The journey changes him. Consciously or not, willingly or not, selectively if not in every respect, he absorbed much of what he breathed along the way. We have seen Muslims embrace Bolshevism and acquire Bolshevik "technologies" of power. We will now see Bolshevized Muslims turn away from their recent communist faith and shift to a form of political Islam, but bringing with them what they have imbibed in the process. In the case of the Soviet Muslims, the hybrid at one point received the name of "national communism." "Sultangalievism," as the Soviet state called this movement, proved to be a critical conveyor belt for transferring the new Bolshevik "technologies" to the world of Islam.

How significant was the turn to Bolshevism of the Muslims of the Russian Empire? In the first place, it was an essential element in the victory of Soviet arms in the vicious civil war that bloodied the country starting in 1918, and from which the Bolsheviks emerged as the unlikely winners. Almost 50 percent of the 6th Red Army, which held the Siberian front, one of the main fronts in the war, consisted of Muslim soldiers and officers. "At the time when the Civil War was at its peak on the Eastern and Turkestan fronts, the proportion of Tatar combatants in the Red Army exceeded fifty per cent of the total... and in certain units (for example the 5th Army) even reached up to seventy or seventy-five percent.... The courses for [Muslim] military leaders... trained thousands of Red Tatar military leaders."[175] By July 1918, the 6th Army had enrolled 50,000 Tatar and Bashkir fighters, and by early 1919, the number of Muslims fighting in the ranks of the Red Army totaled 225,000 to 250,000, "virtually all under the command of Muslim officers." They fell under the control of the Central *Muskom*, Muslim Central Committee, and the Muslim military Collegium. Muslim troops were indeed the decisive factor that tilted victory in the direction of the Bolsheviks.

The surprising alliance grew out of the racial and religious chauvinism of the "White" leadership, which utterly alienated the Muslims of the empire. The strategic obtuseness and "supercilious attitude" of Admiral Aleksandr

[175] Ibid., pp. 29, 143.

Kolchak and General Anton Denikin "pushed [the Muslims] into the arms of the Bolsheviks."[176] To the contrary, Lenin, and especially Stalin, took great care in offering a "new deal" to the Muslims. On November 17, 1917 – two weeks, that is, after the Bolshevik putsch – the new authorities issued an "Appeal to All Toiling Muslims of Russia and the Orient:" "We declare that from now your beliefs, your traditions, your national and cultural ways will be freely exercised and inalienable. Arrange your national life as you intend and decide. This is your right. You must be the masters of your own countries. You yourselves must organize your life in your own way and desires."[177] As befits Bolshevik statecraft, the intent, as summed up by one of the Bolsheviks' prominent expert handlers of the Muslims, was one of instrumentalizing the new friends: "In the East, [Muslim] nationalism is in full development. We must not try to stop this natural movement, but we must try to canalize it," wrote S. Dimanshtein.[178] With some exaggeration, but not wholly out of step with reality, the same depicted the situation in the vast Muslim communities of the empire: "Even the most hardened clericals and reactionaries were transformed into socialists."[179]

The Russian Revolution, by obliterating Russia's age-old institutions, had released all inhabitants of the empire from their traditional allegiances. It created a classic situation of anomie, where the components that have been let loose by the dissolution of old bonds seek new identities, new loyalties, and new institutions as pegs on which to hang these.

The Bolsheviks faced two constraints: They needed to mobilize the Muslims, without whom they would not be able to maintain themselves in power, but at the same time guard against their indispensable ally's possible wish to set themselves free, or even to constitute an autonomous power. This explains why Soviet policy toward "domestic" Muslims went through two distinct phases. At first, as with all other layers of the population courted by Lenin, all was sweet pleasantness. This "policy of meeting the minorities half-way [was] instituted by Lenin and expressed itself in using the Muslim . . . groups on the basis of cooperation and promises allowing them . . . complete freedom of religion and education. Some of this

[176] Gerhard von Mende, *Der nationale Kampf der Russlandtürken. Ein Beitrag zur nationalen Frage in der Sovietunion*, Berlin, Weidmannsche Buchhandlung, 1956, p. 139.

[177] Quoted in ibid., p. 147.

[178] Quoted by Benningsen and Wimbush, *Muslim, National Communism*, 75, from *Metody Revoliutsionnoi: Kommunicheskoi propagandy na Vostoke,* Zhizn Natsionalnostei, vol. 8, no. 14 (1922).

[179] S. Dimanshtein, *Revoliutisiia I Natsionalny Vopros*, vol. 3, Moscow, 1930, 288, quoted by Benningsen and Wimbush, *Muslim National Communism*, p. 22.

propaganda was couched in Pan-Islamist phraseology."[180] Another testimony states: "The Communist Party proceeded only with caution toward Islam.... A Central Committee circular letter dated Feb. 24, 1920, advises to behave cautiously regarding the [religious] beliefs of the masses."[181] For Lenin, and for Stalin who had built his Commissariat for Nationalities (*Narkomnats*) into a powerful network of power within the Soviet structures, one major task of the Muslim organizations and leaders was to Bolshevize the Muslim masses; they were "genuine schools of Marxism."[182] More immediately, Stalin "understood that to win the allegiance or neutrality of the non-Russians was to take a giant step toward winning the Civil War.... Stalin succeeded in securing the participation of a number of prominent Muslim leaders. Typically, they were former nationalists who viewed this new Soviet institution as the stage on which they could act out their national demands."[183]

The Muslim leaders made their flocks available to the Red Revolution for their own reasons. As Hanafi Muzaffar, a prominent Volga Tatar radical intellectual, put it: "[A] considerable number of Muslims viewed the revolution in Russia – and hence the Bolshevik cause – as the first step toward the liberation of Islam from European and Russian encroachments."[184] The Muslim "national socialists" were aware of the antireligious character of their Bolshevik partners, but "rationalized that an alliance with the Russian proletariat was possible because the Communism of the latter was in fact compatible with Islam." Explaining how they could have believed that, Muzaffar wrote: "Muslim people will ally themselves to Communism. Like Communism, Islam rejects narrow nationalism. Islam is international and recognizes only the brotherhood and the unity of all nations under the banner of Islam."[185] A Kazakh leader, Ahmed Baytursun, believed that the Kazakhs "will accept Communism even before all other peoples, because its traditional way of life is already close to Communism."

In a book that was the Muslim National Communists' breviary, Hanafi Muazzar proffered a broad outline of the Muslims' complex motivations:

> The essential point for us is the survival of our nation, and even more broadly, the survival of all Muslim peoples and all colonial peoples who are oppressed and threatened by European imperialism. But as long as Europe can use its might to

[180] Landau, *Pan-Islam*, pp. 161–2.
[181] Mende, *Der nationale Kampf der Russlandtürken*, p. 181.
[182] Benningsen and Wimbush, *Muslim National Communism*, p. 22.
[183] Ibid., pp. 27, 29.
[184] Ibid., p. 29.
[185] Ibid., p. 36.

maintain its imperialistic policy [in the East] our situation will remain hopeless.... It would be a great mistake for us people oppressed by Europe to fail to recognize that Marxism is fighting imperialism. As the Communist Party is fighting the same imperialism in Russia and abroad, we must accept the anti-religious character of the dictatorship of the proletariat because the alliance between the Russian proletariat and the Muslims could deal a death blow to Europe.[186]

The last clause is fundamental: The Muslim leaders were fully aware of the Bolsheviks' hostile attitude to all religions, but for tactical purposes, *Paris vaut bien une messe* ("Paris is well worth a [Catholic] mass," said the Protestant Prince Henri IV of France before converting to become king.) Marxism looked powerful, viable, conquering. Bolshevism was a formidable energizer; it was the guiding ideological force behind the battlefield victories. "These tangible manifestations of power and success reinforced in the mind of the native radicals the belief that Marxism was action as well as ideas. All other ideologies appeared bankrupt in comparison."[187] In the calculus of profit and loss made by the Muslim leaders, the ability of Bolshevism to destroy the "European" order exceeded the damage it was able to inflict on Islam. Islam would gain in the bargain. Musa Jarulallah, then the greatest living leader of Russian Islam, not only lauded this potential alliance but envisaged Communism as a springboard for a deeper penetration of Islam in Asia. "A great revolution has triumphed in Russia, giving birth to a regime of justice and equality instead of the former tyrannical regime. There Muslims enjoy equality, unity and peace.... We must take advantage of this situation to promote the Quranic Unity of Believers."[188]

As a result, "the Red Army was for the non-Russian, non-Proletarian peoples their first school of political action.... For them, the psychological impact of this army in motion was overwhelming. Massive numbers of them rushed to join its ranks, and, subsequently, the ranks of the Russian Communist Party.... [T]he Socialist army [was] as [a] political machine."[189] Even by the gruesome standards of civil war the world over, the Russian Civil War was exceptionally callous and brutish. The Bolshevik school of "politics" was a school of terror, mass murder, countless summary executions, mutilations, and torture. Those were the techniques of war, and

[186] Ibid., p. 29.

[187] Ibid., from Hanafi Muazzar's unpublished 1922 book *Din ve Millet Meseleri [Religious and National Problems]* as quoted in A. Arsharuni and Kh. Gabidullin, *Ocherki Panizlamizma I Panturkisma v Rossii*, Moscow, 1931.

[188] Interview in *Bombay Chronicle*, August 1, 1925, quoted in A. Battal-Toymas, *Musalla Jarullah Bigi*, Istanbul, 1958, p. 23.

[189] Benningsen and Wimbush, *Muslim National Communism*, p. 27.

what recruits and officers were trained and encouraged to do. As a school for political action, the Bolsheviks' Red Army taught that untrammeled violence was the supreme power. As Benningsen and Wimbush persuasively argue: "Submerged in revolution and civil war, . . . the Soviets experienced the unleashing of forces which had been suppressed and repressed for many decades. It was as if Dostoyevsky had created his Grand Inquisitor and his most famous dictum for this one Russian Apocalypse that he could not foretell: 'God is dead; all things are permitted.'"[190] For Russia's many Muslim cadres, officers, and soldiers, the Red Army was a school of terror, and a school of government by violence and terror.

Lessons so learned were overlaid on the earlier layers of jihad. In the Caucasus, for example, the tradition was the anti-Russian jihad of Sheikh Shamil and his *murids*. More broadly among the Muslims, the fighting heritage of the Sufi *tariqa* [brotherhoods] was renewed and revitalized. By a curious paradox some brotherhoods adopted revolutionary and even Socialist ideas. This was especially true of the Naqshbandi *tariqa*, which had a long and violent history of opposition to Russian power. In Socialism, some adepts found new arguments to buttress their traditional holy war against infidels. The convergence, or congruence, was not limited to technical aspects. Marx's historical materialism, with its predetermined course of history, was in some way akin to *kismet* ("fate"). Supranational communism was embodied in a "Soviet Union" that was not a nation-state, and was therefore analogous to the *über*-national *umma*. Hanafi Muazzar had written in this respect that "in the national question [w]e can point by point be at one with then Marxists, for from the viewpoint of Islam nationalism does not exist. In Islamic doctrine, the national question as it is understood today has no standing. In Islamic doctrine, there is but one *Islamiyyat*, only one brotherhood, with unity of all nationalities under the banner of Islam."[191] The similarity extended to a pseudohistory that pitted European "imperialism" against all other nations, that ascribed the origin of Western wealth to the "exploitation" of the others, and reconciled this newfangled theory of imperialism with the past, Islamic and non-Islamic, of Central Asia: "The invasions of Europe by Tamerlane, Dzhingis Khan, and the other Mongol princes, in all the cruelty of their devastating strength, pale before what the Europeans have done," wrote the leading figure of Muslim Bolshevism, Mir-Said Sultan Galiev. From Marx's and Engels's assertion that "all recorded history

190 Fydor Dostoyevsky, *The Possessed*, Chapter 5.

191 Mende, *Der nationale Kampf der Russlandtürken*, 156, quoting from A. Arsharuni in *Ocherki*.

is the history of class struggle" to Iran's Islamo-Marxist hero Ali Shariati's rewriting of history, the line is one.[192] Bolshevik ideas were "nationalized," or, to give it its proper name, Islamicized.

Mir-Said Sultan Galiev (1880–1939) joined the Bolshevik Party in November 1917. Thanks to his exceptional gifts as an organizer, he rapidly became the highest ranking Muslim in the party hierarchy – a member of the Central Muslim Committee, chairman of the Muslim military collegium, member of the Little Collective of the *Narkomnats* (Commissariat of Nationalities), editor of the *Zhin Natsionalnostei*, the official organ of the Narkomnats, and member of the Central Executive Committee of the Tatar Republic.[193] Even more important, however, was Sultan Galiev's gradual evolution of the doctrine of "national communism," which transformed Bolshevik Muslims into modern Islamists. As such, Galiev was the forerunner of the new species of Islamo-Bolshevik jihadis.

Stalin and the Bolsheviks started to rein in the Muslims as early as they could. The party was already trying to bring under control the communist political organizations of the Muslims by the end of 1918, and was doing the same inside the Red Army. In turn, the Nationalist Communists (Muslims) became radicalized. In the period between 1919 and 1923, Sultan Galiev elaborated his "Eastern Strategy" and lay the foundations of a "Colonial International" which was to be based in a projected "Republic of Turan," thus reviving Ender Pasha's dream kingdom with the same Pan-Islamist outlook. By the spring of 1920, Sultan Galiev and his cohorts were meeting secretly and establishing clandestine organizations – which they called *Ittihad ve tarakki* ("Union and Progress"), just like the Young Turks' own secret organization!

As the exile Turkmen leader Mustafa Chokay-Oglu wrote in 1935, "There was a time when we were ready to believe what the Moscow Bolsheviks were telling us, and we did believe them. The author of these lines defended Lenin, Trotsky and Stalin against their own Turkmen agents, who were plundering and murdering the Turkestani natives."[194] As the devastations perpetrated by the Bolsheviks in the Muslim areas spread and worsened, and as state repression increased, the disillusionment accelerated. The revolt of the Basmachis – a Sufi-led popular insurrection against Soviet power – was one of the most powerful manifestations of the break between Muslims and Soviets. At the 12th Congress of the Bolshevik Party in April

[192] Mir-Said Sultan Galiev, in *Zhizn Natsionalnostei*, vol. 42 (50) (1919), quoted by Benningsen, and Wimbush, *Muslim National Communism*, p. 134.

[193] Ibid., p. 207.

[194] Mende, n. 3, p. 147.

1923, a general campaign was launched against Sultan Galiev and his ideas. "Sultan Galiev was thoroughly vilified, accused of deviations and treason, and ejected from the Communist Party." He was arrested in May, but released in June; Moscow could not go too far yet in confronting the Muslims. But a new category of crime had appeared – that of "Sultangalievism."[195] In 1928 Sultan Galiev was accused of plotting to carve a "Turanian Empire" out of the Muslim and Turkic territories of the Soviet Union (Tatarstan, Bashkiria, Kazakhstan, Kirghistan, Uzbekistan, Turkmenistan, Tadzhikistan, the Volga Tatar territories).[196] He was arrested again, summarily received a ten-year sentence and was deported to the Arctic Circle subzero Solovki Island death camp. It is presumed that he died around 1939.

Sultan Galiev's doctrine, which started as the quite improperly named National Communism, rapidly developed as a hybrid between Bolshevism and Pan-Islamism. "Nonproletarian nations can bypass the capitalist stage of development and leap directly from precapitalism to socialism," he wrote. Since this was exactly the argument Lenin had used, in subversion of orthodox Marxism, to justify the Bolshevik Revolution, this carried an irony the Russians failed to notice, or appreciate. Some of Lenin's self-justificatory bickering was particularly appealing, in particular the notion that backwardness, once a stumbling block to socialist development, now was an asset. "All Muslim colonized people are proletarian peoples and as almost all classes in Muslim society have been oppressed by the colonialists, all the classes have the right to be called 'proletarian.' ... Muslim peoples are proletarian peoples.... [I]t is legitimate to say that the liberation movement in Muslim countries has the character of a Socialist revolution."[197] According to his cohort Veli Iskhakov, "The Tatars objectively are more revolutionary than the Russians, because they have been more heavily oppressed by Czarism than the Russians."[198] This was a remarkable anticipation of the cluster of ideas that were to develop fully in the form of "Castroism," "Guevarism," "thirdworldism" and "Arab Socialism," or the Mao–Lin Biao doctrine of the encirclement of the cities by the countryside as well as the doctrine of "the oppressed" and victimhood expressed later by Ali Shariati and Ayatollah Khomeini himself. Or, rather than an anticipation, was this not the influence of the forerunners?

[195] Ibid., pp. 66, 85, 87.

[196] Mende, p. 156.

[197] Mir-Said Sultan Galiev, Speech at the Regional Congress of the Kazan Organization of the Russian Communist Party (Bolshevik), March 1918, quoted by Arsharuni and Gabidullin, *Ocherki*, 78. From Benningsen and Wimbush, *Muslim National Communism*, p. 42.

[198] Benningsen and Wimbush, *Muslim National Communism*, p. 43.

"If a revolution succeeds in England, Sultan Galiev wrote, the proletariat will continue oppressing the colonies and pursuing the policy of existing bourgeois governments.... In order to prevent the oppression of the toiler of the East, we must unite the Muslim masses in a communist movement that will be our own and autonomous."[199] Under the veneer of Marxian phraseology, Sultan Galiev had returned to the antinomy of *dar al-Islam* versus *dar al-Kufr*, or rather he recombined both to create the new doctrine. He went even further: His neo-*umma* would have to extend to the entire world. "Soviet Russia is a transitory phenomenon. The hegemony of the Russian people over other nations necessarily must be replaced by the dictatorship of those same nations over the Russians" in a first stage.[200] Further, the movement "charted a theoretical course which, if successful in practice, would guarantee them supremacy not only over the Russians, but over the whole industrial world. What emerged was an 'Eastern strategy.' The thrust was...that the revolution should be exported beyond the borders of the former czarist empire, incorporating into the National Communist universe millions of oppressed peoples – mostly Asian Muslims."[201] According to their Bolshevik opponents, they "acted as the standard-bearers not only of Tatar nationalism but also of Pan-Islamic democracy."[202] Sultan Galiev was rapidly developing his doctrine of a "Colonial International" and the ambitions it carried.

> The sovietization of Azerbaijan is a highly important step in the evolution of Communism in the Near East. Just as Red Turkestan is playing the role of the revolutionary lighthouse for Chinese Turkestan, Tibet, Afghanistan, India, Bukhara, and Khiva, Soviet Azerbaijan with its old and experienced proletariat and its party – the *Hümmet* Party [of Azerbaijan] will become the Red lighthouse for Persia, Arabia and Turkey.[203]

Collaborators of Sultan Galiev who controlled the government of the Tatar Republic in 1922 created within the commissariat of justice a special Sharia commission, entrusted with the task of reconciling and coordinating Soviet and Quranic law! The integration of Islam into a form of Bolshevism, or vice-versa, was working apace. Sultan Galiev and his comrades were not

199 Ibid., 46. From Z. I. Gimranov, 9th Conference of the Tatar Obkom, 1923, published in *Stenograficheskii otchot 9oi obstnoi konferentsii Tatarskoi organisatsii, RKP(b)*, Kazan, 1924, p. 130.

200 Quoted by Tobolev in *Kontrrivolütsiyon soltangaliëvchekele karshy*, Kazan, 1929, 39, in Benningsen and Wimbush, *Muslim National Communism*, p. 47.

201 Ibid., p. 52.

202 Quoted by Benningsen and Wimbush, *Muslim National Communism*, from L. Rabinstein, *V borbe za Leninskuiu Natsionalnuiu politiku*, Kazan, 1930, pp. 37–9.

203 Benningsen and Wimbush, *Muslim National Communism*, 54. From Tobolec, p. 14.

traditional Pan-Islamists, but hybrids representing the new species of Pan-Islam in the Era of Terror and Revolution. Stalin's interventions in 1923 to liquidate them politically show how dangerous they were considered to be. As their biographies, or their obituaries, testify, many of the Muslim National Communists were purged in the late 1920s and executed in the Great Purges of the 1930s.

"After the liquidation of the NCs, their ideas... muted in the Soviet Union, lived on, and while the Republic of Turan was not realized in their lifetimes... their ideas found other springboards to the underdeveloped world, leaving them a legacy."[204] The legacy was "a body of ideas or disconnected notions about the past which float through the collective memory of society." Further, the ideas developed by the Soviet Muslims

> about the synthesis of Nationalism and Communism, about the complementary nature of Marxism and Islam, about Asia's role as the progenitor of revolution and about the division of the world into oppressed and oppressors in one variant or another has penetrated into virtually every corner of the Third World. It is impossible to say with certainty that in each instance these ideas were carried beyond Soviet borders by intimate personal contacts with the Muslim Communist leaders themselves.[205]

But the transmission occurred – organically, as it were, through KUTVa, most of whose teachers were of that persuasion, including the leading Muslim figures of the Bolshevik Party; through the KUTVa alumni who returned to their own countries; through the Communist Parties that continued to preach more orthodox forms of the doctrine; through Muslims who left the USSR and settled elsewhere. KUTVa leaders and professors, such as the Dutchman Hj. F. M. Sneevliet (Maring), M. N. Roy, the Persian Sultan Zade, and others – many of whom, like Roy, subsequently broke with Stalin and communism – spread those ideas farther after their disillusionment with Soviet communism.

The ambiguity of the hybrid ideology was captured in an article written by Sultan Galiev in 1921 entitled "The Methods of Antireligious Propaganda among the Muslims." His definition of Islam was light-years away from the accepted Marxist–Leninist canon, and fell afoul of the unceasing outpouring of atheist propaganda by the Bolsheviks' League of the Godless:

> The essential factor which determines the position of Islam is its youthfulness. Of all the "great religions" of the world, Islam is the youngest and therefore the most solid and the strongest as far as influence is concerned.... Islam has best preserved social and political elements, whereas other religions emphasize above all ethnic

[204] Benningsen and Wimbush, *Muslim National Communism*, p. 58.

[205] Ibid., pp. 108–9.

and religious elements. [Regarding] Muslim law – the *shariat* –... many of its prescriptions have a clear-cut, positive character.... Islam penetrates the spirit of the believer more deeply than other religions; it is therefore a more difficult and delicate task to combat its influence. The best proof of that lies in the personal position of Muslim clergymen, which is much more solid than that of representatives of other religions.... The Russian priest, appointed by superior authorities, certainly has a lesser authority over his flock than does the Tatar mullah or the Uzbek [*alim*].... The latter consider themselves to be "servants of the people" and lend an attentive ear to their wishes. They are more democratic and closer to the people and exert a greater influence on them than does the village priest over the Russian muzhik."[206]

Along with this pseudosociology went a pseudohistory of anti-imperialist victimhood according to which:

[D]uring the course of the last century the whole of the Muslim world was exploited by European imperialism and served as the material base for its economy. The fact has profoundly marked the religion of the Muslims. The expansion of Western imperialism manifested itself first in the form of the Crusades and later by economic conquest. But the majority of Muslims always felt this battle to be a political conflict, that is to say a battle against Islam as a whole. Moreover, the reverse would have been impossible, for in the eyes of the Muslims, the Muslim world forms an indivisible whole, without distinction, nationality or tribe. Because of this, Islam was and still is, at least in the eyes of Muslims, an oppressed religion forced to be on the defensive. In other words, the historical evolution of Islam fosters a feeling of solidarity among the diverse groups of the faithful and lands.... These conditions make the anti-Islam campaign a difficult one.... We must repeat that Islam is different from other religions in substance."[207]

Was this the plea of an atheist to the Bolsheviks to go soft on Islam for tactical reasons, or an Islamist's manipulation of the Bolsheviks' tactical need to go soft on Islam? Of course, the reality of the Bolshevik attitude toward religion – and non-Russian peoples – was far removed from their sanctimonious rhetoric. Regarding the principle of national self-determination which Lenin had fought tooth and nail throughout the history of the party, his disciple Nikolai Bukharin had said in a somewhat unguarded moment:

If we accept [the principle] and proclaim it regarding all the colonies, all these Hottentots, Bushmen, Blacks and Hindus and all the rest, we will lose nothing at all. To the contrary, we will gain, for all these national masses in motion will go against foreign imperialism and their struggle will merge with the general struggle against

[206] "The Methods of Antireligious Propaganda among the Muslims," *Zhizn Natsionalnostei*, vol. 29, no. 127 (1921) and vol. 30, no. 1128(192), quoted in Benningsen and Wimbush, *Muslim National Communism*, pp. 145–7.

[207] Ibid., pp. 147, 157.

imperialism. Thus, as resolutely nationalist a movement as that of the Hindus only brings grist to our mill inasmuch as it applies to the destruction of British imperialism.

The leading Bolshevik intellectual Riazanov chimed in: to him the salvation of Soviet power lay with "unleashing the hunting pack of the oppressed nations against the imperialist wolves."[208]

In the end, it was not the intent but the result that mattered. For many years, the party leadership gave Sultan Galiev and his friends a rather unrestricted mandate to do as they saw fit, to expound their "mutated Marxism" in party theoretical and political journals, and to train more cadre in this spirit. The arguments used, at any rate, were standard talking points of Muslim apologetics; there is little new in the grand historical narrative proffered by a Sayyid Qutb, a Maududi, a Shariati, or a bin Laden compared to this Manichean travesty of history, an ahistorical morality tale of self-justification.

What the National Communist experience of the Soviet Muslims established was that on the Muslim side, it was not necessary to espouse the whole of Bolshevism – "dialectical materialism," "historical materialism," and the philosophical mumbo-jumbo that go with them – to acquire what was most essential to that creed: the techniques of power through terror, of the management and manipulation of masses, of politically organizing people. Bolshevism and Islam may make strange bedfellows – but at bottom, it was not unreasonable of French sociologist Jules Monnerot to describe communism as the "Islam of the 20th century."[209] Had he lived longer, he could have added that Islam was the communism of the twenty-first century.

Ideological Infectors: Communist Parties in the Middle East

If "Sultangalievist" heterodoxy was ruthlessly crushed within the borders of the Soviet Union, Soviet power found high-value forms of the virus to export. It was admittedly never an easy thing for the Bolsheviks to do so, even in their Stalinist incarnation. For any form of "national" communism carried

[208] Quoted by B. Nikitine, "Le problème musulman selon les chefs de l'émigration russe" in "Le Bolchévisme et l'Islam," II. Hors de Russie, *Revue du Monde Musulman,* (décembre 1922) 55–82, from V. Chernov, *Revoliutsionnaya Rossiya*, vol. 3 (February 1921).

[209] Jules Monnerot, *Sociologie du Communisme*, 3rd ed., Paris, Gallimard, 1949, esp. chapter 1.

with it the threat of a "nationalist deviation," meaning a loss of Moscow's direct control over the local communist forces. On the other hand, the ability to mimic, chameleon-like, local nationalisms and to leverage religion-based discontent and rebellion was too precious a political instrument to be neglected altogether.

In practice, this meant extremely sharp zig-zags in Moscow's marching orders to local communists, oscillations between "united front" tactics with native peoples and organizations, and sectarian retrenchment on a Moscow-only party line. Still, as time went on, and especially as a result of the seventh World Congress of the Communist International in 1935 and its emphasis on "Popular Fronts," Sultangalievism-for-export gained currency, notably in the Middle East.

Politics in the region was a very fluid and inconstant concept. Ideologies tended to be factional markers, or flags, rather than coherently embraced world outlooks, as in the case of European political parties.[210] An adviser to President Anwar Sadat once said that states in the Middle East, save Egypt, are tribes draped in national flags. The same could be said for parties that very rarely transcended the boundaries of a given religious or ethnic affiliation. As usual in the region, family, clan, and tribe trumped other considerations. "Left" and "right" were alien vestments that uneasily fit the body politic of the region. One could jump without compunction from being a socialist to a fascist, a Nazi to a communist, and a Muslim all the while; nobody cried wolf! The adjustment was not that big – the outer garment changed, not the fundamentals.

Most Middle Eastern politics, though, were possessed of a few common denominators. The peoples there "want[ed] their own government – not good government;"[211] "'Anti-imperialism'... more often than not, cover[ed] an *impérialisme manqué*;" and

> the climate of opinion in the Middle East in the late 1930s was vaguely pro-Fascist as it is now [in 1956] vaguely pro-Communist. This does not mean that all the main tenets of totalitarian ideology were or are accepted by most of the people. But there was and is a conviction that Fascism (and Communism), apart from certain excesses,

[210] A comparison may be made with Lucian Pye's analysis of the various *guanxi* networks of influence inside the Chinese Communist Party. It is the *guanxi* that elects an ideological marker to differentiate itself from other contenders for power, rather than ideological differences that determine the formation of a guanxi network. See Lucian Pye, *The Spirit of Chinese Politics*, Cambridge, MA: Harvard University Press, 1992.

[211] Walter Z. Laqueur, *Communism and Nationalism in the Middle East*, New York, Praeger, 1956, p. 11.

ha[d] somehow a good kernel, that it fill[ed] people with enthusiasm and rejuvenates nations, that it gets things done, and that, in short, the future belongs to the dynamic movements.[212]

Communist Parties in the Middle East never assumed power; when they took part in government, they were but the junior partners of stronger, and better armed, forces. More often than not, their allies cast them out as soon as they were dispensable. They often were kept in a tame state, as interfaces with either some part of the local population that had to be co-opted, or as interfaces with the Soviet Union. The only exception, a party that was a genuine mass party and came closer to political power, was the *Tudeh* in Iran, of which more later. But the role assigned by Soviet Russia to the Middle Eastern communist parties was not primarily to be contenders for power. They were Moscow's conveyor belts, and they conveyed crucial Soviet ideas and practices, which were avidly lapped up by the target audiences.

In this context, whether Middle Eastern communist parties bought Moscow much or little influence matters little. The question here is whether – and if so, how much of – their messages and behaviors were assimilated through various channels by the socioideological forces on which modern jihad has rested.

On the one hand, "Communist leaders [in the Middle East] have pointed out ever since the period of the Popular Front in the mid-1930s that early Islam was indeed communistic (or at least democratic)." On the other hand, "Attempts to find Socialist or Communist parallels in the Quran have been made by the left wing of the Muslim Brotherhood in Egypt and Syria."[213] A common hatred toward the West and a deep-seated ideological kinship explain the convergences; the claim by both to be the exclusive owner of absolute truth accounts for their bitter enmity. "Communism and extreme nationalism, frequently without a clear dividing line, [were] the two main forces among academic youth in the Arab countries. Members of orthodox Muslim organizations and right-wing extremists collaborated closely with the Communists under the framework of various 'fronts' [because] a radical change [could] be effected only by means of an authoritarian regime, a dictatorship." [214]

The ideologist of the Muslim Brotherhood Sayyid Qutb wrote in 1952: "I have demanded liberty for the Communists under the same conditions

[212] Ibid., p. 259.
[213] Ibid., p. 6.
[214] Ibid., p. 17.

as for all others who fight against tyranny. I have claimed this liberty for them, considering them honest men who are to be met with arguments, not bullets."[215] Considering Qutb's penchant to recommend hails of bullets toward all *jahili* forces, the compliment was significant. Cooperation was a pattern. "The Middle East has been a successful experimental field for Communist front organizations of various kinds.... Communist collaboration with other political parties and movements began in the late 1920s when the party line was to collaborate with the left wing of national movements," the course Stalin and M. N. Roy had defined.[216] Partnership with Muslim extremists and Arab nationalists went far beyond the left. The Grand Mufti of Jerusalem Amin al-Husayni, who is often better known as a Nazi collaborator, was the object of assiduous courting from the Communist International over a period of time spanning several decades. The role Moscow ascribed to the Communist Party of Palestine had profound, long-term, and largely unanticipated consequences on the Arab and Muslim world.

Lenin had carried out virulent polemics against all attempts by oppressed minorities within the czar's empire to constitute their own parties. One of the main targets of his venom had been the organization of Jewish socialist workers, the *Bund*, ever treated as a "splintering" proletarian force. Nations were passé; nationalism was reactionary. Animus against Zionists was ever greater, for theirs was a bourgeois, or petit-bourgeois ideology. If Lenin was not particularly anti-Semitic (as long as Jewish workers were kept in their place), Stalin was devoured by the passion. The Communist International's Middle Eastern policy bore witness to the legacy of both.

The Communist Party of Palestine (CPP) had been tasked with "Arabization." "Out of the Jewish ghetto!" Karl Radek proclaimed – a slogan that remained in force for many years.[217] Success depended on the party becoming an Arab mass party. In November 1924, Bedouins and fellaheen violently attacked Jewish settlers arriving in the valley of Jezreel. The CPP had called on the Arabs to fight the Jews on the eve of their settlement, charging that they intended "to colonize the country of the ruins of the fellaheen village." Although no villager had been displaced by the Jewish National Fund's land purchase – Afula was considered an uninhabitable swamp – "the Communists claimed that the Arabs were the rightful owners of the country, that the Jews were imperialists, and that the fight against them was part of the general anti-imperialist struggle in the

215 *Al Akhbar*, Aug. 15, 1952, quoted by Laqueur, *Communism and Nationalism*, p. 239.
216 Laqueur, *Communism and Nationalism*, p. 236.
217 This entire subsection will follow Walter Laqueur's narrative.

colonies. The Afula pattern returned frequently during the late 1920s and 1930s."[218]

Even though the Communist Party (CP) called on its members to support the extremist wing of the Arab national movement, the latter's leaders Musa Kasim and Amin al-Husayni, did not initially reciprocate. The CP nonetheless persisted. In 1928, addressing the seventh Arab Conference, Communist Party leaders stated, "The homeland of a Jew is wherever he happens to be born, while Palestine belongs to the Arabs.... It is our sacred duty to fight side by side with the Arabs and to arouse the people of the world against the Zionist danger." The CP was ever trying "to give additional impetus to the Arab demonstrations and [armed] attacks as 'a link in the chain of peasant uprisings against imperialist colonization in all colonial countries.'" The Arabic-language periodicals of the CP "called on every patriotic Arab to go out and fight to save his honor and country against the invaders."[219]

In 1929, Amin al-Husayni set off bloody riots against the Jewish communities of Palestine, during which 133 were killed and 300 wounded, mostly in Hebron and Safed. For the German Communist daily *Rote Fahne*, "the anti-Jewish concomitant of the [Arab] revolt was a natural development that should not be regretted." In a programmatic document, the CPP stated: "In a country like Palestine a revolutionary movement without pogrom is inevitable." Leaflets called on Arabs to rise against their Zionist and British oppressors. In later "self-criticism," the party blamed itself for having been insufficiently bloody-minded: "The party has forgotten that the fellaheen and bedouin waited for leadership and wanted to be shown what to do with their knives and revolvers." "The CP had, in fact, become a part of the most extreme wing of the Arab national movement." It was actively inciting pogroms and killings. "But the day is near when the Arab peasant will rise again and no imperialist force, no Jewish fascist cohort, will be able to prevent this explosion," a communist paper wrote in 1930. The party even criticized Amin al-Husayni for being too moderate. It called on the Arabs to march on Tel Aviv and to use force against the "Nazi Histadrut" (the Jewish labor union).

The CP worked closely with the newly formed *Istiqlal* [independence] Party and especially its left wing, led by Hamdi Husayni from Gaza, who had visited Russia in the early 1930s. The party overall was led by members of the mufti's Arab Higher Committee, in particular religious aides of the

[218] Laqueur, *Communism and Nationalism*, p. 78.
[219] Ibid.

mufti such as Sheikh Muzafir. Together, they violently opposed the inflow of German Jews fleeing the Third Reich. In 1934, the latter were branded a "Zionist-Imperialist-fascist army." Communist literature heavily insisted on "the remarkable identity between Nazism and Zionism." The next year, the CP announced a new "Arab Revolt" and denounced the "Zionist Fascists and chauvinists for waging war on the Arab people and killing fellaheen." The Jewish self-defense force, the *Haganah*, ought to be outlawed and disbanded, the party said. On the eve of the major riots that then broke out and started the bloody Arab Revolt (1935–37), "representatives of the party met the [Grand] Mufti in order to hammer out a working agreement." This occurred after the party executive had decreed that "the Arab Communists should actively participate in destroying Zionism and imperialism, while the Jewish members should do their share by weakening the [Jewish side] from within." Two communists were attached to the general staff planning and coordinating the revolt, one as the intelligence chief of the Arab militias and another as a field commander.

"The Jewish minority in Palestine is a colonizing minority by its very nature," the party insisted. It sent members to commit terror acts against the "Zionist and imperialist" camp on behalf of the "progressive Arab" side. By the midsummer of 1937, the party press denounced the "mad, chauvinist, militarist incitement of the Zionists." The party's support for the Arab leadership, the grand mufti, "reached the stage of full identification," even as al-Husayni by then was receiving substantial support from fascist Italy and Nazi Germany. When the British authorities deported him, the party organized protests. Even after World War II, when Amin al-Husayni "escaped" from Paris with the help of various Western intelligence services intent on employing his valued services, and found shelter in Cairo, the Communists kept in close contact with him. "The Arab people, which has remained faithful to its leaders, celebrates . . . throughout the country."

In sum, starting in the 1920s and 1930s, the Communist Party of Palestine was the great instructor of the Pan-Islamist nationalist movement led by the Grand Mufti Amin al-Husayni in the fine arts of Communist agitprop, the conveyor of crucial Marxist–Leninist concepts, such as "imperialism" and "colonialism." It pioneered the application of European political categories to the Middle Eastern scene in general, and the Jewish–Arab conflict in particular. Most of the ugly repertoire of modern Arab and Muslim anti-Semitism came from the Soviet Union (with only the racial-biological component added by the Nazis). The CPP taught the Arab extremists the use of Bolshevik rhetorical devices previously unknown. The "anti-imperialism" so imported by the communists was remarkably ingested by the Muslim extremists, to the point of becoming integral to their conceptions and expression. It merged with traditional jihadi views that animated the Arabs of the region. In the amalgamation of Bolshevism with jihad that turned out to be so crucial to modern jihad, this was crucial to training the Arabs in Soviet-style politics.

Communist cadres and promising leaders had been sent to Moscow for training. Starting in 1927, groups of Arab Communist students went there for a prolonged course at the Communist International academy. Between 1929 and 1935, more than such cadres went to the USSR, some for three years – the duration of the course for future party leaders at the International Lenin School. Among them were all leaders of the party in the 1930s. Many communist leaders and cadres left the party and found themselves new political homes. Their training did not go to waste but spread farther afield into those new homes, whether these were those of pan-Arab nationalist or Muslim extremist movements.

Communist "united front" tactics had already advanced this kind of relationship.

> The political allies which the Communists have found in recent years came from different quarters: the extreme-right wing and fanatical religious camp, such as the Muslim Brotherhood and Ahmad Husain's "Socialist" party in Egypt, the *Istiqlal* in Iraq, and other groups elsewhere. Each particular tie of this kind could probably be explained as a freak, an interesting phenomenon but nevertheless atypical. But the fact that such collaboration has not been restricted to one particular country but has taken place everywhere in the Middle East makes generalization and the drawing of certain conclusions imperative. It cannot be mere coincidence that the main proponents of fascism in Egypt, Syria and Iraq cooperate nowadays with the Communists in the framework of sundry national, anti-imperialist and "peace" fronts.[220]

The pattern, as the adventures of the Khilafat movement have shown, was not incidental, but rather systematic. Whatever the ultimate differences in ideologies, cooperation and interpenetration were rife.

Likewise, in Egypt, in the last years of King Faruq's rule, Communists and Muslim Brothers shared prison cells, giving the latter their first opportunity to meet the former in the flesh. It is in "the internment camps at Huckstep and Abukir... that the foundations for the 'National Front' of 1951–52 were laid through which the Communists achieved their greatest successes in the history of their movement." Already in 1950, the other communist front organization, "Partisans of Peace" ("Peace Movement" in

220 Ibid., p. 236.

Europe), collected 12,000 signatures for the "Stockholm Appeal," and a year later another 100,000 for successor appeals. Leaders of the semifascist right Ahmad Husain and Fathi Ridwan attended Peace congresses, while the secretary-general of the Peace organization was Yusuf Hilmi, earlier of the pro-fascist wing of the Nationalist Party. The *Mouvement démocratique de libération nationale*, a Communist front, began a period of intense collaboration with Ahmad Husain and the Muslim Brotherhood, and in 1953 reached an agreement for joint action with them against the military regime. The Egyptian quasi-fascists became "neutralists." The "progressive" wing of the Muslim Brothers affirmed the necessity of collaborating with the communists against imperialism. By July 1954, Sayyid Qutb and the other Brotherhood leaders were cooperating with the Communist Party against Nasser, and a common political platform was ironed out. "Not a few members of the *Ikhwan* [Brotherhood] went over to the Communists."[221] The communists' allies also included the already mentioned Fathi Ridwan and Ahmad Husain, once leader of *Misr al-Fatah* (Young Egypt), or "Green Shirts," a paramilitary organization directly modeled on Nazi and fascist movements. Husain had asserted: "We are infinitely closer to Rome and Berlin than to Paris and London." His movement continued its violent activities during the war. By 1945, though, articles favorable to the Soviet Union and communism started appearing in the movement's press. By 1949, "Socialism" was a staple notion. Fathi Ridwan was now minister for propaganda – and an honored member of the Peace Movement. By 1951, fascistic Yusuf Hilmi had progressed to be the president of the Egyptian Partisans of Peace and Ahmad Husain the publisher of the journal *Ishtirakiyya*, "Socialism," which could be "compared only with the early writings of Adolf Hitler in the *Völkischer Beobachter* of 1921 and 1922. Incitement to kill all foreigners, together with anti-feudal slogans, an anti-Jewish hate campaign, threats against the Western 'plutocrats,' demands for agrarian reform, and defense of religion and the interest of the Holy Fatherland."[222]

The same scenario transpired in Syria. The "Islamic Socialist Front" "offered interesting parallels to both the Muslim Brotherhood and Ahmad Husain's 'socialism,'" and it was the local front for the Muslim Brotherhood. Its leader Sheikh Mustafa al-Sibai demanded that Syria "adopt an Eastern [pro-Soviet] orientation," as he orated at a mass demonstration held in 1950 to honor Joseph Stalin. "We shall fight the West regardless whether its pressure continues or not; we shall cooperate with the Russians

[221] Ibid., p. 242.
[222] Ibid., p. 250.

and ask them for help." Front leader Muhammad Mubarak averred: "We shall welcome the idea of Islamistan on condition that it is not directed against the Soviet Union." And to crown the whole affair, another leader of the Islamic Socialist Front (ISF) stated: "The I.S.F. is a Marxist drink in a Muslim cup." The leader in question was Maaruf Dawalibi, an old associate of Amin al-Husayni, the Nazi mufti, who had spent the Second World War churning out pro-Nazi propaganda in Berlin while political secretary to al-Husayni. He was now "the leading exponent of a pro-Soviet orientation."[223] "The Arab countries would prefer to become a Soviet Republic rather than a Jewish state," he said, and Israel was "tantamount to establishing an American colony in the Middle East." No wonder that the Soviet front organization the Partisans of Peace was such a hit in Syria: 60,000 signed the first Stockholm Peace Appeal, in 1950, and 265,000, a successor the next year. This included a majority of the members of parliament and large numbers of prominent divines. A wide network of communist front organizations was spawned, for students, artists, lawyers, and youth. One of the leading Damascus ulama was Sheikh Muhammad al-Ashman, a former gang leader in the Palestinian revolt of 1936–9. He had gone to Moscow and returned to head the Peace Movement.

Alongside the Syrian party, the Communist Party of Lebanon was one of the strongest of all CPs in the Middle East, though the confessional nature of Lebanese society ever prevented it from conquering power. It operated as "a sort of foster-parent to the other [Communist] parties in the Arab world."[224] Relations between both parties were especially close, both having been part of the French Mandate in the interwar years. Khalid Bakdash and a group of cadre had spent several months in Moscow, taken part in the Seventh World Congress of the Communist International, and undergone training in Marxism–Leninism, agitation and propaganda. The "Anti-Fascist League," established in 1938 by party honcho Antun Thabit, held its first congress in 1939. As the war went on, "Everyone in the Levant was in favor of friendship with Russia so soon as it became clear who was going to win the war.... Communist progress in Lebanon was spectacular, notably in the intelligentsia." At the time, the CP ruled the streets of Beirut: "The Communists had almost no competition in street demonstrations because in Lebanon, as in the other Arab countries, political parties in the Western sense did not exist... [and did] not maintain a party apparatus capable of competing with the Communists."

[223] Ibid., p. 256.
[224] Ibid., p. 137.

The party and its front organization made the "struggle for peace" their prime aim. Many of the great names in Lebanese life, the heads of the *grandes familles* who were the lead notabilities under the Ottomans and the political leaders thereafter, affixed their names to the Stockholm Appeal – former president Alfred Naccache, Sami al-Sulh, Hamid Franjieh, Pierre Gemayel, the Maronite patriarch, the Greek Orthodox bishop, the mufti. Laqueur underlines that "the leaders of the Syrian and Lebanese Communist Parties have shown a larger measure of political acumen than their colleagues at the helm of other Middle East parties.... [T]hey have shown much adaptability to national exigencies and traditions. They have quoted the Quran and the *hadith* and made a wide use of Arab history and tradition."[225]

In Iraq, the Communist Party was close to the "great national movement" of the pro-Nazi regime of Rashid Ali Gailani. Indeed, when Gailani and his backers, the Nazi "Four Colonels," took power in 1941, the Soviet Union was the first country in the world – before the Third Reich! – to extend the new government diplomatic recognition. The CPP leader Fuad Nasir, later first secretary of the Communist Party of Jordan, belonged to the entourage of the Grand Mufti al-Husayni, who had resided in Baghdad since October 1939 and was an important leader of the putschists' operation. The mufti declared jihad against Britain. Several leading Iraqi communists worked in the regime's department of propaganda, led by the fascist leader Sadiq Shinshil – who ten years later again collaborated with the Communists as head of the *Istiqlal* Party. That party was the reincarnation of the Iraqi fascists' prewar and wartime movement, but from 1951 it worked directly with the Communist Party. Saddam Hussein's own family bore witness to this fluid cooperation. He was raised by his uncle, profascist Khairullah Tulfah; joined the Baath Party, which was an eclectic mix of Nazi and communist themes; and built a regime that was a favorite partner of Moscow's.

Communism was often a transitional faith, a temporary substitute. Secular ideologies among the Arabs kept their religious substratum, which allowed many of the *pro tempore* Marxists and the transient communists to return to Islam after some years spent immersed in pro-Moscow or other communist organizations.[226] They did not return to the fold as if nothing had happened. They had been steeped in Soviet ideas concerning the nature of politics, the manner in which propaganda and agitation should

[225] Ibid., p. 167.

[226] Fouad Ajami, *The Dream-Palace of the Arabs: A Generation's Odyssey*, New York, Pantheon Books, 1998; Fouad Ajami, *The Arab Predicament: Arab Political Thought and Practice Since 1967*, Cambridge, MA, Cambridge University Press, 1981.

be carried out, the way in which people should be organized – the practice of the united front, the acceptability of terror and mass murder as legitimate tools, the overriding importance of the secret police, contempt for the rule of law and other "formal liberties" that only "bourgeois prejudice" respected, and the notion that masses are only malleable dolts in the hands of the self-proclaimed vanguard – in brief, all the governing shibboleths of Leninist–Stalinist communism. "A Marxist drink in a Muslim cup," Dawalibi had said. Yet that Syrian figure, first and foremost a radical Islamist who in turn found himself happily working with Nazis, and then communists, testifies to the contamination of the cup by the drink.

The Young Turks' impact on the entire region once ruled by the Ottomans, had been clear-cut: "The brutalization of public life by violence, repression and terror; the intrusion of the army into politics, leading to the twin evils of a militarized government and a politicized command... [a] wretched cycle of plot and counterplot, repression and sedition, tyranny, humiliation, and defeat."[227] The brutalization played itself into the modern Middle East by way of Ottoman-trained Arab military officers and the political role they played.[228] The next wave, or the next cycle, of brutalization, of internalization of terror as the principal tool of politics in general and of government in particular, had come from the Soviet contributor. An additional donor brought components as toxic as those thrown in by the Soviets: National socialism was no less than Bolshevism present at creation in the genesis of modern jihad.

The Nazi Contribution

Soviet communism and national socialism are kith and kin. Both are utopian enterprises that aim at radically reshaping human nature and the world and propelling them into a final state of perfection inhabited by their respective version of the "New Man." The principle excludes any other consideration. Those who know the principle are the Elect, and the stupendous import of their cosmic mission gives them exorbitant rights. They are the law unto themselves, the rest is chattel, liable to be used or exterminated at will. As we examined in Chapter 2, both communism and national socialism in turn were the echoes in modern European society of the ancient Gnostic creeds, and of the collective Gnostic mass movement that had wreaked havoc for centuries in medieval Europe.

[227] Lewis, *The Emergence of Modern Turkey*, p. 227.
[228] Kedourie, *Politics in the Middle East*, esp. pp. 277ff, 295ff.

As the world of Islam by necessity became aware of European doctrines and practices, some interest went to the Liberal tradition – on and off during the *Tanzimat* period of the Ottoman Empire, as well as in the remarkable efforts of Sir Sayyed Ahmad Khan in the Indian raj. Guns were readily assimilated into military forces, but liberal democracy was not; in the Arab world, interest was fleeting at best. What borrowing took place almost exclusively concerned the authoritarian, dictatorial, and totalitarian ideologies.[229]

Antagonism toward the West, itself identified with Liberalism, played a role. My enemy's enemy is my friend; my friend's ideology is the enemy of my enemy's ideology. The apparent "efficiency" of the totalitarian model to mobilize society's resources also had an impact: If it was possible for many in Western society, with its experience of democracy, to believe that the totalitarian regimes "worked better" than liberal democracy, it was all the more so in regions that had no experience of it at all. But the assimilation of ideas and practices went beyond mere fashion or misreading. There was enough of an essential similarity between donor and recipient to allow the ready acquisition of many components of the donor's worldview and modus operandi. Besides Bolshevism, the other principal twentieth-century influence on modern jihad, accordingly, was German national socialism – two ideologies that competed for the same turf while sharing many of their core tenets.

The intellectual influence of Romantic-reactionary German nationalism in the Middle East, from Fichte to the ideologues of Wilhelminian Germany, has been abundantly documented. We have also examined the political story of "Jihad Made in Germany." Germany's direct intervention in the Middle East, however, receded in step with the relative stabilization of Germany in the 1920s. When Hans von Seeckt was forced to retire from his command of the Reichswehr in 1926 (and seek new adventures as Chiang Kai-shek's senior military adviser), the Weimar Republic's geopolitical interest in the region vanished altogether. For the Middle East, Germany was merely an important trade partner: "[T]he Germans were attractive partners especially for Middle Eastern nationalists who looked for alternative suppliers."[230]

Hitler's policy toward the Middle East originally resembled Bismarck's. He accepted the reality of the British Empire, thought colonial outposts to be "nothing but trouble," and was happy for his ally Benito Mussolini to have his way in the eastern Mediterranean, Africa, and the Arab world. Additionally, his racially conditioned views of the Arabs and of Islam were

229 Hourani, *Arabic Thought in the Liberal Age,* esp. Chapter XI, pp. 310–23.

230 Schwanitz, "The German Middle East Policy," p. 10.

not flattering. He referred to them as "painted half-apes, who want to feel the whip."[231] He had only a jaundiced view of the use the Reich could have for the Muslims:

> The "Holy War" can produce in our German muttonheads the pleasant thrill that now others are ready to shed their blood for us, because that cowardly speculation has, to speak bluntly, been the silent father of all such hopes – but in reality it will meet a ghastly end under the fire of English machine guns and the hail of explosive bombs.[232]

Accordingly, the Middle East occupied but a secondary place in Hitler's geopolitical schemes, far second to what he foremost coveted – the Russian *Lebensraum*. "An examination of German Middle Eastern policy under Hitler confirms that the region was of no concern to him."[233] It was only if and when the region became a major war theater that it would matter: "German planners were interested in French and British-influenced territories and immediate neighbors of Russia such as Afghanistan and Turkey." The Middle East would thus be a drain on British resources in manpower and material and a potential staging area for attacks on the USSR. "Just for this eventuality, Jihad made in Germany became important again." The now-ancient Max von Oppenheim even updated his World War I plan and memorandum for the benefit of the German Foreign Office. The Reich was however hampered by its Italian ally's own designs. Hitler's *Order #32* called for German Middle East plans to pave the way for later battles against the British. There, too, he would inflict an "uncompromising war against the Jews." Thanks to the new friends of the Reich, "the Arabs will liquidate them," was Berlin's opinion by 1937.[234] As a result, "The formation of a Jewish state... under British mandate is not in Germany's interest, since a Palestinian state... would create an additional position of power for international Jewry.... Germany therefore has an interest in strengthening the Arab world as a counterweight against such a possible increase in power for world Jewry," an instruction from Foreign Minister Konstantin von Neurath read.[235]

[231] Quoted by Lewis, *Semites and Anti-Semites: An Inquiry into Conflict and Prejudice*, New York, W. W. Norton & Co. 1987, p. 140.
[232] Quoted in Kramer, *Islam Assembled*, p. 158.
[233] Schwanitz, "The German Middle East Policy," p. 12.
[234] Lewis, *Semites*, p. 142.
[235] Lukasz Hirszowicz, *The Third Reich and the Arab East*, London, Routledge & Kegan Paul; Toronto: Toronto University Press, 1966, p. 30.

Accordingly, as early as 1937, the "half-apes" were upgraded by the *Völkischer Beobachter* to the lofty status of proto-Aryans, thanks to Armenian and Circassian blood. Nazism was becoming a highly attractive and fashionable ideology.[236] Radical Pan-Arab and Pan-Islamist Arabs, Michel Aflaq and a small group of the founders of the *Baath*, Antun Saada of the Syrian National Socialist Party, Ahmad Husayn, Young Egypt and its Green Shirts, to name but a few, were enthralled. "One party, one state, one leadership," the latter proclaimed. "Their ideology and form of organization and activity [were] thoroughly Nazi, including such devices as fascist salutes, torchlight parades, leader worship" and "most characteristically, their use of gangs of toughs to terrorize and silence their political opponents."[237]

Still, financial aid to Arab rebels led by Amin al-Husayni against the British and the Jews was still "small and irregular." German radio broadcasts in Arabic were begun in the summer of 1938, "and proved immensely effective.... Supplemented by other forms of propaganda... they evoked a powerful response."[238] In 1934, "when the anti-Jewish Nuremberg Laws were promulgated, telegrams of congratulation were sent to the Führer from all over the Arab and Islamic worlds.[239]

There were of course old networks of sympathy, acquaintance, and agentry to supply an infrastructure. German intelligence had developed an extensive network of agents in the Arab world. According to a CIA report declassified in 1976, in Egypt, General Aziz Ali al-Masri (who also was a close associate of Ahmad Hasan of Young Egypt), a "prestigious Arab nationalist,"[240] a close friend of Muslim Brotherhood Supreme Guide Hasan al-Banna, "formed and led an espionage ring to work for German intelligence."[241] A number of the officers who took part seem to have had connections with Young Egypt. The ex-Khedive Abbas Hilmi, already active in Oppenheim's World War I jihad network, was of their number. Werner Otto von Hentig, another veteran of German operations in the Great War, was posted at the German embassy in Constantinople and maintained an impressive network of contacts. Al-Azhar University professor Sheikh Ali Hasan Abdelqader was to chair the Central Islamic Institute in Berlin in 1939. Al-Azhar leader Sheikh al-Maraghi was more sympathizer than agent. Dr. Mustafa al-Wakil,

[236] On this subject, see Murawiec, *The Mind of Jihad*, I, *passim*.

[237] Lewis, *Semites*, p. 149.

[238] Lewis, *Semites*, p. 144.

[239] Lewis, *Semites*, p. 148.

[240] Olivier Carré and Gérard Michaud [Michel Seurat] (présenté par), *Les Frères musulmans 1928–1982*, Paris, Julliard, 1983, p. 22.

[241] Lewis, *Semites*, p. 149.

a.k.a. Kurt Hoffmann, was to be the grand mufti's personal secretary in Berlin, and had been a leader of the Green Shirts.[242]

According to the same source, several of the top advisers of Saudi King Abdulazziz ibn Saud were agents. These included Khalid Abulwalid al-Hud, who visited Hitler on the king's behalf; Fuad Hamza, wartime envoy to Vichy France; Sheikh al-Ardh Midhat; and Sheikh Yusuf Yasim, the king's personal secretary.[243] Iraq

> was the Arab nation in which the German intelligence service [GIS] expended the most efforts and met with the most willing response.... [H]elped by ties which had been developed during World War I, the GIS began building up contacts there in the early 1930s. Since 1939, Iraq was the epicenter of the Pan-Arab nationalist movement, not only because Iraqis themselves were ardent supporters of the Movement, but also because many radical Arab nationalists had fled there.[244]

In Baghdad, senior members of the military and the bureaucracy were members of a "semi-secret Iraqi Nazi organization," including the same Dr. Sami Shawqat, director-general of the Ministry of Education who but a few years earlier had exalted "the manufacture of death." The grand mufti's secretary Osman Kamal Hadded, a.k.a. Max Müller, worked for the GIS in Baghdad, with the assistance of the chief of Iraqi military intelligence, Col. Hamid Rafat.[245] Palestinians and Jordanians, including the grand mufti's nephew Sawfat al-Husayni and other family members, were part of the political intelligence and spy network. In Syria, Maarouf Dawalibi, Muslim Brother, future communist fellow-traveller, spent part of the war as a radio-propagandist operating from Zossen, outside Berlin.[246] There also was the ubiquitous Sheikh Shakib Arslan (b. 1869) from a prominent Syria Druze family. This soulmate of the grand mufti had been a friend of Enver Pasha before World War I, a member of the Young Turk Committee Union and Progress, and an envoy of Enver's to Berlin. In 1921 he went to Moscow with Enver, returned to Germany and then settled in Geneva. This restless agitator worked for Abbas Hilmi, was a close friend of Karl Radek's own national-Bolshevik friend Count Ernst von Reventlow, became a regular acquaintance of Benito Mussolini as early as 1922, and, in 1930,

[242] "Study of German Intelligence Activities in the Near East and related areas prior to and during World War II," pp. 34 and 41. Secret. Declassified 27 September 1976, declass.#NND943072. National Archives, RG263 records of the CIA, "Formerly security classified Special Studies relating to foreign intelligence agencies." Box 2.

[243] Ibid., 29.

[244] Ibid., 106.

[245] Murawiec, *The Mind of Jihad*, I, p. 42.

[246] "Study of German Intelligence Activities in the Near East," 161.

established the periodical *La Nation arabe*.[247] Publication continued as long as the flow of Italian and German funding continued – he was a fully paid agent of German military intelligence, the *Abwehr*.[248] The periodical's tone was "extremely violent, it aimed at galvanizing the readership." At the request of Rashid Rida, this "*mujahid* of the quill" wrote several pamphlets on the causes of the backwardness of the Arab world, and presented Mussolini as the example for Muslims to follow. He also whitewashed Mussolini of any imperial designs over the Arabs, pushing mendacity into unexplored heights. Sheikh Arslan's influence was great in Algeria, where the leading anti-French ulama were under his spell. He is credited with having turned the most important proindependence figure, Messali Haj, away from communism and into the embrace of Pan-Islamism. "At the beginning of the war, Shakib Arslan received specific marching orders from Germany." He went to Berlin in September 1939 "as a technical adviser to the Reich's propaganda to Arab countries."[249] *Reichspropagandaminister* Joseph Goebbels moved the German government to make him an *Ehrenarier* ("Honorary Aryan") and citizen of the Reich. Arslan had met Amin al-Husayni in 1934; the two men struck a lifelong association.

"[Amin] Al-Husayni was regarded by the Axis as one of their top-level assets"[250] even though until 1941, "Arab nationalists like the Grand Mufti of Jerusalem were more interested in [Hitler] than vice versa."[251] Al-Husayni had been working for the *Abwehr* since before the war.[252] He maintained "close ties" with Fritz Grobba, the *Auswärtiges Amt*'s pioneer spy – diplomat-agitator in the region,[253] who was orchestrating action. "[I]n cooperation with influential natives like Shakib Arslan of Greater Syria, [Grobba would] organize the uprisings that would weaken British positions in Egypt and India. A government under the leadership of Amin al-Husayni should be established in Palestine, and only the Jews who had lived there before the First World War should be allowed to stay."[254] The mufti had taken up contact with the authorities of the Reich in 1933, shortly after Hitler's seizure of power. The alliance he sought had not only political and geopolitical aims

[247] Much of this information is from E. Lévi-Provençal, "L'Emir Shakib Arslan," Cahiers de l'Orient contemporain, 4è année (IX–X), 1er–2è trimester 1947, pp. 5–19.
[248] "Study of German Intelligence Activities in the Near East," 6, p. 154.
[249] Kramer, *Islam Assembled*, p. 149.
[250] "Study of German Intelligence Activities in the Near East," pp. 148–9.
[251] Lewis, *Semites*, p. 142.
[252] "Study of German Intelligence Activities in the Near East," pp. 9, 148.
[253] Ibid., p. 4.
[254] Pol. Archiv, AA, Nachlass Werner Otto von Hentig, vol. 84, Memo Max von Oppenheim, 25.07.40, 7 pp., quoted in Schwanitz, "The German Middle East Policy," p. 18.

but also ideological ones. His purpose was "conceived not so much in pan-Arab as in Pan-Islamic terms, for a Holy War of Islam in alliance with Germany against world Jewry, to accomplish the final solution to the Jewish problem everywhere."[255]

Haj Amin al-Husayni (1897–1974) concentrated in his own person, action, and legacy the conscious adhesion of Arab Muslim elites to the totalitarian extremism that arose on European and East European soil in the twentieth century. We have observed him in cahoots with the Communist International. We shall now watch him in league with Nazism and Italian fascism, remaining all the while the chief of the Muslim Brotherhood's Palestinian operations. Husayni had enjoyed "personal ties" with leaders of the Khilafat movement of India, the Ali Brothers, themselves successively pro-German and proBolshevik. He had organized the pogroms and risings in Palestine, and, in the 1936–39 Arab Revolt in Palestine, the systematic assassination of thousands of Palestinians inclined to compromise with the Jews. The Palestinian Arab Party he established in 1935 was "inspired by German Nazism." Its youth group for a time called itself the "Nazi Scouts."[256]

Husayni had been instrumental in organizing several "World" Islamic conferences in the 1930s. The 1931 Congress was a great success, as it attracted prominent Muslim figures such as Rashid Rida; Abdal Rahman Azzam, future head of the Arab League; the Syrian Riyad al-Sulh; later prime minister and future president Shuqri al-Kuwwatli; the prestigious figure of Sir Muhammad Iqbal; the former Iranian prime minister Ziya al-Din Tabatabai; and even a noted Twelver Shiite cleric, Sheikh al-Ghita.[257]

In the course of their "Congresses of Collaboration," "the disciples of Afghani and heirs of Rashid Rida cast their lot with the rising forces of totalitarianism, in the conviction that it would rid the Muslim world of two seemingly greater evils, colonialism and imperialism."[258] In the summer of 1940, Husayni organized an inter-Arab mission to travel to Berlin "to establish direct contact with the German government at the highest level. [It] included government-appointed representatives" from independent Arab states, such as Iraq and Saudi Arabia, and national committees from Allied-controlled ones.[259] Husayni moved his operations from Palestine to Lebanon

[255] Lewis, *Semites*, p. 147.
[256] Becker, *The PLO*, p. 19.
[257] Kramer, *Islam Assembled*, pp. 124–34.
[258] Ibid., p. 155.
[259] Lewis, *Semites*, p. 150.

and, in October 1939, to Iraq. In Baghdad, Prime Minister Nuri al-Said received him well and added to the subsidies he was receiving from Rome and Berlin. "Germany enjoyed a degree of confidence among the Muslims seldom manifested toward unbelievers," wrote General Hellmuth Felmy, who was in charge of training Arab and Muslim warriors fighting in the German Army.[260]

In tandem with the German Legation, Husayni promptly proceeded to plot against his pro-British host. The grand mufti was one of the prime movers in the pro-Nazi coup led in April 1941 by Rashid Ali al Gailani, who was trying to extend the Germans' influence to other Arab countries, starting with Syria. Gailani, a Nazi sympathizer, had been an Abwehr agent prior to the war, while the "Four Colonels" who were the power behind the throne, were ideological Nazis. The grand mufti "helped the Germans by declaring a jihad against the allies in broadcasts to the Middle East."[261] Having failed to kill all the Jews of Palestine, the grand mufti took his revenge by organizing the bloody pogrom of June 1 and 2 in Baghdad: 600 Jews were killed, official sources reported; many more, said unofficial ones. "The massacre was carried out by troops, police, and other elements incited by the fallen Rashid Ali regime and seeking vengeance for its regime."[262]

After the British reclaimed control of Iraq, Husayni fled to Iran, was sheltered there by Axis embassies, in October 1941 went to Rome where he was hosted by the regime, and at the end of the year arrived in Germany. In Rome, Mussolini himself greeted him.[263] Claiming to be the head of a secret Arab nationalist organization with branches in all Arab countries, Husayni volunteered to join the Axis war against Britain "on the sole condition that they recognize in principle the unity, independence, and sovereignty of an Arab state of a Fascist nature, including Iraq, Syria, Palestine and Trans-Jordan."[264] On October 27, 1941, the *duce* met the mufti, and a draft agreement with the Axis was prepared. On November 6, Husayni arrived in Berlin, where he met Ernst von Weizsäcker, Ribbentrop's second in command at the Foreign Office. But the declaration ended up being "no

260 *General der Flieger* Hellmuth Felmy, "Part One" in "German Exploitation of Arab Nationalist Movements in World War II," Historical Direction Headquarters U.S. Army Europe, Foreign Military Studies Branch, MS#P207, National Archives, p. 2.

261 Schwanitz, "The German Middle East Policy," p. 15.

262 Lewis, *Semites*, p. 158.

263 Lewis, *Semites*, pp. 150–1.

264 Daniel Carpi, "The Mufti of Jerusalem, Amin al-Husayni and His Diplomatic Activity during World War II (October 1941–July 1943)," *Studies in Zionism*, vol. 5, no. 7 (Spring 1983), quoted by Lewis, *Semites*, p. 151.

more than a bland statement of general principles." The only concrete clause was Axis agreement to the elimination of the Jewish National Home in Palestine.[265] Still, the way was opened to future parleys – which started soon: on November 28, 1941, the Mufti was to meet with Hitler.

The mufti needed Hitler more than Hitler needed him. Hitler gave him generalities. The issuance of the Axis declaration on the Middle East was postponed. What agreement was finally made was limited and was to be kept secret. The mufti nonetheless stuck to his guns and continued to work on behalf of the Axis, notably through the "Arab Bureau" in Berlin. He had thrown his weight with Nazism for keeps. He had fully assimilated and accepted the ideology in overlay with radical Islam. Various training programs for Arab and Muslim fighters, guerrillas, and spies were begun. In September 1942, the mufti proposed the formation of Arab irregulars for sabotage, and regular Arab military units to assist Axis military operations."[266] In the following years, he and Rashid Ali shuttled between Rome and Berlin. Fritz Grobba "released weekly talks for Arabic broadcasts from Germany to the Middle East and coached Grand Mufti Amin al-Husayni in declaring Holy War against the Allies. Thus Grobba uncorked a magic bottle of warfare under cover of religion."[267] Radio Zossen, located south of Berlin, tried its best to inflame the Muslim world.

If Hitler had damped down the mufti's great expectations – he considered himself nothing short of the voice of worldwide Islam and its leader – "Amin al-Husayni made a far deeper impression upon the *SS-Hauptamt* and the *Ostministerium*," the fiefs of Heinrich Himmler and Arthur Rosenberg, the race theorist, respectively.

> Both were responsible for the political mobilization and military recruitment of Muslims in German-occupied territories, and offered Amin al-Husayni another opportunity to fill the role of Muslim spiritual leader. It was on behalf of the *SS-Hauptamt* that he embarked upon a recruitment campaign among Bosnian Muslims in 1943, a success which owed much to ties forged in earlier Muslim congresses with leaders of the Bosnian Muslim community.

As a result of Husayni's entreaties, Turkic POWs joined the SS in large numbers. The mufti also helped found a school for SS Muslim chaplains in

[265] Lewis, *Semites*, p. 152.

[266] "Study of German Intelligence Activities in the Near East," p. 6.

[267] Wolfgang G. Schwanitz, "The Jinnee and the Magic Bottle: Fritz Grobba and the German Middle East Policy, 1900–1945," pp. 86–117, in Wolfgang G. Schwanitz and Bernard Lewis, eds., *Germany and the Middle East*, Princeton Papers, vols. X–XI, Princeton, NJ, Marcus Wiener Publishers, 2001.

Dresden, which opened in April 1944 – Husayini delivered the inaugural address.[268] Beginning in the summer of 1943, "the SS leadership discovered the Muslim Arab and Turanian fount of manpower." Himmler and al-Husayni met in Berlin in July 1943 "for a long, detailed exchange that ended with mutual assurances of covert cooperation. In late July, there followed concrete negotiations between the mufti and the chief of the SS Main Office, Gottlob Berger." The battalion Imams "under al-Husayni's close supervision during frequent visits, developed into the backbone of the Muslim units of the *Waffen-SS*."[269] At the Nuremberg Trial, SS Dieter Wisliceny, an aide to Adolf Eichmann, Hitler's executive manager for the extermination of Europe's Jewry, declared to the Court that "the Mufti was a friend of Eichmann and had in his company gone incognito to visit the gas chamber at Auschwitz."[270] Husayni "made his own not insignificant contribution to the destruction of European Jewry."[271]

In his dying days, Hitler rued his strategic mistake of underutilizing the Arabs and the Muslims: "We had a great chance of pursuing a splendid policy with regard to Islam. But we missed the bus.... Alone Germany could have aroused the enthusiasm of the whole of Islam."[272] "A bold policy of friendship with Islam had still been possible until 1941."[273]

After the defeat of the Reich, the French interned the mufti, who, after all, had continuously incited their Muslim populations to revolt against their masters. Yet since he was anti-British, the French let him go. U.S. Secretary of State Dean Acheson explained, or explained away, "We cannot indict him." In both cases, it was clearly more convenient to use the war criminal than to prosecute him. Instead the mufti was welcomed raptly into Egypt by King Faruq, where he was able to resume control of his "Army of Salvation" paramilitary organization. After the defeat of the Arab onslaught against Israel in 1948, the mufti set up a "government of all [Mandatory] Palestine" under Egyptian auspices. In 1951, it was one of his agents who murdered the Jordanian King Abdallah in Jerusalem, inside the Al-Aqsa Mosque.[274]

[268] Kramer, *Islam Assembled*, p. 158.

[269] Karlheinz Roth, "Berlin – Ankara – Baghdad: Franz von Papen and German Near East Policy During the Second World War," in Schwanitz and Lewis, *Germany and the Middle East*, pp. 181–214, 203–4.

[270] Lewis, *Semites*, p. 156.

[271] Lewis, *Semites*, p. 155.

[272] *The Testament of Adolf Hitler*, in *The Hitler-Bormann Documents*, February–April 1945, p. 71, quoted by Martin Kramer, *Islam Assembled*, p. 163.

[273] Schwanitz, "The Jinnee and the Magic Bottle," p. 100.

[274] Becker, *The PLO*, pp. 29–31.

But the mufti was not only a megalomaniac and a fanatic. He was a man with a plan, and a substantial network of influence. When he claimed, as others have before and after him, that the entire Muslim world, or merely the whole Arab world, was supporting him to a man, he was delusional. But his secret network, the *Al-Umma'l Arabiyya*, was real. Originally established in 1911 as *al-Fatat* and at first not anti-British, it seems to have been a club and coordination committee at an elite level. Amir Hussein of Mecca, the Hashemite, was a founder; Nuri Said of Iraq was a member as was King Faisal of Iraq. During the early stages of the Palestine War of 1936–39, *al-Umma* radicalized in an anti-British direction, its Anglophile elements purged. "By the end of 1936, *al-Umma* had become wholeheartedly anti-British,"[275] Husayni told SS *Obergruppenführer* Erwin Ettel who was debriefing him in Rome. According to his inflated report, *al-Umma* had members in all Arab countries; each country had an executive committee whose members were also members of the Supreme Committee. He, the mufti, had been a member of *al-Fatat* since World War I, and chosen as successor at the insistence of King Feisal of Iraq. Ertl wrote in his report: "*Al-Umma* ... was a compelling force behind every Arab move for unity and independence. It directed the Palestine War in 1936–39, and engaged the 1941 Iraqi coup by first gaining direct control of the Iraqi army and through the Muslim church [*sic*], the tribal leaders and the youth movement." Membership required lifelong loyalty, based on an oath on the Quran. It is difficult to know whether the mufti was merely embellishing the picture of his personal associates, grandly shaping them into a huge Pan-Islamic organization able to move mountains, taking *ex post facto* credit for events, and ascribing his own action to the power of said organization, or whether it really existed as such. Unraveling this riddle requires more archives to surface – notably the mufti's personal archives, which the CIA has kept under wraps for decades for reasons unstated and rather unspeakable.

Members of the Supreme Committee included Rashid Ali al-Gailani (an increasingly tense rivalry developed between al-Husayni and him); Nadji Shawqat the Iraqi Nazi; the Palestinian Ishaq Derwish, a leader in the 1936–9 Palestinian insurgency and a member of the extended Husayni family; other leaders of the insurgency recycled in Egypt and elsewhere; as well as King ibn Saud's advisers al-Qarqani, Yusuf Yasim, Sheikh Shakib Arslan, his brother Amir Adil Arslan, and Sami al-Sulh.[276]

[275] "Study of German Intelligence Activities in the Near East," pp. 2ff.
[276] Ibid., pp. 4–6.

The grand mufti attended the great anti-imperialist conference of the Third World held in Bandung, Indonesia, in 1955. In the early years of the regime of Gamal Abdel Nasser, "the Nazi sympathies of the new rulers of Egypt were undisguised."[277]

The legacy lived on through the modern Palestinian movement, as well as the senior places where one found Iraqi Nazis, pro-Nazi Egyptians, and Muslim Brothers in general. The coordinator of information about German propaganda in the Muslim world at the Office of Strategic Services (OSS) wrote toward the end of 1941:

> The Arabs are united on one general purpose, to free their world from the domination of French and British masters. Some Arabs are blinded to Italian imperialism and to German domination of Europe by their anxiety to get rid of the foreign control. This arises not only from a desire to play all European powers off against each other but from a naïveté which assures that any one who is against their masters is a friend of the Muslims. They fail to realize that, in case of a British defeat, there would be a substitution of Axis for the British or the French domination.[278]

On October 23, 1970, the following ad appeared in a European newspaper:

> Wanted! Courageous comrades to join us for a tour or several months in the Middle East as war correspondents to study the WAR OF LIBERATION of Palestinian refugees to reconquer their homeland. If you have tank experience, apply at once. Money is no obstacle. What matters is a comradely spirit and personal courage. Information on the PLO free on request.

The ad appeared in the *Deutsche Nationalzeitung*, the unequivocally neo-Nazi German weekly newspaper. The text was replete with code words appealing to the SS spirit. In killing Jews, "the radical right [had been] there first. Europe's Black International had not only discovered the anti-Zionist cause a good quarter century earlier; it worked side by side with the same slogans, promising the same services, dealing with the same Palestinian agents."[279]

The *Nouvel Ordre Européen*, which operated out of Paris – and organized a secret meeting between the fascist "Black Prince" Valerio Borghese and Giangiacomo Feltrinelli, a senior Committee for State Security (KGB)

[277] Lewis, *Semites*, 160. See also Joel Fishman, "The Big Lie and the Media War Against Israel: From Inversion of the Truth to Inversion of Reality," Jerusalem Center for Public Affairs, 29 July 2007.

[278] Lewis, *Semites* p. 102.

[279] Claire Sterling, *The Terror Network: The Secret War of International Terrorism*, New York, Holt, Rinehart Winston, 1981, p. 113.

coordinator of terrorist networks that spanned Cuba, Latin America, eastern and Western Europe, and the Middle East – held a "summit" meeting on the Palestinians' behalf in Barcelona on April 2, 1969.

> The Barcelona meeting dealt with several of Fatah's requests. The delegates talked about raising money, organizing efficient arms traffic, providing ex-Nazi military instructors to help the guerrillas get started, recruiting White Caucasian youths to beef up Fatah's forces in the Middle East, and collecting elements disposed to collaborate in acts of sabotage in Europe. They also discussed a propaganda campaign outlining all-purpose slogans – "Long live the glorious Palestinian fighters against Imperialism!" – with anti-Semitic classics like the *Protocols of the Elders of Zion* and a volume about Israel called *The Enemy of Man.*

There were several Black Summits for the Palestinians after that, in Paris in 1970, in Munich in 1972 – ten days after the Palestinian outrage at the Olympic Games. The 600 delegates cheered Black September and also praised Sirhan Sirhan, the assassin of Robert F. Kennedy. Another summit took placed in Rome in 1974. Ironically, the cream of the Red International rushed to Palestinian camps for training, while Palestinians flocked to Black International camps in the mountains of Spain and Italy. "The ultra-Left sponsored a huge rally for Arafat in Milan, and Italy's most flamboyant neo-Nazi, Franco Freda, held one to honor Arafat's Fatah in Padua."[280]

Just as the Young Egypt movement borrowed from the *National Sozialistische Deutsche Arbeiterpartei* (NSDAP), so did the radical Islamist movement as a whole, "its racism and anti-Semitism. This included support for Nazi philosophy, viciously anti-Jewish propaganda in the party press."[281] Islamic extremists acquired the perverse modern form of racism, biological racism and racial theory. Nasser himself told the *Deutsche Nationalzeitung*, "[D]uring the Second World War, our sympathies were with the Germans.... [T]he lie of the six million murdered Jews is not taken seriously by anybody."[282]

[280] Ibid., p. 116.
[281] Lewis, *Semites*, p. 149.
[282] *Deutsche Nationalzeitung*, May 1, 1964. Quoted in Lewis, *Semites*, p. 162.

6

The Mutated Virus

"Islamic Revolution"

> A further reason for my hatred of National Socialism and other ideologies is quite a primitive one. I have an aversion to killing people for the fun of it. What the fun is, I did not quite understand at the time, but in the intervening years the ample exploration of revolutionary consciousness has cast some light on this matter. The fun consists in gaining a pseudo-identity through asserting one's power, optimally by killing somebody – a pseudo-identity that serves as a substitute for the human self that has been lost.
>
> Eric Voegelin[1]

Stealthy Borrowing

Prior to the twentieth century, the term *revolution* had never been applied to Islam or things Islamic. The juridical and theological framework of Islam radically preclude any notion of "revolution."

Islam conceives of itself as the perfect political system, since it flows from a perfect revelation. It derives its entire body of law from God's *expressis verbis* prescription. There is no conceivable change in a system of that kind. As Ayatollah Khomeini famously said, "You have no need for new legislation; simply put into effect that which has already been legislated for you. This will save you a good deal of time and effort.... Everything, praise be to God, is ready-made for use."[2] Either a polity is ruled by God's law, Sharia, in which case it is Muslim, or it is an infidel, pagan, a *jahili* society. If Sharia is

[1] Eric Voegelin, *Autobiographical Reflections*, Columbia, University of Missouri Press, 2006, pp. 46–7.

[2] Quoted in Martin Kramer, "Political Islam," from Ayatollah Ruhollah Khomeini, *al-Hukuma al-Islamiyya (The Islamic State)*, p. 134.

not being followed, this is a prima facie case of *fitna* ("sedition," "disorder," "troubles") a highly charged term describing an appalling situation wherein the normal course of things must urgently be reestablished.

In a situation where un-Islamic accretions have disfigured "genuine" (original) Islam, allowance is made for the *mujaddid*, the renovator said to appear every century to cleanse the body of Islam. The notion is based on a particular hadith: "Surely, Allah will send for this *Umma* at the advent of every hundred years a person (or persons) who will renovate its religion for it."[3] This "renovation" makes it "as new," it does not renew it. The distinction is fundamental: after the advent of the seal of the prophets, Muhammad, no adjunction is licit or even possible; the renovation, *tajdid*, restores the original beliefs and practices. The *mujaddid* is not like the prophet or the Messenger. He is the one who recreates and demarcates the authentic sunna from the counterfeit *bida*. Islam makes provision for what it terms "reform," a radical return to its postulated roots, the "ready-made" Islam.

Given this, revolution in the Islamic polity is a theoretical impossibility. There may be vicissitudes of fortune for the ruler, or the wheel of fate may favor some other leader; there may be rebellion or insurrection; but there will be no revolution.[4]

In the European sense that spread to the rest of the world and was adopted by it, revolution is opposed to mere rebellion, or rising, or disorder. It implies a radical change. The *Jacqueries* of yore were revolts; the French Revolution intended and partially succeeded in changing the order of things. But in turn, revolution was vested by history with two different meanings. The French Revolution intended to change human nature (Robespierre's "dictatorship of virtue") whereas England's Glorious Revolution and the American Revolution intended to bring the political order into conformity with the natural rights of man, and took full account of human nature to compose the new institutional arrangements.[5] Thenceforward, revolutions in the West and elsewhere were either of the one or the other type: the Anglo-Saxon "liberal" model intended to create equality of opportunity or

[3] Another hadith reports Muhammad as having said: "Verily, at the end of every century, Almighty Allah will send such a person to the *Umma*, who will revive the religion for them." Yet another one says: "Allah has indeed raised a *mujaddid* at the beginning of every century" or "Allah will raise a *mujaddid*."

[4] Bernard Lewis, Islamic Concepts of Revolution," *in* P. J. Vatikiotis, ed., *Revolution in the Middle East and Other Case Studies*, Totowa, NJ, Rowman & Littlefield, 1972, pp. 30–40.

[5] In particular, *Federalist Papers*, in George W. Carey and James McClellan, eds., *The Federalist*, Indianapolis, Liberty Fund, 2001, p. 10.

the French model with its equality of outcomes.[6] The former was built on tradition; the latter intended a *tabula rasa*.[7]

In the political language of Islam, "there was no positive term for the violent replacement of one regime by another until modern times, when the influence of the French Revolution, and of other European revolutions that followed it, percolated into Muslim political thought and language." The word *thawra* ("rising," "excitement," "rebellion") ended up as "the universal Arabic term for good or approved revolution."[8]

Still, the Shiite Islamists who triumphed in Tehran in 1979 spoke of it as their "Islamic Revolution." In a far-reaching statement of intent, the Ayatollah Khomeini had written: "Both the Shariah and common sense dictate that we do not let the existing governments persist in their [wrong] ways.... They have suspended the Shariah of God. For this reason it is the duty of all Muslims of the world, wherever they may happen to be, to rise up for the Islamic Revolution."[9] Moderate Islamist Ibrahim Yazdi concurred: "Our revolution is Islamic. Let no one be in error about that."[10] Article 2.5 of the Constitution of the Islamic Republic of Iran clearly refers to the unorthodox notion of the "revolution of Islam" as follows, "continuous leadership (*imamah*) and perpetual guidance, and its fundamental role in ensuring the uninterrupted process of the revolution of Islam."[11]

Abul Ala al-Maududi, one of the most influential figures of Sunni radicalism in the twentieth century, incessantly spoke of the need for an "Islamic Revolution."

> There is no doubt that all the Prophets of Allah, without exception, were Revolutionary Leaders, and the illustrious Prophet Muhammad (SAAS) was the greatest Revolutionary Leader of all. But there is something which distinguishes these Revolutionary Leaders who worshipped Allah alone, from the general, run-of-the-mill, worldly revolutionaries: these worldly revolutionaries, however honest and sincere their intentions may be, can never attain to a perfect level of justice and moderation,

he wrote in 1939. He added: "'Muslims' is the title of that 'International Revolutionary Party' organized by Islam to carry out its revolutionary program.

[6] Tocqueville, *La démocratie en Amérique*, *Œuvres, II*, Paris, Ed. de la Pléiade, Gallimard, 1992; Tocqueville *L'Ancien régime & la Révolution*, *Œuvres, III*, Paris, Ed. de la Pléiade, Gallimard, 1992.

[7] See Gertrud Himmelfarb, *The Roads to Modernity: The British, French, and American Enlightenments*, New York, Knopf, 2004.

[8] Lewis, *The Political Language of Islam*, pp. 95–6.

[9] Ayatollah Khomeini, "An Islamic State – Point of View," in *Concept of the Islamic State*, London, Islamic Council of Europe, 1979, p. 7.

[10] Kramer, "Political Islam."

[11] Mr. Ramin Parham brought this point to my attention.

'Jihad' refers to that revolutionary struggle and utmost exertion which the Islamic Nation/Party brings into play in order to achieve this objective."[12]

The same was true for his Egyptian friend and counterpart Sayyid Qutb, the ideologue of the Muslim Brotherhood. "No God but God is a revolution against the worldly authority that usurps the first characteristics of divinity," writes Qutb, using the word *thawra*. Revolution to him is "the only credible instrument of attaining social justice and of applying the *sharia*."[13] He insists on "the necessity of revolution as the only proper remedy for decaying societies. *Zalzalah* (shaking) or revolution is the word used to describe the first step in the process of building a new society." Prophet Muhammad led the greatest revolution, Qutb insists, and this should be repeated. He calls for "the comprehensive revolution in the government of man in all its forms, shapes, systems and situations, and the complete rebellion against every situation [contrary to the principles of Islam] on the whole earth."[14]

To say the least, the convergence of such authorities of radical Islam, both Sunni and Shia, on an un-Islamic concept emanating from the West, is paradoxical. Coming from compulsive haters of everything Western, the choice may not be simply ascribed to a desire to imitate, or to Islamic leaders and thinkers taking a leaf from the "secular nationalists" of the Arab world, whom they spent lifetimes insulting and combating when not slaughtering or being slaughtered by each other – the Nassers, Assads, and Saddam Husseins. Their word choice, for sure, betrayed their intent to signal how radical the change they intended to wreak was since they seized on a word the twentieth-century *Zeitgeist* propagated everywhere. Still, Islamists eager to eradicate any *bida*, any innovation and accretion on the holy body of Islam posterior to the Golden Age, should not have been hobnobbing with the *Zeitgeist*. Yet hobnobbing they were.

In intercultural exchanges, the first elements adopted and absorbed by a culture from another one are those easiest to perceive and assimilate. In turn, those elements that are easiest to perceive and to assimilate are those most similar to the adopting culture. The greater the cultural distance, the greater the difficulty in assimilating. Facing European culture, it turned out that the Muslim and especially the Arab Middle East did not assimilate liberalism,

12 Sayyid Abul Ala Maududi, *Jihad fi sabilillah (Jihad in Islam)*, Huda Khattab, ed., translated by Prof. Khushid Ahmad, London, UKIM Dawah Center, n.d.

13 This and following quotes from Ahmad S. Moussalli, *Radical Islamic Fundamentalism: The Ideological and Political Discourse of Sayyid Qutb*, Beirut, American University of Beirut, 1992, pp. 200–3.

14 Qutb, *Maalim fi al-Tariq [Milestones]*, pp. 69–71.

democracy, constitutionalism, pluralism, or federalism but hastily discarded them all as inefficient.[15] When the world stage was dominated by the rivalry between the "Anglo-Saxon" culture of pluralist democracy, and Prussian-inspired authoritarianism, the heart of the Arab elites throbbed for the latter. When this was vanquished, its tyrannical successors, Soviet Bolshevism, Italian fascism, and German national socialism became the rage of the Arab and much of the Muslim world – in succession or simultaneously.

Muslims were attracted to those elements they recognized. Political pluralism was inconceivable in the cultural and intellectual terms of reference of the Muslim Middle East: Power there has ever been one, centralized and indivisible. Muslim culture is a culture of the One – *tawhid*, the unity of God, is reflected by unity on earth. The *umma* is and must be one; the Caliph is "God's shadow on earth," and thus sole ruler; all political relationships converge on a center.

The appeal of totalitarianism came not only from the efficacy ascribed to the totalitarian regimes; it also was culturally far easier to understand. *Ein Reich, ein Volk, ein Führer* had more allure than parliamentary debates, as had Stalin's Five-Year Plan and NKVD (People's Commissariat for Internal Affairs) and Mussolini's *stato totale* and the cries of *Duce*! *Duce*! That oneness was akin to something well understood in Islam, *tawhid*. As Maxime Rodinson, a French Marxist with strong feelings of sympathy for Islam, analyzed:

> Islam has been totalitarian to an extreme. Indeed, in principle, it dominated every act and every thought of the faithful. This domination was symbolized, for instance, by the reciting of the *basmala* [*bismillah*] during even the most trivial actions, and by the hadith's universal relevance. All actions, even those arising out of the most elementary biological needs, such as excretion and coition, were regulated by the ideological system. Even social actions of the kind which other cultures considered outside the realm of religion, be they technical, economic or artistic, were integrated into the system and interpreted in terms of it.... This totalitarian aspect of Muslim ideology persisted for a considerable time.[16]

As the conveying of European concepts to the Middle East proceeded, the transfers concerned in priority those elements that were compatible with Middle Eastern culture.

[15] See especially Hourani, *Arab Thought in the Liberal Age, 1798–1939*, Oxford, Oxford University Press, 1962; Kedourie, *Democracy and Arab Political Culture*, London, Frank Cass, 1994.

[16] Maxime Rodinson, *Marxism and the Muslim World*, translated by Michael Pallis, London: Zed Press, 1979, pp. 41–2.

How did revolution come to the jihadis? What else did they borrow? What mixture came out of the witches' cauldron where the new ingredients were mixed with the jihad of old? These are the questions we will now try to answer by looking at Sayyid Abul Ala Maududi, founder of Pakistan's *Jamaat-i Islami*, the intellectual godfather of the modern radical Islamist movement, the correspondent of Sayyid Qutb and Ruhollah Khomeini, and the original standard-bearer of the "Islamic Revolution."

Maududi, the Terrible Simplificateur

In the Islamic universe Maududi is the purest modern embodiment of medieval Europe's millenarian prophetae. His person and work concentrate almost all the characteristics of the Gnostic ideologue and leader described in Norman Cohn's *Pursuit of the Millenium*. Maududi, like the prophetae of old, was largely self-taught, and "never felt himself tied to any school of theological thought as are the *ulama* who graduate from the great traditional establishments of Deoband or Lucknow."[17] He was a déclassé, whose aristocratic lineage and family intimacy with the Moghol court had given way to lean times; he had to leave school at 15 to earn his keep. The self-developed intellectual undertook "to reconstruct the religious thought of Islam" on grounds he alone selected.[18] Unshackled by obeisance to tradition, conceiving of himself as a self-created, "born-again" Muslim. ("In reality, I am a new Muslim."[19]) Maududi practiced his own *ijtihad* without being acknowledged by the Sunni world as worthy of this rare badge. He "overthrew the authorized interpreters of the Law.[20] He acted and thought like a prophet, and, as we will see, as a quasi-Mahdi. The dimension of his mission was unlimited: "Now the only way open for reform and resuscitation is to rejuvenate Islam as a movement and to revive the meaning of the word Muslim anew," Maududi wrote.[21]

His undertaking was based on a novel consideration, namely that "Islam is one rational whole." This he did by "reconstructing the entire history

[17] Marcel Gaboriau, "Le néo-fondamentalisme au Pakistan: Maududi et la Jamiaat Islami," in Olivier Carré and Paul Dumont, *Radicalismes islamiques*, vol. 2, *Maroc, Pakistan, Inde,Yougoslavie, Mali*, Paris, L'Harmattan, 1986, pp. 33–76.

[18] Gaboriau, "Le néo-fondamentalisme au Pakistan," loc.cit., pp. 38, 40.

[19] Quoted by Seyyed Vali Reza Nasr, *Maududi and the Making of Islamic Revivalism*, Oxford: Oxford University Press, 1996, p. 31.

[20] Gaboriau, "Le néo-fondamentalisme au Pakistan," p. 46.

[21] Abul Ala Maududi, *Musalman awr mawjutah siyas*, Lahore, Kashmakash, 1940, 3:31, quoted in Nasr, *Maududi*, p. 55.

and thought of Islam in order to make it a rational whole. His presentation may seem to be simplistic and highly logical. He isolates the . . . cornerstone ideas of Islamic thought and orders them in a clear synthesis."[22] Like the propheta, he needed to rebuild the entire edifice of his belief structure in ways that uniquely suited him:

> Islam is not merely a religious creed or compound name for a few forms of worship, but a comprehensive system which envisages to annihilate all tyrannical and evil systems in the world and enforces its own program of reform which it deems best for the well-being of mankind. Islam addresses its call for effecting this program of destruction and reconstruction, revolution and reform not to just one nation, but to all humanity.[23]

His construct was an abstract-logical reconstruction that excluded considerations of facts. It was a "shocking method of argument and treatment of facts . . . [and] writing to a predetermined conclusion."[24] *Islam and the World*, Maududi's magnum opus, is a strange compendium of bite-size tidbits of knowledge, mythographic pseudohistory, Quranic quotes, and peremptory assertions, all designed to prove his overarching point. In order to do that, Maududi needed to "erase thirteen centuries of history with all the social and political arrangements that intervened in that period. . . . Between his doctrine and the traditional sources of law [*fiqh*] and theology, there is nothing: no school of thought, no mystical tradition, nothing, save Maududi himself."[25]

Maududi does away with the depth of history between the Prophetic Age of Muhammad and the "well-guided caliphs," and his "break with the past allows the irruption of modern and innovative aspects."[26] But in order to do so, the charismatic leader of the *Jamiaat Islami* had to make himself into a *mujaddid*, the renovator of Islam for a century. In his words, which amount to a self-portrait:

> Though a *mujaddid* is not a prophet, yet in spirit he comes very close to prophethood. He is characterized by a clear mind, penetrating vision, unbiased straight thinking, special ability to see the right path, clear of all extremes, and keep balance, power to think independently of the contemporary and centuries-old social and other prejudices, courage to fight against the evils of the time, inherent ability to lead and

[22] Gaboriau, "Le néo-fondamentalisme au Pakistan," p. 44.
[23] Sayed Abul Ala Maududi, *Jihad in Islam*, Lahore, Islamic Publications, 1998–2001, p. 19.
[24] Nasr, *Maududi*, p. 130.
[25] Gaboriau, "Le néo-fondamentalisme au Pakistan," p. 70.
[26] Gaboriau, "Le néo-fondamentalisme au Pakistan," p. 58.

guide, and an unusual competency to undertake *ijtihad* and the work of reconstruction.[27]

For a Muslim, a claim of "coming very close to prophethood" comes very close to blasphemy. This was one of the reasons why the Deobandi school ultimately pronounced the *takfir* against their former favorite, declaring Maududi to be a *kafr*, an unbeliever.[28] Yet Maududi went even further. He insisted that "[t]he ideal *mujaddid* (or *Imam al-Mahdi*) can be a true successor to Prophethood" and added: "If the expectation that Islam eventually will dominate the world of thought, culture, and politics is genuine, then the coming of a Great Leader under whose comprehensive and forceful leadership such Revolution is to come about is also certain." This millenarian self-appointment as quasi-prophet and great leader has no limits.

> In my opinion the Coming One [the Mahdi] will be a most modern Leader of his age possessing an unusually deep insight in all the current branches of knowledge, and all the major problems of life.... Most probably he will not be aware of his being the promised Mahdi. People, however, will recognize him after his death to be the one who was to establish 'Caliphate after the pattern or Prophethood' as mentioned in the prophecies.

Maududi's personal role was of messianic proportions. "With extensive study and practice one can develop a power and can intuitively sense the wishes and desires of the Holy Prophet.... Thus... on seeing a *hadith*, I can tell whether the Holy Prophet could or could not have said it."[29] This extraordinary claim turned Maududi into the pinnacle and center of the world, the decisive historical figure of the age, which in turn gave him unlimited rights. He "was" Islam. His Islam was "a universal ideology."[30] His party was the party of God (*Hizb Allah*). The party was so tasked:

> We must... create out of nothing a minority of pure upright and educated men, in the image of the first Companions of the Prophet. In short, people who, like Muhammad himself... will rebuild from top to bottom the edifice of the State.... There must exist an upright community devoted to the principle of truth, and whose sole goal in the world is to establish, to safeguard and to realize correctly the system of Truth.[31]

27 Abul Ala Maududi, *A Short History of the Revivalist Movement in Islam*, Lahore, 1963, p. 35, quoted in Nasr, *Maududi*, p. 136.

28 Gaboriau, "Le néo-fondamentalisme au Pakistan," p. 70.

29 Abul Ala Maududi, *Mizajshinasi rasul*, Lahore, Tafhimat, 1965, 1:102, quoted in Seyyed Vali Reza Nasr, *Maududi*, p. 137.

30 Abul Ala Maududi, *Toward Understanding Islam*, 14th ed., 176, quoted in Gaboriau, "Le néo-fondamentalisme au Pakistan," p. 43.

31 Abul Ala Maududi, *Moral Foundations of the Islamic Government*, quoted in Gaboriau, "Lenéo-fondamentalisme au Pakistan," p. 51.

Let us sum up: a déclassé semi-intellectual with a powerful, charismatic personality sets himself up as a figure of Messianic qualities whose cosmic mission is to establish perfection on earth on behalf of and according to the prescriptions of God. He is the quasi-peer of the great prophetic figures, and is possessed of extraordinary abilities. He is also possessed of a complete knowledge of how to move the world from its present, desolate *nadir* to the zenith of perfection: He is a man with a plan. He expounds that plan, which encompasses all aspects of life. He will radically transform the entire order of the world and replace the destroyed old order by a new one according to the plan. His total knowledge allows him to pay no heed to traditions and their present bearers, since he is clearly vested by God with this stupendous mission. He is in charge of the immense bloodshed God requires for the Plan to be implemented. A population group is selected as representing Satan, and is liable to be destroyed.

In 1941, Maududi created the *Jamat-e-Islami* to implement the plan outlined here. In his conception, "[R]evolution did not involve society as a whole, it was *inqilab-i Imamat*, revolution in leadership." Also: "[S]ocieties are built, structured, and continued from the top down by conscious manipulation of those in power."[32] For all practical purposes, his party was established on a Leninist–Stalinist model. The Jamaat was a highly centralized party led by an *amir*, with a consultative council (central committee) and an executive committee (politburo). It had central departments for finances, propaganda, welfare, education and research, and parliamentary affairs, and parallel professional organizations for students, youth, labor, peasants, and ulama. The party's nucleus was a core of professional revolutionaries, with a first circle of committed sympathizers and a second circle of more loosely connected supporters. The party recruited in the first place lower middle class semi-intellectuals who had not yet made it in the "modern" (English-speaking) sector of the economy. "In sum, most of the members of the Jamaat-i Islam came from layers of society that had a veneer of education but little means and little success."[33]

The resemblance to the Soviet model was not limited to organizational similarities, as Maududi repeatedly expressed his admiration for totalitarian movements and parties, communist and fascist alike. His ambition was no less universal than theirs: "Islam has prescribed that through a systematic effort (*jihad*) – if necessary by means of war and bloodshed – all these [corrupt] governments should be wiped out. In their stead must be

[32] Quoted in Nasr, *Maududi*, p. 77.

[33] Gaboriau, "Le néo-fondamentalisme au Pakistan," pp. 51–8.

erected a just and equitable government based on the fear of God and established on the basis of the canons He ordained."[34] "In short, not only was 'Revolution'... an axis around which Maududi conducted his debate," but he "appropriat[ed] the myth of revolution" to apply it to "a utopian sociopolitical order," a biographer writes.[35] "Revolution" was not just a semantic loanword. In his *Jihad in Islam*, Maududi waxes endless on the subject:

> Islam is not the name of a "religion," nor is "Muslim" the title of a "Nation." In reality, Islam is a revolutionary ideology and program which seeks to alter the social order of the whole world and rebuild it in conformity with its own tenets and ideals. "Muslim" is the title of the revolutionary party organized by Islam to carry into effect its revolutionary program and "jihad" refers to that revolutionary struggle and utmost exertion which the Islamic party brings into play to achieve this objective.[36]

Revolutionary jihad is defined:

> Like all revolutionary ideologies, Islam shuns the use of current vocabulary and adapts a terminology of its own, so that its own revolutionary ideals may be distinguished from common ideals. The word "jihad" belongs to this particular terminology of Islam. Islam purposely rejected the word *harb* and other Arabic words bearing the same meaning of "war" and used the word "jihad" which is synonymous with "struggle."... The sole intent of Islam is the welfare of mankind. Islam has its own particular ideological standpoint and practical program to carry out reforms for the welfare of mankind. Islam wishes to destroy all states and governments on the face of the earth which are opposed to the ideology and program of Islam regardless of the country or the nation that rules it.[37]

Never one to spare emphasis, Maududi adds, "Islam requires the earth – not just a portion, but the whole planet." A "mental revolution" is needed; "a revolution in the system of life." Islam is a "revolutionary creed": "[It] was the call for a universal and complete revolution.... [T]he call of the Prophet was never a metaphysical proposition; it was a charter of social revolution.... There is no doubt that all the Prophets of God without exception were Revolutionary leaders, and the illustrious Prophet Muhammad... was the greatest revolutionary leader."[38]

Maududi politicizes religion. If Lenin and Hitler replaced God with a secular religion, Maududi turns religion into a political cause. "These men

34 Abul Ala Maududi, *Al-Jihad fil Islam*, quoted in Gaboriau, "Le néo-fondamentalisme au Pakistan," p. 59.

35 Quoted in Nasr, *Maududi*, pp. 71, 76.

36 Abul Ala Maududi, *Jihad in Islam*, Lahore, Islamic Publications, 1998–2001, p. 8.

37 Ibid., pp. 9–10.

38 Maududi, *Jihad in Islam*, pp. 13, 14, 17.

who propagate religion are not mere preachers and missionaries, but the functionaries of God (so that they may be witnesses for the people), and it is their duty to wipe out oppression, mischief, strife, immorality, high-handedness and unlawful exploitation from the world by the force of arms." What the communist utopia desired – the classless society, the liberation from the realm of necessity and the advent of the realm of freedom; what Nazism wanted – the unimpeded rule of the Race; Maududi's Islam equally calls forth. All evils shall disappear, harmony will prevail, all troubles will vanish. God's kingdom will be realized on earth.

What is so distinctive about Maududi and his co-thinkers – Sayyid Qutb, Ruhollah Khomeini, and their like – is the central role they award the state in their overall scheme. Islam does not separate "Mosque and State" in the sense that the same law, Sharia, applies to the public and the private realm, and the state is tasked first and foremost to ensure the implementation of Sharia. Islam is not a *theo*cracy but a *logo*cracy. And Quran, hadith, and Sharia are the only law.[39] But there has long been a pragmatic separation between the affairs of the state, the preserve of dynasts, and the affairs of religion, the realm of the *ulama*. The latter have traditionally shunned the affairs of state, the only condition being that the caliph, or any ruler for that matter, must not go against divine law. Even an impious scoundrel will legitimately be recognized as caliph, provided he does not try to hinder Sharia, says Sunni orthodoxy. It is a political quietism. As the great codifier of that orthodoxy al-Ghazali had it, any revolt was illegitimate, even against an oppressive and evil ruler, since it would likely generate anarchy and chaos. The radicals decisively broke with that hallowed doctrine and made the conquest of the state the central objective of their political action, as if Lenin's *The State and Revolution* had become their bedtime reading.

So Maududi's claim: "Hence this party [of God] is left with no other choice except to capture state authority."[40] Why is this so? "Apart from reforming the world it becomes impossible for the party itself to act upon its ideals under an alien state system. No party which believes in the validity and righteousness of its own ideology can live according to its precepts under the rule of a system different form its own": the absolutist claim of ideology to have unlimited writ. The example Maududi chooses to illustrate his assertion is noteworthy: "A man who believes in Communism cannot order his life on the principles of Communism while in England or in America, for the

[39] On logocracy, see Jean-Paul Charnay, *La charia et l'Occident*, Paris, Ed. de l'Herne, 2001.
[40] Maududi, *Jihad in Islam*, p. 21.

capitalistic state system will bear down on him with all its power and it will be quite impossible for him to escape the retribution of the ruling authority," he writes, not without some semantic legerdemain. He adds:

> Likewise, it is impossible for a Muslim to succeed in his intention of observing the Islamic pattern of life under the authority of a non-Islamic system of government. All rules which he considers wrong; and taxes that he deems unlawful; all matters which he believes to be evil. The civilization and way of life which, in his view, are wicked; the education system which seems to him as fatal – all these will be so inexorably imposed on him, his home and his children that evasion will become impossible. Hence a person nor a group of persons are compelled by the innate demand of their faith.

As a result of all this, "the acid test of the true devotion" of the believer is that he commits himself to world revolution.[41]

Maududi the Leninist elaborates on his concept of "World Revolution," which he sees as synonymous with "jihad:"

> [T]he objective of the Islamic "jihad" is to eliminate the rule of an un-Islamic system and establish in its stead an Islamic system of state rule. Islam does not intend to confine this revolution to a single state or a few countries: the aim of Islam is to bring about a universal revolution. Although in the initial stages it is incumbent upon the members of the party of Islam to carry out a revolution in the state system of the countries to which they belong, but their ultimate objective is no other than to effect a world revolution. No revolutionary ideology which champions the principles of the welfare of humanity as a whole instead of upholding national interests can restrict its aims and objectives to the limits of a country or a nation. The goal of such an all-embracing doctrine is naturally bound to be world revolution.[42]

This was vintage Lenin, with a strong whiff of Trotsky added. As a biographer noted, "Maududi's program did indeed sound revolutionary in intent and possibly Marxist in origin when he wrote in *The Process of Revolution* "Islam is a revolutionary ideology with a revolutionary practice, which aims at destroying the social order of the world totally and rebuilding it from scratch . . . and jihad denotes the revolutionary struggle."[43]

Maududi appropriated the image and concept of "Revolution," this potent myth of the twentieth century, in the sense the French radical anarchosocialist Georges Sorel gave to the word in his *Réflexions sur la violence*: Given the violent and irrational motivations of social and economic conduct,

41 Ibid., pp. 21–2.
42 Ibid., pp. 22–4.
43 Nasr, *Maududi*, p. 70.

a deliberately-conceived "myth" must be concocted to sway masses into concerted action. The revolutionary mobilization of the masses

> could not be produced in a very certain manner by the use of ordinary language; use must be made of a body of image which, by intuition alone, before any considered analyses are made, is capable of evoking as an undivided whole the mass sentiments which correspond to the different manifestations of the war undertaken by socialist agitation against modern society. This problem [is solved] perfectly by concentrating the whole of socialism in the drama of the general strike; there is no longer place for the reconciliation of contraries in the equivocations of the professors; everything is clearly mapped out, so that only one interpretation of Socialism is possible. The method has all the advantages which the "integral" knowledge has over analysis.[44]

For Sorel, the shibboleth was "the general strike"; for his disciple Mussolini, it was "the total State"; for Lenin, "communism" and "The Revolution"; for Hitler, the "Aryan Race"; and for Maududi, "The Islamic world revolution." Different creeds used the same structure: The myth is the actualization of redemption in the here and now. All were Manicheans and Gnostics. All cultivated the drama that overwhelmed analysis and placed the mass under the sway of the propheta. Based on his sociopolitical reading of the Quran, Maududi redefined Islam from faith to ideology and converted religion into a mass movement fostering the drama of world Islamic Revolution.

The starting point to identify lines of communication through which Leninist thought came to Maududi is Maududi's active membership in the Khilafat movement at the very early age of 16.

> From the *Khilafat* activists he learned about the West and about politics; he learned the value of social mobilization and political propaganda, as well as the utility of putting Islamic slogans and symbols to communalist and political use. Many of the ideas of the *Khilafat* movement, such as its anti-imperialism, its effort to unite the various expressions of Islam in India, its appeal to Pan-Islamist sentiment, and its belief in the viability and desirability of resuscitating the institution of the Caliphate remained hallmarks of Maududi's political thought.[45]

In turn, we have seen how leading figures in the Khilafat movement were mesmerized by and attracted to Bolshevism, and how at the same time the Deobandi school drew close to Moscow. The conclusion, if needing to be fleshed out, is: However inescapable it was that the multifarious Bolshevik influence we have charted found potent ways to shape Maududi's thinking,

[44] Georges Sorel, *Réflexions sur la violence*, 8th ed., Paris, Marcel Rivière, 1936, pp. 122–3.
[45] Nasr, *Maududi*, p. 19.

as it did many other Muslim leaders and intellectuals, at the hand of this terrible simplificateur, jihad and world revolution became one.

Sayyid Qutb, the ideologist for the Muslim Brotherhood in Egypt, was Maududi's disciple. He in turn made Maududi's absolute dichotomy between Islam and un-Islam into the cornerstone of his revolutionary Islamist ideology.

Gnostic Mullahs and Smaller Satan

> The nationalism of the Arab-Muslim peoples [has a] double profile. On the one hand, it presents itself as a nationalistic movement of the conventional European style, based on a sense of racial kinship, and with certain general claims that are justified on historical grounds. On the other, it is a thinly disguised Mahdist movement aimed at forcible purification of Islam and at the revival of the traditionally demanded imperialism of the Umma. The interlocking of those two activistic drives gives [the movement] its strength.[46]

Jihadis of all stripes in the modern age share the same highly toxic mix of messianism, revolution, and the cult of blood and violence. Modern jihad is the tapestry resulting from the weaving together of different warps and woofs: Pan-Islamism and Bolshevism, Nazi and fascist ideology and practices, and Gnostic–Manichean beliefs within Islam. Originally distinct and distant threads have been woven together by artisans. We have so far described the German, Ottoman, Russian, Indian, and some Arab craftsmen of the weaving. We will now examine the Iranian threads, and how they were woven into the tapestry.

Khomeini and the militant clerics aimed at establishing an Islamic state by means of an Islamic revolution: "[T]he proponents of Islamic traditionalism had appropriated the most potent myth of modern politics, the myth of the revolution."[47] They had to learn the art of accessing the masses from the Iranian Communist Party, the *Tudeh* ("Masses"). In bringing about a fusion of Marxism and the Gnostic tradition of Shia Islam, they received the invaluable input of Ali Shariati and Muhammad Navab Safavi. Safavi showed them how to make terror a principal instrument of politics, much of which he had learned from Hasan al-Banna and Sayyid Qutb. Ayatollah Motahhari merged the lessons learned from his friend Shariati and from his other friend Navab Safavi. With spectacular cunning, Ayatollah Khomeini

46 Grunebaum, *Modern Islam*, p. 224.

47 Said Amir Arjomand, *The Turban for the Crown: The Islamic Revolution in Iran*, Oxford: Oxford University Press, 1988, p. 105.

used them all to develop his revolutionary Mahdism, a doctrine he had in part learned form his correspondent Abul Ala Maududi.

The militant clerics led by Khomeini were avid readers of the writings of Sayyid Qutb and of Maulana Abul Ala Maududi. "Their influence is unmistakable in the revolutionary slogans and pamphleteering" in Iran.[48] In his preface to *Social Justice in Islam*, Qutb's clerical translator praised the author for having established "a living and invaluable ideology."[49] The Iranian Islamists readily acknowledged their intellectual debt to the Sunni revolutionaries. Had Navab-Safavi, Khomeini's old terrorist acolyte, not consorted with the Muslim Brothers in Cairo as early as the 1940s? "Maududi ... had met the chiefs of the Muslim Brotherhood. ... The Iranian *fedaiyan-e Islam* had serious relations with the Muslim Brothers of Egypt, Syria [and] Jordan. ... Khomeini's 'Islamic Revolution' is a resurgence of that of the defunct *fedaiyan* movement. Ali Shariati's ideas, which are explicitly claimed by the heroes of the Iranian Islamic revolution ... [they] are close to Sayyid Qutb's."[50]

Navvab Safavi, Iran's First Modern Propheta

Muhammad Navvab Safavi, nee Sayyid Mujtaba Mir-Lowhi (b. Tehran 1924), was the purveyor of al-Banna's brand of fascistic Islamism to Iran. This "young and not very well educated cleric," who had spent two years at the Najaf Seminary, established the *Jamiyat-e Fedaiyan-e Eslam* ("those who sacrifice their lives for Islam") in 1945. The movement rapidly attracted a large membership of lower class and urban poor, and the religious middle class, and acquired powerful protectors among wealthy bazaar merchants and influential clerics. At its peak, the organization of the charismatic Navvab Safavi boasted 7,000 members.[51] It quickly emulated the Muslim Brotherhood's terror campaigns and murders of "corrupt," pro-Western political figures. All the atrocities perpetrated by his group were blessed by prominent clerics. Ayatollah Murtaza Motahhari, a student, disciple, and trusted lieutenant of Ruhollah Khomeini, was a close friend and associate. The first killing was that of the modernizer Ahmad Kasravi, an author whose 1946 assassination was signed off on by Khomeini himself; by Ayatollah

[48] Ibid., p. 97.
[49] Ibid., p. 94.
[50] Olivier Carré, "Introduction," in Carré and Dumont, *Radicalismes islamiques*, 8.
[51] Mahmood T. Davari, *The Political Thought of Ayatollah Murtaza Mutahhari: An Iranian Theoretician of the Islamic State*, London & New York: Routledge Curzon, 2003, p. 20.

Abdol Hoseyn Amini, who issued a fatwa calling for the elimination of the "Satanic" writer; by cleric Mohammad-Hasan Taleqani, who provided the money; and by the most prominent political leader of the Iranian clergy of the time, Ayatollah Kashani, speaker of the *Majlis*, the Iranian Parliament, who was to make extensive use of Navvab Safavi's murderous services in years to come.[52] Clerical pressure forced the government to let the killer go with but a slap on the wrist.[53]

Kashani gave the upstart plebian cleric a serious religious cover and in return acquired the support of an organization able to mobilize activists. After a failed assassination of the shah, the top clerics again protected the fugitive Navvab Safavi, who hid at the house of Ayatollah Mahmud Taleqani, while the young killer of Kasravi now killed the minister of the court. The *fedaiyan*'s rampage went on undisturbed. The prime minister, the tough General Ali Razmara, fell victim to one of their assassins, who again was protected by Kashani. The organizer of the targeted assassinations, Navvab Safavi was now a celebrity, granting menacing interviews and meeting Arab heads of states in the course of a late 1953–early 1954 tour of the Middle East. He was feted in Cairo by the Muslim Brothers and treated as a guest of honor by the Egyptian government.[54] When he returned to Iran, the Shah tried to co-opt him, even as the fedaiyan openly called for the shah's death: "[T]he Shah was a usurper of Islamic rule and the government was illegitimate; the usurper of Islamic rule must be killed and the illegitimate government banished."[55]

Navvab Safavi now published a manifesto that foreshadowed the Islamic state that arose in Iran after 1979. Bearing some resemblance to Italian fascist and German national socialist propaganda, it was a curious jumble of reactionary–romantic nostalgia for an idealized past, violent rejections of anything modern or Western, panicked fear of female sexuality, statist and redistributionist economic and social views, and radical demands for clerical executive power. Society was to be placed under "the university of the Quran" and "the barracks of Islam." The manifesto described an idyllic Islamic state, "where the government would be the father of the people, where nobody would fear the state's representative nor the thieves, where stores and houses had no more locks and keys. Sexual passions are released

[52] Davari, *The Political Thought of Ayatollah Murtaza Mutahhari*, p. 21.

[53] Yann Richard, "L'organisation des *fedaiyan-e Eslam, mouvement intégriste musulman en Iran (1945–1956)*, in Carré and Dumont, *Radicalismes islamiques*, pp. 24–8.

[54] Richard, "L'organisation des *fedaiyan-e Eslam*," pp. 35, 40, 51.

[55] Davari, *The Political Thought of Ayatollah Murtaza Mutahhari*, p. 22.

in marriage" – though temporary marriage must be promoted – "there is no more unreason, no alcohol, no binges. Truly it would be a paradise."[56] Of course, the pathway to paradise was brutal: "Reform can only be achieved under the shadow of force; force is sacrifice, and sacrifice is but under the shadow of Islamic education. Hence, we, children of Islam, with God's help, we can achieve these reforms through our own sacrifice." War was necessary and beautiful: "Human wars come from ignorance, and Islam's wars come from God's command." With this creed, Safavi recruited very young men – was Ayatollah Khomeini later not to say that "people over 20 were already contaminated by Satanic civilization"?[57] These candidates for martyrdom were "processed" by Navvab Safavi himself, in a functional equivalent of brainwashing, a technique that was later refined for mass use by the regime.[58]

The charismatic Navvab Safavi was finally executed in 1956. He "left a deep imprint on the religious opposition to the regime."[59] He was the first incarnation of the Gnostic propheta in contemporary Iran, but he was by no means the last. In 1963, barely seven years after his death, three activist religious groups, which he had deeply influenced, coalesced to form the *Heyat-e Motafelehye Eslami*. Composed of bazaar people and youngsters, it was led by a four- or five-man clerical committee appointed by Ayatollah Khomeini, including Ayatollahs Beheshti and Motahhari, and able to deploy about 500 activists. The clerics issued guidelines to propagate Islam, to extend Islamic "ideology," to establish classes to that effect, and to establish groups for training speakers and teachers. They started to organize members into semisecret ten-person groups. By November 1964, the leadership had decided to establish a military branch for targeting the regime's anti-Islamic figures. The following year they succeeded in killing Prime Minister Hasan Ali Mansur after the clerical committee issued a fatwa to that effect.[60] The *Vehme* assassinations executed in the early 1920s by the German *Freikorps* had found an echo.[61]

Navab Safavi's fellow *Fedaiyan-e Eslam* Sayyid Mahmud Taleqani (1910–79), a genuine scholar of Islam, has been called "The Father of

[56] Richard, "L'organisation des *fedaiyan-e Eslam*," pp. 54–63.

[57] Taheri, *Holy Terror*, p. 81.

[58] See Farhad Khorokhavar, *Les nouveaux martyrs d'Allah*, Paris, Flammarion, 2002, passim.

[59] Richard, "L'organisation des *fedaiyan-e Eslam*," p. 81.

[60] Davari, *The Political Thought of Ayatollah Murtaza Mutahhari*, p. 39; Arjomand, *The Turban for the Crown*, p. 95.

[61] Robert G.L. Waite, *Vanguard of Nazism: The Free Corps Movement in Postwar Germany 1918–1923*, New York, W. W. Norton, 1969.

the Revolution."[62] Many of the themes and doctrines he originated or formulated became common property of most revolutionary groups and individuals in later decades. To discuss private proper, "he adopt[ed] and islamicize[d] patently Marxist terminologies.[63] He proposed that "the East" was virtually exempt from "Western" class struggle. His famous 1963 speech on holy war and martyrdom was seminal to much elaboration of the matter in later years. So was his Orwellian theory treating knowledge as a "veil that prevent[s] direct thinking about and seeking guidance from the [Quranic verses]."[64] Like many of his fellow radicals, Taleqani's voluminous exegesis of the Quran was a crucial power in a reengineering of Islam into a revolutionary creed. His Quran had created "a new man,"[65] as it was geared "to manifest the hidden intent of the Quran."[66] No wonder that his followers later established the Organization of People's Guerrilla![67]

How to Organize Masses: The Tudeh

Iran is possessed of a long tradition of urban and rural uprisings. In 1913, in the northern region of Ghilan which abuts the Caspian Sea, an anti-imperialist uprising with "radically Pan-Islamist" leanings had taken place against Russian and British encroachments, under the leadership of a religious figure, Mirza Kuchik Khan. The Muslim warriors were supported, funded, and armed by the Germans and the Ottomans. Shortly after the collapse of the czar's army in Iran, in 1917, "socialist ideas reached the Jengeli," and contacts were made with Red movements in Azerbaijan and Persia. In June 1920, the Soviet commander of the Red Fleet in the Caspian, and member of the Central Asian Bureau of the Communist International, Admiral Raskolnikov, proclaimed an alliance with the Jengeli, as the insurgents were known. The Soviet Socialist Republic of Ghilan was "the first Soviet satellite outside the Soviet Union."[68] Less than a year later, having chosen to turn Reza Shah into an ally, Moscow betrayed its Jengeli allies and established diplomatic relations with Tehran. In retaliation, Kuchik slaughtered the entire leadership of the Iranian Communist Party; he was then hunted down by the Iranians.

[62] Dabashi, *Theology of Discontent*, p. 220.
[63] Ibid., p. 225.
[64] Ibid., p. 237.
[65] Ibid., p. 246.
[66] Ibid., p. 263.
[67] Ibid., p. 267.
[68] Benningsen and Wimbush, *Muslim National Communism*, pp. 79–80.

This first experience with Soviet trustworthiness did not prevent the establishment, in September 1941, mostly by intellectuals, of an Iranian Communist Party. To avoid alienating the mullahs, the party's provisional program of February 1942, in typical "united front" manner, kept Marxist-tainted demands out. Stating its attitude toward religion, the party explained: "The *Tudeh* party has sincere faith in the true religion of Islam. Most of the members . . . of our party are Muslims by background and believe in the religion of Muhammad. We shall never divert from the straight path of Islam." *Dar barih-i Eslam*, a party manifesto addressed to the clerics, averred: "Not only is the *Tudeh* party not against religion in general, but we feel a particular allegiance and deep respect toward Islam. We do not see any contradiction between the teachings of Islam and the principles that our party is advocating. We follow the same path and struggle for the same objectives. We hope that the *ulama* of Islam join us in this holy struggle and assure them of our loyalty to the true faith."[69] The Islamic technique of *taqiyeh*, dissimulating the truth to advance the cause and protect its partisans, was clearly not lost on the Tudeh.

In August 1946, as Soviet power rose and rose, three party members received cabinet positions in the government. The party was outlawed in 1949 but reemerged in 1951–2 in the complex game played by multiple actors – the shah, the clerical party, the bazaaris, the Soviet Union, the United States, and Britain – over the issue of the nationalization of Iran's oil. *Tudeh* supported Dr. Mohammad Mosadeqh on and off, as suited its own goals, just as did the clerical party. Having built a remarkable apparatus to mobilize masses, the party was an essential player. It had established a large array of front organizations, each of which published periodicals openly propagating Marxist causes: youth, women, peasants, an association to fight illiteracy, a society for a Free Iran, workers, journalists, a society against the imperialist oil companies, a society of the Partisans of Peace, high-school students, lawyers, teachers, engineers, civil servants.[70] The party was the first force ever in Iran to organize in this "European" manner, directly inspired by the way socialists and especially communists organized various layers of society. The party's ascent was not even dampened by Stalin's failed test-operation of setting up a satellite Soviet republic in a part of the Soviet wartime occupation zone of Iran closest to the USSR, Azerbaijan. When the puppet state collapsed, its leaders fled to the Soviet Union, where they were rounded up and either executed or shipped to Siberia. In the 1960s,

[69] Arjomand, *The Turban for the Crown*, pp. 24–25.
[70] Ibid., p. 25.

the survivors returned to Iran. "Most remained true to their Communist ideal, although their faith in the Russians was spent. It was possible that their influence on the Communist movement in Iran is responsible for the emergence in the *Tudeh* party of a strong religious-national wing which in a curious way attempts to reconcile radical Islam and Marxism," researchers were able to report in 1979.[71] In that, the Iranians were rather successful – if not to the benefit of communism, certainly to that of radical Islam.

In July 1952, a few days before the resignation of Premier Mosadeqh, the Communist Party appealed to all anti-imperialist groups to join in a united front and "specifically requested [Ayatollah] Kashani to take the initiative toward this goal. When Kashani sent an appeal to the working and youth members of the *Tudeh* party, the Tehran press reported that an alliance had come into being between the *ulama* and the Iranian Communist Party." The day Mosadeqh effectively resigned, "Kashani sent a public letter to the pro-*Tudeh* organizations thanking them for their invaluable contribution to the national victory." The meanders of on-and-off alliances and enmities that mark the period are of little interest here – *Tudeh* now supported Mosadeqh, Kashani opposed him, but the communists' influence and power grew by leaps and bounds. Three of its leaders again were members of the cabinet. By July, the *Tudeh* was the strongest and best organized political force in the country.[72] It was demanding official recognition for the Communist Party as such and the expulsion of American military advisers. When Stalin died, in March 1953, huge marches were organized along the breadth and length of the country. *Tudeh* was even recruiting prominent clerics, such as Sayyed Ali Akbar Burqai who campaigned for the Partisans of Peace. After the pro-Western countercoup, Tudeh was banned but maintained a prominent and efficient clandestine presence.

Even though Khomeini ranted against Marxism and materialism, he allowed and encouraged his supporters to ally and cooperate with *Tudeh*. In turn, the latter sycophantically supported the Ayatollah. All the way into the 1979 Islamic Revolution and thereafter, this was true of Khomeini's trusted faithful who ran the mass organizing: "The *Tudeh* ideologues, from whom the IRP [Islamic Revolutionary Party] cadre took many of their cues," were in a partial symbiosis with the Communists. This persisted until the Imam decided to ban the party, arrest its members by the thousands, and exterminate its cadre. When that happened, in April 1983, the regime discovered several hundred Tudeh infiltrators in the military. The crackdown was

[71] Benningsen and Wimbush, *Muslim National Communism*, pp. 111–12.
[72] Davari, *The Political Thought of Ayatollah Murtaza Mutahhari*, pp. 26–7.

probably motivated less by the party's influence in the intelligentsia, which lay supine under the Imam's spell or his killers' ways, but rather "the party's ideological impact on the clerics while they were novices in Iranian politics." In fact, "The militant clerics learned many of their political and journalistic tricks and tactics – first used during the anti-liberal, anti-nationalist smear campaign following the occupation of the American Embassy, their coining of political slogans and their models for political analysis from the *Tudeh* party."[73]

Ali Shariati's Theology of Liberation

The revolutionizing of radical Islam in Iran did not follow one line of communication only. We have already explored the cult of blood and redemptive violence that is a hallmark of Shariati's "Islamo-Marxism," the doctrine he called *tashayyo-e sorkh* ("Red Shiism").[74] We will now examine his doctrine and actions from the vantage point of their contribution to the transfer of Marxism and Marxian existentialism into radical Islam. Shariati is one of the most significant of the Gnostic *prophetae* of the contemporary age. This "most furious revolutionary among the ideologues of the Islamic revolution" managed "to capture the revolutionary imagination of an entire generation" and extended far and wide into the entire spectrum of radical Islam, Shiite and Sunni alike.[75]

The modern myth of revolution is a modern form of the millenarian creed. Earthly redemption and the millennial kingdom, preached by all the totalitarian movements of the twentieth century, found especial resonance among religious masses whose creeds incorporated massive doses of apocalyptical and eschatological beliefs, such as the peculiar Mahdism of Shia Islam. In Twelver Shia, the dominant sect of Shiism, the starting point of Mahdism is the unbroken continuity of the Prophet's family's Imamate, through Fatima, Ali, Husayn, and Hassan. It did not end with the disappearance of the Twelfth and last Imam.

Muhammad al-Mahdi ("the guided," b. 868, d. ?), hidden since birth, appeared at the age of 6 to assert his claim to the Imamate, only again to disappear, this time down a well, to avoid his father's and grandfather's sad fate. For the next seventy years he maintained contact with his followers through a succession of four assistants, each known as *Bab* ("Gate"). On

[73] Arjomand, *The Turban for the Crown*, pp. 157–9.
[74] Murawiec, *The Mind of Jihad*, esp. pp. 47–57, 130–7, 215–23.
[75] Dabashi, *Theology of Discontent*, pp. 107, 103.

his deathbed in 941, the fourth Bab, as-Samarri, produced a letter from the Imam stating that there should be no successor to the latter and that henceforward the Mahdi would not be seen until he reappeared as champion of the faithful in the events leading to the Judgment Day. This long period, which has not come to an end yet, is known as the Greater Occultation. Some titles of the Twelfth Imam include: Master of the Age (*Sahib az Zaman*), Master of Command (*Sahib al Amr*), the one to arise (*al Qaim*), remnant of Allah (*Bagiyyat Allah*), and the awaited Imam (*Imam al Muntazar*).[76] This belief-structure was the perfect foundation on which to generate Gnostic–eschatological expectations, in short, Mahdism. In turn, the great renovator of Mahdism in the modern age – its prophet, the man who turned it into a political religion – Jamal al-Din al-Afghani, was a far-reaching influence on Shariati.[77]

Shariati's Mahdist historiography is a hagiographic fairy tale made for the edification of the credulous. His supposed familiarity with Western intellectual currents is shallow, his sociology is sophomoric, and his scholarship is embarrassingly feeble: He is an ideologue who nibbles on bits and pieces of history, philosophy, and sociology. Shortly before his premature death, he entrusted his (still unpublished) testament to Mohamad Reza Hakimi, a noted follower of Khomeini's, who in turn reported: "Of Shariati, let us first and foremost retain his potent and delicate gift as a communicator; with just a few words, simple slogans, he succeeded in radicalizing the mass of the people, which the clergy had been trying to do for a thousand years."[78] He cites one such slogan coined by Shariati at the time, "The martyr is the heart of history." The homology of Shariati's role and self-conception with that of Europe's medieval prophetae could not be more striking. He is "the intellectual who knows the formula for salvation from the misfortunes of the world and can predict how world history will take its course in the future,"[79] though it would be more appropriate to call him a semi-intellectual: As J. W. Goethe wrote in his *Die Wahlverwandtschaften*: "Fools and intelligent people are equally harmless. It is only the demi-fools who are really dangerous."

The "Third International" merged with Russia, the "Third Rome" the "Third Reich" merged with the "third age" (Age of the Spirit) in the

[76] Encyclopedia of the Orient, http://lexicorient.com/e.o/12thimam.htm, accessed Jan. 1, 2006.

[77] Nouchine Yavari-d'Hellencourt, "Le radicalisme chiite de Ali Shariati," in Carré Dumont, *Radicalismes islamiques*, p. 113. Also Dabashi, *Theology of Discontent*, p. 131.

[78] Yavari-d'Hellencourt, "Le radicalisme chiite de Ali Shariati," p. 117.

[79] Eric Voegelin, *Science, Politics & Gnosticism*, Washington, DC, Regnery, 1977, p. 67.

Gnostic parody of Christianity; likewise Shariati, like an alchemist, blended Islamic Mahdism with Marx's Manichean millenarianism. Two Gnostic traditions intersected, recognized one another, and recombined their compatible strands. A suggestive simile to his undertaking was a group of Bolshevik leaders and intellectuals, today rather forgotten, but who individually and collectively played a major role in the Russian Revolution and the development of the Bolshevik Party. It is not uncommon – "Revolution devours its children" – for such groups to create an intellectual atmosphere conducive to the mobilization of revolution only to be discarded by the new masters once they are securely in power.

This Russian group called itself the "God Seekers;" its leaders were the proBolshevik writer Maxim Gorki, the engineer and Bolshevik leader Alexksandr Bogdanov, and the future People's Commissar for Culture Anatolii Lunacharsky. These three had adopted Nietzsche's perspective of the "superman." In his hatred for "individualism," Gorki had dreamed of a Russian Superman who would lead the masses in a struggle for liberation. Lunacharsky and Gorki during the 1905 revolution developed a Marxist surrogate religion of *Bogostroitel'stvo* (God building). It extolled the heroic proletariat as savior of humanity, preached worship of collective humanity, and promised collective immortality to encourage people to risk death fighting for socialism, and to inspire heroism and self-sacrifice. It was in large part a response to Nietzsche, as was the obsession of the Russian radicals, from Chernychevsky onward, with creating a new culture and a New Man (*chelovek*) who would shed human nature and become more than the normal humans.[80] In the 1950s, Shariati was a member first of the "Movement for the Islamic Renewal," and then the *Nezhat-e Khoda parastan-e Sosyalist*, the "Movement of the Socialist Worshippers of God."[81] Like the Russian he emulated, Shariati loathed Christianity as a "religious individualist" faith and praised Islam as "religious collectivism."[82] To him, "monotheism" (Islam) and "polytheism" (including Judaism and Christianity) were expressions of class struggle, and congruent with his invented polarity of disinherited and oppressors.[83]

Shariati's children Ershan and Sarah Shariati, both professors in France today, report their father's fondness for his correspondent, the revolutionary

[80] Luciano Floridi, *Nietzsche: Impact on Russian Thought*, London: Routledge, Chapman & Hall, 1988. http://lists.paleopsych.org/pipermail/paleopsych/2006-August/005656.html, accessed Aug. 8, 2006.

[81] Yavari-d'Hellencourt, "Le radicalisme chiite de Ali Shariati," p. 111.

[82] Dabashi, *Theology of Discontent*, p. 116.

[83] Ibid., p. 144.

Frantz Fanon, and his conception of "creating a new man." The raw material of the dream was to be "the oppressed masses." To convey that imitation of Marxian class struggle, Shariati borrowed Fanon's expression of "*les damnés de la Terre*," "the wretched of the earth," and translated it into Persian by reviving the Quranic term of *mostazafin* ("the disinherited") – "a term that was to occupy a central position in the Islamic revolutionary rhetoric," since Shariati, even posthumously, was its leading sloganeer.[84]

Shariati also borrowed from the Quran and the stories of Muhammad's companions. In his fictionalized biography *Abuzar Qaffari the Socialist Worshipper of God*, he fished out this figure from relative obscurity to embody his theology of "liberation:" "I am the disciple of Abuzar, my doctrine, my Islam, my Shiism, my yearnings, my anger and my ideals are his. My purpose begins like his: in the name of God, God of the oppressed (*mostazafin*)."[85] Elsewhere, Shariati develops the fiction: "Abuzar, Companion of the Prophet, disciple of Ali.... He is a great revolutionary who fights against aristocracy, authoritarianism, capitalism [*sic*], misery, and segregation. His word is higher than that of Proudhon."[86] And yet more:

> A poor Bedouin, illiterate and rebellious to the idolatry of his time.... His material misery has endowed him with a keen sense of social justice; a man from the desert, remote from the depravation of the city, his illiteracy sheltered him from any reference other than Islam; his 'primitive' revolt against idolatry made him a proto-Monotheist, a *hanif*; his Islam is pure and coarse.[87]

Abuzar, in other words, was a good savage, the degree zero of humanity: he was nothing, a man without attribute; therefore he was dispossessed and ready to become the apotheosis of super-humanity, the martyr. Of course, the Westernization, or modernization, of Iran, was a grievous attempt at further dispossessing the good savage of his authentic identity, culture, and religion.

Taking all the leaves from Fanon's book, Shariati hammered: "I hate modernism." He hated as well its effect on Iran, *qarbzadegi* ("plagued by the West"), or in Jalal Al-e Ahmad's word, "Westoxication." The later, an early communist leader, was a born-again Muslim who rediscovered the might of religious myth and superstition, "the most real of all realities" against the hateful, alien, artificial modernity which, like a disease,

84 Arjomand, *The Turban for the Crown*, p. 94.

85 Ali Shariati, *Che bayaad kard?*, Tehran, Complete Works, 20, 1982, p. 249, quoted in Yavari-d'Hellencourt, "Le radicalisme chiite de Ali Shariati," p. 86.

86 Ali Shariati, *Baz-gasht*, Tehran, Hoseiniye Ershad, Complete Works, 4, 1978, p. 308.

87 Quoted by Yavari-d'Hellencourt, "Le radicalisme chiite de Ali Shariati," p. 87.

caused all evils.[88] Branded "the majesty of all men of letters" by Ayatollah Ali Khamenei, Al-e Ahmad was the most influential essayist of post–World War II Iran and the creator of "a language for social criticism."[89] Identity politics, which played a central role in mobilizing for the 1979 revolution, was rooted in his influence. He had the borrowed ugly term *Westoxication* from the Iranian standard-bearer of German existentialist philosopher and Nazi Martin Heidegger,[90] Ahmad Fardid (1912–94), who in turn may have borrowed it from the ideologue of reactionary post-modernism Enrst Jünger.[91] Shariati burdened his imaginary "West" with all the sins and flaws, social and moral, marital and political, economic and religious. In contast with this "satan" stood his demigods, Muhammad, Ali, Husayn.

Prophet Muhammad himself was a revolutionary, but a Gnostic one who intended to establish God's perfect order on earth *hic et nunc*, just as Shariati: "The Prophet does not talk of a 'virtuous city,' of a 'divine city,' or of a 'promised land,' he implements it. It is not a theoretical construct but an objective one. The virtuous city of Islam is a real community (*Umma*). It is the city of the Prophet."[92] To him, the Quran was the blueprint for the perfect social life. Muhammad was "this revolutionary shepherd of the people."[93] Like his Bolshevik predecessors, and just as Dostoyevsky's "Possessed" equated God and the People, Shariati divinized the People: "Jihad in the way of God is jihad in the way of the People."[94] It was a "radically populist theory of revolution."[95] His "man" is Godlike; his ethics are those of The Perfect Man.[96] He is a propheta: "He was convinced, like no other one in his historical vicinity, that he had ... to the fullest extent seen the light."[97] Marxism was a rival rather than an enemy. He himself was the great enlightener, endowed with a sacred mission, to redeem Iran from "cultural colonialism" and therefore redeem the Iranians to their true nature.

88 In Dabashi, *Theology of Discontent*, pp. 47–92, passim.

89 Ibid., p. 74.

90 See Emmanuel Faye Heidegger, *L'Introduction du Nazisme dans la philosophie – Autair des séminauis indits de 1933–1935*, Paris, Albin Michel, 2005.

91 See Daryush Shayegan, "Heidegger en Iran," Le Portique, numéro 18, 2006.

92 Shariati, *Che bayad kard?*, 417, quoted in Yavari-d'Hellencourt, "Le radicalisme chiite de Ali Shariati," p. 90.

93 Ali Shariati, *Jehat-giri-e tabaqati-e eslam*, Tehran, Complete Works, 10, 1980, quoted in Yavari-d'Hellencourt, "Le radicalisme chiite de Ali Shariati," p. 96.

94 Ibid., p. 89.

95 Arjomand, *The Turban for the Crown*, p. 93.

96 Dabashi, *Theology of Discontent*, pp. 120, 132.

97 Ibid., p. 145.

In a double movement, the Gnostic actualizes the Absolute by establishing Perfection in the finite and imperfect human world and mobilizes the strivings of people for the same Absolute and Perfect. What is properly Gnostic in this double process is the claim that man can escape his condition, abolish his finite character – in other words, change his nature. This is the myth of revolution as embodiment of eschatological millenarianism. A utopia is essentially empty: It consists only of the desires projected into it by believers. So it had been for the Bolshevik Revolution of 1917, for the National Socialist Revolution of 1933, for the Chinese Revolution of 1949, and so it was to be in 1979 for the Islamic Revolution of Iran.

Shariati's ideas contributed directly to the revolutionary outbreak through his influence on Iranian students and young intellectuals, especially the highly organized and motivated *Mojahedin-e Khalq*, who did some of the decisive fighting in the fateful days of February 1979. His ideas also had an important influence on the writings of the clerical pamphleteers and preachers, who were quick to take up the rhetoric of social justice and the cause of the disinherited. Furthermore, Shariati's writings won over a substantial part of the lay intelligentsia to Khomeini's side by leading them to believe the Islamic Revolution would be "progressive." Presumably, as a reformer Shariat was a model to be followed; he had written that Prophet Muhammad had preserved the form of traditional norms but had changed their contents in a revolutionary manner.[98]

This was Muslim Brother Maaruf Dawalibi's "Marxist drink in a Muslim cup" all over again. The Islamic Revolution was the Shiite millennium, the Imam-Mahdi reappearing in the shape of Ayatollah Khomeini.

Shariati's concept of the party as the instrument of revolution was a Leninist one: the party was the locus where belief (faith: *iman*) connects with revolutionary action (jihad). Shariati

> succeeded to re-Islamicize a youth to which the religious leaders had lost access.... He transmogrified the Westernized youth into Islamic fighters. This psychological and behavioral transformation expressed itself as an increasing rejection of the Western model.... Shariati made himself the "bridge" connecting the dynamic element of the [Islamist] middle class, the educated youth, and the people traditionally led by the clergy.

This "triangle" carried out the revolution.[99]

[98] Arjomand, *The Turban for the Crown*, p. 94.

[99] Yavari-d'Hellencourt, "Le radicalisme chiite de Ali Shariati," p. 110.

Now, Shariati – the young Islamist disciple of semi-Marxists Herbert Marcuse, Jean-Paul Sartre, and Frantz Fanon – was a darling of the radical Shiite clergy. "Very early on, the revolutionary clerics are in contact with him and throughout his life bestowed him with marks of respect and protection. The best-known *mujtahids* ... ayatollahs Taleqani, Tehrani, Beheshti, Mofatteh and especially Ayatollah Motahhari collaborated closely with him."[100] When clerical agents of the regime asked him to condemn Shariati, Ayatollah Khomeini pointedly refused. Khomeini's point-man Motahhari maintained a close friendship and collaboration with Shariati. In 1965, Motahhari (whose functions in the *Hetyat* included pronouncing on the killing of "enemies of Islam") cofounded the *Huseiniyeh-ye Ershad* institute for research and education which later "played a major role in the religious movement of young activists before the Islamic Revolution." In November 1967, Motahhari sent a letter to Shariati asking him to contribute to a book about the life of the Prophet the institute was going to publish, and soon afterward, he invited Shariati to come lecture there. "His lectures were livered with emotion, firing his audience with enthusiasm and were warmly welcomed by the young students, His teachings, too, had a major influence among the older men and women students. This essentially turned the Ershad Institute into the most attractive religious center in the country." In a letter Motahhari wrote to the trustees, he depicted Shariati's lectures as "so popular during the four years [in question] that it exerted an influence on all groups of the country from the Grand Ayatollahs to the government officials."[101] Only Shariati's early death – probably at the hands of agents of SAVAK, the regime's secret police – prevented a continuation of his collaboration with Motahhari: "In his late texts and lectures.... Shariati sought to modify his views and present an affirmative view of the *ulama* by mentioning their revolutionary and anti-imperialist role in contemporary Islam."[102] Shariati had journeyed to the West and brought back the worst he could find, which he then placed in the service of the Islamists' spirit of destruction.

Shariati's heirs were many, although in the end the legacy was channeled exclusively in the direction approved by the mullahs. Established at the beginning of the 1970s, the "Iranian People's Guerrilla," *Fadai-ye Khalq-e Iran*, which took its name from Navvab Safavi's old group, had started as a student group at Tehran University a half a dozen years before. Members became Marxists, read and discussed Che Guevara, Régis Debray, and

[100] Ibid., p. 101.
[101] Davari, *The Political Thought of Ayatollah Murtaza Mutahhari*, pp. 42–4.
[102] Ibid., p. 63.

the Brazilian theorist of urban guerrilla Carlos Marighela. Their theoretical pamphlets extolled guerrilla warfare, mass spontaneity, and heroic activities; they added Castro, Mao, and Giap to their repertoire. Another group, the *Guruh-e Furqan*, also established by Tehran University students, was the origin of the later Mujahideen. They read the Quran, Bazargan, and Taleqani but also literature on modern revolutions – Russia, China, Cuba, Algeria. A favorite was Algerian FLN (Front de libération nationale) ideologue Ammar Ouzegane's book *Le meilleur combat* (*The Highest Struggle*). Ouzegane, a former communist, argued in his book that Islam was a revolutionary, socialistic creed and that the only way to fight imperialism was to resort to armed struggle and appeal to the religious sentiments of the masses. After years of study and debate, the Mujahideen assembled a team to provide its membership with their own theoretical handbook. They wrote a series of pamphlets, which included very primitive discussions of the theory of evolution, Marx's theory of value, and "historical materialism," as well as a two-volume introduction to Quranic studies (*The Principle of Quranic Thinking*). Here they wrote that God is absolute evolution, not perfection; prayer is the connection between party members; the visible and invisible worlds are two hidden and overt stages of struggle and revolution; and the afterworld is a socioeconomic system of a higher world. They interpreted Quranic verses according to class struggle and concluded that property was nothing more than a colonial phenomenon. This was very much in keeping with the pseudohistory that is always to be heard from the Gnostic revolutionaries from wherever they hark, and which Shariati, Maududi, and Qutb had refined to a great art.

The Mujahideen also issued two large booklets on the history of the prophets and on Imam Husayn. The interpretation was that of class struggle between rich and poor, ruled and rulers.[103] One of the Mujahideen's leaders summed up their syncretic effort:

> Our original aim was to synthesize the religious values of Islam with the scientific thought of Marxism ... for we were convinced that true Islam was compatible with the theories of social evolution, historical determinism, and the class struggle.... [W]e say "no" to Marxist philosophy, especially to atheism. But we say "yes" to Marxist social thought, particularly to its analysis of feudalism, capitalism and imperialism.[104]

[103] The foregoing is a paraphrase of Davaris's report on the matter, ibid., pp. 75ff.

[104] Quoted by E. Abrahamian, *Radical Islam: the Iranian Mojahedin*, London, Tauris, 1988, p. 92.

The Mujahideen represented the inherent radicalism of Shiism, a form of socialism, a Muslim renaissance and reformation. They advocated an alliance with the Soviet Union. They were Shariati's "third way" to development.

The Mujahideen courted Ayatollah Khomeini. The story of their dealings sheds a fascinating light on the Islamic Revolution. The Mujahideen sent two members of their ideological team to Najaf in 1972 to ask Khomeini to give them his public support. With them they had letters of introduction from Ayatollahs Taleqani and Montazeri, and from Ayatollah Motahhari, who was in effect Khomeini's operational chief in Iran. The pair held twenty-four secret audiences with Khomeini, who urged them to de-Marxify themselves. He failed to grant his support, but he wrote letters to some of his followers in Iran urging them to support the families of Mujahideen who had been hurt by the shah's repression. The *Mujhideen* and Khomeini were now in a united-front relationship. The Mujahideen had created an aura of organizational efficiency, of revolutionary fervor, of religious martyrdom around themselves. They made headways into the religious seminaries at Khunsar, Qom, and Tehran; they debated with Taleqani and Shariati. One of their best-known slogans was "*Bi nam-e Khuda va be Nam-e Khalq-e Qahraman-e Iran*" ("In the name of God and in the name of the People of Iran"). This infuriated the orthodox Gnostics, as it "gave God an associate" – the people – the very definition of the sin of polytheism in Islam.[105]

After some bloody internal conflicts, the Mujahideen published a "vehemently anti-Islamic manifesto" which discarded Islam in favor of Marxism-Leninism.[106] Khomeini's associate Motahhari blasted the Mujahideen for their "new stratagem" and branded them "Batinists," an old insult denoting those who see allegorical and esoteric meanings in the Quran. The increasingly radicalized *Furqan* followed in the footsteps of the medieval millenarians in developing a vision of an Islam without institutionalized leadership. They targeted and assassinated a number of the leading ulama and officials, starting in May 1979 with Murtaza Motahhari himself.[107] Khomeini unleashed on them the full fire of his fury, calling them *munafiqun* ("hypocrites") – worse than unbelievers.

The falling out was inexorable. The chemical combination of Islam and Marxism is an unstable and explosive one, but its syncretic-Manichean

105 Davari, *The Political Thought of Ayatollah Murtaza Mutahhari*, p. 79.
106 Ibid., pp. 76–7.
107 Ibid., pp. 81–2.

content is indisputable. Even when they slaughtered one another, they all promoted – Ayatollahs and lay prophetae – the same fundamental Gnostic gospel. Their views on who should preach it and be in power differed, as different mafia gangs compete for the loot but fight together against the authorities. The "Mobilization" (*Basije*), the regime's organization for the recruitment of the 12- to 14-year-old volunteers for death and martyrdom, was intellectually the joint offspring of both, of clerical and of lay revolutionaries. Likewise, the first president of the Islamic Republic, Abolhasan Bani-Sadr, left-winger, demi-Marxist, "monotheist economist," was a Manichean doctrinaire of strong Gnostic leanings, the author of a utopian, and rather preposterous economic theory deeply rooted in reactionary German romantic tropes, one altogether free from any constraint that reality might have imposed. His 1971–2 *Manifesto of the Islamic Republic* gave a name to the dreams of leftists and Islamists alike – it was a cosmic, neo-Manichean program for his "economy of the Imam."[108]

Jihad and Revolution: Ayatollah Motahhari

Motahhari the cleric was no less of a Gnostic than his lay friend and rival Shariati. Although human history externally consisted of wars and contradictions between the poor and the rich, or between the ruling and the ruled classes, internally these were wars between right and wrong, good and evil. Outwardly Motahhari was a semi-Marxian cleric, but inwardly he was a Gnostic-Manichean.[109] As he wrote in his discussion of martyrdom: "A martyr's motivation is different from that of ordinary people. His logic is the blind logic of a reformer, and the logic of a Gnostic lover.... A martyr's logic is unique. It is beyond the comprehension of ordinary people. This is why the word martyr is surrounded by a halo of sanctity."[110] But as a thinker, Motahhari also was in a form of constant dialogue with Marxism, as if no clerical doctrine could be developed which did not, point by point, face and answer Marxism. In his biographer's words, "The importance of Motahhari's works is based, first, on their comprehensiveness and complexity. While similar to Marxist totalism," [holism] they challenge it, since he "presents an alternative total Islamic system, Islamic world-view and

[108] Dabashi, *Theology of Discontent*, pp. 220–5.

[109] Davari, *The Political Thought of Ayatollah Murtaza Mutahhari*, p. 48.

[110] Morteza Motah-hari [Murtaza Mutahhari], *The Martyr*, Houston, Free Islamic Libraries, 1980, p. 14.

social-political ideology." How much he felt the urge to meet Marxism, rival but not enemy as Shariati had put it, emerges from his anguished interrogation regarding the attractiveness of Marxism for the young:

> Today, it is more or less established in the minds of youth that one must either be a theist – a peacemaker, complacent, calm, motionless, neutral – or a materialist – active, rebellious, opposed to colonialism, exploitation and despotism. Why has such an idea infiltrated the minds of young people?... They observe that it is just the supporters of materialism who lead uprisings, revolutions, battles and struggles, while theists are mostly static and neutral. [...] At present, the majority of heroic struggles against despotism [and exploitation] are guided by persons with more or less materialistic feelings. Undoubtedly, to a high extent, they have occupied the heroic trench.[111]

In order to reoccupy the heroic trench and regain the youth in it from Marxism, Islam had to marxify itself. While it may be doubted whether Motahhari and his fellow clerics would have seen the matter in this light, the wholesale adoption of Marxian categories to analyze the world and of Marxist–Leninist rhetoric to transform it, encapsulated in slogans a thousand times repeated, created an Islamo–Marxist hybrid – a monstrous laboratory experiment that was unleashed on the body of Iran and thence the rest of the world of Islam. The clerical agents of that innovation thought their immutable Islam immune to the loan-ideas, and probably saw themselves as both responding to urgent tactical requirements and cunningly borrowing effective devices from their rivals. The issues caused "a considerable division between the militant *ulama*." A delegation was sent to Najaf to ask Khomeini's ruling. "Although Khomeini took a cautious position and did not issue a statement, he privately supported Motahhari."[112]

Motahhari's project was to create an Islamic ideology, every bit as "holist" as Marxism. Just as Afghani before him, and Maududi, and Qutb, he sought an "ideologization" of Islam, to turn Islam into a political ideology similar to the secular religions of twentieth-century totalitarianism, though couched in the Islamic cultural idiom. The new Islamist ideology

> meant the arrangement of readily available maxims constituting the sources of the Islamic tradition, the Quran and the sayings of the Prophet and the [Shiite] Imams, in accordance with a new pattern suggested by the Western total ideologies such as Communism and Fascism. A number of clerics took up the challenge of constructing the requisite Islamic total ideology. They were quick to learn the art of constructing an ideology from the lay intellectuals. They learned this art both from their

[111] Davari, *The Political Thought of Ayatollah Murtaza Mutahhari*, pp. 64–5.
[112] Ibid., p. 63.

opponents – most notably the ideologues of the *Tudeh* party – and their allies lay Islamist reformers such as [Mahdi] Bazargan and Shariati. Here, the importance of intense ideological debate between the *Tudeh* ideologues and the militant clerics in the Shah's prisons in the 1960s should be noted.[113]

In the economic and social planks of his total Islamic ideology, Motahhari was a corporatist socialist, keen on limiting economic freedom and eager to confiscate and nationalize wealth. The ambit of cases justifying state takeover was so huge and its terms so vague that it amounted to confiscating everything but the bazaar and peasants' lands.[114] Rarely did Motahhari, and most others, bother reading the original Western sources that they knew only from bowdlerized versions. His judgments on the West are thunderous, but slipshod, his knowledge vague and superficial; his contempt for such a thinker as Aquinas is based on an utterly trivial detail.[115] He taught classes on Marxism, culled from the Farsi translations of third-hand and third-rate Western authors. But "because Marxism appeared to be the main alternative, Shia writers developed a dual attitude toward it: on the one hand, they tended to argue their own case through refutation of Marxism while, on the other, they tried to interpret Islamic laws and traditions as being no less revolutionary than Marxist ideals."[116]

Motahhari's Marxian graft took to the Islamic stem. The project worked: "The major achievement of the clerical activists was to [offer] an ideology attractive to the intelligentsia and of maintaining their intellectual authority and leadership over the latter."[117] *Tudeh* and others had been the laboratory experiment, but the corporate interest reaping the fruit of their labor was the Islamic Revolution. The new jihad would be the result. Motahhari's "three sacred concepts" of "faith, *hijrat* [migration] and jihad" were now applied to political struggles through their Marxist repatterning.[118] Materialism and monism were *tawhid* ("the unity of God"); together they meant fighting against oppressors, the *taghut* ("idolaters"); the Marxist proletariat was the Islamic *mostazafin* ("the disinherited"); the shah was the anti-Christ, *ad-Dajjal* in the Muslim apocalyptic tradition; and Khomeini his messianic counterimage. All the facile dichotomies of a Gnostic worldview that erases differences and rubs out complexities were mobilized. Bevies of useful idiots from the Left, the intelligentsia, and the good society enthusiastically joined

[113] Arjomand, *The Turban for the Crown*, p. 97.
[114] Davari, *The Political Thought of Ayatollah Murtaza Mutahhari*, pp. 103–6.
[115] Dabashi, *Theology of Discontent*, p. 155.
[116] Davari, *The Political Thought of Ayatollah Murtaza Mutahhari*, p. 87.
[117] Arjomand, *The Turban for the Crown*, p. 97.
[118] Motahhari, *The Martyr*, p. 78.

the Islamic Revolution, typified perhaps by the first president of the Islamic Republic Abolhasan Bani-Sadr, one of the muddled ideologues of Islamo-Marxism. In the end, another slogan expressed the reality of the situation: *Shah raft Imam amad* ("The Shah has gone, the Imam has come"). Among the illiterate and the young urban professionals oscillating between past and present, between Islamic identity and modernization, Motahhari was an immense influence, notably through his popular 1960 collection of stories and anecdotes from the Muslim prophetic tradition, canonical sources, and ethical vignettes. After he aired the stories on national radio, starting in the month of Ramadan in 1963, "millions" were reportedly "glued to the radios."[119] Motahhari was thus doing in practice what the left-wing intelligentsia was clamoring for, the reinjection of Islam into society.

Motahhari systematically plied the meetings and sessions of the "Islamic societies" that attracted young urban professionals; his reengineering of the Shiite doctrine was a critical element in putting Iran's Shiite body on a war footing against the regime of the shah. He was instrumental in developing the revolutionary image of "Karbala," the venue of the martyrdom of Ali's grandson Husayn – "Karbala is not only in one day, it always is," summed up the doctrine that abolished time and space and helped transfer the minds of millions from the real world into the "second reality" of myth. This radical reinvention of tradition opened the way to revolution. As early as 1968, Qom religious scholar Salihi Najaf-Abadi's book *The Immortal Martyr* had triggered a major debate among religious circles. Prefaced by Ayatollah Montazeri, the 500-page tome was "the first serious, daring and semi-scholarly attempt to transform the quiescent character of the Karbala paradigm into an active, worldly oriented drama," and to politicize what had been a "mystical, lyrical and emotional" interpretation.[120]

As the Islamic Revolution triumphed, it established a totalitarian apparatus of rule that came directly from the book of Hitler's, Lenin's, Stalin's, and Mao's dictatorship. The militant clerics manned the Islamic Revolutionary Committees (*komiteh*), which meted out summary "justice" to the "enemies of God" and the "corruptors on earth," as the Cheka's flying three-men tribunals and later the Gestapo's *Blockwart* system once had. The clerics created and manned the "Political-Ideological Bureaus" in the various branches of the armed forces – like the Red Army's *politruk* and the structure of political commissars. In 1979, they created an equivalent to the SS, the Corps of the Guardians of the Islamic Revolution (*Sepah-e Pasdaran-e Enqelab-e*

119 Dabashi, *Theology of Discontent*, p. 157.

120 H. Enayat, *Modern Islamic Poloitical Thought*, Austin, University of Texas, 1982, p. 184.

Eslami). In 1984, they established the Vigilante Patrols for Combating the Forbidden (*Gashta-ye Mobarazeh ba Moukarat*), a modern variation on the traditional moral police – the *mutawwa*, under the Central Bureau of the Revolutionary Committees. A ministry of intelligence – a KGB or SS Sicherheitsdienst, or better, the Nazi Reichssicherheitshauptamt (RSHA) – was established in 1983, along with a supreme command of Islamic propaganda that imitated the Soviet Central Committee's agitprop department. Islamic societies "were established in all organizations and enterprises of consequence to act as watchdogs for Islamic conformity" – precisely what Soviet party cells were designed to do. Islamic societies of ministries and government departments like the teachers, the military, and factory workers have been particularly important. They have formed nationwide organizations, and there is even a committee for the coordination of the Islamic societies of governmental departments and agencies. There is also a council for the coordination of Islamic propaganda.[121]

The "oneness" so prized by Islamists of all sorts under the rubric of the "unity of God" (*tawhid*) was eerily redolent of the Soviet *jedinstvo* or the National Socialist unity. A sermon pronounced in 1980 by Ayatollah Montazeri, one of the great luminaries of the Islamic Revolution, stated:

> The entire nation is coming to the Friday prayers.... All classes come and they have one slogan: and their slogan is based on the faith in God, in Islam. All are saying "God is the greatest." All kneel down before God. They have one slogan: the slogan of Islam, of God, of religion, and they follow one leader who stands before them. When he kneels down, all kneel down, when he bows, all bow. He obeys, all obey unitedly [and] in harmony.

Ein Reich, ein Volk, ein Führer, all under one God.[122]

But Khomeini went further. By 1980, he launched an "Islamic Cultural Revolution" aimed at re-Islamicizing society, reshaping the people and the state, desecularizing the educational system, and fully establishing the Islamic Republic as an ideological state. The cultural revolution, "an interesting extension of the modern myth of revolution due to Mao Zedong and the repercussions of the Chinese Revolution," was designed to eradicate all traces of Western cultural influence from high schools and universities. "It was natural for [Khomeini and his clerical activists] to look at the latest model of revolution, with added features. Khomeini therefore ordered the

[121] Arjomand, *The Turban for the Crown*, 163, 165, 170. Also Ram, *Myth and Mobilization*, p. 24.

[122] Ram, *Myth and Mobilization*, 200–1, sermon of January 4, p. 1980.

creation of the Committee for Cultural Revolution to take charge of the Islamicization of the universities."[123]

The relationship between Islam and Marxism, between Islamists and communists, Marxists and sundry ideologues, was never free of tensions, but ever an unstable coalition of Gnostics whose ideologies were convergent enough to permit cooperation and interchange but divergent enough to cause strain and conflict. As long as they all fought uphill to oust the shah, Khomeini cunningly kept silent or even encouraged the Leftist revolutionaries and gave his clerics a wide mandate to work with them.

The Imam–Mahdi of the Revolution

In Iran's second presidential "election," in 1981, about 5 percent of the vote, or 400,000 ballots, were cast for the Twelfth Imam, the Mahdi. The myth was becoming flesh. In the event, the Mahdi did not become president, but he had a readily available substitute: Over many years, with the fevered help from his flock, Ayatollah Khomeini had painstakingly boosted himself to be the next best thing to the Twelfth Imam – a quasi-Mahdi.

Shiism owed its establishment in Iran to the supreme leader of an aberrant millenarian warrior order. The founder of the Safavid dynasty in the sixteenth century had claimed Mahdihood for himself. The intense personalization of the cosmic drama in Shiism – around the doomed figures of Ali, Husayn, and Hasan – was a powerful, inherent booster to millenarian eschatology. The orthodox interpretation given over the ages by the clerics kept the millenarianism within bounds: The last Imam, the Mahdi, had gone into hiding and would return at some unspecified time in the remote future; societies cannot exist in a permanent state of eschatological expectation, everlastingly suspended to a hypothetical. The millennium was a hope, not a daily matter. It was thus contained but not eradicated: The chiliastic belief lay now dormant, now fully reawakened. "As part of the general revival of religion in the late 1960s and 1970s, there was a marked increase in the popularity of *duaye nodbeh*, the supplication for the return of the Hidden Imam as the Mahdi, and special sessions were being arranged for its recital."[124] The etiology of millenarian upsurges needs social dislocation and mental disorientation as preconditions and catalysts for its emergence as a mass phenomenon. Especially after the oil manna upset all norms and shook all rules as a result of the 1973 oil crisis, the shah's Iran qualified as a society

[123] Ibid., pp. 142–3.
[124] Ibid., p. 101.

gripped by anomie. A fundamental dimension of the Islamic Revolution was the systematic exploitation, not least by Khomeini, of nostalgia for the old times, for the old stability.

The Egyptian Muslim Brotherhood had developed with a notion of supreme leadership – Hasan al-Banna was *al-Murshid* ("the Guide"). The charismatic Persian divine Musa al-Sadr, had organized the Lebanese Shiite community around a novel mix of social activism, truculent identity politics and the fanning of millenarian expectations, and was called *Imam* by his followers. He was a harbinger of the future Khomeini as "leader of the Good in [the Lebanese Shiites'] Holy War against the forces of Evil."[125] Influenced by those examples, by 1970 Khomeini's militant followers were calling him *Imam*: "The acclamation of Khomeini as *Imam* by his followers was a startling event in Shiite history in Iran. Never since the majority of Iranians had become Shiite in the 16th century had they called a living person *Imam*. The term had hitherto only been used in reference to one of the twelve holy *imams* and its connotations in the minds of the Shiite believers as divinely-guided, infallible leaders undoubtedly worked to build up Khomeini's charisma."[126] It was now suggested that the Ayatollah was linked to the Hidden Imam of the Age, the Lord of Time.

"An unmistakably apocalyptic mood was observable during the religious month of Moharram 1399 (December 1978) among the masses of Tehran. Intense discussions were raging as to whether or not Khomeini was the Imam of the Age and the Lord of Time."[127] Khomeini's face was allegedly seen on the moon in provincial cities. Without claiming to be the returning Mahdi, Khomeini ingeniously exploited the messianic yearning by encouraging his acclamation as the *Imam*. He suggested that he was the forerunner of the Mahdi.

The slogan most frequently chanted by the "Followers of the Line of the *Imam*" was: "O God, O God, keep Khomeini until the Revolution of the Mahdi."[128] In September 1982, a clerical member of the Majlis, the parliament, predicted the imminent Advent of the Mahdi. A soldier wounded at the front during the war between Iran and Iraq reported that he had seen the Mahdi who had spoken to him thus: "Your prayer . . . has expedited my Advent by a few hundred years." The story was printed in *Sorush*, the intellectual journal of the Islamic militants in November 1982.

[125] See Taheri, *Holy Terror*, pp. 65–73.
[126] Arjomand, *The Turban for the Crown*, p. 101.
[127] Ibid.
[128] Ibid., p. 152.

The influential Ayatollah Saduqi of Yazd reported a miracle performed by Khomeini many years earlier: The Imam had created a spring in the middle of the desert under a scorching sun.

Khomeini's self-appointment as quasi-Mahdi was rooted in the revolutionary doctrine he had developed, that of the "government of the jurist," *velayat-e faqih*. In Islam, the law is *fiqh* and the jurist is the *faqih*. This covers a much wider ambit than is connoted by the English words, since "in Islam, theology is law and law is theology," a conception that derives seamlessly from the undivision of the religious and the political sphere. Khomeini now claimed absolute political power for the *faqih*, that is, himself. His theory overthrew centuries of accepted Shiite doctrine: During the Occultation of the Twelfth Imam – that is, until his Advent – the ulama's mandate does not extend to the political sphere, and their mandate is a collective mandate, not one vested with any one individual. Khomeini rode roughshod over traditions and objections. From the 1963 riots onward, Khomeini and his followers stirred up the masses with the perspective of a political revolution; "to secure the leadership of this political revolution for themselves, they... revolutionized the Shiite political ethos."[129]

In January 1988, Khomeini asserted his God-given, absolute mandate to rule and govern as "the most important of the divine commandments [with] priority over all derivative divine commandments, even over prayer, fasting and pilgrimage to Mecca."[130] This was an extraordinary innovation in Islam, since the "derivative" commandments have always been considered the "Pillars of Islam." This clerical absolutism (hierocracy) exercised by one man, the quasi-Mahdi, became, as it were, Gospel truth in the Islamic Republic. Then-President Khamenei, now Supreme Guide himself – though lower in the scale of Mahdihood – asserted that the commandments of the ruling jurist, *valiye faqih*, "are like the commandments of God." He added: "It is the ruling jurist who creates the order of the Islamic Republic... and requires obedience to it. Opposing this order has become forbidden as one of the cardinal sins, and combating the opponents of this order has become a... religious duty."[131]

Khomeini even set himself up on a par with Prophet Muhammad and Caliph Ali, "the Perfect Man," if not religiously, which would have been blasphemous, but politically, also arguing that the Islamic Republic was a community superior to the Prophet's own in Medina and later Mecca:

[129] Ibid., p. 181.

[130] Ibid., p. 182.

[131] *Jomhuri-ye Eslami*, January 1988, in Arjomand, *The Turban for the Crown*, p. 183.

"Our people are better than the community of the Apostle," he dared[132] – the flirtation with blasphemy was intense. His tortuous rhetoric relentlessly advanced the notion that the jurist (*velayat-e faqih*), that is, himself, was the deputy of Muhammad, that as replacement for the occulted Imam, he was the inheritor of the Prophet, and therefore "ha[s] the same authority as the Prophets . . . [is] like [the] Prophets."[133]

This extraordinary innovation had been enabled by, and was rooted in, the status of leadership in twentieth-century totalitarian states. In the Muslim world, Hasan al-Banna's role as *al-Murshid* had been one of the conveyors of this conception, but Antun Saada's Nazi-modeled Syrian Socialist National Party in Lebanon,[134] Ahmad Hasan in Egypt, and others had shared and propagated it. *Al-Murshid* was a notion with an old Sufi pedigree; it merged and blended with the *Duce* leading his *stato totale*, with Hitler's *Führerprinzip*, and with Stalin as the *Vozhd*. Ayatollah Khomeini in his incarnation as the *velayat-e faqih* was the very embodiment of Carl Schmitt's decisionist leader, as well as a repeat of the great medieval prophetae of Europe, Thomas Müntzer, or the Anabaptist "king" of Münster. When in 1982 Khomeini ordered twenty-five Islamic organizations to merge into one "party of Allah," *Hezb-Allah*, it stood to reason, or unreason, that the slogan should be "Only one party, the party of Allah! Only one leader, Ruhollah!" It rhymes in Persian, with a ring similar to "*Ein Reich, Ein Volk, Ein Führer*!" and "Proletarians of all lands, *unite*!" Khomeini "represent[ed] Allah's will on earth," just as Hitler was the Will of the Race and Stalin the Will of History and The People.[135] The Iranian regime orchestrated the same type of spectacular collective ceremonies that Albert Speer had arranged for Hitler at Nuremberg and Berlin and that Stalin had organized on Red Square, with a keen eye on manipulating masses in order to mobilize them.[136]

Even though he was a politician of great cunning, Khomeini displayed the coarse brutality of a *Cheka* commissar or a Herman Goering. His ruthless cruelty was based on his very conception of Islam: "Muhammad was not only instrumental in bringing the Islamic law, he was also its first executioner. He cut off hands, chopped off limbs, stoned adulterers to death."[137]

The results have been of the same order. The rampant jihad that has radiated from Tehran since 1979 has been one of the principal causes of

[132] Ram, *Myth and Mobilization*, p. 112.
[133] Dabashi, *Theology of Discontent*, pp. 413, 445.
[134] Becker, *The PLO* p. 114.
[135] Taheri, *Holy Terror*, p. 80.
[136] Ram, *Myth and Mobilization*, pp. 17–18.
[137] Quoted by Dabashi, *Theology of Discontent*, p. 440.

destabilization and destruction in the region since; it has fanned the flames not only of Shiite jihad but also of Sunni jihad. Indeed, Sunni-Shiite revolutionary and jihadi collaboration started the minute Khomeini returned to Tehran in 1979. Further, the Saudi–Wahhabi nexus was startled and frightened by the jihadi eruption across the Persian Gulf. The Kingdom's legitimacy as Custodian of the Holy Places was under relentless attack. The storming and seizure of the huge complex of the Great Mosque in Mecca, on November 20, 1979, the first day of the fifteenth century according to the Muslim calendar, shook the royal family to its foundations. The assailants had a Saudi core, but included in their ranks Egyptians, Kuwaitis, Sudanese, Iraqis, and Yemenis, among others. They had received military and tactical training in Libya and South Yemen from East German, Cuban, and Palestinian (members of the Popular Front for the Liberation of Palestine) instructors. They also included a contingent of apprentice terrorists trained in Iran.[138] The International Brigades of the new jihad were at work. As befits things modern, they had been born in a test-tube – the Palestine Liberation Organization – with a mad scientist operating the laboratory – the Soviet Union.

[138] Laurent Murawiec, *Princes of Darkness: The Saudi Assault on the West*, Lanham MD, Rowman & Littlefield, 2004, esp. Chapter 2.

7

Jihad as Terror

> [A] section of our opinion . . . thinks obscurely that the Arabs have acquired the right somehow to slit throats and to mutilate.
>
> Albert Camus

> We must above all keep our hatred alive and fan it to paroxysm. Hate as a factor of struggle, intransigent hate of the enemy, hate that can push a human being beyond his natural limits and make him a cold, violent, selective and effective killing machine.
>
> Ernesto "Che" Guevara

Algeria: A How-To of Modern Jihad

The Soviets had strongly advised the Palestinian movement to emulate the "Algerian model." By forcing the French out of Algeria, the Algerian insurrection had been a signal success. The Algerian insurrectionists became the poster boys of the anti-imperialist, anti-colonialist struggle of the "oppressed and exploited people – the living embodiment, in other words, of Leninist ambitions – the Baku Congress come to life. After the victory of the Viet Minh against the French Army in 1954, the Algerian War was the next great nexus of the third world revolt against "capitalism." Support for the Algerian cause was the main headline at the 1955 Bandung Conference of the Non-Aligned Movement.[1] Propaganda poured out of Nasser's Cairo, notably on the waves of "Voice of the Arabs" radio, and along with the multitudinous organs of Pan-Arabism, incessantly drummed up the glories of the Algerian FLN.

[1] See Léon Poliakov, *De Moscou à Beyrouth: Essai sur la désinformation*, Paris, Calmann-Lévy, 1983, pp. 85–6.

The victory of the Vietnamese communists – who posed as nationalists – had been for Arabs and for Muslims a great and heartening example of the "small oppressed people" throwing off the yoke of a "great Western power." It was as much myth as reality – the cover and sanctuary accorded the Viet Minh by Russia and China had been crucial to their victory – but it gave Muslim revolutionaries great confidence that the world and history were going their way. The Vietnam War may have been inspiring, but it was emotionally remote: Culturally and intuitively, Arabs and Muslims had little in common with Ho Chi-Minh's cohorts. They were able to learn from them to some extent, but Asia's conditions and traditions were distant. The war waged by fellow-Arabs and fellow-Muslims in Algeria was much closer to their hearts; it was easier to understand and easier to imitate. During his first trip to postwar Algeria, Arafat's oldest companion Abu Iyad confirmed that the Algerian "revolution," for the Palestinian movement, "symbolized the success we dreamed of."[2]

On the international stage, the Algerian War was presented as a national liberation movement. Moscow broadcast it as such, and foreign correspondents were writing it; to Algerian Muslims, it was presented as a jihad. The FLN's initial proclamation of November 1954: "To the Algerian People" announced the "launch [of] the true revolutionary struggle" and made it clear that it was "freeing itself from any possible compromise." It stated its goal as "national independence through ... the restoration of the Algerian state, sovereign, democratic and social, within the framework of the principles of Islam." It also proposed external objectives, "internationalization of the Algerian conflict," and the "pursuit of North African unity in its national Arab-Islamic context." Christians and Jews would be dhimmis in the projected new Algeria, and the Berbers, a large proportion of the population, would be second-class persons.[3] To make the point explicit, the name of the FLN's flagship newspaper was *al-Moudjahid*.

Arab and Islamic, the insurgency did not hide its colors – at home.

> When the Algerian revolution calls itself Arab, it concerns a reaction – of a cultural-linguistic nature ... – against the influence of the French, or more generally, Western culture. When the Algerians accentuate their Arab civilization and ethnic origins, it is an attempt to give a content ... to a nationalism which is still too new to be able to set itself up as autonomous in any other way than by opposing the cultural presence of France.... When it calls itself Muslim ... "Islamism," then consists in showing that a certain feeling of equity, of solidarity, of social justice, is common

[2] Rubin and Rubin, *Yasir Arafat*, p. 30.

[3] Horne, *A Savage War of Peace*, p. 95.

to the teaching of the Prophet and to Socialist conviction; at a more subtle level it is maintained that the revolution is nothing more than the modern way of realizing the aims of religion.[4]

The FLN leadership was more pragmatic than ideological, it mixed Islam and Marxism, or rather Islam and Leninist techniques.[5] "Essentially inward-turned the FLN leaders as a whole do not impress one as having been well-read on revolutionary practice and theory; if they had absorbed the techniques of the Viet Minh, it was through the direct experiences some had had as members of the ill-fated French forces in Indochina."[6] The "Nine Historical," the group of leaders that launched the insurrection, "deeply admired Ho Chi Minh."[7] They were shortly to be Mao's guests of honor in Beijing, and "placed ostentatiously . . . to the right of Mao" for the October 1 Revolution Day parade.[8] Tito's Yugoslavia gave "staunch support both in arms and on international platforms."[9] And, as soon as Fidel Castro came to power, "the Cubans were counted among the warmest friends of the Algerians."[10] The leading theoretical voices in the FLN were the former Communist Ammar Ouzegane, who was especially close to Ahmed Ben Bella, and Frantz Fanon, the Gnostic inspiration for Ali Shariati.

As might be expected, there also was a significant Nazi contribution to the FLN. A number of FLN cadres were former Nazis, like Mohammed Said, leader of the *wilaya 3* (one of the six regions into which the FLN had divided its operations), who had joined the Muslim SS Legion formed by the mufti of Jerusalem during World War II. "In 1943, he was parachuted into Tunisia as an *Abwehr* [German military intelligence] agent." Always coiffed with a Wehrmacht steel helmet, he made no secret about his wartime commitment: "I believed that Hitler would destroy French tyranny and free the world."[11]

The FLN carried out its jihad by way of three principal means: The first was the systematic and gruesome slaughter of large numbers of Muslims

[4] Roger Le Tourneau, Maurice Flory, and René Duchac, "The Revolution in Algeria," in P. J. Vatikiotis, ed., *Revolution in the Middle East*, p. 114.

[5] Horne, *A Savage War of Peace*, p. 74. Horne's impressive study has used the best literature available on the subject, and confirms what, for instance, Yves Courrière's highly valuable contribution had reported. I have therefore chosen to use his book as the source for most of the incidents mentioned in this section; they are present in most of the other published accounts of the Algerian War.

[6] Ibid., p. 407.

[7] Ibid., p. 78.

[8] Ibid., p. 405.

[9] Ibid., p. 406.

[10] Tourneau et al., "The Revolution in Algeria," p. 91.

[11] Horne, *A Savage War of Place*, p. 131.

to show everybody, French and Muslims, who was boss; the second was atrocious terror against the French *pied noirs* (native to Algeria); the third was to court support from the international communist movement, the Non-Aligned, and all Westerners who for whatever reasons found it convenient or expedient to support the future winners against the French.

The first act of the Algerian War occurred nearly ten years before its effective outbreak, in 1945. In the city of Setif, on VE Day, graffiti on the walls loudly proclaimed: "Muslims, awaken!" "It's the Muslim flag that will float over North Africa!" "*Français*, you will be massacred by the Muslims!" A report on those days' events states:

> As violence erupted, small groups of killers, the scent of blood in their nostrils, now fanned out by taxi, bicycle or even on horseback into the surrounding countryside, spreading the word that a general jihad . . . had broken out. . . . For five dreadful days the madness of demonstrators run amok, killing, rape and pillage, continued. . . . The accepted casualty reports made grisly reading: 103 Europeans murdered and another hundred wounded, a number of women brutally raped. . . . Many of the corpses were appallingly mutilated: women with their breasts slashed off, men with their severed sexual organs stuffed into their mouths.[12]

When the insurrection started for real, on All Saints' Day 1954, its first strike was highly symbolic: a bus was stopped in the middle of the countryside. FLN fighters ordered the passengers to disembark, and killed two civilians, a Left-leaning French schoolteacher, and a Muslim notable. The symbol could not have been clearer.

"At first, the [FLN] terrorism was aimed mainly at the Muslims, in order to dissuade them from cooperating with the French authorities or to enroll them by force, and to make them respect, out of fear, the orders given to the population."[13] It was a permanent and systematic modus operandi through the eight years of that "savage war of peace." The doctrine was very similar to that developed in Latin America by Brazilian Communist leader Carlos Marighela: "It is necessary to turn political crisis into armed conflict by performing violent actions that will force those in power to transform the political situation of the country into a military situation. That will alienate the masses, who, from then on, will revolt against the army and the police and blame them for this state of things." Marighela's strategy demanded blind terrorism to polarize and exacerbate the situation, which would eradicate the "soft center." In effect, he wanted to create violent persecution

[12] Ibid., pp. 24–6.
[13] Tourneau et al., p. 89.

against those in whose name he was supposed to fight.[14] Marighela was the accomplished communist Gnostic: He knew better than them what was good for them, and how to get there, in the name of the Doctrine that he (not them) knew to be True. The same went for the FLN. As we shall now see, they needed to terrorize the Algerian masses into becoming subservient to their "saviors."

By the winter of 1954–5, "[f]ear was everywhere. The bodies of loyal Muslims would be discovered, often appallingly mutilated or having been subjected to slow deaths." For instance, "the village policeman was found with his throat slit and eyes gouged out, a scrap of paper signed 'FLN' pinned to his skin."[15] By 1955, "[t]error had taken hold" in the whole country, wrote the French governor General Jacques Soustelle. French countermeasures diverted the FLN from hardened or risky targets. "Brutal murders of Muslim 'friends of France,' from caids [judges] to humble village constable, multiplied, totaling 88 in April [1955] alone, with a similar number hideously mutilated – as terrible warning to the rest." The FLN ordered all to stop smoking or drinking. The penalty for a first offense was the cutting off of lips or nose; for the second one, the slitting of the throat."[16] The massive use of the weapon of terror and savagery propelled the FLN to worldwide fame, resulting in the new organization being invited to the Bandung conference. The conference condemned colonialism in particular, and in general, and then unanimously adopted an Egyptian motion proclaiming Algeria's right to independence. There the FLN leaders met Ho Chi Minh, ever ready to supply his own recipes, among which mass murder and terror featured prominently. Five months later, the "Algerian Question" was formally inscribed on the agenda of the United Nations General Assembly. Terror paid. Soustelle, an old left-winger, pointed out that the FLN "never sought to attach the rural populations to their cause by promising them a better life, a happier and freer future; no, it was through terror that they submitted them to their tyranny."[17] The initiation ritual for new recruits was the killing of a designated Muslim "traitor" or French petty official. "In their actual techniques of liquidation FLN operatives consciously endeavored to achieve the gruesome. A loyal rural constable would be found tied to a stake, his throat cut." Marching orders were: "Kill the *caids*.... Take their children and kill them. Kill all those who pay taxes and those who collect them.

[14] Horne, p. 118.
[15] Ibid., p. 101.
[16] Ibid., p. 112.
[17] Ibid., p. 134.

Burn the houses of Muslim NCOs away on active service.... Liquidate all personalities who want to play the role of *interlocuteur valable*.... Kill any person attempting to deflect the militants."[18] Over the first two and a half years of the war, the FLN killed six Muslims for every one Frenchman. It was not even only pro-French "collaborators" whose death was ordained. In the summer of 1955, the cruel *wilaya* head Ait Amouda, a.k.a. Amirouche, had his forces encircle a *maquis* run by the Algerian National Movement (MNA) in East Kabylia; all 500 guerrillas were slaughtered. In a village near Bougie (today's Annaba), Amirouche ordered the liquidation of 1,000 or more "dissident" Muslims. Any Muslim beneficiary of land grants in the framework of the French-initiated land reform was ordered to be killed.

At the 1956 "Soummam" leadership summit of the FLN, which adopted a strongly Marxist-oriented platform, "indiscriminate terrorism was espoused."[19] On May 31, 1956, the French authorities announced that the *mechta* ("village") of Melouza had been the theater of a frightful massacre: "Three nights earlier, the FLN had rounded up every male above the age of 15 from the surrounding area, herded them into houses and into the mosque, and slaughtered them with rifles, pick-axes and knives: a total of 301 in all.... Sickened by the massacre, world opinion... for a brief time animadverted against the FLN."[20]

The precision is important: Anaesthetized by the holy cow of "anti-colonialism," press correspondents who covered the war soon reverted to their apologies of the Noble Savage in his struggle against Evil incarnate, and the unspeakable massacre soon faded into oblivion, while every atrocity committed by the French Army – and those were not few – found its place in the automatic pigeonhole that fit the overall narrative. No less a figure than Albert Camus, a left-wing pied noir with a passionate love for Algeria, exploded in saddened anger against "a section of our opinion [which] thinks obscurely that the Arabs have acquired the right somehow to slit throats and to mutilate."[21] Prominent parts of the cult in support of the right to slit throats were Jean-Paul Sartre, who made it into a theory in his 1961 introduction to Frantz Fanon's *Les damnés de la terre*, [22] and Simone de Beauvoir, who compared the French army to the Nazis (it was easier to bad-mouth the French army in 1960 than oppose the real Nazis during

[18] Ibid., p. 135.
[19] Ibid., p. 214.
[20] Ibid., pp. 221 –2.
[21] Albert Camus, *Actuelles III, Chronique algérienne*, 1939–1958, Paris, Gallimard, 1958.
[22] Frantz Fanon, *Les damnés de la terre*, introduction by Jean-Paul Sartre, Paris, F. Maspéro, 1961.

World War II – which they had carefully abstained from). Their confederate Francis Jeanson, who organized a logistical support network for the FLN, explained that Stalin's crimes were "made almost unavoidable by the hostility of the entire world." This attitude was not unique to wayward French intellectuals. Prominent British Labour Party left-wing leader Barbara Castle explained on the "Algeria Day" decreed on the Soviet model that "terrorism was the result of repression, not its cause."[23] The Algerian War was indeed a model for much of what was to come.

Arab corpses mattered only if killed by the French. By 1957, the FLN had begun a vicious war in mainland France – against fellow Muslims who opposed the FLN, or were merely neutral, but especially against the MNA. By 1960, this campaign had already claimed several thousand lives, "[T]he killings reached a crescendo as the FLN stepped up its campaign to achieve total ascendancy. Barely a day went by without a corpse fished out of the Seine or found hanging in the Bois de Boulogne . . . a blanket of terror successfully imposed by the FLN."[24] The climax was reached right after "independence," when anywhere between 30,000 and 150,000 *harkis*, Muslim auxiliaries of the French, and their families, were exterminated by the victorious FLN. In total, it is estimated that if the French killed 141,000 FLN male combatants, the FLN killed 172,000 to 232,000 male Muslims.[25]

Wilaya 2 commanders decided "to launch a total war on all French civilians, regardless of sex and age." Justifying it, the *wilaya* commander Youssef Zighout declared: "To colonialism's policy of collective repression, we must reply with collective reprisals against the Europeans, military and civilian, who are all united behind the crimes committed against our people. For them, no pity, no quarter!"[26] The hapless small town of Philippeville was chosen to highlight this commitment. In August 1955, the FLN mobilized: "The largest possible number of Algerians, even hastily armed with only sticks, pitchforks, axes, sickles and knives, was to be involved." It was a typical mafia tactic: Make the people accomplices to the crime, make them burn their bridges. Here is what happened:

> Muslims of both sexes swarmed into the streets in a state of frenzied, fanatical euphoria. Grenades were thrown indiscriminately into cafés, passing European motorists dragged from their vehicles and slashed to death with knives or even razors. Altogether, some 26 localities came under sudden attack. The peak of horror was reached

[23] Horne, *A Savage War of Peace*, pp. 235, 238, 244.
[24] Ibid., p. 408.
[25] Ibid., p. 538.
[26] Ibid., p. 119.

at Ain-Abid, 24 miles east of Constantine, and at el-Alia . . . close to Phlippeville. The attackers [at el-Alia] went from house to house, mercilessly slaughtering all the occupants regardless of sex or age, and egged on by Muslim women with their *you-you* chanting. . . . In some of the attacked towns, the muezzins even broadcast from their minarets exhortations to slit the throats of women and nurses in the cause of the "Holy War."

When the French army arrived on the scenes, "an appalling sight greeted them. In houses literally awash with blood, European mothers were found with their throats slit and their bellies slashed open. . . . Children had suffered the same fate, and infants in arms had had their brains smashed out against the wall."[27]

At Ain Abid, an entire pied noir family called Mello perished atrociously:

a 73-year-old grandmother, and an 11-year-old daughter, the farmer killed in his bed, with his arms and legs hacked off. The mother had been disemboweled, her five-days-old baby slashed to death and replaced in her opened womb. There were similar scenes of such revolting savagery in attacks elsewhere that day, and what heightened the horror . . . was the carefully premeditated planning which clearly lay behind them."[28]

Bodies strewed the streets.

French reprisals were atrocious, and the number of Muslims who perished perhaps ten times higher. The FLN had "succeeded": They ardently desired that a river of blood separate the two communities. It did. The same awful scenario was replayed in the terrible defeat suffered by the FLN with the Battle of Algiers in 1957, which the French won, if at a terrible price. There, the FLN called a general strike, and the French army broke it. But the 1,400 operatives of the terror network were laying bombs in cafés, dancing bars, at the General Post Office of Algiers. "The casualties of the innocent were . . . almost equally divided between Muslims and Europeans." Only, in the mind of the jihadis waging total war, "there are no innocents," as the Palestinian Marxist George Habash later said. The bombing campaign "struck equally at ordinary, working-class Muslims and at Europeans."[29] Mass arrests, mass torture – the French military harvested all the actionable intelligence they needed, and nabbed or killed virtually the entire FLN organization, including its leadership. Algiers would be relatively peaceful for several years.

[27] Ibid., p. 120.
[28] Ibid., p. 121.
[29] Ibid., pp. 128–9.

De Gaulle's absolute commitment to liquidate the French presence in Algeria, and to liquidate the war, so as to reshuffle the country's entire foreign policy, tore the guts out of the French military victory. De Gaulle wanted France to be the leader of the Non-Aligned while being covered by the American nuclear umbrella. To be loved by the third world, the Arab world in particular, which he was going to spend much of his foreign policy efforts attempting, he needed to leave the Algerian theater. Starting negotiations with the FLN demoralized the pro-French forces among the Algerians, who knew they could not expect mercy from a victorious FLN, infuriated the pied noir community who saw no future under an FLN government, and maddened the officer corps. It led to full parleys, and in 1962, to independence. "*La valise ou le cercueil*" ("Your choice is to pack your bags or get a coffin") was the FLN's promise to the pieds noirs. Here is a typical, all-too-familiar FLN killing in 1961: "they killed a shop inspector in his car, a man who had never done anything to anyone. They sliced open his skull, took out his brains, and carefully placed them on the ground – like a milestone on the roadside."[30]

The Kabyle writer and friend of Albert Camus Mouloud Feraoun wrote in dismayed tones: "There is French in me, there is Kabyle in me. But I have a horror of those who kill.... Vive la France, such as I have always loved! Vive l'Algérie, such as I hope for! Shame on the criminals! Shame on the cheaters! When Algeria lives and raises her head again... it will remember France and all it owes to France." Alas, Feraoun was machine-gunned by those Frenchmen who had become as beastly as their enemy, the OAS (Organisation de l'Armie Secrete). Hopes for the kind of enlightened brotherhood he had in mind had been murdered along with all the civilians. The FLN's view was voiced by Frantz Fanon: "Come now, comrades, the European game has finally ended; we must find something different. We today can do everything, so long as we are not obsessed by the desire to catch up with Europe. Europe now lives at such a mad, reckless pace that she has shaken off all guidance and all reason."[31] This Gnostic response – *everything is possible, everything is permitted* – was indeed the break with what Europe had to offer on its best side, but also an embrace of Europe's worst.

The war against Algerian Muslims waged by the FLN was completed by a war of terror carried out against French civilians; Muslims were the softest of targets, only followed by French civilians. After the Battle of

[30] Ibid., p. 497.

[31] Ibid., p. 526.

Algiers and General Challe's highly successful military campaign, the FLN was liquidated as a military force. Its organized military forces huddled in Tunisia, the prime sanctuary enjoyed throughout the war by the FLN, and stopped trying to cross the mined and electrified "Ligne Morice" erected by the French. In the dying years of the war, terror was as essential to the FLN strategy as it had been in its early years.

First under the lunatic socialist despotism of Ahmed Ben Bella and then under the implacable military dictatorship of Houari Boumediene, the triumphant new class looted Algeria to the bone. The victorious *mujahdin* of yesterday confiscated power and riches. The new Algeria was ruled under a pale of silent terror where people disappeared and did not come back. It was gradually, but forcibly Arabized at the expense of the few remaining Europeans, and mostly at the expense of the Berbers of Kabylia, it was Islamicized. The non-Arab, non-Muslim population was increasingly treated as dhimmis.

After three decades of misrule that squandered the nations' oil and natural gas wealth and forced a large part of the population to emigrate – mostly to France! – the youth rose in revolt under the leadership of the only available alternative, the very Islamists that the regime had encouraged to destroy the influence of Western culture. The callous Algerian military leadership was ready to repeat its wartime exploits in order to keep power. In the atrocious civil war of the 1990s, perhaps 150,000 were slaughtered, either by the military or by the Islamists – it was often very difficult to know who the culprits were. The very methods used by the FLN were now repeated either by its heirs or by its challengers, this time without an extraneous third party: Villages were exterminated, busses were stopped and passengers were gunned down or killed by slitting their throats, entire families were murdered during "house visits," babies were slaughtered, thousand of young women were raped. The GIA (Groupe Islamique Armé) and the "Salafist Group for Preaching and Combat" had assimilated the lesson taught by the FLN: He who wants to rule must terrorize and despise human life as an incidental instrumentality to his quest for power. The FLN won the Algerian War at the price of "freeing" the country from its most educated and skilled element, of purging a large part of the population, of creating a permanent dictatorship, of making it incapable of sustaining its population, and, perhaps worst of all, of durably imprinting terror as the favored means of political action in the souls of surviving Algerians. This nightmare that haunted the nation without apparent end was the curse of the Algerian War. The means used by the FLN to accomplish its goal predetermined the face of the future Algeria: It was to be an endless repeat of the same nightmare.

This is the model of which Arafat and his friends "dreamt." The Tricontinental, the entire international Left, the Soviet propaganda apparatus, never stopped singing the praise of the Algerian revolutionaries. The Iranian clerics and the lay intellectuals, the entire Palestinian movement, empathized with them and studied their actions. As late as 1980, Ayatollah Khamenei, in a sermon delivered in Tehran to praised the mosque as "the fire of revolution" recalled how "the enemy experienced the role of the mosques in Algeria."[32]

Many of the Soviet-allied networks that supported the rise of Palestinian terror coalesced during the Algerian War (1954–62). After the victory of the Algerian insurgents, Algiers became a place of pilgrimage for revolutionary kooks, charlatans, academics, Messiahs and killers, Black Panther Eldridge Cleaver and Cuban hero Che Guevara, Nazi international leader François Genoud and old *Komintern* hands.

Coda: The PLO–Soviet Incubator

Russia's inextinguishable thirst for territorial conquest propelled the czar's armies into Chechnya in 1829. In self-defense, the Sufi Brotherhood, the *Naqshbandiya-Muridiyya*, declared a holy war. After their first leaders Gazi Molla and Sheikh Mansur Ushirma were killed, a new leader emerged, Sheikh Shamil, whose role in the spread of Pan-Islamism has been examined earlier. Early Soviet literature "adopted a positive view of Shamil," as shown by textbooks of the time: "He was hailed as an able administrator, reformer, military leader and a patriot." This was in keeping with the original alliance between the Bolsheviks and the Pan-Islamists.[33] World War II saw a renewal of this favorable view, as Stalin contemplated ordering the Muslim religious leaders to declare a jihad against the Germans; in its aftermath, however, Shamil was the object of a virulent anti-Islamic campaign. His rehabilitation had to wait until after the Communist Party's Twentieth Congress in 1956. Soviet policy toward the Muslim world and the Middle East was undergoing a great new change. Shamil's symbolic value had to be activated.

The ultimate strategic failure of this renewed Soviet thrust in the world of Islam does not imply at all that it failed to have a powerful impact in that world, or that its effects were insignificant. A Soviet-centered analysis, as most approaches of the subject have been, will conclude that the strategy was a gigantic sinkhole for Soviet treasure and energy. An Islam-centered analysis will show a mighty penetration of Soviet ideas and practices, as has

[32] Ram, *Myth and Mobilization*, sermon of July 11, 1980, p. 31.
[33] Karpat, *The Politicization of Islam*, pp. 38–9.

already been developed regarding the rise of Muslim national communism and the Bolshevik jihad.

Like the treatment of Shamil in Soviet literature, Soviet attitudes toward Islam followed the tactical meanders of Moscow's strategies. The World Peace Movement, founded in 1949 as the Soviets' premier front organization, scored resounding successes in the Middle East. Yet it did not preclude massive anti-Muslim persecutions within the USSR under the premiership of Nikita Khrushchev, whose policy was to eradicate all religions. Still, Khrushchev showed a notable ability to exploit developments in the third world, the Muslim world inclusively. "The world was going our way," in the KGB's own words.[34] The Movement of the Non-Aligned convened its Bandung Conference in 1955. In spite of its bombastic name this group was strongly "anti-imperialist" and hence anti-American. It was also highly responsive to the Soviets. With leaders such as Fabian socialist Jawaharlal Nehru and the communist Josip Broz "Tito," philo-communism was a given – a point proven by the delirious welcome granted Chinese prime minister Zhou Enlai. With the Suez fiasco of 1956, the Soviets had the wind of history in their sails.

Accordingly, in the same year was established the Soviet Afro-Asian Solidarity Committee.

Moscow was developing its great proxy policy. Since the Warsaw Pact could not conquer Europe by conventional forces lest it set off a nuclear war that had been assessed to be virtually impossible to win, Soviet strategy would bypass and undermine the stalemate on the central front by weakening the periphery. It was a classic case of indirect strategy. As much as possible of the third world would be the great proxy for Moscow's irregular warfare against the United States.

Delegations of Peace Partisans from the Arab world flocked to Cairo for the first Afro-Asian Solidarity Conference. Soviet participation was significant, with the Soviet Union presenting itself as a "brotherly Muslim country."[35] In 1958, a first Muslim religious delegation led by the chief mufti of Syria was in the USSR. "The desire of Soviet Muslims to volunteer to defend Arabism and Islam against Israeli imperialism" was stressed. The frequency of this kind of journey increased: The chief mufti of Egypt, the grand mufti of India, and others made the pilgrimage to the Third Rome. The same year,

[34] Christopher Andrew and Vassili Mitrokhin, *The World Was Going Our Way: The KGB and the Battle for the Third World*, New York, Basic Books, 2005, esp. pp. 139–261.

[35] Alexandre Benningsen, Paul B. Henze, George K. Tanham, and S. Enders Wimbush, *Soviet Strategy and Islam*, New York, Saint Martin's Press, 1989, p. 32.

Nasser went twice to Moscow and began receiving a huge aid package, comparable over the next fifteen years only to what Cuba received. Soviet per capita nonmilitary aid to Egypt was fifteen times what India received and twenty times what China obtained, while the military aid was even larger. In 1964, Khrushchev journeyed to Alexandria: "The reception when he landed was quite indescribable. Many elements combined to make it a unique occasion. Nasser's prestige was at its height, and Khrushchev had become a legendary figure.... I saw there were tears in his eyes. Never anywhere had he been received as the Egyptian crowds had received him that day," reported Nasser's confidante Mohammed Heykal.[36]

"The Soviets presented themselves as the self-proclaimed protectors of colonized people and oppressed minorities."[37] As Khrushchev said,

> The Soviet attitude is clear and precise: shackled with the chains of colonialism in Asia, Africa, Latin America or any other area of the globe. All peoples must be free! There is a close interconnection between the struggle of national liberation and the struggle for disarmament and peace. The struggle for general disarmament facilitates the struggle for national independence. The achievements of the National Liberation Movements, in their turn, promote peace and contribute to the struggle for disarmament.[38]

Accordingly, the Kremlin toned down the anti-Muslim campaign at home and began to create an Islamologic and Arabologic policy establishment. They of course discovered that "Islamic society... may become a revolutionary anti-capitalist reformist movement."[39]

In brief, the wheel was being rediscovered, namely Stalin's and Sultan Galiev's original policy. The policy went through three channels: official – government, party, communist youth, trade unions, universities, the Academy of Sciences, and professional organizations, such as the writers' union; KGB front organizations, such as the Partisans of Peace, and binational friendship societies; and properly Islamic channels run through the Muslim Spiritual Directorates.[40] The latter was sending Soviet muftis as middlemen in delegations abroad; they were received by the religious authorities of the visited countries, and in turn they received the latters' contacts in the Soviet Union.[41]

36 Mohammed Heykal, *The Sphinx and the Commissar: The Rise and Fall of Soviet Influence in the Middle East*, New York, Harper & Row, 1978, pp. 134–5.

37 Roberta Goren, *The Soviet Union and Terrorism*, London, Allen & Unwin, 1984, p. 76.

38 *Soviet News*, July 11, 1962, quoted in Goren, *The Soviet Union and Terrorism*, p. 86.

39 Quoted in Benningsen et al., *Soviet Strategy and Islam*, p. 37.

40 Quoted in ibid., p. 38.

41 Quoted in ibid., pp. 41–8.

The Central Committee's International Department (ID) controlled the Soviet-sponsored Afro-Asian Solidarity Committee. The department was essentially the old Communist International (cosmetically dissolved in 1943 to please the Anglo-Americans), now directly integrated into the Central Committee apparatus. It was the leading voice in analyzing and formulating Soviet foreign policy. Run for decades by veteran Komintern functionary Boris Ponomarev, the ID also was the "orchestrating arms of the [Party] for the activities of the [military intelligence service] GRU, diplomats and related personnel abroad, and even KGB residencies abroad."[42]

In 1964, the party leadership, Politburo, and I.D. decided to reestablish the "International Lenin School" (or Institute) that up to the purges of the late 1930s had operated as the top-level cadre school for international communism, but had been terminated by Stalin. The school's main focus was the third world, in particular the Muslim world. Under the general supervision of Boris Ponomarev and his deputy Karen Brutents, the first head of the school was Fyodor Rizhenko, former head of the MGIMO diplomatic school, the prestigious State Institute for International Affairs in Moscow. Rizhenko championed nontraditional methods of teaching for his special student body. The emphasis was on adapting the Marxist–Leninist creed to "local conditions," including religion and ideologies. As Rizhenko stated to the faculty: "Do not preach under the banner of Marxism–Leninism, use the Quran as a revolutionary book."[43] The school was training future secretary-generals and high-level leaders of Communist Parties, leaders of PFLP (People's Front for the Liberation of Palestine), PDFLP (Democratic Popular Front for the Liberation of Palestine), the *Tudeh*, the *Baath*. The Patrice Lumumba University was a reprise of the old KUTVa; it trained lower level personnel and screened "candidates" for higher destinies and terror careers. It established a coherent phalanx of communist-terrorist cadre, trained in the crafts of "psychological warfare, subversive use of the media, as well as Marxist–Leninist ideology."[44] At the same time that the Politburo decided to establish the Lenin School, it also decided – as reported by Czech General Jan Sejna who defected to the West in 1968 – drastically to increase Soviet investment in terrorist enterprises, by a tenfold factor.[45]

[42] Goren, *The Soviet Union and Terrorism*, pp. 102–3.

[43] Personal report to the author from a participant.

[44] "Annual of Power and Conflict," 1973–4, London, Institute for the Study of Conflict.

[45] U.S. Congress, Judiciary Committee, U.S. Senate Hearings on Terroristic Activity, Part 4, 94th Congress, 14 May 1975; Jan Sejna, *We Will Bury You*, London, Sidgwick & Jackson, 1982; Claire Sterling, *The Terror Network*, p. 14.

In that framework, the rise of the Castro regime was a boon for Soviet strategy. Cuba was to be a cover, a proxy, and a redispatching center for the indirect strategy. It would be an essential coach, educator, and mentor for subversive, terrorist and related activities in the third world. The OSPAAAL (*Organisatión de solidaridad de los pueblos de Asia, Africa y America latina*)/Tricontinental established under the sponsorship of the Cuban *barbudos* gave a new luster to long-tarnished Soviet enterprises; it allowed for the recruitment of new layers inaccessible to direct Soviet entreaties. It provided an appropriately colored point of entry into the third world as well as an elixir of revolutionary romanticism that Soviet bureaucrats had long been unable to grow. It is through Cuba and the Tricontinental that the test tubes of modern Soviet terrorism – its cadre force, its methods – were cultivated. Top-fight Soviet agents such as Giangiacomo Feltrinelli, Henri Curiel, "Carlos" the Venezuelan, the Red Brigades of Italy, the Red Army Fraction of Germany, the Irish Republican Army (IRA), and the Basque Euzkadi ta Askatasuna (ETA) rubbed shoulders under the aegis of the KGB, the East German *Stasi*, the Czech *Státní bezpečnost* (STb), Bulgarian intelligence, the Romanian *Securitate*. All of them in turn played a role in shaping, training, and deploying Palestinian terrorism as well as Arab terror in general.

The Kremlin, for example, was extending its operations to the newly independent North Yemen, starting with a friendship pact with its pro-Nasser regime. At the Soviet Embassy in Saana, the job of the first secretary "was to organize and direct guerrilla operations in Aden[,] . . . control the embryonic liberation movement in Oman and Saudi Arabia and interface with the Front for the Liberation of South Yemen."[46] But far-away Yemen was a sideshow, too primitive, too remote from the heartlands of Arabism and Islam. It may have been a useful training ground for future Soviet operations, but its usefulness rarely went beyond that of a strategic support station. Gradually, as Arab states disappointed their Soviet partners, notably after the Six Days' War of 1967 and after Anwar al-Sadat expelled thousands of Soviet advisers from Egypt, Soviet policy deemphasized state-to-state relations and increasingly turned to the indirect approach: The ascent of the PLO had begun.

The Palestinian national movement had a double pedigree line grafted onto its Islamic origins. Grand Mufti of Jerusalem Amin al-Husayni, as we have seen, maintained a far-reaching cooperation with the Communists of Palestine from the late 1920s through the 1930s. He also gradually forged

[46] Quoted in Benningsen et al., *Soviet Strategy and Islam*, 105. See also John B. Kelly, *Arabia, The Gulf and the West*, New York, Basic Books, 1980, esp. Chapter 1, pp. 1–45.

solid links of collaboration with the Axis powers, first by way of Rome and then by way of Berlin. His distant relative Yasser Arafat connected all sides, from his youthful membership in the Muslim Brotherhood in his native Cairo to his lifelong partnership with the Soviet intelligence service, the KGB.

There is no point here in rewriting the history of the PLO and its longest serving leader, which authoritative historians and journalists have already covered in detail.[47] What is presently of concern is the transfer to, and acquisition of, the Soviet art of terror by the Palestinian movement, and the role played in turn by this movement as a test-tube experiment for which methods worked and which did not – the lessons learned by its Soviet sponsors, by the movement itself, and by the Arab and Muslim world as well. For one of the keys to unlocking the mysteries of modern jihad is the Palestinian *cause célèbre.*

The notion of "terrorism" as a series of more or less connected individual attacks carried out especially against civilians is an utter misnomer, a misleading label that warps and disguises the nature of the phenomenon beyond recognition. Terrorism is not the list of discrete bombings, gunnings, knifings, hostage-takings, and homicides perpetrated by small groups or networks of groups to protest this or that grievance or obtain redress. The Palestinian movement learned especially from its Soviet partners and sponsors what terror in the modern sense is. In the Soviet panoply of statecraft, terror was an instrument aimed at shaking, destabilizing, demoralizing, and cowing into submission an opponent one is not able or willing to attack frontally. The enemy's power will be eroded, rather than broken in one or several decisive battles, but in the end, or so the doctrine goes, the indirect approach will annihilate the enemy's will – the concept is Clausewitzian through and through.

This doctrine is a standard tenet of Marxist–Leninist doctrine: It is the "people's war," whose chief instrument is terror. Let us examine the Soviet conception of terror before advancing to people's war. Lenin rejected individual terrorism, such as was practiced by the Narodniki and the Socialist Revolutionaries (SR) of Russia. But he repeatedly pointed out that rejecting terrorism out of principle was "philistine." To receive his license of approval, terrorism had to be part of an overall, concerted plan of action designed by

47 See inter alia, Dobson, *Black September*; Goren, *The Soviet Union and Terrorism*; Becker, *The PLO*; Karsh, Rubin and Rubin, *Anti-Americanism*; and Ion Pacepa, *Red Horizons: The True Story of Nicolas and Elena Ceawces au: Gimes, Lifestyle and Corlaytion*, Washington, DC, Regnery Gateway, 1987.

the party. As he wrote in *Left-Wing Communism*, "Of course, we rejected individual terror only on grounds of expediency, whereas people who were capable of condemning 'on principle' the terror of the French Revolution, or in general the terror employed by a victorious revolutionary party which is besieged by the bourgeoisie of the whole world, had always been ridiculed and laughed in scorn by revolutionaries."[48] In 1916, he emphasized: "We do not at all oppose political killing." So little did he, indeed, that the Bolsheviks in power launched a civil war and terror of proportions hitherto unknown in human history. The history of the Russian Civil War is one of countless atrocities perpetrated by both sides, but the very special contribution of the Bolsheviks was the systematic and deliberate mass murder of civilians not for what they did, or even for what they believed, but for what they were, from a "class standpoint." In civil wars throughout history, the opponent has been callously attacked on grounds of his belonging to the other camp, and on grounds of his religion: no innovation there. But the Bolshevik political police, the Cheka, launched a methodical campaign of extermination against the "bourgeois" class – men, women, old, and young. The Cheka spent the day arresting the "guilty" and the night slaughtering them by the dozens and the hundreds, in the local or regional headquarters of the organization – a bullet in the neck, and mass graves in the forest.[49] Every leader and member of the party shared Lenin's concept. Trotsky even wrote a fervent glorification of terror, *Terrorism and Communism*, which equated revolution with war, and terror with both. "The main object of revolution, as of war, is to break the will of the foe . . . if required, by terrorism."[50]

What distinguishes the totalitarian regimes of the twentieth century from their predecessors in despotism is that the terror they applied on their way to power did not abate as their grip on power consolidated; it worsened. Terror became a bureaucratically organized activity, sanctioned by parodies of laws and caricatures of tribunals. Mass graves were pushed eastward, to the archipelago of the Gulag. The terrorization of society paradoxically reached a climax after the 1934 Bolshevik Party congress that had named itself "The Victors' Congress." The show trials of the mid-1930s presented terror in iconic form. They embodied terror's "crime and punishment' in the form of

48 Quoted by Goren, *The Soviet Union and Terrorism*, p. 22.

49 The most graphic depiction of Cheka terror in the civil war is in an autobiographical novella written by the bolshevik chief of the Cheka in the large city of Omsk during the Civil War: *Zazubrin, Shchepka*, published in French translation as *Le tchékiste*, Paris, Chr. Bourgois, 1990; see also Pipes, *The Unknown Lenin*.

50 Leo Trotsky, *Terrorism and Communism*, Ann Arbor, MI, AA Paperback, 1961, p. 58.

a bloodthirsty morality tale: Anyone opposing even in the secret of his own mind the untrammeled rule of Stalin was a dead man. The terrible years of the great purges saw terror breaking into families and mowing people down by the hundreds of thousands. Society was truly terrorized.[51] Marx's analytical concept that "violence is the great midwife of history" had now turned to a prescriptive mandate. Just as the medieval millenarians had demanded "torrents of blood," the Goddess Revolution wanted its innumerable pounds of flesh. An Italian terrorist of the 1970s inspired by bolshevik terror wrote: "Violence is the auroral, immediate, vigorous affirmation of the necessity for Communism. [. . .] A live animal, ferocious with his enemies, savage in its considerations of itself and its passion – that is how we like to foresee the constitution of a Communist dictatorship."[52] Terror as a permanent tool of statecraft – this is what the Soviets bequeathed their students. Rather than any particular tactics employed, this is the nature of "terrorism" – the piecemeal if spectacular killing of civilians designated as the enemy of a given group.

An eerie similarity unites the Marxist–Leninist and the Islamic world outlook. For the former, aggression is organic and specific to class society – by definition, the Soviet Union was peaceful, and capitalist societies were aggressors. Likewise, as we have seen in Maududi's and Qutb's writings in particular, Islam is axiomatically peaceful, since it represents the "Peace of Allah," the state of utter perfection on earth, whereas un-Islam is axiomatically troubling the peace by its very existence. The Orwellian inversion is permanent: Any move taken in self-defense by the Other is ipso facto characterized as an attack on the One. Terror is therefore seen and proclaimed as an instrument in self-defense. He who represents either History and the Will of the People, or Allah's sovereignty "has no other choice," as the expression endlessly recurs in Islamist literature, but resort to terror. For one example in a thousand, the Palestinians judged in Athens for having fired into a crowd at the airport addressed the United States in a courtroom speech: "We have decided to adopt your criminal methods and teach the first lesson to the people who are undertaking a campaign of extermination against us. We have discovered that in order to make you understand us and realize our right to live, we must begin to defend ourselves against all those who seek to exterminate us."[53]

[51] Robert Conquest, *The Great Terror: Stalin's Purge of the Thirties*, New York, Macmillan, 1973.

[52] Quoted by Goren, *The Soviet Union and Terrorism*, pp. 212–13.

[53] Quoted by Dobson, *Black September*, pp. 152–53.

The Cuban intelligence service (DGI) played an essential role in the grooming of the Palestinian movement. The January 1966 Tricontinental conference was held in Havana, with 513 delegates from 83 third world groups, Communist countries, and "national liberation" movements. "The Palestinians, soon to become a second great magnetic pole for apprentice terrorists, began sending their own apprentices to Cuba in 1966. Cuban instructors have taught in the Middle East *fedayeen* camps since the early 1970s. Closing the triangle was Soviet Russia itself, arming and training Palestinians on its own territory and turning out professional terrorists by the thousands."[54] This was no "spontaneous" terrorism, but rather state-conceived and state-organized and state-backed terrorism. The Soviet aim was "to do everything possible to exacerbate Arab alienation and anger with the West... and to embark on a vast expansion of subversion and terrorist operations."[55] The Soviets did not seriously expect that regimes similar to theirs would take root in the region and did not aim at achieving that. "Rather they seemed to be aiming at the preservation and intensification of a state of chaos that could dangerously weaken their American enemy."[56] Defector Vladimir Zakharov confirmed: "The Soviet goal is to keep the conflict boiling on a low fire and to drag the Palestinians along. If everything was settled, how would the Soviets manipulate the Arabs?"[57]

Soviet interest in the Palestinians apparently started in earnest around the same time as their decision to change tack in their Middle Eastern policy. In other words, they went shopping for groups that would fit the particular bill they had in mind. It is likely, but not essential, that Arafat, with some of his Cairo acolytes, had taken part in the World Youth Conference held in Prague in 1956 that the intelligence services of the Soviet block used like a fishing pond for recruitment. The Palestine Liberation Organization had been established in 1964, at the behest of Nasser, at an Arab League Congress – and was meant by the Egyptian rais to be a weapon directed primarily against King Hussein of Jordan. By May 1966, the garrulous leader of the PLO, former Saudi civil servant and Egyptian agent Ahmad Shuqairy, was meeting with Soviet Prime Minister Aleksei Kosygin. In January 1965, Arafat's al-Fatah had been set up by the Syrian intelligence service as a rival to Nasser's operation. Army intelligence deputy chief Ahmad Sweidani

[54] Sterling, *The Terror Network*, p. 15.

[55] Benningsen et al., *Soviet Strategy and Islam*, p. 89.

[56] Ibid., p. 91.

[57] Vladimir Zakharov, *High Treason*, New York, Ballantine, 1981, p. 251, quoted in Benningsen et al., *Soviet Strategy and Islam*, p. 91.

recruited would-be fedayeen in Palestinian camps in Lebanon. One of his agents was approached by a member of a group of eight, grandly entitled "Movement for the Liberation of Palestine," of which Arafat was one. On Sweidani's assignment, it carried out its first terrorist raid in January 1965.[58] Bulgaria, Czechoslovakia, and East Germany offered scholarships to members of the General Union of Palestinian Students, Arafat's fief.[59] The Soviet strategists singled out al-Fatah as a prime channel for their operations, and "Arafat appears to have been singled out as a focal point to effect that centralization."[60]

There were other groups. Every Arab country insisted on the honor of having its own Palestinian group. Splinter groups abounded, claiming their differences to be ideological (generally Marxist) ones, though in reality they were sectarian, tribal, and geographical. George Habash and his Popular Front for the Liberation of Palestine went from being pro-Chinese to being pro-Soviet. He had been sought out by the Tricontinental in Beirut in 1967 and persuaded to go international.[61] Ahmad Jibril and his Palestine Liberation Front were fully KGB from the start. The PFLP was the most adept at absorbing Soviet ideology, or phraseology. It imitated Soviet rhetoric, calling Israel a "bridgehead for old and new imperialism" led by the United States, and it linked Zionism, racism, and world imperialism.[62] Nayef Hawatmeh and his PDFLP "had the longest and the closest ties to the USSR of all the PLO factions."[63] The KGB's own Henri Curiel, a founder of the Egyptian Communist Party, was running an international support and logistics network for Latin American, Arab, European, and Japanese terrorists out of Paris.[64]

For their own reasons, each and every Arab state was contributing to the PLO and the myriad splinter or pseudo-splinter groups that gravitated around it. The Saudi monarchy funded the PLO as a gesture of "Arab solidarity," and to prevent Nasser and the other contenders for "Arab leadership" – the hackneyed but ever-new shibboleth of inter-Arab politics – from cornering the prestige that emanated from the Palestinian "market." The Gulf Emirates, led by the Kuwaitis, funded the PLO as an insurance policy to protect themselves against the racket: Orienting Palestinian and Pan-Arab sentiment against Israel was the safer way. Syria, Iraq, and in the

58 Becker, *The PLO*, pp. 41, 43.
59 Goren, *The Soiviet Union and Terrorism*, pp. 106–7.
60 Ibid., p. 108.
61 Sterling, *The Terror Network*, p. 39.
62 Goren, *The Soviet Union and Terrorism*, p. 109.
63 Ibid., p. 119.
64 Sterling, *The Terror Network*, pp. 54ff.

end everybody wanted a piece of the action all the more after 1956, 1967, and 1973 had shown that challenging the Israelis militarily was a quick way to be badly mauled. The PLO was in effect a joint venture of Soviet and Arab shareholders: There seldom or never was a shareholders' face-to-face meeting; the executive was unreliable and unaudited; but everybody found their interest in its continued promotion.

After the Six Days' War, some Soviet statements advocated an "Algerian" strategy against Israel. They suggested that there was a need for the Arabs to prepare for protracted guerrilla warfare and "a real people's war."[65] During the period known as the Total Liberation Phase (1969–74), the PLO culturally and politically found its place in the ranks of other socialist anti-colonial liberation movements.[66] It called for a people's war, inspired by guerillas in Algeria, China, Cuba, and Vietnam. The PLO's target in Israel, however, was not merely a government but the people themselves. Thus, since the PLO was at war with a society – not an army or simply the post-1967 occupation – every aspect and member of Israeli society was a legitimate target. The PLO's aim "is not to impose our will on the enemy," explained the PLO magazine *Filastin al-Thawra* in 1968, "but to destroy him in order to take his place . . . not to subjugate the enemy but to destroy him."[67]

The Palestinians sought to emulate the Algerian revolutionary experience and received expert advice in presenting their case. "Until they had consulted with the Algerians, the main Palestinian propaganda theme was 'throwing the Jews into the sea.' Under Algerian guidance, they introduced different terminology and themes" – such as "democratic, bi-national state" and other fictions.[68] The Palestinians' new mentors underlined that French public opinion and that of France's major allies had played a key role in the outcome of the war, as a result of the FLN's external propaganda. After the Six Days' War, M'hamed Yazid, minister of information in two Algerian wartime governments (1958–62), imparted the following principles to Palestinian propagandists:

> Wipe out the argument that Israel is a small state whose existence is threatened by the Arab states, or the reduction of the Palestinian problem to a question of refugees; instead, present the Palestinian struggle as a struggle for liberation like the others.

65 MER, vol. 3 (1963), 3 quoted by Goren, *The Soviet Union and Terrorism*, p. 107.

66 Hussam Mohammad, "PLO Strategy: From Total Liberation to Coexistence," http:/pij.org/site/vhome.htm?g=a&aid=4282.

67 Barry Rubin, *Revolution until Victory? The Politics and History of the PLO*, Cambridge, MA: Harvard University Press, 1994, p. 24.

68 Joel S. Fishman, "Ten Years since Oslo: The PLO's 'People's War' Strategy and Israel's Inadequate Response," *Jerusalem Viewpoints*, No. 503, 1–15 September 2003, Jerusalem Center for Public Affairs, http://www.jcpa.org/jl/vp503.htm, accessed May 12, 2005.

> Wipe out the impression... that in the struggle between the Palestinians and the Zionists, the Zionist is the underdog. Now it is the Arab who is oppressed and victimized in his existence because he is not only facing the Zionists but also world imperialism.[69]

In 1970, China and Vietnam "reached out" to the PLO, inviting Yasser Arafat and Abu Iyad for a discrete visit. Zhou Enlai received them in China and granted them his country's full support.[70] In Vietnam, where Arafat and Abu Iyad remained for two weeks, they were hosted by General Vo Nguyen Giap, the master of insurrectionary warfare of his generation. It is reported that Abu Iyad asked the Vietnamese why public opinion in the West considered the Palestinian armed struggle to be terrorism, while the Vietnamese struggle enjoyed praise and support. In response, the Vietnamese counseled the PLO to work for their goals in phases, which would conceal their real purpose, permit strategic deception, and give the appearance of moderation. They also coached the Palestinians on the manipulation of the American news media. Giap exhorted Arafat: "Fight by any method which can achieve victory.... If regular war can do it, use it. If you cannot win by classical methods, don't use them. Any method which achieves victory is a good one. We fight with military and political means and with international backing."[71] Abu Jihad, who later ran the PLO's military operations, had already visited China and North Vietnam, where he studied the strategy and tactics of guerilla war. He testified that these visits affected his military thinking for years to come to such an extent that he later preached the need for "a people's liberation war."[72] Al-Fatah translated the writings of Giap, Mao, and Che Guevara into Arabic.[73]

The Soviets had unexpectedly found their panacea. Even though they were involved up to their eyeballs in funding, training, arming, and

[69] Raphael Danziger, "Algeria and the Palestinian Organizations," in *The Palestinians and the Middle East Conflict*, Gabriel Ben-Dor, ed., Tel Aviv, Turtledove, 1979, pp. 364–5, quoted by Fishman, "Ten Years since Oslo."

[70] Abu Iyad [Salah Khalaf] with Eric Rouleau, *My Home, My Land*, translated by Linda Butler Koseoglu, New York, Times Books, 1978), pp. 65–7. Quoted by Fishman, "Ten Years since Oslo."

[71] Fishman, "Ten Years since Oslo."

[72] See entry of Khalil al-Wazir in Guy Bechor, ed., *The PLO Lexicon*, Tel Aviv, Ministry of Defense, 1991, p. 90. See also "Biography of Khalil al-Wazir (Abu Jihad)," *Encyclopedia of the Palestinians*, Philip Mattar, ed., New York, Facts on File, 2000, Quoted by Fishman, "Ten Years since Oslo."

[73] Y. Harkabi, "Al Fatah's Doctrine," in Walter Laqueur and Barry Rubin, eds., *The Israel-Arab Reader: A Documentary History of the Middle East Conflict*, New York, Penguin Books, 1991, p. 395.

supporting Palestinian terror and even though they provided it with permanent media, political, and diplomatic cover, with sanctuary and every resource imaginable, Moscow could still deny its own "direct" involvement. The very chaos that the PLO was – this Brownian motion of fiercely competing rivals who literally raced for the honor of killing – favored Soviet designs, as it helped obfuscate the central strategy and role of the mastermind: Arafat was meeting on a weekly basis with Soviet ambassador Aleksandr Soldatov, "generally regarded as a leading expert on urban guerrilla warfare," whose previous posting had been in Cuba.[74] The PLO was a major hub for Soviet operations and, under Soviet protection, was able to transfer Soviet methods and concepts to the entire region, bypassing borders and states that were often the prisoner of their declaratory pro-Palestinian stance (until the PLO crossed the line, and the Arab supporters slaughtered the Palestinians with gusto and in great numbers – the game of balance was fragile). The use of an endless string of soubriquets, which all included the words "Palestine," "liberation," "democratic," or more colorful Arabic words, was but more sand in the eyes of the credulous beholders. For whoever wished to see with their eyes, there was of course no obfuscation or confusion, but the West's general attitude was to accept the Soviets' bold-faced lies: Why compromise and endanger détente over a few casualties in the Middle East, or even in Europe?

A few days after the shah's flight and Khomeiny's return in February 1979, Arafat arrived in Tehran. His retinue chanted: "Today Iran, tomorrow Palestine!" Arafat's association with Khomeiny had begun in 1970 when the Ayatollah was an exile in Iraq.[75] A great many Iranian revolutionaries had trained in Palestinian camps in Lebanon, including Khomeiny's own son.[76] The PLO had lent assistance to Musa al-Sadr's new paramilitary force, which later turned into Hezbollah's military wing. They had exchanged personnel. In November 1979, shortly after the takeover of the U.S. Embassy in Tehran, Arafat had ordered all Fatah cadres to help the Iranian Revolution – with terror operations in particular. The PLO had lent many of its Lebanese assets to Iran, the most effective one being Imad Mugniyah of the PLO's elite Force 17. Mugniyah was an important Fatah intelligence figure in his own right and later headed Hezbollah's terror apparatus.[77] It was Fatah and Iranian intelligence that planned and organized the 1983 destruction of the U.S.

74 Goren, *The Soviet Union and Terrorism*, pp. 140–1.

75 Ibid., p. 132, n.154.

76 Rubin and Rubin, *Yasir Arafat*, p. 84.

77 Ibid., p. 97.

Embassy in Beirut and the October bombing of the Marine Corps barracks. Arafat had not been mendacious when he had declared on his arrival in Tehran in 1979:

> The path we have chosen is identical; we are moving forward on the same path; we are fighting the same struggle, the same revolution; our nation is one, we have always lived in the same trenches for the same goal and the same slogan, Our slogan is: we are all Muslims; we are all Islamic revolutionaries, all fighting for the establishment of one body of Islamic believers. We will continue our struggle against Zionism and move towards Palestine alongside the Iranian revolutionaries.[78]

[When Khomeiny set up a three-man committee to create the Iranian terror network under the leadership of Hodjatoleslam Fazlallah Malahati, several PLO-trained advisers served in a senior capacity in the venture.[79]

The PLO was the great educator of Middle Eastern jihad, the principal transmitter of the Soviet art of terror. The lessons learned were of primordial importance for the jihadis and were duly assimilated and replicated in years and decades to come. Arafat and his companions taught that violence was glamorous; that maximalism, an all-or-nothing policy, paid off because it frightened Western leaders; that "blood and iron" was the only way; and that "armed struggle restores a lost personal and national identity. An identity taken by force . . . can only be restored by force."[80]

Arafat applied Guevara's concept of the revolutionary *foco* to all the places he succeeded to dominate for a time, whence hords of terrorists then went to plague other countries, whether in Europe or the Middle East.

Arafat relentlessly explored and pushed the limits of lawlessness, as in the case of the "Black September" movement that he created, as yet one more terror group "which I do not control" – the group was made up entirely of Fatah intelligence personnel, using Fatah's facilities and funds![81] He showed that armed gangs were above any law, order, and authority, above any tradition and norm: The Cause was "sacred" and therefore surpassed any conceivable human and divine conception. Few crimes were not committed in the name of the Cause under his authority. "The PLO was free of all checks and accountability, secular or religious. There were neither written nor custom-established laws to which the rulers had to refer."[82] "The absence of any territorial parameters allowed the PLO to set up [quasi-

[78] BBC/ME, February 21, 1979; quoted *in* Kramer, "Political Islam," p. 14.
[79] 635 Taheri, *Itoly Terrors*, pp. 88–9.
[80] Quoted by Rubin and Colp Rubin, *Yasir Arafat*, pp. 27–8.
[81] Ibid., p. 61.
[82] Becker, *The PLO*, p. 141.

military] facilities in many countries and endowed it with a larger potential for the unacceptable without the possibility of any retribution from the society of nations."[83]

Arafat showed the power of egregious threats. In the summer of 1995, he stated to his Israeli interlocutor: "I know there are two ways to reach a Palestinian state, through the negotiating table and through a war of independence. We can accept a lot of casualties, 30,000 martyrs. Can you accept 500 Israeli soldiers killed?"[84]

Arafat showed how timorous the most famed Western leaders were, and how they could be made to pay ransom. European governments freed imprisoned killers as their planes were being hijacked and their nationals kidnapped and slaughtered. European airlines – Air France, Lufthansa, and others – submitted to the PLO's racket so that their airplanes would not get into trouble. The British Foreign Office, the Austrian chancellor, socialist Bruno Kreisky, the Socialist International leader Willy Brandt, the U.S. Department of State, and every French president fell over themselves to make nice to the PLO and pretend that they believed Arafat's solemn assurances that he condemned terrorism. Henry Kissinger wrote in 1973: "The PLO had potential for causing trouble all over the Arab world; we wanted it to be on its best behavior during the early stages of our approaches to Egypt and while we were seeking Saudi support."[85] Recently declassified archives have shown that the U.S. government had direct and incontrovertible evidence of Arafat's personal orchestration of terror against the United States, including the cold-blooded murder of a U.S. ambassador, but chose to ignore it for diplomatic reasons.[86]

Arafat also unwittingly taught another lesson that the jihadis emulated: He was – his people were – the prisoners of their own web of delusion. They had conjured up a maze of fiction that they mistook for reality, and then willed themselves to act according to this self-deception. When Arafat clashed with reality and lost – as he always did, in Jordan, in Lebanon, in Tunis, in Ramallah – he invented new fictions that further alienated him and his faithful from reality by explaining away their failures. But it was also the case that "despite actual failure, he achieved symbolic success by persuading his followers that it had been a victory."[87]

[83] Goren, *The Soviet Union and Terrorism*, p. 181.

[84] Quoted by Rubin and Rubin, *Yasir Arafat*, p. 157.

[85] Henry Kissinger, *Years of Upheaval*, New York, Simon and Schuster, 1982, pp. 626–7.

[86] See, for example, Caroline Glick, "The Longest-Running Big Lie," *Jerusalem Post*, January 1, 2007.

[87] Quoted by Rubin Colp Rubin, p. 41.

In brief, Arafat demonstrated that a high-risk, high-reward strategy paid off. He operationally established a new price/earning ratio (PER) for terror: For the PLO, the expenditure required to win the kind of victories it craved was minimal; for its enemies, the expenditure to be incurred to hunt down the PLO was huge, the benefits always tenuous in the short term that Western politics, especially, indulged in. The PLO was the first school and its chief the headmaster of international jihad. The rewards for this unending series of crimes were international accolade: Arafat's pistol-wearing appearance at the United Nations' General Assembly of 1974 and, twenty years later, the Oslo Agreements with a Nobel Peace Prize thrown in. In 1966, in his message to the first conference of the Tricontinental, Che Guevara had said: "We must above all keep our hatred alive and fan it to paroxysm. Hate as a factor of struggle, intransigent hate of the enemy, hate that can push a human being beyond his natural limits and make him a cold, violent, selective and effective killing machine."[88]

Osama bin Laden's aide Abu Ubeid al-Qurashi reported that the model for the September 11, 2001, operation had been the PLO's Munich massacre of the Israeli Olympics athletes. "Munich," he averred, "was the perfect media victory."[89]

"Strike Terror in the Heart of the Enemy"

The word "jihad" conjures up the vision of a marching band of religious fanatics with savage beards and fiery eyes brandishing drawn swords and attacking the infidels wherever they meet them and pressing them with the edge of the sword.
Maududi Abul Ala[90]

General Zia ul-Haq took power in a military coup in Pakistan in 1977, after a tenure as chief of Army staff, the country's highest ranking military officer. A devout Deobandi, Zia maintained a close relationship with Saudi Arabia and the Wahhabi, such that in the terse formulation of compatriot Shahid Mahmud, "If it had been possible, Zia would have imported all the sands of Saudi Arabia to make Pakistan resemble it."[91] Abul Ala Maududi was a political partner, an adviser, a guru.

In 1979, the newly minted dictator wrote a foreword to a book, *The Quranic Concept of War*, written by his subordinate Brigadier S. K. Malik.

[88] Che Guevara, Message to the Tricontinental Conference, cited in the *Brigate Rosse*'s *Contro Informazione*, July 1978, quoted by Sterling, *The Terror Network*, p. 8.

[89] Al-Ansar, February 27, 2002, translated by MEMRI, #353, March 12, 2002.

[90] Maududi, *Jihad in Islam*, p. 5.

[91] http://www.tolueislam.com/Bazm/Shahid/SM_001.htm.

Zia's foreword was short and to the point: "I ... commend Brigadier Malik's book ... to both soldier and civilian alike. *Jihad fil sabil Allah* is not the exclusive domain of the professional soldier, nor is it restricted to the application of military force alone."[92] Former justice minister of Pakistan Allah Bukhsh K. Brohi wrote the preface to the book. "The most glorious word in the vocabulary of Islam is jihad," he intoned.[93] The former advocate-general of Pakistan gave a more than extensive definition of the *casus belli* that must provoke jihad: "When a believer sees that someone is trying to obstruct another believer from traveling on the road that leads to God, [the] spirit of jihad requires that such a man who is imposing obstacles should be prevented from doing so and the obstacles placed by him should also be removed."[94] The definition was exactly that given by Maududi and Sayyid Qutb: Just about anything and anyone was liable to fall within the purview of the *casus jihadi.*

This is the definition used by Osama bin Laden and the other jihadis: the very existence of the Other and the lowliness of Islam's stature in the world are the causes of jihad. Brohi continued:

> Defiance of God's authority by one who is His slave exposes that slave to the risk of being held guilty of treason and such a one, in the perspective of Islamic law, is indeed to be treated as a sort of that cancerous growth on [the] organism of humanity.... It thus becomes necessary to remove the cancerous malformation even if it be by surgical means (if it would not respond to the other treatment), in order to save the rest of humanity.[95]

As a result, our Islamic jurist concluded, "The believers have no option, but in sheer self-defense, to wage a war against those who are threatening aggression." To make sure that the point was not missed, he added, "[The Muslims'] role on earth is to communicate the same message of God and his practice (*Sunnah*) which they have inherited from their Prophet and if there be anyone who stifles their efforts and obstructs them from communicating the Message it will be viewed as constituting membership in *darul Harb* and liable to be dealt with as such."[96]

This is a warrant for mass murder. Brigadier Malik supplied the theory, the Quranic concept of war. The ISI (*Inter-Service Intelligence*, the

92 Brigadier S. K. Malik, *The Quranic Concept of War*, Lahore, National Book Foundation – M/S Istiqlal Press, 1979, p. xi.

93 Malik, *The Quranic Concept of War*, p. xiii.

94 Ibid., p. xiv.

95 Ibid., p. xix.

96 Ibid., pp. xxi–xxii.

all-powerful military intelligence service that largely runs the country) and the army of Pakistan – creators of the Taliban, the power behind the Kashmir jihad, patrons of Mollah Omar, and protectors of Osama bin Laden – absorbed it. The book, *The Quranic Concept of War*, was highly commended in the Pakistani military. Zia's Islamic theory of war written by S. K. Malik has been a compulsory course for indoctrination of its army and the ISI, wrote Air Marshal Malik, vice-chief of staff (no relation).

The brigadier, after a long scholastical retreading of quotations from the Quran and hadith on the subject, lists the cases in which jihad will be invoked, and must be. They are so extensive as to constitute an unlimited mandate, provided forms are respected. "Punitive, retaliatory and preventive purposes" as well as "unbearable and provocative manner" on the part of the enemy are casus belli, while Muslims should "enter into armed hostilities in sympathy with their brethren living in another state," but of course "but only after scrutinizing each case on its own merit and not as a matter of general rule."[97] Quranic rules "revolutionized warfare" and "conferred upon the Muslim armies a complete and total protection and immunity against all the psychological and moral attacks that the enemy could bring to bear upon them.... [They] became immortal and invisible."[98] So, what is jihad? "Jihad is total strategy," the brigadier answers. It is

> the near-equivalent of total or grand strategy.... Jihad entails the comprehensive direction and application of "force." Jihad is a continuous and never-ending struggle waged on all fronts including political, economic, social, psychological, domestic, moral, and spiritual to attain the object of policy. It aims at attaining the overall mission assigned to the Islamic state, and military strategy is one of the means available to it to do so. It is waged at individual as well as collective level; and at internal as well as external front.[99]

Having defined the function of jihad, Malik then defined the aim of jihad:

> The Quranic military strategy thus enjoins us to prepare ourselves for war to the utmost in order to strike terror into the hearts of the enemies, known or hidden, while guarding ourselves from being terror-stricken by the enemy. In this strategy, guarding ourselves against terror is the "Base," preparation for war to the utmost is the "Cause:" while the striking terror into the hearts against the enemies is the "Effect." The whole philosophy revolves there.... In war, our main object is the opponent's heart or soul, our main weapon of offense against this object is the strength of our own souls, and to launch such an attack, we have to keep terror away from our own hearts.[100]

97 Ibid., pp. 23–4.
98 Ibid., p. 41.
99 Ibid., p. 54.
100 Ibid., p. 58.

The phrase "strike terror (into the hearts of) the enemies of Allah and your enemies" is a well-known verse from the Quran (8:60). Malik then waxes Sun Zi-like: "So spirited, zealous, complete and thorough should our preparation for war [be] that we should enter the 'war of muscles' having already won the 'war of will.' Only a strategy that aims at striking terror into the hearts of the enemies for the preparation stages can produce direct results."[101] War is peace, and peace is war, he insists. Peacetime preparation for jihad is "vastly more important than the active war."

> [Preparation] must be to the utmost, both in quality and in quantity. It must be a continuous and never-ending process. Preparation should be at the plane of total strategy, that is, jihad and not the military instrument alone.... The lesser the physical resources the greater must be the stress and reliance on the spiritual dimensions of war. Terror struck into the hearts of the enemies is not only a means, it is the end in itself. Once a condition of terror into the opponents' heart is obtained, hardly anything is left to be achieved. It is the point at [which] the means and the end meet and merge. Terror is a means of imposing decision upon the enemy, it is the decision we wish to impose upon him.[102]

Brigadier Malik concludes, in pure Gnostic fashion, with a strong dose of Leninist voluntarism, or Nietzschean *Wille zur Macht*:

> Terror cannot be struck into the hearts of an enemy by merely cutting its lines of communication or depriving it of its route of withdrawal. It is basically related to the strength or weakness of the human soul. It can be instilled only if the opponent's Faith is destroyed. Psychological dislocation is temporary; spiritual dislocation is permanent. Psychological dislocation can be produced by a physical act but this does not hold good of the spiritual dislocation. To instill terror into the heart of the enemy, it is essential... to dislocate his faith. An invincible faith is immune to terror. A weak faith offers inroads to terror.[103]

The mind of jihad has spoken.

[101] Ibid., p. 58.
[102] Ibid., pp. 58–9.
[103] Ibid., p. 60.

Conclusion

Modern jihad erupted in full force with the Islamic Revolution in Iran in 1979 in both the Shiite and the Sunni world. It was a reflection, a result, and a concentrate of all the main political pathologies of the twentieth century, led by the parade of motley totalitarian ideologies, but transformed by its absorption into the Islamic cultural matrix.

What a striking historical paradox this was: The world of Islam was falling behind the fast-paced progress made by the modern world and those areas of the world that had taken up the challenges of modernity. It was falling behind not only because it did not invent modernity or espouse it, but because it actively rejected it. On the other hand, it avidly absorbed the dark shadow of modernity, its evil side – the totalitarian ideologies that sprung up as the corruption of modernity, Bolshevism, fascism, Nazism, postmodernism.

Some parts of the world of Islam accepted at least components of modernity – Turkey in the first place, and others to lesser degrees. These all occurred in "hybrid" civilizational areas outside the Arab core of Islam where those in power accepted to borrow other, more constructive creations of the West. Those who did not went shopping in Europe for nihilism, the destructive hatred and the self-destructive passions that neo-Gnosticism had loosed on the continent.

The European totalitarian ideologies themselves were an echo from older times, a secularized form of pseudoreligion. They were largely the violent spasms that responded to the torments and dislocations of modernity, and were rooted in the medieval, millenarian, apocalyptical, eschatological insurgencies that wreaked havoc in Europe from the eleventh through the early sixteenth centuries. Just as the medieval sectarians had lived in a "second reality" of their own making, their messianic successors in modern Europe made class or race or state the divinized ordering point of their delusional world. Both the medieval and the modern sectarians shed torrents of blood to bring about their version of perfection on earth.

Likewise, modern jihad, which massively drew on the modern sectarians, has its roots in traditional jihad, and has stirred the tidal messianic hopes of disoriented Islamic masses, their dislocated lives, and their incensed ruminations and is twice promising them the Gnostic Paradise, in Allah's kingdom erected on earth, and in Paradise as martyrs. Modern jihad is the modern form of Mahdism. It is Islamic in its cultural idiom, form, and content. There is no firewall between Mahdism and mainstream Islam, since it is all "in the Book," in the Quran, in the vast hadith literature, in the fiqh, in the jurisprudence derived from both, in the folktales and collective memory of Muslim peoples.

Grafted onto a tribal social structure – in the sociology of society, in the structure of the religion, in the minds of its members – a toxic combination of jihad and totalitarianism appeared on the market, conveyed by numerous and complex contacts and cooperation between the European retailers and the Islamic purchasers. It was expressed in and symbolized by the jihadis' worship of violence, their predilection for blood, and their cult of death: "We love death more than you love life." This was a society going terminal and descending into a nihilistic frenzy of destruction.

This is the mind of jihad. This is the enemy we are facing in the great war declared on us on September 11, 2001. This is his way of war.

Index

Abbasid (dynasty), 103, 113, 117–18, 174
Abd-al-Ilah, Crown Prince, 23
Abdallah (King), 252
Abdelqader, Ali Hasan (Sheikh), 246
Abduh, Muhammad, 30–2, 125
Abdülaziz (Sultan), 174
Abdülhamid I (Sultan), 174
Abdülhamid II (Sultan), 174–6, 178, 179, 192
Abdullah, Mohammed (Sheikh), 182
Abdülmejid (Sultan), 187
Abel, 44, 101
Abélard, Peter (scholastic philosopher), 85
Abo, Husni, 25
Abraham, 20
Abu Abbas, 8
Abu Bakr, (Caliph), 113
Abu Ghraib prison, 135
Abu Jihad, 187, 191, 316
Abuzar Qaffari the Socialist Worshipper of God, 279
Abwehr, 248, 250, 297
Aceh (a territory of Indonesia), 174, 176
Acharya, M.P.B.T., 217, 220
Acheson, Dean (Secretary of State), 252
Achille-Lauro (cruise ship), 8
Ada, 152
Adam, 160
ad-Dajjal, 109, 115, 121, 287
Adonis, Ali Ahmad Said Asbar (poet), 169
Aflaq, Michel, 39, 40, 104–5, 246
Afro-Asian Solidarity Committee, 308
Afula, 236
Ahab (King), 20
Ahl al-Dhimmi, 100
Ain-Abid (city of Algeria), 302
Ait Amouda. *See* Amirouche
Akhuwat, 198
al Haramayn, 160
al-Afghani, Jamal al-Din, 29–32, 38, 125–7, 173, 177–8, 195–6, 198, 249, 277, 286
al-Ardh Midhat (Sheikh), 247
al-Asabadi, Jamal al-Din. *See* al-Afghani
al-Ashari, Abdul Hassan, 154–5
al-Ashman, Muhammad (Sheikh), 241
al-Assad, Hafez, 24, 104
al-Assad, Rifat, 24–5
al-Awaji, Mohsin (Sheikh), 27
Alawites (sect of Shiite Islam), 150
Al-Azhar (University), 32, 36, 57, 170, 246
Al-Azhar, Shaykh, 100
al-Banna, Hassan, 30, 32–3, 35–7, 39, 41, 59, 100, 103, 117, 135, 246, 269–70, 291, 293
al-Dawa (Iraqi Shiite movement), 90, 161

al-Din, Nadir (Shah), 29–30
Al-e Ahmad (Iranian writer, social and political critic), 279–80
Aleppo (city of), 24–5
Alexander II (Tsar), 6
al-Fatat, 253
al-Gailani, Rashid Ali, 39, 253
Algerian National Movement (MNA), 300
al-Ghazali, Abu Hamed Mohammad ibn Mohammad, 177, 266
al-Ghita (Sheikh), 249
al-Hanafiyya, Muhammad ibn, 115
al-Hassan, Mahmud (Sheikh al-Hind), 220
Al-Hilal (journal), 198
al-Hud, Khalid Abulwalid, 247
al-Husayni, Sawfat, 247
al-Husri, Sati, 39
Ali, ibn Abi Talib (first Imam), 44–5, 49–50, 102–3, 112, 115, 118, 120, 276–81, 288, 290, 292
Ali, Mehmet, 125
Ali, Muhammad, 51
Alids (members of the dynasty of Ali ibn Abi Talib), 102, 115
Aligarh College, 196
alim, 185, 195, 232
al-Jazeera, 9
al-Jihad, 37, 100
al-Jundi, Sami, 104
al-Kuwwatli, Shuqri, 249
All-India Muslim League, 196
al-Mahdi, Muhammad, 263, 276
al-Manar, 31, 33, 55
Al-Manshwai mosque, 27
al-Maraghi (Sheikh), 246
Al-Masri, Abu Hamza (Sheikh), 57
al-Masri, Aziz Ali (General), 246
al-mawt fann, 34
Almohades (dynasty), 119
Almoravid (dynasty), 119
al-Moudjahid (newspaper), 296
al-Mulk, Nizam, 122
al-Murshid, 291, 293
Al-Mutanabbi, Abou-t-Tayyib Ahmad ibn al-Husayn (poet), 132
al-Qadir, Abd (Algerian Islamic scholar, political and military leader), 147
Al-Qaeda, 11
al-Qarqani, Khalid al-Hud, 253
Al-Qassem, 55
al-Qurashi, Abu Ubeid, 320
al-Rahman Azzam, Abd,
al-Sabah, Hasan ibn, 45, 106
al-Sadr, Musa, 291, 317
al-Said, Nuri (Prime Minister), 23, 250, 253
al-sharaf, 136
al-sharaf al-arabi, 132
al-sharaf al-Muslimi, 132
al-Sibai, Mustafa (Sheikh), 240
al-Sulh, Riyad, 249
al-Sulh, Sami, 242, 253
Al-Tayyeb, Ahmad dr. (Sheikh), 57
al-Tell, Wasfi, 21
Al-Umma'l Arabiyya, 253
al-Urwa al Wuthqa Journal, 30
al-Wahda al-Islamiyya. See Wahdat al-Islam
al-Wahhab, Muhammad ibn, 97, 124
al-Wakil, Mustafa Dr., 246
al-Zarqawi, Abu Musab, 9
Amanullah (Shah), 194, 206, 219
American Airlines Flight 11, 8
American Revolution, 257
Amini, Abdol Hoseyn (Ayatollah), 271
amir al-Muminin, 179
Amir Hussein, 253
Amirouche, 300
Anabaptists, 70, 79–81
Anarchist, 7
Anatolia (region of), 147, 179, 210
an-Nashashibi, Nasri ad-Din, 28
anthropology, 2, 123
Anti-Fascist League, 241
Aquinas, Thomas, ii, 61, 287
Arab League, 39, 249, 313
Arab Revolt, 238, 249
Arafat, Yasser, 51–3, 55–6, 255, 296, 305, 310, 313–14, 316–20
Archangel Jibril, 92
Archangel Michael, 72
Arianism, 96

Arif, Abdul Salam, 23
Aristotle, 61
Arius (Bishop), 96
Army of God, 204, 207, 220
Army of Liberation, 218
Army of Salvation, 252
Arslan, Amir Adil, 253
Arslan, Shakib (Sheikh), 247–8, 253
asabiyya, 139–41, 146–8, 160
Ashkhabad (capital city of Turkmenistan), 217, 221
Ashura (celebrations), 50, 168
as-Samarri, 277
Atlantic Ocean, 171, 205
Atta, Muhammad, 19
aubach, 168
Auftragstaktik, 163
Augustine, Saint, 61, 66, 86
Auschwitz, 252
Auswärtiges Amt (German Foreign Office), 248
Azad, Maulana Abul Alam, 197–8
Aztecs, 19
Azzam, Abdal Rahman, 39, 249
Azzam, Abdullah, 10, 56, 58, 105

Baal (Phoenician god), 19–20
Baath Party (the original secular Arab nationalist movement), 38–9, 104, 242
Baathist, 24
Bab, 276
Babur (Emperor), 193
Bagdash, Khalid, 222
Baha'i (religion, founded in the 19th Century, Persia), 167
Bakdash, Khalid (leader of the Syrian Communist Party), 241
Baku Congress, 217, 220, 222, 295
Bakunin, Mikhail, 6
Bal Gangadhar Tilak, 197
bandits d'honneur, 165
Bani-Sadr, Abolhasan, 285, 288
Barakatullah, Muhamamad, 195, 219, 220
barbudos (revolutionary guerillas), 309
Barelvi, Said Ahmad, 124
Barkat-Ullah. *See* Barakatullah
Basije (paramilitary volunteer force), 50, 285
Basiret, 177
Basra (city of Iraq), 189
Batinists, 284
Battle of Algiers, 302, 304
Bay of Bengal, 171
Baytursun, Ahmed, 225
Bazargan, Mehdi (Iranian leader), 283, 287
Beauplan, Guillaume Le Vasseur de, 162
Beauvoir, Simone de, 300
Bedouins, 139, 144, 146, 149–50, 157, 236
Behesht Zahra, 26
Beheshti, Mohammad (Ayatollah), 272, 282
Ben Bella, Ahmed (President of Algeria), 297, 304
Benevolent Islamic Society, 180, 192
Benningsen, Alexandre (scholar of Islam), 227, 273, 275, 306–7, 309, 313
Benost-Méchin, Jacques, 39
Berg, Nicholas, 8, 9
Berger, Gottlob, 252
Bhattacharya, Narendra Nath. *See* Roy, M. N.
Biazar-Shirazi, Abdul-Karim, 49
bida, 257, 259
bin Laden, Osama, 10, 19, 56, 58, 105, 125, 134, 145, 209, 233, 320–2
Bismarck, Otto von, 181, 244
Black International, 254–5
Black Plague of 1348, 69
Black Sea, 171
Black September, 51, 255, 318
Black Shirts (Italian fascist paramilitary groups), 38
Blackwater Co., 11
Bloch, Ernst, 81
Blockwart system, 288
Blok, Alexander, 212
Blount, W. S., 30
Bockelson, Jan, 81

Bogdanov, Aleksandr, 278
Bogostroitel'stvo (God-building), 278
Bolshevik, 4, 178, 195, 199–203, 206–12, 214–15, 218–19, 221–6, 228–32, 238, 249, 268, 278, 280–1, 306, 311
pl. Bolsheviks, 3, 146, 161, 166, 196, 200, 202–4, 208–11, 213, 216–17, 219–24, 226–8, 231–3, 305, 311
Bolshevism and the Islamic Body Politick, 219
Bonaparte, Napoléon, 135
Book of a Hundred Chapters, 72
Borghese, Valerio, 254
Borodin, Mikhail, 208
Bosch, Hieronymus (painter), 108
Bosnia, 10
Boukhobza, Hammed dr., 25
Boumediene, Houari, 304
Brandt, Willy, 319
Brest-Litovsk (city of), 204
Brodie, Bernard, 2
Brohi, Allah Bukhsh K., 321
Bruck, Moeller van den, 88
Brutents, Karen, 308
Buddha, 102
Bukhara (city in Uzbekistan), 178, 230
Bukhari, Sahih, 152
Bukharin, Nikolai (Soviet politician), 232
Bund, 236
Bund der Asienkämpfer (Union of Asian Fighters), 205
Burns, Robert (poet), 217
Burqai, Sayyed Ali Akbar, 275
Bush, George W., 133
Busher (city of Iran), 189
Bushido (Samurai code of conduct), 136
Buyids (dynasty of), 117

CAB (Central Asia Bureau), 218
Cain, 44, 70, 101
Caliphate, 18
Calvin, John, 75
Camus, Albert, 295, 300, 303
Canal Zone, 35
Čapek, Jan,
Caputiati, 71
Carlos the Venezuelan, 309
Carranza, Venustiano, 208
Carthaginians, 20
Caspian Sea, 204, 273
Castle, Barbara, 301
Castro, Fidel, 283, 297, 309
Catechism of a Revolutionist, 6
CBS (Columbia Broadcasting System), 134
Cemal, Ahmad (Pasha), 186–7, 202
Central Asia Bureau (CAB), 218
Cervantes, Miguel de, 146
chaku-kechan, 168
Challe, Maurice (General), 304
Champakraman Pillai, 208
Charter of Hamas, 53
Che Guevara, Ernesto, 282, 305, 316, 320
Chechnya, 10, 211, 305
Cheka, 218, 288, 293, 311
Chernychevsky, Nikolai (Russian radical), 278
Chiang Kai-shek, 244
Chicherin, Georgy, 216, 217
Chokay-Oglu, Mustafa, 228
Churchill, Winston, 1
CIA (Central Intelligence Agency), 11, 246, 253
City of God, 66, 85, 86
Clausewitz's doctrine, 25
Cleaver, Eldridge, 305
Cohn, Norman, 88, 261
Colonial International, 228, 230
Commissariat for Nationalities (Narkomnats), 225
Commission on the National and Colonial Question, 208
Committee Union and Progress, 38, 179, 247
Communist *agit-prop*, 238
Communist International, 202, 206, 210–11, 215, 218, 222, 234, 236, 239, 241, 249, 273, 308
Communist University of the Peoples of the East, 216
Comte, Auguste, 88

Confucius, 102
Congress of the People of the East, 206, 215
Congress of the Toilers of the East. *See* Congress of the People of the East
Constantinople *or Istambul* (city of Turkey), 181–2, 193, 198, 200, 202, 246
Coriolanus, 136
Corneille, Pierre (French dramatist), 136
Corps of the Guardians of the Islamic Revolution, 288
Council of High Learning, 184
CPP (Communist Party of Palestine), 236
Crimea (an autonomous republic of Ukraine), 184
Crimean War, 190
Cromer, Lord, 63
Crone, Patricia (scholar, author and historian of early Islamic history), 157
CUP (Committee Union and Progress), 38, 179–80, 186–7, 206
Curiel, Henri, 309, 314
Cyrenaica (the eastern coastal region of Lybia), 147, 180

dais, 117
dar al-Dawa, 161
dar al-Harb (house of War), 3, 89, 160–2
dar al-Islam (house of Islam), 3, 89, 92, 159, 160, 162, 170–1, 174, 198, 230
dar al-Jahiliyya, 159
dar al-Kharaj, 161
dar al-Kufr, 159, 230
dar al-sulh, 161
Dar barih-i Eslam, 274
Dar-ul Uloom, 220
darululum (school), 199
Darwish, Mahmud, 28
dawa, 122, 161
Dawalibi, Maaruf, 241, 243, 247, 281
Debray, Régis, 282
Declaration of War, 56, 134
Democratic Popular Front for the Liberation of Palestine (PDFLP), 314
Deng Xiaoping, 222
Denikin, Anton (General), 224
Deobandi, 124, 195, 220, 263, 268, 320
Derwish, Ishaq, 253
Deutsche Nationalzeitung, 254–5
DGI (intelligence agency of Cuba), 313
Dharr, Abu, 57
dhimmi, 161, 197
  pl. *dhimmis*, 49, 93, 97–8, 296, 304
Die Revolutionierung des islamischen Gebiete unserer Feinde, 188
Die Wahlverwandtschaften, 277
Diodorus (Greek historian), 19
Dir Jarir (village of), 11
Djavid Bey, 202
Dobson, Christopher, 23
Don Quixote, 146
Dostoyevsky, Fyodor, 5, 6, 227, 280
Duba-Yort, 10
Durkheim, Emile, 118, 153
Dutch Indies, 192, 198

Ebert, Friedrich, 217
ed-Din, Jamal (Sheikh), 30
Eichmann, Adolf, 252
Einsatzkommandos, 16
el-Alia (city of Algeria), 302
Elijah, 20
Engels, Friedrich, 81, 227
Enteharis, 51
Enver, I'smail (Pasha), 180, 185–9, 193, 202–6, 210–11, 213–14, 216–18, 247
Ershad Institute, 279, 282
Erzurum (city of Turkey), 194
esprit de corps, 139–40
ETA (Basque armed nationalist separatist organization), 309
Ettel, Erwin, 253

F.T.H. Filistin Tahrir Hezb, 52

Fadai-ye Khalq-e Iran. See Iranian People's Guerilla
Faisal (King), 39, 253
Fallujah (city in Iraq), 11
fann al-mawt, 34
Fanon, Frantz, 32, 44–5, 51, 53, 102, 104, 279, 282, 297, 300, 303
Faraj, Abd-al Salaam, 37, 100
Fardid, Ahmad, 280
Faruq (King), 33, 239, 252
Fatah (Palestinian political group), 51–2, 255, 313–14, 316–18
Fatima (the Prophet's daughter), 111, 115, 118, 276
Fatimids, 118
fatwa (Islamic religious edict), 129, 183–5, 197, 271, 272
Fayad, Shafiq, 25
fedaiyan, 270–2
Fedayeen of Islam, 41
Felmy, Hellmuth (General), 250
Feltrinelli, Giangiacomo, 254, 309
Feraoun, Mouloud, 303
Fichte, Johann Gottlieb, 38, 87, 146, 244
Fidai-e-Islam, 32
Filastin al-Thawra (magazine), 315
Filistin Tahrir Hezb, 52
fiqh, 152, 262, 292, 325
Fitrah, 62
Flagellants, 70, 74
Flandin, Eugene, 167
FLN (National Liberation Front), 26, 283, 295–304, 315
Foucault, Michel, 32
Fountain of Blood, 26
Four Colonels, 242, 250
Four Schools of Law, 34
Franjieh, Hamid, 242
Freda, Franco, 255
Free Hindustan Movement, 194
Freikorps (paramilitary organizations), 272
French Revolution, 257–8, 311
Führerprinzip, 293
futuwwah, 164–5, 167, 168
Gailani, Rashid Ali, 242, 250
Gaith, Suleiman Abu, 53
Galiev, Mir-Said Sultan, 223, 227–31, 233, 307
Gandhi, Mahatma, 196–8
Gaulle, Charles de, 39, 303
Gaza (city of), 12, 52, 237
Gemayel, Pierre, 242
Genghis Khan (fouder and emperor of the Mongol Empire), 212
Genoud, François, 305
German Communist Party (KPD), 203
Germany, 272
Gestapo (the secret police of Nazi Germany), 288
ghazawat, 213
ghazw, 143
Ghilan, 273
GIA (Groupe Islamic Armé), 56, 304
Giap, Vo Nguyen, 283, 316
GIMO (State Institute for International Affairs), 308
GIS (German Intelligence Service), 247
Glorious Revolution, 257
God Seekers, 278
Goddess Revolution, 312
Goebbels, Joseph, 248
Goering, Herman, 293
Goethe, Johann Wolfgang von, 103, 277
Gog and Magog, 67, 109
Golden Horde, 171
Goltz, Colmar von der (General), 181
Gordon, Charles George (General), 126, 189
Gorki, Maxim, 278
Gorodetsky, Sergei, 214
Gospel of Barnaby, 96
Gospel of Childhood, 96
Gospel of Thomas, 96
Great Mutiny, 174, 190
Great Purges of the 1930s, 231
Great Rebellion of 1857–59, 124
Great War in Europe, 190
Greater Occultation, 277

Green Shirts *or Misr al-Fatah* (paramilitary organization), 240, 246–7
Gregory VII (Pope), 67
Grobba, Fritz, 248, 251
GRU (Russian intelligence agency), 308
Grunebaum, G.E. von, 269
Guardians of the Revolution, 168
Guénon, René, 32, 45
guerrilla, 21, 41, 283, 309, 315, 317
Guilani, Muhammad Muhamadi (Ayatollah), 49
Gulag (penal labor camp in the Soviet Union), 311
Guruh-e Furqan, 283

Habakkuk (prophet in the Hebrew Bible), 162
Habash, George, 53, 55, 104, 302, 314
Habibullah (King), 194
Hadded, Osman Kamal, 247
Hadramut (region of the Arabian Peninsula), 191
Haganah, 238
Hail (city in Saudi Arabia), 147
Hajaru 'l-Aswad, 160
hajj (pilgrimage to Mecca), 176, 180, 210
Hakimi, Mohamed Reza, 277
Hama (city of), 25
Hamas (Islamic Resistance Movement, a Palestinian Islamist Sunni organization), 12, 134
Hamza, Fuad, 247
Hanbalite, 31, 37
Hanson, Victor Davis, 2
haram, 160
Harb, Said Shaykh Ragheeb, 51, 159, 198–9
Harfleur (town in France), 17
Hariri, Rafiq, 133
Hasan, Ahmad, 246, 293
Hasan, Qasim ibn, 100, 102, 106, 117, 123, 290
Hasan-I Sabbah, 20, 39, 122–3. *See* ,
Hashemite monarchy, 23
Hassan, Margaret, 8
Hawatmeh, Nayef, 314
Hedin, Sven, 187
Hegel, Friedrich, 87
Heidegger, Martin, 86, 280
Helphand, Alexander, (a.k.a "Parvus"), 202–3
Henry V, 17
Hentig, Werner Otto von, 193, 246
Heyat-e Motafeleh-ye Eslami, 272
Heykal, Mohammed, 307
Hezbollah, 55, 133, 167, 317
High Caliphal Period, 165
Hijaz (region in Saudi Arabia), 111, 118, 121, 220
Hijrat (movement), 198
Hikmet, Nazim, 130–1, 222
Hilmi, Abbas, 188, 194, 246–7
Hilmi, Yusuf, 240
Himmler, Heinrich, 16, 251–2
Hintze, Paul von (Admiral), 207
Historical Role of Islam:An Essay on Islamic Culture, 207
Hitler, Adolf, 104, 240, 244–5, 247, 248, 251–2, 265, 268, 288, 293, 297
Hizb Allah, 263
Ho Chi Minh, 222, 296–7, 299
Hobbesian war, 63
Hobsbawm, Eric, 166
Hoffmann, Kurt. *See* al-Wakil, Mustafa Dr.
hudud, 170
Hujja, 116, 122
Hümmet Party, 230
Husain, Ahmad, 239–40
Husain, ibn Ali (Imam), 30, 44–5, 48, 50, 101, 120
Husayni, Amin, 215, 236–8, 241–2, 246, 248–53, 309
Husayni, Hamdi, 237
Hussein (King of Jordan), 313
Hussein, Saddam, 104, 128, 134, 242

I.D. (International Department), 308
I.S.F. (Islamic Socialist Front), 241
Ibadi Imamate (political leadership), 147

ibn Bijad, Abd Al-Rahman Al-Athari (Sultan), 134
Ibn Hazm, Abul, 154
Ibn Khaldun, 109, 111, 139, 140, 148, 157
Ibn Saud, Abdulazziz (King), 27, 37, 124, 188, 247, 253
Ibn Tumart, Abu Abd Allah Muhammad, 119
ijma, 153
ijtihad, 34
Ikhwan, 240
Ilim, 25
Imam Mahdi, 113
iman, 179, 281
Imperial Guarded Dominions, 183
Incas, 19
India Revolutionary Committee, 193–4, 198–9
Induskii kurs, 221
Inqilabiun-i Hind, 220
Insulindian archipelago, 171
International Department, (I.D.), 308
International Lenin School, 239
Iqbal, Mohamed, 199, 249
IRA (Irish Republican Army), 309
Iranian People's Guerrilla, 282
Iranian Revolution, 106, 123, 317
Iran-Iraq War, 40, 129
Iraq, 8, 10, 23–4, 36, 63, 111–12, 125, 129, 135, 164
Iraqi, 11, 24, 32, 38–9, 44, 90, 239, 242–3, 247, 249–50, 253, 291, 314, 317
Irish Fenians, 194
IRP (Islamic Revolutionary Party), 275
Is An Invasion of India Possible?, 206
Isa, Prophet, 109, 113
Isaac, 20
Isfahan (city of), 167
Ishtirakiyya (journal), 240
ISI (Inter-Service Intelligence), 321–2
Iskhakov, Veli, 229
Islam and the World, 262
Islamic Republic, 168, 258, 285, 288–9, 292
Islamic Revolution, 168, 256, 258, 261, 269–70, 275, 281–2, 284, 287–9, 291, 324
Islamic Socialist Front (I.S.F.), 240
Islamiyyat, 227
Ismail, Khedive, 30
Ismaili Aga Khan, 196
isnad, 157
Istiqlal, 239, 242, 321
Istiqlal party, 237
Ittihad ve tarakki (Union and Progress), 228
Ittihad-i Islam. See Wahdat al-Islam
Iyad, Abu (a.k.a. Salah Mesbah Khalaf), 296, 316

Jacob (monk), 71, 173
jacquerie, 257
Jamiaat Islami, 261–2
Jamiat-i Hizbollah, 198
Jamiyat-e Fedaiyan-e Eslam, 270
Jarulallah, Musa, 226
Jeanson, Francis, 301
Jeddah (city of Saudi Arabia), 189
Jemal (Pasha), 180
Jephthah, 20
Jewish National Fund, 236
Jewish National Home in Palestine, 251
Jibril, Ahmad, 314
jiziya, 98
Joachim de Fiore, 70, 87, 88
John Paul II (Pope), ii
Johnson, Paul, 8
Jonas, Hans, 82
Juj and Majuj *(Gog and Magog)*, 121
Jund al-Rabbaniyya, 220
Jünger, Ernst, 280
jus consuetudinis, 157

kaaba, 160
Kabyles, 142
Kabylia (region of Algeria), 300, 304
kafir, 159, 263
Kaganovich, Lazar, 218
Kamil, Kibrisli Mehmed (Pasha), 186
Kant, Immanuel, 20
Karakhan, Lev, 210

Karbala (city in Iraq), 50, 288
Kashani, Abol-Ghasem (Ayatollah), 271, 275
Kashgar (city in China), 178, 199
Kasim, Musa, 237
Kasravi, Ahmad, 41, 270–1
Kazan (city of), 184
Kedourie, Elie, 39, 260
Kemal, Mustafa, 38, 305
Kennedy, Robert F., 255
Kerbala (city of Iraq), 189
KGB (Committee of State Security of the Soviet Union), 254, 289, 306–10, 314
Khairi, Abdal Jabbar, 198
Khalkhali, Sadeq (Ayatollah), 49
Khamenei, Ali (Ayatollah), 47–8, 280, 292, 305
khamsa, 143
Khan, Mirza Husain, 30
Khan, Sayyid Ahmad, Sir, 244
khandjar (curved dagger), 19
khaniqahs, 166
Kharijites, 51, 96, 116
Khartoum (capital of Sudan), 189
Khayri Efendi, 183
Khilafat, 220, 239, 249, 268
Khilafat Manifesto, 197
Khiva (city of Uzbekistan), 184, 230
Khomeiny, Ruhollah Musawi (Ayatollah), 32, 41, 43–4, 47, 50, 62, 292, 293
Khosrokhavar, Farhad, 22
Khrushchev, Nikita, 306–7
khulafa, 171
Khurasan (province of), 164
kismet, 227
Kissinger, Henry, 319
Klinghoffer, Leon, 8
Kokand (city in Uzbekistan), 178
Kolchak, Alexandr (Admiral), 224
Komintern (Communist International), 202, 305, 308
Komitehs (armed Islamic revolutionary group), 168
Kopp, Viktor, 216
korban (sacrifical offering described and commanded in the Hebrew bible), 20
Korkmasov, Djamalutdin, 213
Kostring, Ernst, 206
Kosygin, Aleksei (Prime Minister), 313
KPD (German Communist Party), 203, 208
Kreisky, Bruno, 319
Kuchik, Mirza (Khan), 273
Kufa (city in Iraq), 96–7, 115, 121
kufr, 97, 121, 161
Kun, Bela, 214
Kuni, Konca, 25
KUTVa (The Communist University of the Toilers of the East), 222, 231, 308

L'Intransigeant (newspaper), 126, 178
La Description d'Ukraine, 162
La Nation arabe, 248
Lake Chad, 175
Laqueur, Walter Zeev, 26, 242, 316
Lares, 137
Lawrence, Thomas Edward, 190
Laws of War, 14
Le Cid, 136
Le meilleur combat, 283
League of Islamic Revolutionary Societies, 206
League of the Godless, 231
Left-Wing Communism, 311
légion d'honneur, 136
Lenin School, 308
Lenin, Vladimir Ilyich, 3, 77, 80, 87, 104–5, 201–5, 207–10, 216–19, 222, 224–5, 228–9, 232, 236, 265, 267–8, 276, 288, 308, 310–11
Les damnés de la terre, 300
Lessing, Gotthold Ephraim, 87
Lewis, Bernard, viii, 20, 158, 257, 258
Liddell Hart, Sir Basil (military historian), 163
Liebknecht, Karl, 203
Liu Shaoqi, 222
Louis IX (King), 71
Löwith, Karl, 87

LTTE (Liberation Tigers of Tamil Eelam), 105
Lunacharsky, Anatolii, 278
Luther, Martin, 75
luti, 167–8
Luxemburg, Rosa, 203

Ma'an (city of Jordan), 189
Mahalati, Fazlallah (Ayatollah), 48, 318
Mahdi, Ibrahim (Sheikh), 52
Mahdiyya (social and political movement), 147
mahdur addamm, 49
Maher, Ahmad, 34
Mahfuz, Naguib, 5
Mahmud of Ghazna (Sultan), 193
Makiya, Kanan, 24
Malik, Nur (Air Marshal), 322
Malik, S.K., 17, 18, 320–3
Manifesto of the Islamic Republic, 285
Mansur, Hasan Ali (Prime Minister), 272
Mao Zedong, 166, 229, 283, 288–9, 297, 316
Marcuse, Herbert, 45, 282
Marighela, Carlos, 283, 298–9
Maring. *See* Sneevliet, H.J.F.M.
Maronite, 242
Marx, Karl Heinrich, 45–6, 101, 146, 227, 278, 283, 308, 312
Massignon, Louis, 44
Maududi, Abu Ala, 3, 124, 233, 258–9, 261–270, 283, 286, 312, 320–1
mawali, 140
Mello (family), 302
Melouza (village of), 300
Mensheviks, 202
Mephistopheles, 103
Mesha (king of Moab), 19
Messali Haj, Ahmed Ben, 248
Mexican Socialist Party, 208
Milestones, 134
millet, 148
Mir-Lowhi, Sayyid Mujtaba. *See* Safavi, Navvab
Misr al-Fatah (Green Shirts), 240
MNA (Algerian National Movement), 300, 301
Moabit prison, 203
Mofatteh, Mohammad (Ayatollah), 282
Moghol (dynasty), 261
Moghul Empire (imperial power in India), 171
Mojahedin-e Khalq, 281
Molla, Gazi, 305
Moloch (Phoenician god), 19
Moltke, Helmuth von, 181
Moltke, Helmuth von, Jr., 187–8
Mongols, 13, 20, 45, 67, 103, 163
Monnerot, Jules, 233
Montazeri, Hosein-Ali (Ayatollah), 284, 288–9
Montesquieu, Charles de Secondat, baron de, 1
Moplah Rebellion, 198
Mosadeqh, Mohammad Dr., 42, 274, 275
Mosque, Ijlin (Sheikh), 52, 129, 266
mostazafin, 279, 287
Mosul (city of), 23
Motahhari, Morteza (Ayatollah), 46, 269, 270, 272, 275, 282, 284–8
Mouvement démocratique de libération nationale, 240
Movement of the Non-Aligned, 306
Muazzar, Hanafi, 225, 227
Mubarak, Muhammad Hosni (President of Egypt), 63, 241
Mudeiris, Ibrahim (Sheikh), 54
muezzin, 32
Mugniyah, Imad, 317
Muhajirun (migrant Muslims), 199, 219, 221
Muhammad, 257
Muhammad Ali, 195
Muhammed, Ahmad, 175
mujaddid, 116, 257, 262–3
mujahid, 8, 46, 248
mujahideen (pl. mujahid), 10–11, 16
Mujahideen Shura Council, 11
mujtahids, 152, 282
Mukhtar, ibn Abi Ubayd al Thaqafi, 115

mullahs, 167–8, 222, 269, 274, 282
Müller, Max. *See* Hadded, Osman Kamal
munadi, 121
munafeqeen, 48
Munich massacre, 320
Müntzer, Thomas, 79, 81, 88, 293
murids, 166, 227
Muslim Brotherhood, 25, 30, 32–3, 63, 95, 100, 130, 132, 135, 235, 239–40, 246, 249, 259, 269–70, 291, 310
Muslim National Communists, 231
Muslim World League, 129
Muslims in Entente, 193
Mussolini, Benito, 38, 104, 244, 247–8, 250, 260, 268
mustakbar, 48
mustanbat, 48
mustazaf, 48
mutawiya, 27
mutazila, 155
Muzaffar, Hanafi, 225
Muzafir (Sheikh), 238

Naccache, Alfred, 242
Nachrichten, 189
Nachrichtenstelle für den Orient, 186
Nahhas, Mustafa (Pasha), 35
Najaf (city of Iraq), 41, 270, 284, 286, 288
Najaf Seminary, 270
Najaf-Abadi, Salihi, 288
Nanotvi, Maulana Abul Qasim, 124
Naqshbandi (one of the major Sufi orders of Islam), 227
Naqshbandiya-Muridiyya, 305
Narbutabekov, Thaspolat, 213
Narkomnats (Comissariat of Nationalities), 225, 228
Narodniki (Russian revolutionaries), 310
Narody Vostoka, 215
Narrenschiff ("Ship of Fools", a common image in late Medieval Renaissance times),
Nasir, Fuad, 242
Nasrallah, Sayyed Hassan, 55, 133
Nasrullah Khan, 194
Nasser, Gamal Abdel (second president of Egypt), 39, 104, 128, 132–3, 209, 240, 254–5, 295, 307, 309, 313–14
natiq, 116
Navarre, Marguerite de, 75
Nazi (National Socialist), 16, 38–9, 41, 49, 129, 234, 236, 238, 240–3, 246–7, 250, 253–5, 269, 280, 289, 293, 297, 305
Nazi Scouts, 249
Nazim, Hüseyin (Pasha), 186
Nazism, 39, 238, 246, 249, 266, 272, 324
Nechaev, Sergei, 6–7, 68, 105
Nehru, Jawaharlal, 306
Nestorian missionaries, 112
Neurath, Konstantin von, 245
New Man (*chelovek*), 278
Nicolai, Walter (Colonel), 185
Niedermayer, Oskar von, 194–5, 210, 216–17
Nietzsche, Friedrich, 5, 278
nihilism, 50, 324
Nihilism, 5, 103
Nihilists, 6, 8
Nikolaev (city of), 203
Nile (river of), 189, 199
niyyah, 42, 77
Nizarat al-Marif, 220
NKVD (secret police of the Soviet Union), 260
Northern Alliance, 22
Nouvel Ordre Européen (racist movement), 254
NSDAP (National Socialist German Workers Party), 255
Nuremberg Laws, 246
Nuremberg Trial, 252
Nuri Pasha (General of the Ottoman Army), 204

OAS, Organisation de l'armée secrète (Organization of the Secret Army), 303

Obeidullah, Maulvi, 195, 220
Ode to a Mouse, 217
Odessa (city of), 203
Office of Strategic Services (OSS), 254
Oman (Sultanate), 147, 309
Omar, Mullah, 125, 322
Oppenheim, Max von, Baron, 182, 187–91, 193, 210, 218, 245–6
Origen (early Christian theologian), 65
Oslo Agreements, 320
OSPAAL (Organization of Solidarity of the People of Asia, Africa and Latin America), 309
Ostministerium (East Ministry), 251
Ottoman Janissaries, 146
Ouzegane, Ammar, 283, 297

Pact of Umar, 100
paganism, 8, 37, 159
Pahlevi (dynasty), 168
Palestine Liberation Front, 8, 53, 314
Palestine Liberation Organization (PLO), 294, 313, *see PLO*
Palestinian, 8, 12, 16, 28, 51–4, 56–7, 215, 238, 241–2, 245, 249, 253–5, 294–6, 302, 305, 309–10, 313–17, 319
Palestinian National Charter, 52
Papen, Franz von, 195
Partisans of Peace, 274–5, 307
Partovi-Sabzevari, Muhammad-Taqi, 49
Parvus (Alexander Helphand), 202, *see Helphand*
Pascal, Blaise, ii
Pasdaran, 168, 288
Pasha, Nahhas, 35
Pastoureaux, 70
Patna (city in India), 124
Patrice Lumumba University, 308
Paul, Saint, 83
PDFLP (Democratic Popular Front for the Liberation of Palestine), 308, 314
Peace Partisans, 306
Pearl, Daniel, 8
Peloponnesian War, 5
Peshawar (city in Pakistan), 124
Peshawari, Abd al-Rab, 220
Peter the Hermit (priest of Amiens), 68
Peters, Jakob, 218
PFLP (People‘s Front for the Liberation of Palestine), 53, 55, 308, 314
Philippeville, 301
Picardy (province of France), 71–2
pied-noir (French inhabitant of Algeria), 300, 302, 303
pîrs, 165–6, 197
PLO (Palestine Liberation Organization), 8, 21, 51–2, 254, 305, 309–10, 313–20
Pol Pot (Prime Minister of Cambodia), 100, 161
Politburo, 308
Ponomarev, Boris, 308
Popper, Karl (philosopher), 83
Porete, Marguerite, 75
Porte (court of the Ottoman Empire), 176, 178, 186, 190
Pratap, Kumar Mahendra, 193, 195
Predication and Combat (radical group), 22
Proto-Gospel of James, 96
Pseudo-Methodius, 66
Punjab (area of South Asia), 124
Pursuit of the Millenium, 261
putsch, 3, 39, 180, 199, 224

Qaim, 121, 277
Qajar (dynasty), 168, 171
Qaradawi, Yussuf, 57, 135
Qarmats, 45, 106, 166
Qaseem, Abdul Karim, 23
Qatada, Abu, 16
qatl, 37
qibla, 160
Qing (dynasty), 146
qissas (laws of), 44
qital, 34, 37
Qutb, Sayyid, 3, 8, 10, 37, 94–101, 103, 105, 125, 134–5, 153, 233, 235–6, 240, 259, 261, 266, 269–70, 283, 286, 312, 321

Radek, Karl, 202–4, 208, 210–13, 217, 236, 247
Radio Zossen, 251
Rafat, Hamid, 247
Rafsanjani, Afbar Hashemi (Ayatollah), 48
Rahimbaev, Abduqadir, 218
Ramallah (city of), 11, 319
Rashidi (clan), 147
Raskolnikov, Fyodor, 218, 273
Rationalists of Islam, 155
Razmara, Ali (General), 271
Red Army, 205–6, 216–18, 221, 223, 226, 228, 288, 309
Red Army Fraction of Germany, 309
Red Brigades of Italy, 309
Red International, 255
Reflections on Humanity, 101
Réflexions sur la violence, 267
Reichssicherheitshauptamt, RSHA, 289
Res publica, 136
Research Institute on the Social Consequences of the War, 202
Reventlow, Ernst, Graf zu, 208, 247
Revolt of the Basmachis, 228
Revolutionierungspolitik, 182
Reza Shah Pahlavi, 38, 273
Ribbentrop, Ulrich Friedrich Wilhelm Joachim von (Foreign Minister of Germany 1938–1945), 250
Rida, Rashid, 30–3, 37, 97, 248–9
Ridwan, Fathi, 240
Rizhenko, Fyodor, 308
Roberts, Frederick, Lord, 206
Robespierre, Maximilien de, 6, 257
Rodinson, Maxime, 260
Roquetaillade, Franciscan Jean de, 72
Rosenberg, Arthur, 251
Rote Fahne, 237
Roy, M. N., 199, 205–10, 215, 217–22, 231, 236
Russian Civil War, 226, 311
Russian Left, 202
Russian Revolution, 219, 224, 278
Russian Socialist movement, 182, 202
Russo-Ottoman war of 1877–1878, 196
Saada, Antun, 246, 293
Sabri, Ikrimeh (Sheikh), 52, 54
Sadat, Anwar El (president of Egypt), 63, 100, 234, 309
Saduqi, Mohammad (Ayatollah), 292
Safarov, Georgi, 218
Safavi, Navvab, 32, 40–2, 49, 269–72, 282
Said, Nuri, 269, 274, 276, 297
Saladin, Yusuf Ibn Ayyub, (Sultan of Egypt), 11, 118, 128, 182
salaf, 30, 157
salafi, 31
salafism, 30
salafiyya, 31
Salameh, Hafiz (Sheikh), 91
Salha, Aziz, 11
Salonica *or Thessaloniki* (city of Greece), 180, 186
Sanders, Liman von (General), 181
Sanusiyya (Sanussi Brotherhood) (political-religious organization), 147, 176
Saoshyans, 114
Saraya al-difa, 24
sarkha, 32
Sartre, Jean-Paul, 32, 44–5, 86, 282, 300
Sattar, Abdal, 198
satyagraha (movement), 198
SAVAK, (National Information and Security Organization, Iran), 42, 282
Sayyid, Ahmad Khan, Sir, 51, 196
Sayyid, Ameer Ali, 196, 259
Schabinger, Karl, 191
Schlegel, Friedrich, 87
Schmitt, Carl, 158, 293
Scythians, 212
Second World Congress of the Communist International, 208
Securitate (secret police of Communist Romania), 309
sedentary society, 14
Seeckt, Hans von (General), 186, 193, 200, 203–6, 208, 210, 213, 216–18, 244

Sejna, Jan (General), 308
Selim I (Sultan), 174
Sen Katayama, 222
Sepoy Mutiny, 196
Sepoys, 124
Shaban, Buthayna Dr., 135
shahada (martyrs), 10
shahid (martyr), 46, 48
Shakespeare, William, ii, 17, 136
Shakti (a hindu god), 207
Shamil, Imam (political leader), 128, 176, 227, 305–6
sharia (body of Islamic religious law), 18, 91, 97, 152, 156, 172, 174, 210, 230, 256, 259, 266
Shariati, Ali, 32, 44–7, 50–1, 101–6, 228–9, 233, 269, 270, 276–87, 297
Shariati, Ershan, 278
Shariati, Sarah, 278
Shawkat Ali, 197
Shawkat, Sami dr., 38
Shawqat, Nadji, 253
Shawqat, Sami Dr., 247
shaykh al-Turuq, 176
sheikh al-Islam, 183, 188
Shepherds Crusade, 70
Shia, 40, 44, 45, 50, 101, 113, 116, 118, 120–1, 259, 269, 276, 287
Shiatu Ali (partisans of Ali), 112
Shiism, 40, 45, 101, 103, 105–6, 120, 126, 276, 279, 284, 290
Shiite, 29, 32, 40, 42, 44–5, 55, 90, 101, 103, 106, 112, 116–17, 122, 126, 130, 170, 249, 258, 276, 281–2, 286, 288, 291–2, 294, 324
Shinshil, Sadiq, 242
Shukri Mustafa, 100
Shuqairy, Ahmad, 313
Sikhs, 124
silf, 157
Simon, Walter, 217, 319
Sind (Province of), 198
Sirhan Sirhan, 255
Six Days' War, 129, 309, 315
Skliansky, Efraim, 206, 210
Slavophiles, 146
Sneevliet, H.J.F.M. (pseudonym *Maring*), 231
Social Justice in Islam, 270
Socialist Revolutionaries, 310
Soldatov, Aleksandr, 317
Solovki Island, 229
Sondergruppe R, 216
Sorel, Georges, 33, 53, 267, 268
Sorush (journal), 291
Soustelle, Jacques (General), 299
Soviet Afro-Asian Solidarity Committee, 306
Soviet Communism, 3
Spartacus League. *See* German Communist Party
Speer, Albert (Minister of Armament), 293
Spirituals, 70, 75
SPQR, 137
SS (Schutzstaffel), 16, 251–4, 297
SS Obergruppenführer (Nazi Party paramilitary rank), 253
SS-Hauptamt (SS Head Office), 251
Stalin, Joseph, 166, 201, 215, 222, 224–5, 228, 231, 236, 240, 260, 274–5, 288, 293, 301, 305, 307, 308, 312
Stasi (secret police of East Germany), 309
State Institute for International Affairs, 308
STB (Czechoslovak secret police), 309
Storch, Niklas, 79
Suez Canal, 188, 189
Sufi, 44, 74, 106, 125, 127, 149, 165–6, 176, 227–8, 293, 305
Sufyani, 115, 121
suhl, 161
Sultangalievism, 223, 234
Sunni, 3, 29, 31–2, 40, 55, 57, 90, 93, 97, 100–1, 103, 106, 112, 116–18, 120, 122, 129–30, 152, 154, 165–6, 170, 177, 258–9, 261, 266, 270, 276, 294, 324
Svadeshi movement, 190
Svaraj movement, 190

Sweidani, Ahmad, 313, 314
Sybilline Oracles, 66

Tabatabai, Ziya al-Din, 249
Taborite, 78, 88
pl. Taborites, 70, 77
Tabriz (city of Iran), 189
Tafur (King), 69–70
Tafurs, 69
tahwid, 96, 99, 289
Taimiyya, Taqi ad-Din Ahmad ibn, 37, 97
tajdid, 257
takfir, 37, 40, 49, 96–7, 99, 263
Takfir wal-Hijra. *See* Al-Jihad
Takriti (clan), 150
Talaat, Mehmed (Pasha), 180, 186–7, 202–4
Taleqani, Mohammad-Hasan, 271, 283
Taleqani, Sayyid Mahmud (Ayatollah), 271–3, 282, 284
Talibans, 22
Tamerlane, 227
Tamil Tigers, 105
Tan Malaka, 222
Tanchelm of Antwerpen, 67
Tantawi, Muhammad (Sheikh), 57
Tanzimat period, 244
tarikat, 176
tariqa, 166, 227
Tarzi, Mahmad, 194
tashayyo-e sorkh, 276
tathir, 49
tawhid, 260, 287
Tehrani, Mahdi, Hadavi (Ayatollah), 282
Terreur, 6
Teshkilat-i Mahsusa (TM), 185, 214
Teskilat, 192
Thabit, Antun, 241
thawra, 258–9
The Devils, 6
The Highest Struggle. *See* Le meilleur combat
The Immortal Martyr, 288
The Martyr, 46, 285, 287
The Peasant War in Germany, 81
The Possessed. *See The Devils*
The Principle of Quranic Thinking, 283
The Process of Revolution, 267
The Quranic Concept of War, 320–2
The State and Revolution, 266
The World of Islam (newspaper), 180
The Wretched of the Earth, 44
theology, 2, 29, 43, 47, 48, 82, 92, 95, 101, 112, 128, 159–60
Theses on Feuerbach, 46
Third Afghan War, 194
Thucydides (Greek historian), 5
Thug cult of Kali, 19
Tiburtina, 66
Tishrin (newspaper), 25
Tito, Josip Broz (President), 297, 306
Tocqueville, Alexis de, 59, 258
Tokugawa shoguns, 146
Tönnies, Ferdinand, 138
Topkapı Palace, 172
Treaty of Kücük Kaynarca, 174
Treaty of Rapallo, 203, 217
Triad gangs (Chinese underground organizations), 166
Tripolitania (historic region of Libya), 176, 180, 185, 191
Trotsky, Leon, 202, 206, 216–17, 228, 267, 311
Tudeh, 235, 269, 273–5, 287, 308
Tukhachevsky, Mikhail (General), 206
Tulfah, Khairullah, 242
tullab, 167
Turk Yurdu, 202
Turkestan (region in Central Asia), 174, 176, 184, 218, 223, 230
Turkish Compassionate Fund, 196
Turkish Hizbullah, 25
Twelver Shia, 276

ulama, 18, 37, 100, 111, 128, 165, 176–8, 197–9, 213, 222, 241, 248, 261, 264, 266, 274–5, 282, 284, 286, 292
ul-Haq, Zia, 63, 320
Umar (Caliph), 113

Umayyad (dynasty), 96, 102, 115
umma, 31, 36, 56, 59, 164, 172–3, 184, 222, 227, 230, 260
Umma al-Arabiyya, 32
Umma al-Muhammadiyya, 32
Unamuno, Miguel de, ii
Untermenschen ('inferior people', a term from Nazi racial ideology), 161
Urabi, Ahmed (Colonel), 175
Urban II (Pope), 67
urf, 152, 157
Uruba, 31
Ushirma, Mansur (Sheikh), 305
USSR (Soviet Union), 231, 239, 245, 274, 306, 314
usus, 156
Uthman, Amin, 35
Utushev, 214

Vademecum in Tribulations, 72
Vaez-Tabassi, Abbas (Ayatollah), 105
Van (city of Turkey), 189
Vehme assassinations, 272
velayat-e faqih, 292–3
Veli, Mehmed Khan (General), 217
Viet Minh (League for the Independence of Vietman), 295–7
Vigilante Patrols for Combating the Forbidden, 289
Virgin Mary, 71, 74
Voegelin, Eric (philosopher), 84, 88–9, 256, 277
Voigt, Günther, 217
Volk, 49
Völkischer Beobachter, 240, 246
Vozhd, 293

Waffen-SS (Armed SS, elite combat unit), 252
Wahdat al-Islam, 178
wala, 140
Wangenheim, Hans Freiherr, 193
Warsaw Pact, 306
Weber, Max, 77
Weimar Republic, 244
Weizsäcker, Ernst von, 250
Weltanschauung (world view), 158
wilaya, 297, 300–1
Wilhelm II (Emperor), 181–3, 186, 214
Wilhelminian (period), 181, 244
William (Emperor), 44
Wimbush (Enders), 227, 273, 275, 306
Wisliceny, Dieter, 252
World Peace Council, 130
World Peace Movement, 306
World Youth Conference, 313

Xinjiang (East Turkestan), 176

Yajuj and Majuj. *See* Gog and Magog
Yakub Bey, Muhammad, 176
Yark (city in China), 178
Yasim, Yusuf (Sheikh), 247, 253
Yasin, Sheikh, 10
Yazdi, Ibrahim, 258
Yazid, M'hamed, 315
Yemen (country of), 36, 118, 125, 147, 294, 309
Young Egypt, 240, 246, 255
Young Turk, 38, 202, 203, 247

Zade (Sultan), 231
Zahiris, 154
Zakharov, Vladimir, 313
zalzalah, 259
Zamindar, 220
Zaydi (sect, school named after Imam Zayd ibn Ali), 147
Zhizn Natsionalnostei, 228
Zhou Enlai (Prime Minister), 306, 316
Zighout, Youssef, 301
Zimmermann, Arthur, 182
Zinoviev, Grigory, 206, 210–11, 213–14, 217
Zoroaster, 102
zur-khane, 168